Simple
Celebrations

Beta Sigma Phi

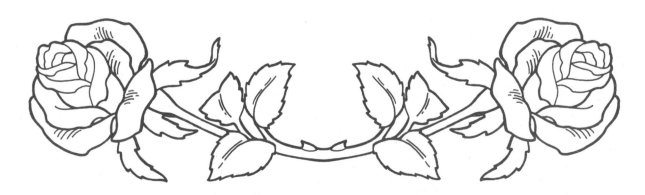

EDITORIAL STAFF

Managing Editor — Mary Cummings

Executive Editor — Debbie Seigenthaler

Editorial Manager — Georgia Brazil

Project Manager — Anita McKay

Editor — Jan Keeling

Associate Editors — Linda Bennie, Ginger Dawson
Elizabeth Miller, Tanis Westbrook
Joy Wilson, Mary Wilson

Typographers — Jessie Anglin, Sara Anglin

Award Selection Judges — Bill Ross, Debbie Seigenthaler
Charlene Sproles

Art Director — Steve Newman

Illustrator — Barbara Ball

Test Kitchen — Charlene Sproles

Essayist — Robin Crouch

Cover photograph: Oregon Hazelnut Board

© Favorite Recipes® Press, A Division of Heritage House, Inc. 1999
  P.O. Box 305141, Nashville, Tennessee 37230

ISBN: 0-87197-478-9

Manufactured in the United States of America
First Printing 1999

Recipes for Cover photograph are on page 211.

Contents

Shanna Groves

Dear Beta Sigma Phi Sisters:

No party in the world compares to a Beta Sigma Phi celebration. Thanks to you, we now have a cookbook with dishes that are fast and festive—a perfect complement to all your sorority socials!

Simple Celebrations is for all of us sisters who like recipes and party ideas that are quick and easy. Forget those parties where your hostess spends all her time cooking in the kitchen! This cookbook is filled with entrée ideas that are low on time, high on taste. Everyone can enjoy the party with *Simple Celebrations!*

Since this cookbook is reasonably priced, buy an additional copy for your Secret Sister—or anyone who enjoys eating and having fun with friends! Better yet, buy extras for your entire chapter, and devote your sorority year's programs to learning a few new recipes. You won't be sorry, and neither will your taste buds!

Here's to all your simply delicious celebrations—enjoy!

Yours in Beta Sigma Phi,

Shanna Groves

Shanna Groves
Editor, The Torch
Beta Sigma Phi International

Quick Creations

Cooking is convenient with five or fewer main ingredients in each *Quick Creations* recipe, providing homemade goodness on drive-through time. Posthaste appetizers and beverages, short-order soups and salads, as well as effortless entrées and desserts are featured herein and sprinkled liberally throughout the pages of **Simple Celebrations.** Select from *Quick Creations* and make mealtimes more manageable with fewer ingredients, whether you're whipping up last-minute dishes or pulling off main-menu venues.

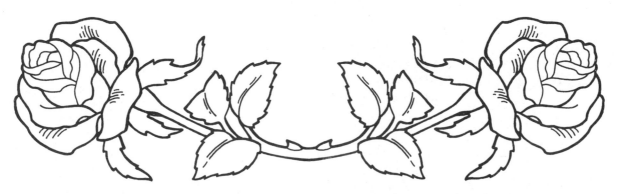

Appetizers

❖ CREAM CHEESE FONDUE

1½ cups milk	1 tablespoon garlic
8 ounces cream cheese,	powder
cubed	¾ cup grated Parmesan
8 ounces cream cheese	cheese
with chives, cubed	Sourdough bread, cubed

Combine the milk, cream cheese, cream cheese with chives and garlic powder in a saucepan. Cook over low heat until blended, stirring constantly. Stir in the Parmesan cheese. Pour the cheese mixture into a fondue pot. Serve with sourdough bread cubes. Yield: 4 servings.

Michelle Young, Alpha Alpha Gamma
Redding, California

HOT BEEF 'N' CHEESE DIP

1½ pounds ground beef	1 tablespoon chile
2 onions, finely chopped	powder
2 (16-ounce) packages	1 teaspoon Tabasco
processed American	sauce
cheese, cubed	2 tomatoes, finely
1 (7-ounce) can chopped	chopped
green chiles	

Brown the ground beef and onion in a skillet until crumbly; drain. Add the American cheese, green chiles, chile powder and Tabasco sauce and heat until mixture is blended, stirring occasionally. Stir in the tomatoes. Serve warm with party crackers, bread cubes or corn chips. Yield: 30 servings.

Mary Beth Watson, Laureate Eta
Rocklin, California

PARMESAN CHEESE DIP

16 ounces cream cheese,	½ cup mayonnaise
softened	⅓ to ½ onion, chopped
1½ cups grated fresh	
Parmesan cheese	

Beat the cream cheese, Parmesan cheese and mayonnaise in a mixer bowl until blended. Stir in the onion. Spoon into a 9-inch glass pie pan. Bake at 350 degrees for 40 to 50 minutes or until light brown. Serve with assorted party crackers. Yield: 15 to 20 servings.

Nancy Nelson, Nu Lambda
Gilbert, Iowa

PRETZEL DIP

This is always a hit. So good, quick, and easy you will want to double it. Simple ingredients can be kept on hand to make at a moment's notice.

8 ounces cream cheese,	1 teaspoon
softened	Worcestershire sauce
1 (5-ounce) jar Old	Dash of garlic salt
English cheese spread	(optional)

Beat the cream cheese, Old English cheese, Worcestershire sauce and garlic salt in a mixer bowl until blended. Serve with mini pretzels. Yield: 10 servings.

Rosalyn Guyton, Psi Master
Ballwin, Missouri

TANGY CHEESE DIP

8 ounces cream cheese	1 tablespoon chives
1 cup shredded Cheddar	1 teaspoon horseradish
cheese	½ teaspoon dry mustard
⅓ cup beer	Dash of cayenne

Place the cream cheese in a microwave-safe dish. Microwave on High for 30 seconds. Add the Cheddar cheese, beer, chives, horseradish, dry mustard and cayenne and mix well. Microwave for 2 minutes or until hot and bubbly. Serve warm with assorted party crackers, fresh vegetables, or French bread cubes. Yield: 15 servings.

Nancy L. Barclay, Laureate Epsilon Phi
Pittsburgh, Pennsylvania

ARTICHOKE DIP

1 (10-ounce) package	1 (14-ounce) can
frozen chopped	artichoke bottoms,
spinach, thawed,	drained, chopped
drained	1 cup mayonnaise
1 (14-ounce) can	1 cup grated Parmesan
artichoke hearts,	cheese
drained, chopped	1 clove of garlic, minced

Combine the spinach, artichoke hearts, artichoke bottoms, mayonnaise, Parmesan cheese and garlic in a bowl and mix well. Spoon into a 9x9-inch baking dish. Bake at 350 degrees for 25 minutes. Serve warm with assorted party crackers. Yield: 15 to 20 servings.

Jeanne Dunagan, Beta Sigma Master
Dallas, Texas

ONION DELIGHT

1 (10-ounce) package   **3 cups shredded Swiss**
frozen chopped   **cheese**
onions   **1 to 2 tablespoons Dijon**
1 cup mayonnaise   **mustard**

Mix the ingredients in a bowl. Spoon into a 9x9-inch baking pan. Bake at 350 degrees for 30 to 40 minutes or until bubbly. Serve warm with assorted party crackers. Yield: 25 servings.

Doreen Ennis, Preceptor Iota Sigma
Templeton, California

CHEESY ONION DIP

This is a great, quick dip for any event.

1 cup sour cream   **2 tablespoons onion**
1 cup mayonnaise   **soup mix**
1 cup Cheez Whiz

Combine the sour cream, mayonnaise, Cheez Whiz and onion soup mix in a bowl and mix well. Serve with bagel chips or breadsticks. Yield: 20 servings.

Michelle Oxrider, Preceptor Zeta Mu
Cincinnati, Ohio

SWEET ONION DIP

This is so simple and tasty. A hit every time it is served.

2 cups sliced sweet   **2 cups cubed Swiss**
onions   **cheese**
2 cups mayonnaise

Combine the ingredients in a bowl and mix well. Spoon into a greased 8x8-inch baking dish. Bake at 350 degrees for 25 minutes. Serve warm with assorted party crackers. Yield: 20 servings.

Trudy Grandt, Beta Omega
Kankakee, Illinois

REUBEN DIP

1 cup Thousand Island   **2 (3-ounce) packages**
salad dressing   **corned beef, chopped**
8 ounces shredded Swiss   **1 (10-ounce) can**
cheese   **sauerkraut, drained,**
4 ounces cream cheese,   **chopped**
softened

Combine the ingredients in a saucepan. Cook over low heat until blended and bubbly, stirring frequently. Serve warm with cocktail rye bread. Yield: 25 servings.

Lynn Moerke, Preceptor Theta Sigma
Sarasota, Florida

RASPBERRY SALSA BLACK BEAN DIP

Great dish to bring to a party for finger food.

1/2 red onion, minced   **1/2 (14-ounce) jar**
1 (16-ounce) can black   **raspberry salsa**
beans, drained   **8 ounces shredded**
8 ounces cream cheese,   **pepper jack cheese**
softened

Layer the red onion, black beans, cream cheese, raspberry salsa and pepper jack cheese in a 9-inch baking dish. Bake at 350 degrees for 20 minutes or until bubbly. Serve warm with tortilla chips. Yield: 15 servings.

Lisa C. Reader, Xi Alpha Zeta
Bentonville, Arkansas

SOUR CREAM SALSA DIP

2 cups sour cream   **1 envelope ranch salad**
1 (8-ounce) jar salsa   **dressing mix**

Combine the sour cream, salsa and salad dressing mix in a bowl and mix well. Chill, covered, until ready to serve. Serve with tortilla chips.
Yield: 15 to 20 servings.

Judy Bradee, Xi Omega
Waukesha, Wisconsin

CREAMY CARAMEL APPLE DIP

8 ounces cream cheese,   **1 teaspoon caramel**
softened   **flavoring**
1/3 cup packed brown   **1 teaspoon vanilla**
sugar   **extract**

Beat the cream cheese, brown sugar, caramel flavoring and vanilla in a mixer bowl until creamy. Serve with sliced red or green apples.
Yield: 10 to 15 servings.

Julie E. Jones, Xi Delta Chi
Broken Arrow, Oklahoma

CRANBERRY DIP

2 cups fresh cranberries   **2 tablespoons orange**
1 cup sugar   **marmalade**
1 tablespoon lemon   **1/4 cup amaretto**
juice

Bring the cranberries, sugar and lemon juice to a boil in a saucepan. Boil for 20 minutes, stirring frequently. Stir in the orange marmalade. Remove from the heat. Stir in the amaretto. Serve with crackers, or pour over cream cheese. Yield: 15 to 20 servings.

Donna L. Thompson, Preceptor Beta Epsilon
Spring Hill, Florida

FRUIT DIP

1 cup whipped topping   *1 cup strawberry yogurt*

Fold the whipped topping into the strawberry yogurt in a glass bowl. Chill, covered, for two hours. Serve with sliced fresh fruit. May spread mixture over shortcake and garnish with sliced fresh strawberries and kiwifruit. Yield: 12 to 14 servings.

Debbie Arseneault, Preceptor Gamma Rho
Kemptville, Ontario (Canada)

PUMPKIN DIP

1 pound confectioners'
* sugar, sifted*
16 ounces cream cheese,
* softened*
1 (30-ounce) can
* pumpkin pie filling*

2 teaspoons cinnamon
1 teaspoon ginger
* powder*

Beat the confectioners' sugar and cream cheese in a mixer bowl until blended. Add the pumpkin pie filling, cinnamon and ginger and mix well. Chill, covered, until ready to serve. Serve with gingersnap cookies. Yield: 7 cups.

Beverly Sue Hicks, Preceptor Gamma
Hannibal, Missouri

CHERRY CHOCOLATE CHEESE BALL

11 ounces cream cheese,
* softened*
1 tablespoon amaretto
1/4 teaspoon cinnamon

1 cup chocolate chips
1/2 (21-ounce) can cherry
* pie filling*

Heat the cream cheese, amaretto, cinnamon and chocolate chips in a saucepan, stirring until blended. Remove from heat. Let stand until cool. Shape into a ball. Make a well in the cheese ball. Spoon cherry pie filling into the well, letting it run down the sides of the cheese ball. Chill, covered, until ready to serve. Serve with chocolate wafers. Yield: 15 to 20 servings.

Pam Carter, Preceptor Epsilon Epsilon
Wentzville, Missouri

BAKED FETA

8 ounces feta cheese,
* crumbled*

1 (26-ounce) jar
* marinara sauce*

Place the feta cheese in a baking dish. Pour the marinara sauce over the cheese. Bake at 250 degrees for 20 minutes. Serve with sliced garlic bread. Yield: 4 servings.

Pat Griffey, Kappa Theta
Pensacola, Florida

CHICKEN CHEESE BALL

1 (5-ounce) can chicken
* or turkey, drained*
8 ounces cream cheese,
* softened*
1 tablespoon chutney

1 tablespoon curry
* powder*
1/2 cup sliced almonds
Dash of salt
Dried parsley

Combine the chicken, cream cheese, chutney, curry powder, almonds and salt in a bowl and mix well. Shape into a ball. Roll the cheese ball in the parsley. Chill, covered, until ready to serve. Serve with assorted party crackers. Yield: 12 servings.

Carolyn Christenbury, Preceptor Epsilon Sigma
Hayward, California

SALMON SPREAD

1 (15-ounce) can salmon,
* drained*
8 ounces cream cheese,
* softened*
1 tablespoon lemon
* juice*

1 teaspoon liquid smoke
1 teaspoon horseradish
1/2 teaspoon onion
* powder*
Salt to taste
Pepper to taste

Combine the salmon, cream cheese, lemon juice, liquid smoke, horseradish, onion powder, salt and pepper in a bowl and mix well. Serve with assorted party crackers. Yield: 8 to 10 servings.

Beverly Thomas, Xi Alpha Phi
Beatrice, Nebraska

SMOKY SALMON CHEESE BALL

1 (7-ounce) can salmon
8 ounces cream cheese,
* softened*

3 drops liquid smoke
3 tablespoons chopped
* green onions*

Drain the salmon, reserving 2 teaspoons of the liquid. Combine the cream cheese, liquid smoke and reserved salmon liquid in a bowl and mix well. Stir in the green onions and salmon. Shape into a ball. Chill, covered, for 2 hours. Serve with assorted party crackers. May roll the cheese ball in chopped pecans. Yield: 12 servings.

Brenda Yates, Xi Upsilon Iota
Tyler, Texas

VEGETABLE SPREAD

4 carrots
4 radishes
2 green onions

1 green bell pepper
8 ounces cream cheese,
* softened*

Place the carrots, radishes, green onions and green pepper in a food processor and process until blended. Add the cream cheese and process until smooth. Chill, covered, until ready to serve. Serve with assorted party crackers or fresh vegetables. Yield: 12 servings.

Mary Frances Emerson, Xi Gamma Beta
Lake Havasu City, Arizona

MEDITERRANEAN OLIVE SPREAD

**1 (10-ounce) jar stuffed
  green olives, finely
  chopped
1 carrot, finely chopped
2 garlic cloves, minced**

**¹/₂ cup olive oil
1 tablespoon red wine
  vinegar
¹/₂ teaspoon pepper**

Combine the olives, carrot, garlic, olive oil, red wine vinegar and pepper in a bowl and mix well. Chill, covered, for 2 hours. Drain the excess oil before serving. Serve with assorted party crackers or cocktail rye bread. Yield: 10 servings.

Dale Stackhouse, Preceptor Epsilon Sigma
Nepean, Ontario, Canada

BAKED CHEESE

**1 (4-count) can crescent
  rolls
2 teaspoons minced
  fresh dillweed**

**8 ounces cream cheese
1 egg yolk, beaten**

Unroll the crescent roll dough to form a 4-inch by 12-inch rectangle on a floured surface, pressing the perforations to seal. Press the dillweed on all sides of the cream cheese. Place the cream cheese in the center of the prepared dough. Wrap the dough around the cream cheese, pressing the edges to seal. Place the dough on a greased baking sheet. Brush with the egg yolk. Bake at 350 degrees for 20 to 27 minutes or until light brown. Cut into thin slices. May be served warm or cold. Yield: 6 to 12 servings.

Peggy Freeman, Beta Delta Mu
Conroe, Texas

BLEU CHEESE PUFFS

**4 ounces bleu cheese
¹/₄ cup margarine**

1 (10-count) can biscuits

Heat the bleu cheese and margarine in a saucepan until blended, stirring frequently. Cut the biscuits into small pieces. Press into a 9-inch glass pie plate. Pour the cheese mixture over the prepared biscuits. Bake at 350 degrees for 15 minutes. Yield: 8 to 10 servings.

Mary Fleming, Preceptor Zeta
Rapid City, South Dakota

CHEESE BRIOCHE

**1 (8-count) can crescent
  rolls**

**1 Gouda cheese round
1 egg, beaten**

Unroll the crescent roll dough. Separate into 2 sections. Place 1 section in a greased 8-inch pie plate, pressing the perforations to seal. Place the cheese on top of the prepared dough. Pull the dough up around the sides of the cheese. Place the remaining dough over the top of the cheese, pressing the perforations to seal. Wrap the dough around the cheese. Brush with the egg. Bake at 350 degrees for 30 minutes or until light brown. Let stand for 10 minutes before slicing. Yield: 8 servings.

Reba Plaisance, Preceptor Epsilon
Baton Rouge, Louisiana

CRAB APPETIZER

**1 (5-ounce) jar Old
  English cheese spread
¹/₄ cup butter, softened
7 ounces crab meat
2 tablespoons
  mayonnaise**

**¹/₂ teaspoon garlic salt
¹/₂ teaspoon seasoned
  salt
1 (8-count) package
  English muffins**

Beat the Old English cheese and butter until blended. Add the crab, mayonnaise, garlic salt and seasoned salt and mix well. Spread the mixture over one side of each of the English muffins. Freeze, covered, until partially frozen. Slice the prepared muffins into fourths. Place on an ungreased baking sheet. Broil for 2 to 4 minutes or until edges are light brown. Yield: 32 servings.

Kay Braaten, Preceptor Phi
Las Vegas, Nevada

PARTY CUCUMBER SANDWICHES

**1 loaf frozen wheat
  bread dough, thawed
8 ounces cream cheese,
  softened
¹/₂ cup mayonnaise-type
  salad dressing**

**1 envelope ranch salad
  dressing mix
Cucumber slices**

Place the bread dough in a greased bread tube. Place the bread tube in an upright position in the oven. Bake at 350 degrees for 1 hour. Cool completely in the bread tube before removing. Slice the bread when completely cooled. Combine the cream cheese, salad dressing, and ranch salad dressing mix and mix well. Spread the cheese mixture on 1 side of each slice of bread. Top with a cucumber slice. Yield: 20 servings.

Pat Miller, Xi Gamma Mu
Aurora, Nebraska

OYSTERS IN WINE SAUCE

This has been a Christmas Eve snack for our family for about 25 years.

1 quart shucked raw oysters	1 teaspoon seasoned salt
1/4 cup flour	Pepper to taste
1 teaspoon garlic powder	1/2 cup butter
	1 cup white cooking sherry

Rinse the oysters and pat dry. Mix the flour, garlic powder, seasoned salt and pepper in a bowl. Melt the butter in a saucepan. Coat the oysters with the flour mixture. Cook the oysters in the butter until brown. Pour in the sherry slowly. Cook until thickened, stirring constantly. Serve warm with crackers. Yield: 6 to 10 servings.

Susie Harbers, Preceptor Mu Kappa
Yoakum, Texas

STUFFED RED PEPPERS

2 red bell peppers	1 teaspoon Beau Monde seasoning
8 ounces cream cheese, softened	1/2 teaspoon garlic

Cut the red peppers in half lengthwise. Wash and remove the seeds. Combine the cream cheese, Beau Monde seasoning and garlic in a bowl and mix well. Spoon the cream cheese mixture into the red pepper halves. Cut the prepared red peppers into 1-inch pieces. Yield: 16 servings.

Donna Root, Laureate Nu
Hamilton, Montana

STUFFED STRAWBERRIES

These are ideal for a party or tea.

18 large strawberries, stems removed	1 1/2 teaspoons confectioners' sugar
3/4 cup whipped cream cheese	1/2 to 1 1/2 teaspoons milk
2 tablespoons finely chopped walnuts	

Cut the tips off of the strawberries and reserve the tips. Scoop out half of the pulp from each strawberry, leaving the shells intact. Blend the pulp, cream cheese, walnuts, confectioner's sugar and milk in a bowl until mixture is of a creamy consistency, adding more milk if necessary. Spoon the strawberry mixture into a decorator tube fitted with a large tip. Pipe into the strawberries. Place the reserved strawberry tips on top. Yield: 18 servings.

Dorothy Sheets, Beta Beta
Eagleville, Missouri

DILL SEASONED POPCORN

12 cups popped popcorn	1 teaspoon dillweed
Butter flavored nonstick cooking spray	1 teaspoon parsley
1/2 cup grated Parmesan cheese	

Spray the popcorn with the cooking spray to coat. Combine the Parmesan cheese, dillweed and parsley in a bowl and mix well. Pour over the popcorn in a large bowl, tossing to mix. Yield: 6 servings.

Betty Ozark, Xi Zeta Epsilon
Kalamazoo, Michigan

GARLIC PRETZELS

My son at college would rather receive a tin of these pretzels than chocolate chip cookies.

1 cup light olive oil	1 teaspoon dillweed
1 envelope ranch salad dressing mix	1 teaspoon lemon pepper
1 teaspoon garlic powder	1 (16-ounce) package hard pretzels, broken

Combine the olive oil, ranch salad dressing mix, garlic powder, dillweed and lemon pepper in a bowl and mix well. Drizzle over the pretzels in a bowl, tossing to coat. Spread the pretzels on an ungreased 10x15-inch baking sheet. Bake at 300 degrees for 20 minutes, stirring once midway through the baking time. Let stand until cool. Store in an airtight container. Yield: 20 to 25 servings.

Jean Pessano
Ocean City, New Jersey

OVEN-ROASTED PECANS

3 tablespoons melted butter	1 teaspoon garlic salt
1 1/2 teaspoons Worcestershire sauce	1 teaspoon Tabasco sauce
	4 cups pecan halves

Combine the butter, Worcestershire sauce, garlic salt and Tabasco sauce in a bowl and mix well. Drizzle over the pecans, tossing to coat. Spread the pecans on an ungreased 10x15-inch baking sheet. Bake at 250 degrees for 1 hour, stirring every 15 minutes. Let stand until cool. Store in an airtight container. Yield: 15 to 20 servings.

Barbara Dyke
San Antonio, Texas

SPICY PECANS

3 tablespoons butter	1/4 teaspoon cayenne
3 tablespoons	pepper
Worcestershire sauce	1/4 teaspoon garlic
Dash of Tabasco sauce	powder
1 teaspoon salt	1 pound pecan halves
1/2 teaspoon cinnamon	

Melt the butter in a large skillet. Add the Worcestershire sauce and Tabasco sauce and mix well. Stir in the salt, cinnamon, cayenne and garlic powder. Add the pecans and toss until coated. Spread in a single layer in a 10x15-inch baking pan. Bake at 325 degrees for 15 to 20 minutes or until golden brown, stirring frequently. Yield: 4 cups.

Michele Applegate, Xi Gamma
Essex Junction, Vermont

SUGARED PECANS

2 egg whites	3 1/2 cups pecans
1 cup sugar	1/4 cup melted butter
1/8 teaspoon salt	

Beat the egg whites in a mixer bowl until stiff peaks form. Add the sugar and salt and mix well. Stir in the pecans and butter. Spread the pecans on an ungreased 10x15-inch baking sheet. Bake at 300 degrees for 30 minutes, stirring every 10 minutes. Let stand until cool. Store in an airtight container. Yield: 12 to 15 servings.

Sandy Anderson, Xi Gamma Mu
Aurora, Nebraska

SWEET CHEX

9 cups Rice Chex cereal	3/4 cup margarine
2 cups pecans	1/4 cup butter
1 cup packed brown	
sugar	

Combine the Rice Chex cereal and pecans in a large bowl. Combine the brown sugar, margarine and butter in saucepan. Bring to a boil, stirring constantly. Pour over the cereal mixture, tossing to coat. Spread the mixture on an ungreased 10x15-inch baking sheet. Bake at 325 degrees for 16 minutes, stirring once midway through the baking time. Let stand until cool. Store in an airtight container. Yield: 35 to 40 servings.

Nancy Natividad, Xi Alpha Zeta
Bentonville, Arkansas

FUNKY CORN CHIPS

1 cup sugar	1 (12-ounce) package
1 cup light corn syrup	corn chips
1 cup creamy peanut	6 (1 1/2-ounce) chocolate
butter	bars

Combine the sugar and corn syrup in a saucepan and mix well. Bring to a boil, stirring constantly. Remove from heat. Add the peanut butter, stirring until blended. Spread the corn chips on a greased 10x15-inch baking sheet. Pour the peanut butter mixture over the corn chips. Place the chocolate bars on the peanut butter mixture in a single layer. Let stand until chocolate is melted. Spread the melted chocolate to form a thin layer. Let stand until cool. Break into 1 inch pieces. Store in an airtight container. Yield: 20 to 25 servings.

Karen Crook, Laureate Alpha Eta
Moses Lake, Washington

Beverages

APRICOT PUNCH

4 cups apricot nectar	2 cups orange juice
4 cups apple juice	3 1/2 cups ginger ale

Combine the apricot nectar, apple juice, orange juice and ginger ale in a punch bowl and mix gently. Serve chilled. Yield: 25 to 30 servings.

Betty D. Thomas, Laureate Gamma Kappa
Lakeland, Florida

CACTUS BLOSSOM PUNCH

1 (16-ounce) bottle	1 (12-ounce) can guava
crangrape	nectar
concentrate	1 (1-quart) bottle seltzer
4 cups water	

Combine the crangrape concentrate, water and guava nectar in a punch bowl and mix well. Stir in the seltzer. Garnish with slices of lime. Serve chilled. Yield: 20 to 25 servings.

Shirley Varnum, Xi Alpha Sigma
Ajo, Arizona

Pennie Goetz, Preceptor Zeta Gamma, Tampa, Florida, makes a delicious all-purpose Special Ladies Punch by mixing 4 bottles of peach chardonnay (minus 2 cups of the wine) and 2 cups of peach schnapps together and adding 6 peaches that have been peeled, sliced and the slices cut into halves. Well chilled this goes well with all kinds of desserts.

CRAN-RASPBERRY PUNCH

I was asked to make punch for our 1998 Fall Ritual. I thought these items sounded great together. So I made it, and it was a big hit. It also was hard to keep the punch bowl full.

1 gallon water
2 cups sugar
2 envelopes raspberry
  drink mix
1 (12-ounce) package
  frozen raspberries

1/2 gallon raspberry
  sherbet
1 (2-liter) bottle
  cranberry soda

Combine the water, sugar and raspberry drink mix in a punch bowl, stirring until the drink mix is completely dissolved. Stir in the raspberries. Spoon the sherbet into the punch bowl. Add the cranberry soda. May use an ice ring. Yield: 50 servings.

Kim McGhehey, Xi Beta Kappa
Carmen, Idaho

MILK PUNCH

1 cup vanilla ice cream
1 teaspoon vanilla
  extract

1/4 cup bourbon
Nutmeg

Combine the ice cream, vanilla extract and bourbon in a blender container and blend until smooth. Pour into glasses and sprinkle with nutmeg.
Yield: 2 servings.

Carolyn Meyer, Xi Delta Omicron
Savannah, Georgia

RED HOT PUNCH

1 (46-ounce) can
  pineapple juice
1 cup red hot cinnamon
  candies

1 (1-liter) bottle ginger
  ale

Combine the pineapple juice and candies in a saucepan. Heat over low heat until the candy is completely dissolved, stirring frequently. Chill, covered, until serving time. Add the ginger ale just before serving. Yield: 15 servings.

Aliene Gribas, Laureate Iota
Havre, Montana

BLUEBERRY LEMONADE

3 cups fresh blueberries
3/4 cup sugar
3 cups cold water

2 cups freshly squeezed
  lemon juice

Purée the blueberries in a blender. Add the sugar and process until blended. Combine the water and lemon juice in a pitcher. Press the blueberry mixture through a sieve into the pitcher and mix well. Garnish with lemon slices. Yield: 4 servings.

Sharlene Wesson, Preceptor Tau
Massena, New York

REGAL ROOT BEER

This is great for Halloween as a witch's brew.

5 gallons water
1 (2-ounce) bottle root
  beer extract

5 pounds sugar
5 pounds dry ice

Combine the water, root beer extract and sugar in a large container and mix well, stirring until the sugar is dissolved. Add the dry ice carefully. Do not let it make contact with the skin. Serve when the mixture stops bubbling. Yield: 50 to 60 servings.

Tracie Cochrane, Delta Mu Gamma
Hemet, California

STRAWBERRY SPARKLE

1 (10-ounce) package
  frozen strawberries
2 cups cranberry juice,
  chilled

1 (750-milliliter) bottle
  champagne, chilled

Place the strawberries in a blender container and process until smooth. Pour the strawberries into a pitcher. Add the cranberry juice and mix well. Add the champagne and mix well. May garnish with sliced fresh fruit. Yield: 12 servings.

Sandi Davison, Laureate Gamma Upsilon
Kansas City, Missouri

ICED MOCHA

2 cups milk
1/3 cup chocolate syrup

1 tablespoon instant
  coffee

Combine the milk, chocolate syrup and coffee powder in a pitcher and mix well. Pour over ice into glasses. Garnish with whipped topping.
Yield: 2 servings.

Norma Albright, Preceptor Phi
Madison, Wisconsin

CARAMEL COFFEE

1 to 1 1/2 cups fresh
  brewed coffee

1 teaspoon caramel
  syrup

Pour the coffee into a mug. Stir in the caramel syrup. Top with whipped topping. Yield: 1 serving.

Laura Schultes, Xi Gamma Kappa
Bowling Green, Kentucky

SPICED WHITE COFFEE

3/4 cup ground coffee
1 1/2 teaspoons cinnamon
1 1/2 teaspoons nutmeg
4 cups water

4 cups milk
3 to 4 tablespoons sugar
Sweetened whipped
cream

Combine the coffee, cinnamon and nutmeg in the filter basket of a drip coffee maker. Brew the coffee to desired strength using the water. Heat the milk and sugar in a saucepan; do not boil. Stir the brewed coffee into the milk mixture. Pour into mugs. Garnish with the whipped cream. Yield: 8 servings.

Emma Pritchard, Xi Pi Exemplar
Columbia, Mississippi

AMARETTO ORANGE TEA

This is a gracious way to end a fun-filled formal evening.

3 cups strong brewed tea
1/2 cup Grand Marnier
1/2 cup amaretto

8 ounces whipping
cream, whipped

Combine the tea, Grand Marnier and amaretto in a teapot and mix well. Pour into teacups. Garnish with the whipped cream. Yield: 4 servings.

Delma J. Waller, Preceptor Alpha Sigma
Waterloo, Ontario, Canada

HOT FLORIDA TEA

4 lemon slices
12 whole cloves
2 1/2 cups apricot nectar
1 cup pink grapefruit
juice

1 cup water
2 tablespoons sugar
2 cinnamon sticks
2 teaspoons instant tea

Stud the lemon slices with the cloves. Combine the apricot nectar, pink grapefruit juice, water, sugar and cinnamon sticks in a large saucepan and mix well. Bring to a boil, stirring occasionally. Reduce the heat and simmer, covered for 10 minutes. Stir in the tea powder. Serve hot. Yield: 6 to 8 servings.

Patricia Toulouse-Tesch, Preceptor Alpha Rho
Albuquerque, New Mexico

HOT RASPBERRY CIDER

1 (48-ounce) bottle apple
cider or apple juice
1/4 teaspoon unsweetened
lemonade drink mix
1/8 teaspoon unsweetened
raspberry drink mix

1 (3-ounce) package
raspberry gelatin
1 (4-ounce) package red
hot cinnamon candies

Heat the cider in a slow cooker. Do not boil. Add the lemonade drink mix and raspberry drink mix and stir until dissolved. Stir in the raspberry gelatin. Add the candies and stir until dissolved. Serve hot. Yield: 12 servings.

Denise Massie
Mt. Vernon, Missouri

Soups

ARTICHOKE SOUP

This is a delicious, low-fat soup. It makes an easy meal when served with bread or crackers and a salad.

1 pound turkey sausage
2 (14-ounce) cans
artichoke hearts,
chopped
3 cups Italian-style
tomatoes, diced
2 to 3 (14-ounce) cans
chicken broth

1 envelope instant onion
soup mix
1/2 teaspoon Italian
seasoning
1/2 teaspoon basil
1/2 teaspoon oregano

Slice the sausage into 1/2-inch pieces. Brown in a large, non-stick skillet. Add the artichokes and tomatoes and mix well. Stir in the chicken broth, onion soup mix, Italian seasoning, basil and oregano. Simmer for 30 minutes. Ladle into soup bowls. May substitute water for chicken broth.
Yield: 6 to 8 servings.

Judy Reid, Xi Tau Psi
Flower Mound, Texas

LOW FAT CABBAGE SOUP

This soup has less than 1 gram of fat, so it is great for anyone. Add French bread and fresh fruit and you have an easy, low-fat meal.

1 (32-ounce) bottle
tomato juice
1 quart water
1 medium onion, chopped
1 small green bell
pepper, chopped

1 (16-ounce) package
coleslaw mix
1 (16-ounce) jar salsa
(optional)

Combine tomato juice, water, onion, bell pepper, coleslaw mix and salsa in a large saucepan over medium-high heat. Bring to a boil, reduce the heat and simmer for 20 minutes. Ladle into soup bowls.
Yield: 8 to 10 servings.

Karen Wagner, Xi Mu Gamma
Manitou Beach, Michigan

CARROT SOUP

5 cups chicken or
    vegetable broth
8 carrots, thinly sliced
2 medium potatoes,
    peeled, chopped
2 medium onions,
    chopped

3 ounces cream cheese,
    cubed
2 cups milk
Salt and pepper to taste

Combine the broth, carrots, potatoes and onions in a large saucepan over medium-high heat. Cook until the vegetables are tender, stirring frequently. Stir in the cream cheese and cook over low heat until melted. Add the milk, salt and pepper and simmer for 3 to 5 minutes. Ladle into soup bowls.
Yield: 6 to 8 servings.

Carol MacKenzie, Kappa Master
Guelph, Ontario, Canada

EASY CLAM CHOWDER

2 (10-ounce) cans cream
    of potato soup
2 (4-ounce) cans minced
    clams, drained

2 (8-ounce) cans
    Mexicorn
2 soup cans milk
Salt and pepper to taste

Combine the soup, clams, Mexicorn and milk in a medium saucepan over medium-high heat. Add the salt and pepper and simmer for 15 minutes. Ladle into soup bowls. Yield: 6 servings.

Marie Robinson, Xi Omega Nu
Sugarland, Texas

COLORADO 4X4 SOUP

1 pound lean ground
    beef
1 (15-ounce) can ranch-
    style beans
1 (10-ounce) can
    minestrone

1 (10-ounce) can
    tomatoes with green
    chiles
Salt and pepper to taste

Brown the ground beef in a saucepan over medium-high heat until crumbly; drain. Stir in the beans, minestrone, tomatoes, salt and pepper. Simmer for 30 to 45 minutes. Ladle into soup bowls and serve with corn bread. May also prepare in a slow cooker.
Yield: 6 to 8 servings.

Gaye Tow, Epsilon
Oklahoma City, Oklahoma

LEEK SOUP

2 medium leeks
3 medium potatoes,
    peeled

8 ounces Polish sausage
1 cup (about) milk,
    heated

Trim the leeks, cut into halves lengthwise and wash under cold water; drain. Chop leeks, potatoes and sausage into bite-size pieces. Combine the potatoes, half of the sausage and a small amount of water in a saucepan and bring to a boil. Add the leeks and remaining sausage and cook until the leeks are tender-crisp. Stir hot milk into leek mixture. Add milk only to the portion of leek mixture being served. Ladle into soup bowls. Serve with hot, crusty bread.
Yield: 3 servings.

Kathleen Urban, Xi Omega
Pewaukee, Wisconsin

OLIVE GARDEN SOUP

1½ pounds ground beef
1 medium onion,
    chopped
2 (20-ounce) cans
    minestrone
1 (16-ounce) can kidney
    beans, drained

1 (10-ounce) can
    tomatoes with green
    chiles
1 soup can water
Salt and pepper to taste

Brown the ground beef and onion in a large saucepan over medium-high heat until crumbly; drain. Add the minestrone, kidney beans, tomatoes, water, salt and pepper. Simmer for 30 minutes, stirring occasionally. Ladle into soup bowls.
Yield: 8 to10 servings.

Patty Smith
Waxahachie, Texas

QUICK FRENCH ONION SOUP

4 cups hot water
4 medium onions,
    chopped
6 beef bouillon cubes

2½ tablespoons butter
1 tablespoon grated
    Parmesan cheese

Combine the water, onions, bouillon cubes, butter and cheese in a large saucepan. Bring to a boil; reduce the heat and simmer for 1 hour, stirring occasionally. Ladle into soup bowls. Yield: 5 servings.

Florence E. Peetz, Laureate Alpha Nu
The Dalles, Oregon

SPICY POTATO SOUP

1 pound ground beef
2 medium onions,
    chopped
3 large potatoes, peeled
    and cubed
3 (8-ounce) cans tomato
    sauce

4 cups water
2 teaspoons salt
1 teaspoon pepper
½ to 1 teaspoon hot
    pepper sauce

Brown the ground beef and onions in a saucepan over medium-high heat until crumbly; drain. Add the potatoes, tomato sauce, water, salt, pepper and hot pepper sauce. Bring to a boil; reduce the heat and simmer for 1 hour, stirring occasionally. Ladle into soup bowls and serve with corn muffins.
Yield: 6 servings.

Patricia Miller, Preceptor Alpha Omega
Coffeyville, Kansas

ZESTY TOMATO SOUP

2 (10-ounce) cans   **2 teaspoons chili**
   tomato soup   **powder**
2²/₃ cups water

Combine the soup, water and chili powder in a saucepan over medium-high heat. Cook until heated through. Ladle into soup bowls and garnish with oyster crackers or shredded Monterey Jack cheese.
Yield: 4 to 5 servings.

Judy Ramer, Xi Beta Xi
North Little Rock, Arkansas

EASY VEGETABLE SOUP

This is an easy, healthy soup on a cold night. I like to serve it with bacon, lettuce and tomato sandwiches.

1 (46-ounce) can   **1 (28-ounce) package**
   vegetable juice   **frozen mixed**
   cocktail   **vegetables**

Combine the vegetable juice cocktail and vegetables in a large saucepan over medium-high heat. Bring to a boil; reduce the heat and simmer until vegetables are tender. Ladle into soup bowls. Yield: 6 servings.

Eloise W. Evans, Laureate Upsilon
Omaha, Nebraska

MEXICAN CHILI

This soup was served at a family gathering for the baptism celebration for my granddaughter, Sydney Wall.

1 pound ground beef   **1 (15-ounce) can**
1 (16-ounce) can kidney   **tomatoes with onion**
   beans, drained   **and garlic**
1 (15-ounce) can white   **2 cups salsa**
   corn, drained

Brown the ground beef in a large saucepan over medium-high heat until crumbly; drain. Add the beans, corn, undrained tomatoes and salsa; mix well. Cook until heated through. May also cook in the oven or in a slow cooker. Add water for desired consistency. Ladle into soup bowls. Top with shredded Cheddar cheese and serve with tortilla chips.
Yield: 6 to 8 servings.

LuAnn Wall, Preceptor Alpha
Cheyenne, Wyoming

Salads

ALMOND GRAPES

1 large bunch of seedless   **¹/₂ teaspoon almond**
   red grapes   **extract**
1 large bunch of seedless   **1 cup chopped toasted**
   white grapes   **pecans**
1 cup sour cream
1 cup packed brown
   sugar

Wash and rinse grapes and set aside. Combine the sour cream, brown sugar and almond extract in a bowl and mix well. Pour the sour cream mixture over the grapes in a large bowl; toss to coat. Stir in the pecans. Chill, covered, overnight for the best flavor.
Yield: 6 servings.

Dinah Wilson
Magnolia, Arkansas

BANANA SALAD

4 medium bananas,   **1 cup sugar**
   mashed   **8 ounces whipped**
1¹/₂ cups buttermilk   **topping**

Combine the bananas, buttermilk and sugar in a bowl; mix well. Fold in the whipped topping. Spread the mixture in a 9x13-inch dish. Freeze until firm.
Yield: 12 servings.

Toppy Bell, Laureate Eta Theta
Richardson, Texas

CHERRY SALAD

This is an easy, delicious salad that was a favorite of my late, 95-year-old mother.

1 (20-ounce) can light   **1 (8-ounce) can crushed**
   cherry pie filling   **pineapple**
1 (14-ounce) can   **16 ounces light whipped**
   sweetened condensed   **topping**
   milk

Combine the pie filling, condensed milk and pineapple in a large bowl; mix well. Fold in the whipped topping. Chill, covered, at least 1 hour before serving, stirring after 30 minutes. Yield: 12 servings.

Virginia Beach, Eta Master
Aurora, Colorado

LAYERED GELATIN SALAD

1 (3-ounce) package
   orange gelatin
1 (3-ounce) package
   lemon gelatin
1¹/2 cups boiling water
14 to 15 large
   marshmallows

3 ounces cream cheese,
   cut into small chunks
1 (8-ounce) can crushed
   pineapple, drained
1 (3-ounce) package
   orange gelatin

Prepare 1 package orange gelatin using package directions. Pour into a 9x13-inch dish and chill until firm. Dissolve the lemon gelatin in boiling water in a bowl. Mix until dissolved. Stir in the marshmallows, cream cheese and pineapple. Let cool. Pour mixture over orange gelatin layer. Chill until firm. Prepare the remaining orange gelatin using package directions. Let cool. Pour over the lemon gelatin layer. Chill until firm. Yield: 12 servings.

Alice A. Swartz, Alpha Delta Rho
Chillicothe, Missouri

MELON AND RASPBERRY SALAD

1 (3-ounce) package
   lemon gelatin
1 cup boiling water
1 cup fresh raspberries

1 cup cantaloupe or
   honeydew melon
   balls

Dissolve the gelatin in boiling water in a bowl. Mix until dissolved. Chill until slightly firm. Fold in raspberries and melon balls. Pour the mixture into a ring mold. Chill until firm. Invert onto a prepared dish to serve. Yield: 6 servings.

Ellen Plossl, Xi Delta Rho
LeRoy, New York

SUNSHINE SALAD

1 (3-ounce) package
   orange gelatin
1 cup boiling water
1 cup cold water

2 tablespoons vinegar
1 cup crushed pineapple
1 cup grated carrots

Dissolve the gelatin in boiling water in a bowl. Mix until dissolved. Add the cold water and vinegar. Chill until slightly firm. Fold in the pineapple and carrots. Pour the mixture into a mold sprayed with non-stick cooking spray. Chill until firm. Invert onto a bed of lettuce and garnish with mayonnaise. Yield: 6 servings.

Donna Deseve, Xi Delta Rho
LeRoy, New York

EASY TOMATO ASPIC

I always serve this salad at Christmas dinner because the red and green is festive and it goes nicely with turkey.

1 (28-ounce) can stewed
   tomatoes
2 (3-ounce) packages
   lemon gelatin

2 green onions, sliced

Heat tomatoes in a saucepan on the stove until boiling. Add the lemon gelatin and stir until dissolved. Remove from heat. Stir in the green onions. Pour the mixture into a mold. Chill until firm. Invert onto a bed of lettuce to serve. Yield: 8 servings.

Stephanie Higgins, Preceptor Gamma Tau
Sorrento, British Columbia, Canada

YOGURT GELATIN SALAD

1 (3-ounce) package
   gelatin (any flavor)
1 cup boiling water
1 cup ice cubes

8 ounces yogurt (any
   flavor)
¹/2 cup whipped topping

Dissolve gelatin in boiling water in a bowl. Add the ice cubes and stir until melted. Add the yogurt and whipped topping and beat at medium speed until light and foamy. Pour into a dish and chill until firm. Try using different combinations of gelatin and yogurt for different flavors. Yield: 5 servings.

Maeanna Blomberg, Alpha Beta Zeta
Lake Winnebago, Maryland

CAULIFLOWER SALAD

1 medium head
   cauliflower
1 (4-ounce) can black
   olives

3 green onions, chopped
Mayonnaise to taste

Clean and cut the cauliflower into bite-size pieces. Combine with the black olives and onions in a bowl and mix well. Stir in mayonnaise to desired consistency. Chill. Yield: 8 servings.

Joyce Garlow, Psi Masters
Loveland, Colorado

Mary D. Stockwell, Xi Lambda, Baton Rouge, Louisiana, makes French Green Bean Salad by mixing 2 well-drained cans French-style green beans, ¹/4 cup each chopped white and green onions, 2 chopped hard-cooked eggs, ¹/2 cup chopped bell pepper and 1 cup shredded Cheddar cheese. Mix in mayonnaise, salt and pepper to taste. Serve on crisp lettuce.

SWEET POTATO SALAD

1 (16-ounce) can sweet
  potatoes, diced or
  3 medium sweet
  potatoes, cooked,
  diced
1 cup mayonnaise
1 tablespoon milk

1/4 teaspoon salt
4 large Red Delicious
  apples, cut in 1/2-inch
  cubes
2 cups chopped celery
1/2 cup raisins
1/2 cup chopped walnuts

Chill the sweet potatoes. Combine mayonnaise, milk and salt in a large bowl; mix well. Stir in the apples, celery, raisins and walnuts. Fold in sweet potatoes. Chill, covered. Yield: 12 servings.

Joyce Ivey, Delta Master
Kalispell, Montana

CILANTRO SALAD DRESSING

1/2 cup sugar
1/3 cup vinegar
2 teaspoons dried
  cilantro

1/4 cup chopped onion
1 teaspoon salt
1 teaspoon dry mustard
1 cup vegetable oil

Process the first 6 ingredients in a blender until smooth. Add the oil gradually, processing constantly until smooth and thickened. Chill, covered, until ready to serve. Yield: 2 cups.

Jan Duggins, Xi Theta Tau
Harrisburg, Illinois

EASY COLESLAW DRESSING

1/2 cup low-fat
  mayonnaise
1/2 cup vinegar

1/2 cup sugar
1/2 cup canola oil

Process all ingredients in a blender until smooth. Chill, covered. Toss with coleslaw mix 10 minutes before serving. Yield: 2 cups.

Ina Bethea, Mu Master
Mt. Vernon, Washington

CREAMY RANCH DRESSING

This makes a great dressing for salads or a dip for vegetables and chips.

1 cup mayonnaise
1/2 cup sour cream
1/4 cup milk
1 tablespoon dried
  parsley flakes

1 teaspoon garlic
  powder
1 teaspoon onion
  powder

Combine the ingredients in a bowl and mix well. Chill, covered, until ready to serve. Yield: 1 2/3 cups.

Kaye C. Lang, Preceptor Eta
Sparks, Nevada

ORIENTAL SALAD DRESSING

A Japanese lady gave this recipe to me many years ago. It is delicious served on salad greens with pine nuts, croutons and Chinese noodles.

1 cup vegetable oil
3/4 cup rice vinegar
1/2 sugar
1/3 cup sesame oil

4 teaspoons MSG
1 tablespoon salt
2 teaspoons pepper

Combine the vegetable oil, rice vinegar, sugar, sesame oil, MSG, salt and pepper in a glass jar with a lid. Cover and shake until well blended. Chill until ready to serve. Shake thoroughly before each use. Yield: 2 cups.

Dorothy I. James, Alpha Epsilon Master
Lakewood, Washington

SALAD DRESSING

This dressing is perfect to use for coleslaw, green leaf salads or potato salads.

1 (14-ounce) can
  sweetened condensed
  milk
2 cups mayonnaise

1 cup sugar
1 cup white vinegar
1 teaspoon salt
1/4 teaspoon pepper

Combine the condensed milk, mayonnaise, sugar, vinegar, salt and pepper in a blender container; process until smooth. Pour into a glass jar with a lid. Chill, covered, until ready to serve. Yield: 5 cups.

Shirley Diane Hicks, Xi Iota Lambda
Shelhina, Missouri

Main Dishes

ITALIAN BEEF

My sister gave me this good, easy recipe.

1 (3- to 5-pound) beef
  roast, trimmed
1 (12-ounce) jar
  pepperoncini

1 pepperoncini jar water
Salt and pepper to taste

Place the roast in a slow cooker. Arrange the pepperoncini over the roast. Pour the water over the pepperoncini. Season with salt and pepper. Cook on High for 6 to 8 hours. Remove the roast to a cutting board. Shred with a fork. Serve on buns. Yield: 12 to 20 servings.

Julie Rothe, Preceptor Gamma Zeta
Ballwin, Missouri

ITALIAN RUMP ROAST

1 (5-pound) rump roast
1 envelope Italian salad
  dressing mix
1 envelope brown gravy
  mix
2 cups water

Place the roast in a slow cooker. Combine the salad dressing mix, gravy mix and water in a bowl and mix well. Pour over the roast. Cook on Low for 8 to 10 hours. Remove the roast to a cutting board. Shred with a fork. Return the beef to the slow cooker. Cook for 6 hours longer. Drain the beef. Serve on buns. May serve undrained beef over mashed potatoes. May add cooked noodles to leftover beef for another meal. Yield: 5 to 10 servings.

Georgetta Stonewall, Preceptor Epsilon Chi
Kingston Mines, Illinois

EXCELLENT AND EASY BRISKET

This is an easy recipe with very little cleanup. It reheats well and is also good cold.

1 (3- to 4-pound) beef
  brisket
1 envelope onion soup
  mix
²/₃ cup brown sugar
¹/₂ teaspoon garlic
  powder
1 cup catsup

Place the brisket on a large piece of foil in a roasting pan. Pour a mixture of the soup mix, brown sugar, garlic powder and catsup over the top. Wrap and seal with the foil, allowing space at the top. Bake at 350 degrees for 3¹/₂ to 4 hours or until tender. Slice the brisket. Serve with the drippings.
Yield: 12 to 16 servings.

Jayne Sivill, Xi Alpha Kappa
Chillicothe, Missouri

EASY STROGANOFF

This is our daughter's favorite birthday dinner.

2 pounds sirloin tip beef
1 (10-ounce) can
  mushrooms
1 (19-ounce) can cream
  of mushroom soup
1 (10-ounce) can cream
  of chicken soup
¹/₃ envelope onion soup
  mix

Cut the beef into ¹/₂-inch cubes. Drain the mushrooms, reserving ¹/₃ cup of the liquid. Combine the soups, soup mix, mushrooms and reserved liquid in a bowl and mix well. Arrange the beef in a 3-quart baking dish. Spoon the soup mixture over the beef. Bake, covered, at 275 degrees for 5 to 6 hours. Serve over egg noodles. Yield: 8 servings.

Anita Syme, Laureate Alpha Xi
North Vancouver, British Columbia, Canada

HODGEPODGE STEW

1¹/₂ pounds ground beef
2 (10-ounce) cans
  vegetable soup
2 (15-ounce) cans pinto
  beans
1 (10-ounce) can
  tomatoes with green
  chiles

Brown the ground beef in a skillet, stirring until crumbly; drain. Stir in the soup, pinto beans and tomatoes. Cook over medium heat for 20 minutes. Yield: 8 servings.

Bobbi Carter, Xi Kappa
Independence, Kansas

FIVE-MINUTE CHILI

My children love this chili because of the tomato soup base. It's fast and easy—perfect for a meal after an afternoon of sledding.

1¹/₂ pounds ground beef
2 (26-ounce) cans
  tomato soup
1 (40-ounce) can chili
  beans
Chili powder to taste

Brown the ground beef in a skillet, stirring until crumbly; drain. Combine the soup, beans and chili powder in a large saucepan over medium heat. Add the ground beef and mix well. Cook until heated through. Serve with corn chips. Garnish with green onion slices and shredded mild Cheddar cheese. Yield: 6 to 8 servings.

Melody Sublette-Peyton, Omicron Chi
Spirit Lake, Louisiana

SUPER-QUICK CHILI

I invented this recipe when I wanted a quick, spicy chili.

1 pound ground beef
1 (14-ounce) can diced
  tomatoes with garlic
  and onion
1 (10-ounce) can Italian
  tomato soup
1 soup can water
1 (15-ounce) can kidney
  beans, rinsed, drained
Salt and pepper to taste

Brown the ground beef in a skillet, stirring until crumbly; drain. Stir in the seasoned tomatoes, soup and water. Bring to a boil. Add the beans and mix well. Add salt and pepper and mix well. Cook over low heat for 20 to 30 minutes. May cook over medium heat just until heated through. Serve with a fresh salad and crusty bread or crackers.
Yield: 4 servings.

Suzanne P. Meyer, Alpha Psi
Radnor, Ohio

EASY CASSEROLE

1¹/2 pounds lean ground
   beef
Salt and pepper to taste
³/4 cup chopped onion
1 (10-ounce) can cream
   of chicken soup

1 (16-ounce) can sweet
   peas, drained
1 (32-ounce) package
   Tater Tots

Press the ground beef evenly over the bottom of a 9x13-inch baking dish sprayed with nonstick cooking spray. Sprinkle with salt and pepper. Layer with chopped onion, soup, peas and Tater Tots. Bake at 375 degrees for 45 to 60 minutes or until ground beef is cooked through and Tater Tots are golden brown. Yield: 8 to 10 servings.

Jeanette Sepulvedo, Xi Zeta Mu
Borger, Texas

HAMBURGER AND GREEN BEAN CASSEROLE

1 pound ground beef
1 (15-ounce) can green
   beans

1 (10-ounce) can tomato
   with rice soup
3 cups mashed potatoes

Brown the ground beef in a skillet, stirring until crumbly; drain. Add the green beans and soup and mix well. Spoon into a 2-quart baking dish. Spread the mashed potatoes evenly over the top. Bake at 350 degrees for 30 minutes or until potatoes are golden brown. Yield: 4 servings.

Gaylene Swearingen, Alpha Rho
Mountain Home, Idaho

MOCK FILETS

2 pounds lean ground
   beef
1 envelope onion soup
   mix

1 egg
4 to 6 slices thick-cut
   bacon

Combine the ground beef, soup mix and egg in a bowl and mix well. Shape into 1-inch-thick patties. Wrap the perimeter of each patty with a slice of bacon, securing with a wooden pick. Broil or grill over low heat until ground beef and bacon are cooked through. Serve with baked potato, corn on the cob and tossed salad. Yield: 4 to 6 servings.

Linda Schlouski, Mu Eta
Jacksonville, Illinois

CRUSTY HAMBURGER PATTIES

1¹/2 pounds lean ground
   beef
2 eggs
¹/4 teaspoon pepper
1¹/2 stacks saltines,
   finely crushed

1 large onion, sliced
Vegetable oil for frying
Salt to taste

Shape the ground beef into 8 thin patties. Combine the eggs and pepper in a shallow bowl and beat well. Dip the patties into the egg mixture. Coat with the cracker crumbs. Heat ¹/4 inch oil in a large frying pan over medium heat. Cook the patties in the oil until cooked through and brown on both sides, turning once. Drain the skillet, reserving a small amount of oil in the skillet. Sauté the onion in the oil until tender and light brown, adding salt to taste. Serve the patties with the sautéed onions. Yield: 8 servings.

Karen Snavely, Xi Alpha Zeta
Lilburn, Georgia

MEAT LOAF

2 pounds lean ground
   beef
1 onion, chopped
2 large potatoes, peeled,
   shredded

3 large carrots, peeled,
   shredded
Salt and pepper to taste
Garlic powder to taste

Combine the ground beef, onion, potatoes, carrots, salt, pepper and garlic powder in a bowl and mix well. Press into a loaf pan. Bake for 1 hour. Serve with mixed vegetables and dinner rolls. Yield: 8 servings.

Sylvia Swanson, Xi Alpha Xi
Burnsville, Minnesota

SIMPLY MEAT LOAF

When I first made this meat loaf, my mother kept asking how it was going to hold together without any eggs.

1 pound extra-lean
   ground beef
1 cup cornflake crumbs

1 (10-ounce) can chicken
   with rice soup

Combine the ground beef, cornflake crumbs and soup in a bowl and mix well. Press into a loaf pan sprayed with nonstick cooking spray. Bake at 350 degrees for 1 hour or until cooked through. Serve with green beans and mashed potatoes.
Yield: 3 to 4 servings.

Amy Thiede, member at large
Kansas City, Missouri

EASY OVEN KALUA PORK

This easy pork recipe is great for a Hawaiian-style social or luau. It's similar to the Kalua or Hawaiian pig served in the islands.

1 (5- to 6-pound) pork butt	1 tablespoon or more sea salt
1 tablespoon liquid smoke	½ to 1 cup water

Score the fatty part of the pork in several places. Rub the pork with the liquid smoke and sea salt. Place in a roasting pan. Add the water to the bottom of the pan. Bake, tightly covered, for 4 hours or until cooked through. Remove the pork to a cutting board. Shred with a fork. Serve with rice.
Yield: 6 to 8 servings.

Joan McDonald, Laureate Omega
Bellevue, Washington

SWEET-AND-SOUR RIBS

3 to 4 pounds country-style pork ribs	½ cup red wine vinegar
½ gallon pineapple juice	1 (16-ounce) jar honey
1 (1-pound) package dark brown sugar	¾ cup cornstarch

Combine the ribs and pineapple juice in a Dutch oven. Bring to a boil. Cook over medium heat for 1 hour. Combine the brown sugar, wine vinegar and honey in a bowl and mix well. Remove the ribs from the pineapple juice, reserving the pineapple juice. Place the ribs in the brown sugar mixture. Marinate, covered, in the refrigerator for 30 minutes or longer. Remove the ribs from the marinade, reserving half the marinade. Grill the ribs over hot coals for 20 minutes, basting frequently and turning once. Add the cornstarch and the reserved marinade to the reserved pineapple juice. Cook over low heat until thickened, stirring constantly. Serve the ribs over hot cooked rice. Spoon the sauce over the rice.
Yield: 4 to 6 servings.

Jeri Martin, Preceptor Beta Psi
La Quinta, California

NORTH OF THE BORDER-STYLE POSOLE

My husband will only eat hominy when it is prepared this way.

4 pork steaks	1 (4-ounce) can chopped green chiles
Salt and pepper to taste	
1 (14-ounce) can hominy, drained	1 teaspoon chili powder
1 onion, chopped	1 garlic clove, chopped

Place the pork steaks in a slow cooker. Season with salt and pepper. Layer the hominy, onion and green chiles over the pork steaks. Sprinkle with chili powder and garlic. Cook on Low for 4 to 6 hours.
Yield: 4 servings

Betty Pederlick, Preceptor Beta Delta
Show Low, Arizona

BAKED PORK CHOPS

6 pork chops	2 tablespoons brown sugar
2 tablespoons vegetable oil	Juice of ½ lemon
2 (8-ounce) cans tomato sauce	½ cup water
½ cup finely chopped celery	1 teaspoon mustard

Brown the pork chops in the oil in a skillet. Arrange the pork chops in a shallow 8x12-inch baking dish. Combine the tomato sauce, celery, brown sugar, lemon juice, water and mustard in a bowl and mix well. Spoon over the pork chops. Bake, covered, at 350 degrees for 1 hour or until tender.
Yield: 6 servings.

Carolyn Honeycutt, Xi Alpha Sigma
Stansbury Park, Utah

PORK CHOP CASSEROLE

1½ cups rice	Salt and pepper to taste
3 cups water	4 to 6 pork chops
1 (10-ounce) can tomatoes with green chiles	

Combine the rice, water, tomatoes, salt and pepper in a bowl. Spoon into a 9x12-inch baking dish. Top with the pork chops. Bake, covered with foil, at 350 degrees for 1 hour. Remove the foil. Bake for 15 minutes longer. Yield: 4 to 6 servings.

Jane Robertson, Xi Xi Nu
Georgetown, Texas

SEVEN-UP PORK CHOPS

6 (1-inch-thick) pork chops	1 envelope onion soup mix
1 (12-ounce) bottle Seven-Up	

Arrange the pork chops in a shallow baking dish. Pour Seven-Up over the pork chops. Sprinkle with the soup mix. Bake at 350 degrees for 1 hour.
Yield: 6 servings.

Barbara Melton, Epsilon Mu
Shreveport, Louisiana

PORK CHOP SCALLOP

4 to 6 pork chops,
   trimmed
Salt and pepper to taste
1 (10-ounce) package
   scalloped potatoes
2 tablespoons chopped
   pimento

Brown the pork chops in a greased skillet. Season with salt and pepper. Remove the pork chops to a plate. Mix the potatoes using the package directions. Spoon the potato mixture into the skillet. Stir in the pimento. Bring to a boil, stirring occasionally. Arrange the pork chops over the potatoes. Cook, covered, over low heat for 30 to 35 minutes or until the potatoes are tender. Yield: 4 to 6 servings.

Lynn Dennis, Beta Alpha Epsilon
Vernon, Texas

CHINESE PORK CHOPS

1/4 cup soy sauce
1/4 cup chili sauce
1 tablespoon honey
Salt and pepper to taste
8 (3/4- to 1-inch-thick)
   pork chops, trimmed

Combine the soy sauce, chili sauce, honey, salt and pepper in a bowl and mix well. Arrange the pork chops in a 9x13-inch baking dish. Spoon the sauce over the pork chops. Bake, covered, at 350 degrees for 30 minutes, basting occasionally with the sauce. Bake, uncovered, for 30 minutes longer, basting occasionally with the sauce. Yield: 6 to 8 servings.

Elizabeth Elden, Omega Theta
Ft. Myers, Florida

PIMENTO PORK CHOPS

4 (1-inch-thick) pork
   chops
Salt and pepper to taste
Garlic salt to taste
1 tablespoon vegetable
   oil
1 large onion, sliced
1 (4-ounce) can whole
   pimentos, coarsely
   chopped
1 (10-ounce) can cream
   of mushroom soup
1/4 cup catsup

Season the pork chops with salt, pepper and garlic salt. Brown the pork chops in the oil in a skillet. Remove the pork chops to a plate. Add the onions to the skillet. Sauté until tender. Return the pork chops to the skillet. Combine the pimentos, soup and catsup in a bowl. Spoon over the pork chops. Simmer, covered, for 50 minutes or until tender, turning occasionally. Serve with au gratin potatoes or rice. Yield: 4 servings.

Shirley Petersen, Laureate Kappa
Beatrice, Nebraska

DELICIOUS EASY PORK CHOPS

6 (3/8- to 1/2-inch-thick)
   center cut pork chops
Salt to taste
2 cups fine bread crumbs
   or crushed cornflakes
Pepper to taste

Line a baking sheet with foil. Spray the foil with non-stick cooking spray. Season the pork chops with salt. Coat with the bread crumbs. Arrange on the foil-lined baking sheet. Sprinkle with pepper. Bake at 400 degrees for 40 minutes or until the bread crumbs are light brown, turning once. Serve with applesauce and seasoned mashed potatoes. Yield: 6 servings.

Norma Gragg, Laureate Delta Pi
Euless, Texas

JUICY PORK CHOPS

1/3 cup flour
1 teaspoon salt
1 teaspoon dry mustard
1/2 teaspoon garlic salt
6 to 8 pork chops
2 tablespoons vegetable
   oil
1 (10-ounce) can roasted
   garlic soup

Combine the flour, salt, dry mustard and garlic salt in a shallow bowl and mix well. Coat the pork chops with the flour mixture. Brown the pork chops in the oil in a skillet. Layer the pork chops with the soup in a slow cooker, ending with the soup. Cook on Low for 6 to 8 hours or on High for 3 to 4 hours, adding water if needed. Serve with rice or mashed potatoes. Yield: 6 to 8 servings.

Dianne Kennedy, Preceptor Theta
Ormond Beach, Florida

STUFFED PORK CHOPS

4 (2-inch-thick) center
   cut pork chops
1 (6-ounce) package
   stuffing mix
1 (10-ounce) can cream
   of mushroom soup
Salt and pepper to taste

Cut a pocket in the side of each pork chop. Prepare the stuffing using the package directions. Grease a 9x13-inch baking pan. Spread a small amount of the stuffing mixture over the bottom of the pan. Stuff the pork chops with the remaining stuffing mixture. Spread the soup evenly over the top. Season with salt and pepper. Bake at 350 degrees for 30 to 45 minutes or until pork chops are cooked through. Yield: 4 servings.

Carol Sizemore, Preceptor Alpha Upsilon
Northfork, West Virginia

THREE-PEPPER SAUSAGE SAUTE

1 large red bell pepper
1 large yellow bell
    pepper
1 large green bell pepper
1 pound hot Italian
    sausage
1 onion, sliced
1 teaspoon dried
    oregano leaves
1/2 to 1 teaspoon
    Tabasco sauce
1/4 cup water

Cut the bell peppers into 1/2-inch slices. Cook the sausage in a large skillet over medium heat until brown on all sides, turning as needed. Prick with a fork. Remove the sausage to a cutting board. Add the bell peppers and onion to the skillet. Sauté for 5 minutes. Cut the sausage into 1-inch slices. Add the sausage, oregano, Tabasco and water to the skillet and mix well. Bring to a boil. Cook, covered, over low heat for 5 minutes. Yield: 4 servings.

Judy Mowrey, Xi Delta Iota
Tucson, Arizona

RED BEANS AND SAUSAGE

I prepare this recipe for my children and grandchildren when we get together to celebrate birthdays.

1 pound smoked sausage
1 cup chopped onion
1 cup chopped green bell
    pepper
1 cup catsup
1 tablespoon mustard
Basil to taste
Oregano to taste
1 tablespoon minced
    garlic
2 (16-ounce) cans light
    red kidney beans
1 kidney bean can water

Sauté the sausage, onion and green pepper in a skillet until the sausage is brown; drain. Add the catsup, mustard, basil, oregano and garlic, stirring to coat the sausage. Add the kidney beans and water. Simmer over low heat for 30 minutes or until thickened. Serve over hot cooked rice. Serve with asparagus stems. Yield: 4 servings.

Patsy Bienvenu, Beta Rho
St. Martinville, Louisiana

KIELBASA WITH A KICK

2 cups instant rice
2 cups water
1 cup salsa
1/2 pound kielbasa,
    thinly sliced

Combine the rice, water, salsa and kielbasa in a bowl and mix well. Spoon into a 2-quart microwave-safe dish. Microwave for 10 minutes or until all of the water is absorbed. Yield: 4 servings.

Angela Helms, Beta Gamma
Lincoln, Maine

SAUSAGE SURPRISE

5 potatoes, peeled, sliced
1 head cabbage, cut into
    wedges
1 pound sausage links,
    cut into 2-inch slices

Arrange the potatoes in the bottom of a slow cooker. Add water to cover. Arrange the cabbage over the potatoes. Add the sausage. Cook on Low for 10 hours or longer. Serve with corn bread. Yield: 8 servings.

George Anne Bedford, Laureate Zeta Gamma
Deer Park, Texas

SAUSAGE AND EGG CASSEROLE

We used to serve this delicious, rich casserole at our annual "Lavender and Lace" rush party.

1 pound bulk sausage
12 eggs
16 ounces Cheddar
    cheese, shredded
2 cups heavy cream

Brown the sausage in a skillet, stirring until crumbly; drain. Break the eggs into a 9x13-inch baking pan. Pierce the egg yolks with a fork. Layer the sausage and cheese over the top. Pour the cream over the cheese. Bake at 325 degrees for 45 to 60 minutes or until set. Serve with cinnamon rolls or muffins and cranberry jello. Yield: 12 servings.

Barb Olson, Preceptor Alpha
Missoula, Montana

SAUSAGE CASSEROLE

I like to make this dish for birthday and potluck breakfasts.

1 pound bulk sausage
1 (8-count) can crescent
    rolls
2 cups shredded Cheddar
    cheese
4 eggs, beaten
3/4 cup milk
Salt and pepper to taste

Brown the sausage in a skillet, stirring until crumbly; drain. Line the bottom of a buttered 9x13-inch baking dish with the crescent rolls, pressing the perforations to seal. Layer the sausage and cheese over the top. Combine the eggs, milk, salt and pepper in a bowl and mix well. Pour over the cheese. Bake at 425 degrees for 25 minutes or until set. Let stand for 5 minutes before serving. May add other omelet-type ingredients if desired. Serve with fruit and coffee. Yield: 4 to 6 servings.

Barbara Accordino, Xi Mu
Louisville, Kentucky

NIGHT BEFORE BRUNCH EGGS

8 slices bread, buttered, cubed
8 eggs, beaten
4 cups milk
1/2 pound Cheddar or Swiss cheese
8 ounces ham, chopped
Salt and pepper to taste

Arrange the bread in an 11x14-inch baking pan. Combine the eggs, milk, cheese, ham, salt and pepper in a bowl and mix well. Pour over the bread. Refrigerate, covered overnight. Bake at 350 degrees for 1 hour or until set. May add peas, chopped onion or chopped green bell pepper. Yield: 8 servings.

Celeste P. Litton, Kappa Omicron
Ballwin, Missouri

SCRAMBLED EGG MUFFINS

1/2 pound bulk sausage
12 eggs
1/2 cup chopped onion
1/4 cup chopped green bell pepper
1/2 teaspoon salt
1/4 teaspoon pepper
1/4 teaspoon garlic powder
1/2 cup shredded Cheddar cheese

Brown the sausage in a skillet, stirring until crumbly; drain. Beat the eggs in a large bowl. Add the onion, green pepper, salt, pepper and garlic powder and mix well. Stir in the sausage and cheese. Spoon by 1/3 cupfuls into greased muffin cups. Bake at 350 degrees for 20 to 25 minutes or until a knife inserted near the center comes out clean. Yield: 12 servings.

Barbara A. Todd, Beta Sigma Phi
Dearborn, Missouri

ENGLISH MUFFIN BREAKFAST

I like to have these on hand for a quick breakfast.

1 pound bulk sausage
4 eggs, lightly beaten
1 (8-ounce) jar Cheez Whiz
6 English muffins, split

Brown the sausage in a skillet, stirring until crumbly; drain. Add the eggs to the sausage in the skillet. Cook until the eggs are set, stirring constantly. Add the Cheez Whiz and mix well. Spoon some of the egg mixture onto each muffin half. Arrange on a baking sheet. Freeze until firm. Store in freezer bags in the freezer. To serve, bake or microwave one or more servings until heated through. Yield: 12 servings.

Pauline Dennis
Dallas, Texas

CHEESE QUICKIES

12 ounces Monterey Jack cheese, shredded
1 bunch green onions, finely chopped
7 or 8 pieces bacon, crisp-fried, crumbled
3 to 4 tablespoons mayonnaise
4 English muffins, split

Combine the cheese, green onions and bacon in a bowl. Add enough of the mayonnaise to bind the cheese mixture together. Spread over each English muffin half. Arrange on a baking sheet. Broil for 3 to 5 minutes or until brown. Yield: 8 servings.

Treva Scott, Beta Beta
Neodesha, Kansas

QUICK CHICKEN AND DUMPLINGS

1 (2- to 3-pound) chicken
1 (10-ounce) can cream of chicken soup
4 or 5 flour tortillas, cut up

Boil the chicken in water to cover in a stockpot until cooked through. Remove the chicken to a cutting board, reserving the broth. Add the soup to the broth and mix well. Shred the chicken, removing the skin and bones. Add the chicken to the reserved broth mixture. Bring to a boil over high heat. Add the tortillas. Cook over medium heat for 15 to 20 minutes; do not stir. Yield: 5 or 6 servings.

Rosemary Hohman, Xi Epsilon Psi
Brookport, Illinois

CHICKEN AND DRESSING

A business acquaintance related this recipe to me over the phone many years ago. It has been a standby for me ever since.

8 boneless skinless chicken breasts
1 (8-ounce) package sliced Swiss cheese
1 (8-ounce) package herb-seasoned stuffing
1 (10-ounce) can cream of mushroom soup
1 (10-ounce) can chicken broth

Arrange the chicken in a 9x13-inch baking pan. Top each piece of chicken with a slice of Swiss cheese. Layer with the stuffing and a mixture of the soup and broth. Bake, covered with foil, at 350 degrees for 1 hour or until the chicken is cooked through. Serve with steamed broccoli. Yield: 8 servings.

Janet Miller, Preceptor Kappa
Ludington, Michigan

STUFFED CHICKEN BREASTS

4 or 5 boneless skinless
   chicken breasts
Salt and pepper to taste
1 cup chopped broccoli
1 small onion, diced
1 tablespoon butter
1 cup shredded Swiss or
   Colby cheese
¼ teaspoon nutmeg
Paprika to taste

Pound the chicken to ¼-inch thickness between waxed paper. Season with salt and pepper. Sauté the broccoli and onion in the butter in a skillet for 5 minutes. Remove to a bowl. Add the cheese and nutmeg to the broccoli mixture and mix well. Spoon some of the broccoli mixture onto each piece of chicken. Fold the chicken to enclose the broccoli mixture. Arrange each piece of chicken seam side down in a lightly greased 8x10-inch baking dish. Spoon the remaining broccoli mixture around the chicken. Sprinkle paprika over the top. Bake at 450 degrees for 20 minutes or until chicken is cooked through. Serve with rice, salad and homemade wheat bread.
Yield: 4 to 5 servings.

Karla Wing, Xi Psi
Jackson, Michigan

POLAR CHICKEN

1 (8-ounce) bottle
   Catalina salad
   dressing
1 (16-ounce) can whole
   cranberry sauce
1 envelope onion soup
   mix
10 chicken breasts

Combine the salad dressing, cranberry sauce and soup mix in a bowl and mix well. Arrange the chicken in a large shallow baking dish. Spoon the salad dressing mixture over the chicken. Bake at 350 degrees for 1 hour. Serve with rice. Yield: 10 servings.

Jill Douglas, Preceptor Epsilon Sigma
Kanata, Ontario, Canada

SWEET-AND-SOUR CHICKEN

1 (12-ounce) jar apricot
   preserves
1 envelope onion soup
   mix
1 (8-ounce) bottle
   Russian salad
   dressing
8 chicken breasts

Combine the apricot preserves, soup mix and salad dressing in a large bowl and mix well. Add the chicken. Marinate, covered, in the refrigerator for 1 to 10 hours. Arrange the chicken in a 9x13-inch baking dish. Bake at 350 degrees for 1 hour or until cooked through. Serve over rice. Yield: 8 servings

Juanell Arthur, Xi Zeta Mu
Borger, Texas

CHICKEN WITH PORK SKINS

1 egg
3 egg whites
4 or 5 boneless skinless
   chicken breasts
1 (2-ounce) package
   pork skins, crushed
1 teaspoon butter
Salt and pepper to taste

Whisk the egg and egg whites in a bowl until blended. Dip the chicken in the eggs. Coat with the pork skins. Sauté in the butter in a skillet over high heat for 5 minutes or until brown on each side, turning once. Arrange in a baking dish sprayed with nonstick cooking spray. Bake at 350 degrees for 25 to 30 minutes or until cooked through. Season with salt and pepper. Serve with green salad and baked acorn squash. Yield: 4 to 5 servings.

Patti Solinsky, Xi Chi Kappa
McKinleyville, California

BROILED CHICKEN CORDON BLEU

My husband buys chicken breasts every other week so that I'll make this for him.

4 boneless skinless
   chicken breasts
¼ cup butter
4 thin slices ham
4 tablespoons honey
   mustard dressing
4 thin slices Swiss
   cheese

Arrange the chicken on a broiler pan sprayed with nonstick cooking spray. Broil 4 inches from the heat source for 3 minutes. Turn the chicken. Broil for 3 minutes. Brush with the butter. Top each with a ham slice. Broil for 1 to 2 minutes. Brush with the dressing. Top each with a Swiss cheese slice. Broil for 1 minute longer. Serve with asparagus. Yield: 4 servings.

Karen Phillips
Menasha, Wisconsin

BAKED HONEY DIJON CHICKEN

2½ cups milk
Salt and pepper to taste
1 (8-ounce) bottle honey
   Dijon marinade
3 tablespoons ranch
   salad dressing
2 boneless skinless
   chicken breasts

Combine the milk, salt, pepper, marinade and salad dressing in a bowl and mix well. Place the chicken in a large sealable plastic bag. Add the milk mixture; seal. Marinate in the refrigerator for 12 to 24 hours. Remove the chicken and marinade to a 7x12-inch baking pan. Bake at 350 degrees for 30 to 45 minutes or until the chicken is cooked through. Serve with corn and steamed broccoli with cheese.
Yield: 2 servings.

Katrina Lane, Epsilon Rho
Pelham, Alabama

SLOW-COOKER SOUTHWESTERN CHICKEN

My mother-in-law first served us this on the day after Christmas last year. It was a nice break from turkey. There weren't any leftovers.

2 (15-ounce) cans whole
kernel corn, drained
1 (15-ounce) can black
beans, rinsed, drained
1 (16-ounce) jar chunky
salsa

6 boneless skinless
chicken breasts
1 cup shredded Cheddar
cheese

Combine the corn, black beans and ¹/₂ cup of the salsa in a slow cooker. Add the chicken and remaining salsa. Cook on High for 3 to 4 hours or until chicken is cooked through. Sprinkle with the cheese. Cook for 5 minutes or until cheese melts. Yield: 6 servings.

Debbie Collaer, Xi Beta
Meridian, Idaho

PARMESAN CHICKEN

1 cup crushed butter
crackers
¹/₂ cup grated Parmesan
cheese

2 tablespoons parsley
4 boneless skinless
chicken breasts
¹/₂ cup melted margarine

Combine the cracker crumbs, Parmesan cheese and parsley in a shallow dish. Dip the chicken in the margarine in a shallow bowl. Coat with the cracker crumb mixture. Arrange in a 9x11-inch baking dish. Spoon the remaining cracker crumbs over the top. Drizzle with the remaining margarine. Bake at 400 degrees for 1 hour. Yield: 4 servings.

Sara Ussery, Xi Delta Rho
Brentwood, Tennessee

BAKED CHICKEN WITH RICE

1 cup rice
1 cup water
1 teaspoon salt
1 teaspoon pepper
1¹/₂ cups milk

1 (10-ounce) can low-fat
cream of chicken soup
4 to 6 boneless skinless
chicken breasts

Combine the rice, water, salt, pepper, milk and soup in a bowl and mix well. Spread over the bottom of an 11x13-inch baking dish sprayed with nonstick cooking spray. Arrange the chicken over the rice. Bake, covered with foil, at 350 degrees for 1¹/₂ hours or until chicken is cooked through. Yield: 4 to 6 servings.

Beatrice Finkemeier, Preceptor Delta Alpha
Lee's Summit, Missouri

LOW-FAT BAKED CHICKEN REUBEN

4 boneless skinless
chicken breasts
1 (16-ounce) can
sauerkraut, drained
4 slices light Jarlsberg
cheese

1¹/₄ cups light or fat-free
Thousand Island
salad dressing

Arrange the chicken in a 9x13-inch baking dish sprayed with nonstick cooking spray. Layer the sauerkraut, cheese and salad dressing over the top. Bake, covered with foil, at 325 degrees for 1¹/₂ hours or until chicken is cooked through. Remove the foil. Broil the chicken for 5 minutes or until brown on top. Garnish with chopped parsley. To reduce the amount of sodium in this dish, rinse the sauerkraut. Serve with hot rolls and tossed salad. Yield: 4 servings.

Jacqueline M. Kaldon, Beta Master
Greensboro, North Carolina

CHILI CHICKEN

4 boneless skinless
chicken breasts
1 (14-ounce) can Italian
stewed tomatoes

1 (15-ounce) can chili
with beans
4 slices Cheddar or
American cheese

Arrange the chicken in a 7x11-inch baking dish. Add the tomatoes. Bake at 350 degrees for 50 minutes or until chicken is cooked through. Spoon the chili over the chicken. Bake for 10 minutes longer. Top with the cheese. Bake for 3 to 4 minutes or until the cheese melts. Serve with flour tortillas and green salad. Yield: 4 servings.

Mary Ann Kinzie, Xi Alpha Alpha Omicron
Ennis, Texas

CREAMY CHICKEN

This is a working girl's easy recipe. It was given to me by one of my co-workers.

8 ounces cream cheese
¹/₂ cup flour
1 (10-ounce) can cream
of mushroom soup

¹/₂ cup water
4 to 6 boneless skinless
chicken breasts

Melt the cream cheese in the slow cooker. Add the flour, soup and water and mix well. Top with the chicken. Cook on Low for 8 hours. Chop the chicken into small pieces with a spoon, stirring to mix with the sauce. Serve over mashed potatoes or noodles. Yield: 4 to 6 servings.

Dorothy Thompson, Laureate Beta Sigma
St. Charles, Missouri

CHICKEN FAJITAS

This makes a light and quick dinner that my whole family will eat.

1 onion, sliced	**Salt and pepper to taste**
2 garlic cloves, crushed	**4 boneless skinless**
1 red bell pepper, sliced	**chicken breasts, cut**
1½ teaspoons cumin	**into strips**
1½ teaspoons chili	**1 tablespoon vegetable**
powder	**oil**
¼ teaspoon oregano	**8 flour tortillas**

Sauté the onion, garlic, red pepper, cumin, chili powder, oregano, salt, pepper and chicken in the oil in a skillet for 8 minutes or until the vegetables are tender and the chicken is cooked through. Spoon the chicken mixture onto the tortillas. Fold the tortillas to enclose the filling. May garnish with salsa and sour cream. Yield: 8 servings.

Berny Suchan, Xi Zeta
Yorkton, Saskatchewan, Canada

CHICKEN CHEESE ENCHILADAS

1 (10-ounce) nacho	**2 cups chopped cooked**
cheese soup	**chicken**
½ cup milk	**1 teaspoon chili powder**
½ cup salsa	**8 (8-inch) flour tortillas**

Stir the soup and milk together in a bowl. Combine the salsa, chicken, chili powder and 2 tablespoons of the soup mixture in a bowl and mix well. Spread about ⅓ cup of the chicken mixture on each tortilla. Fold the tortillas to enclose the filling. Arrange seam side down in a greased 8x10-inch baking dish. Spread the remaining soup mixture over the top. Bake, covered with foil, at 375 degrees for 35 minutes or until hot and bubbly. Serve with salad and Mexican rice. Yield: 4 servings.

Cheryl Schroeder, Beta Theta Psi
Bay City, Texas

CHICKEN IN RED WINE

1 (2- to 3-pound)	**1 cup finely chopped**
chicken, cut up	**onion**
2 tablespoons vegetable	**2 cups red wine**
oil	**Salt and pepper to taste**

Cook the chicken in the oil in a skillet until brown. Add the onion and wine. Simmer, covered, for 45 minutes or until the chicken is cooked through. Serve with buttered rice and green salad. Yield: 4 servings,

Angie Tomko, Chi Zeta
Dunnellon, Florida

LOW-FAT CHICKEN BAKE

2½ boneless skinless	**½ teaspoon oregano**
chicken breasts,	**½ teaspoon basil**
chopped	**½ teaspoon garlic**
1 (16-ounce) jar mild	**powder**
taco sauce	
12 ounces low-fat	
cottage cheese	

Arrange the chicken in a 9x13-inch baking pan. Layer with the taco sauce and cottage cheese. Sprinkle with the oregano, basil and garlic powder. Bake, covered with foil, at 350 degrees for 1 hour. Stir before serving. Serve with rice or noodles. Yield: 4 to 6 servings.

Emma Durost, Beta Omicron
Lebanon, Maine

QUICK CHICKEN

When my son was in college, I would make this for him when he came home to visit.

1 (10-ounce) can cream	**Cracker crumbs to taste**
of mushroom soup	**Poppy seeds to taste**
1 cup sour cream	**½ cup butter, melted**
4 chicken breasts,	
cooked, chopped	

Stir the soup and sour cream together in a bowl. Add the chicken and mix well. Spoon into an 8-inch square baking pan. Cover with cracker crumbs. Sprinkle with poppy seeds. Drizzle with the butter. Bake at 350 degrees for 25 to 30 minutes or until heated through. Serve with baked potatoes, creamed corn and green beans. Yield: 4 to 6 servings.

Judith Ann Omo, Laureate Psi
Siloam Springs, Arkansas

DRESS THE CHICK

1 (6-ounce) package	**1 (10-ounce) can cream**
chicken flavor	**of chicken soup**
stuffing mix	**½ cup sour cream**
2 cups chopped cooked	**1 cup frozen green peas,**
chicken breast	**thawed**

Prepare the stuffing using the package directions. Combine the chicken, soup, sour cream and peas in a bowl and mix well. Spoon into a lightly greased 8-inch square baking dish. Spread with the prepared stuffing. Bake at 350 degrees for 1 hour.
Yield: 4 servings.

Kathie Reichstein, Laureate Kappa
Beatrice, Nebraska

CHICKEN PIE

I like to make this recipe with leftover chicken.

2 cups chopped cooked
  chicken
1 (20-ounce) can peas
  and carrots, drained
1 (20-ounce) can whole
  potatoes, drained,
  cut up

2 (12-ounce) jars home-
  style chicken or
  turkey gravy
2 all ready pie pastries

Combine the chicken, peas and carrots, potatoes and gravy in a bowl and mix well. Line a deep-dish pie plate with 1 of the pie pastries. Spoon the chicken mixture into the prepared pie plate. Top with the remaining pie pastry, sealing the edge and cutting vents. Bake at 400 degrees for 40 to 50 minutes or until golden brown. Yield: 4 to 6 servings.

Velma J. Weaver, Laureate Mu
Salem, New Jersey

WHITE CHILI

1 pound dried Great
  Northern beans
6 cups (or more) chicken
  broth
2 garlic cloves, minced
1 onion, chopped
4 boneless skinless
  chicken breasts, cut
  into 1-inch pieces

1 tablespoon water
1 teaspoon ground
  cumin
1 teaspoon oregano
1/8 teaspoon cayenne
1 teaspoon salt

Rinse and sort the beans. Combine the beans, broth, garlic and half of the onion in a stockpot and mix well. Bring to a boil. Simmer for 2½ to 3 hours or until beans are very tender, adding additional broth as needed. Sauté the chicken and remaining onion with the water in a nonstick skillet until cooked through. Stir in the cumin, oregano, cayenne and salt. Add the chicken to the bean mixture. Simmer for 1 hour. Garnish with sour cream, chopped tomato, chopped green onions and shredded Monterey Jack cheese. Add 4 ounces green chiles for spicier chili. Serve with tortilla chips. Yield: 8 servings.

Diane Kelly, Zeta Eta
Derby, Kansas

Joann Templeton, Preceptor Epsilon Gamma, Pickering, Ontario, Canada, browns 12 Octoberfest sausages, cuts into pieces and combines with 32 ounces sauerkraut and 1 tablespoon caraway seeds in a slow cooker on Low for 4 to 5 hours for Easy Sauerkraut and Sausage.

TURKEY BURRITOS

1 pound ground turkey
1 (20-ounce) can refried
  beans
1/2 cup shredded Cheddar
  cheese

1/2 teaspoon garlic
  powder
Chopped fresh cilantro
  to taste
12 flour tortillas

Brown the ground turkey in a skillet, stirring until crumbly; drain. Add the beans, cheese, garlic powder and cilantro. Spoon about 2 tablespoons of the mixture onto each tortilla. Fold the tortillas to enclose the filling. Cook the burritos in a lightly greased skillet over medium heat until light brown. Serve with sour cream and salsa. Yield: 6 servings.

Sharron deMontigny, Xi Kappa
Corvallis, Oregon

PHEASANT IN WHITE WINE SAUCE

1 pheasant, cut up
2 tablespoons butter
2 (10-ounce) cans
  chicken broth

1 cup sliced mushrooms
1 cup white wine
5 sprigs of parsley,
  chopped

Brown the pheasant in the butter in a skillet. Remove to a 9x15-inch baking dish. Add the broth to the pan drippings in the skillet and mix well. Stir in the mushrooms, wine and parsley. Spoon over the pheasant. Bake, tightly covered with foil, at 325 degrees for 2 to 3 hours or until very tender. Serve with wild rice or pasta and spinach salad. Yield: 4 servings.

Ruth Larsen, Laureate Lambda
Big Arm, Montana

HALIBUT STEAKS WITH COFFEE BUTTER

1/4 cup margarine,
  melted
1 tablespoon lemon
  juice
1/2 teaspoon salt

1 tablespoon instant
  coffee granules
1/4 teaspoon onion
  powder
2 pounds halibut steaks

Combine the margarine, lemon juice, salt, instant coffee and onion powder in a bowl and mix well. Arrange the fish on a grill 3 to 4 inches from hot coals. Brush with the coffee butter. Grill for 10 minutes. Turn the fish. Brush generously with coffee butter. Grill for 10 minutes longer or until fish flakes easily. Brush generously with coffee butter. Serve immediately. Yield: 6 servings.

Margarete Sue Zimmerman, Laureate Gamma Beta
Cameron, Missouri

ORANGE ROUGHY

3 egg whites
6 tablespoons skim milk
3 pounds orange roughy

6 cups fat-free cracker
   crumbs
3/4 teaspoon dry mustard

Combine the egg whites and milk in a bowl and beat well. Dip the fish in the egg mixture. Coat with a mixture of the cracker crumbs and dry mustard. Arrange in a 9x13-inch baking pan. Bake at 425 degrees for 20 to 25 minutes or until the fish flakes easily. Yield: 8 servings.

Carol Lanham, Preceptor Nu Zeta
Visalia, California

SALMON CROQUETTES

1 (15-ounce) can salmon
1/2 cup herb-seasoned
   stuffing mix
1/4 cup chopped onion

1 egg
Pepper to taste
2 tablespoons vegetable
   oil

Combine the salmon, stuffing mix, onion, egg and pepper in a bowl and mix well. Shape into patties. Cook in the oil in a skillet until crisp and brown on both sides, turning once. Remove to a baking sheet. Bake at 350 degrees for 30 minutes. Serve with a cheese sauce and green peas. Yield: 4 servings.

Kimberly Johnson, Preceptor Alpha Tau
Lawton, Oklahoma

SALMON PUFFS

1 (15-ounce) can salmon
1 egg
1/2 cup flour, sifted

Pepper to taste
1 teaspoon (heaping)
   baking powder

Drain the salmon, reserving 1/4 cup of the liquid. Flake the salmon with a fork in a bowl. Add the egg and mix well. Stir in the flour and pepper. Combine the reserved salmon liquid with the baking powder and beat with a fork until tripled in volume. Add to the salmon mixture and mix well. Drop by teaspoonfuls into hot oil in a deep fryer. Cook until golden brown. Yield: 3 to 4 servings.

Jayne Hornsby, Xi Alpha Xi
Hueytown, Alabama

FIVE-CUP DINNER

1 (6-ounce) can tuna,
   drained
1 (5-ounce) can chow
   mein noodles
1 (10-ounce) can cream
   of mushroom soup

1 (10-ounce) can cream
   of celery soup
1 (14-ounce) can Chinese
   vegetables

Combine the tuna, noodles, soups and vegetables in a bowl and mix well. Spoon into a 1 1/2-quart baking dish. Bake at 350 degrees for 40 minutes. Yield: 6 servings.

Roxanne Saathoff, Laureate Kappa
Beatrice, Nebraska

CHEESY TUNA RICE MUFFINLETTES

2 cups cooked rice
1 cup shredded Cheddar
   cheese
1 (6-ounce) can tuna,
   drained
1 tablespoon parsley

1 tablespoon instant
   minced onion
1 teaspoon seasoned
   salt
2 eggs, beaten
2 tablespoons milk

Combine the rice, cheese, tuna, parsley, onion and seasoned salt in a bowl and mix well. Stir in the eggs and milk. Spoon equal portions of the tuna mixture into 6 muffin cups sprayed with nonstick cooking spray. Bake at 375 degrees for 15 minutes or until light brown. May serve with a butter sauce made by mixing 1/4 cup melted butter, 1 tablespoon lemon juice, 1/2 teaspoon seasoned salt and 1/2 teaspoon parsley. Yield: 6 servings.

Barbara Lewis, Alpha Delta
Kettering, Ohio

TUNA PATTIES

1 (6-ounce) can tuna,
   drained
3/4 cup graham cracker
   crumbs

1/2 cup catsup
1 egg

Combine the tuna, cracker crumbs, catsup and egg in a bowl and mix well. Shape into patties. Cook in a lightly greased skillet over medium heat until golden brown on both sides, turning once.
Yield: 6 to 8 servings.

Shirley F. Simon, Iota Master
Quincy, Illinois

FRUITS DE MER

1 cup chopped onion
8 garlic cloves, finely
   chopped
1/2 cup olive oil
4 cups white wine

2 strips of lemon peel
6 sprigs of thyme
72 littleneck clams in
   shells, scrubbed

Sauté equal portions of the onion and garlic in equal portions of the olive oil in each of 2 large skillets over medium heat for 5 minutes. Add equal portions of the wine, lemon peel and thyme to each skillet. Simmer for 3 to 4 minutes. Add equal portions of the clams to each skillet. Simmer, covered, for 7 to 10 minutes or until the clams open, discarding any clams that do not open. Discard the lemon peel and thyme sprigs. Serve over hot cooked Creole rice. Yield: 8 servings.

Pat McKelvy, Preceptor Theta Sigma
Brackettville, Texas

FAKE LOBSTER NEWBURG

1 (10-ounce) can cream
  of shrimp soup
8 ounces cream cheese,
  softened

1 (6-ounce) can lump
  crab meat
1/4 cup dry sherry

Combine the soup, cream cheese, crab meat and sherry in a saucepan over medium heat and mix well. Simmer until thickened, stirring frequently. Serve over toast or rice or in pastry shells. Yield: 4 servings.

Jean Everson, Chi Zeta
Dunnellon, Florida

BARBECUED SCALLOPS WITH BACON

My sorority sisters love this recipe. Their significant others always want them to bring home the leftovers.

9 slices bacon
18 large scallops

1/2 cup honey-flavor
  barbecue sauce

Cut each slice of bacon into halves. Wrap each scallop with a piece of bacon, securing with a wooden pick. Arrange on a broiler pan. Brush with barbecue sauce. Broil for 8 to 10 minutes or until scallops are white and edges of bacon are crisp. Yield: 18 servings.

Ginny Nichols, Omega Zeta
Winter Haven, Florida

SAVANNAH LOW-COUNTRY BOIL

In Savannah everyone loves a "boil."

3 to 4 bay leaves
1 tablespoon (heaping)
  Old Bay seasoning
Red new potatoes

Smoked sausage, cut
  into chunks
Corn on the cob
Unpeeled shrimp

Fill a stockpot 3/4 full with water. Bring to a boil over high heat. Add the bay leaves, Old Bay seasoning and potatoes. Cook just until the potatoes are tender. Add sausage, corn and shrimp in order, returning to a boil after each addition. Cook until shrimp turn pink; drain. Serve with melted butter, Tabasco sauce and cocktail sauce. Yield: variable.

Susan Parsley, Xi Eta Delta
Savannah, Georgia

GARLIC CHEESE SHRIMP WITH RICE

1 roll of garlic cheese
1 (10-ounce) can
  cream of shrimp
  soup

1/2 teaspoon curry
  powder
6 ounces frozen peeled
  salad shrimp, thawed

Combine the garlic cheese, soup and curry powder in the top of a double broiler. Cook over high heat until the garlic cheese is melted, stirring frequently. Rinse the shrimp using the package directions. Add the shrimp to the cheese sauce, stirring to mix. Serve over hot cooked rice. Yield: 4 to 5 servings.

Janie Gresham
Clarksville, Arkansas

GRILLED SHRIMP AND CHEESE

1/2 cup lime juice
1/2 cup olive oil
1 1/2 pounds shrimp,
  peeled

1 pound Colby-Jack
  cheese, sliced
2 pounds bacon

Combine the lime juice and olive oil in a bowl and mix well. Add the shrimp to the lime juice mixture. Marinate, covered, in the refrigerator for 2 to 3 hours. Remove the shrimp from the marinade. Place a cheese slice between 2 pieces of shrimp. Wrap a piece of bacon around the shrimp and cheese, securing with a wooden pick. Repeat the procedure until all of the shrimp are used. Grill or broil for 15 minutes or until the shrimp is pink and the bacon is crisp. Yield: 4 to 6 servings.

Patricia Taylor, Laureate Theta Kappa
Garden Grove, California

CHEESY MOSTACCIOLI

1 (16-ounce) package
  mostaccioli
1 1/2 pounds ground beef
1 (10-ounce) can
  Cheddar cheese soup
1 (32-ounce) jar
  spaghetti sauce

1 teaspoon Italian
  seasoning
1 teaspoon pepper
3 cups mozzarella
  cheese

Cook the mostaccioli using the package directions. Brown the ground beef in a skillet, stirring until crumbly; drain. Combine the soup, spaghetti sauce, Italian seasoning, pepper and 2 cups of the cheese in a bowl and mix well. Add the ground beef and mostaccioli and mix well. Spoon into a 3-quart baking dish. Top with the remaining cheese. Bake at 400 degrees for 25 minutes or until hot and bubbly. Yield: 8 to 12 servings.

Diane Hakala
Virginia, Minnesota

CHILI BURGER CASSEROLE

This recipe is quick and easy, making it great for working mothers.

1 pound ground beef
1 (15-ounce) can chili
1 (8-ounce) can tomato
  juice
1 cup macaroni shells,
  cooked
4 slices American cheese

Brown the ground beef in a skillet, stirring until crumbly; drain. Add the chili, tomato juice and macaroni shells and mix well. Spoon into a 9x12-inch baking dish. Bake at 350 degrees for 25 minutes. Arrange the cheese slices over the top. Bake for 5 minutes longer. Use an iron skillet for the stovetop preparation and baking to save on cleanup. Yield: 6 servings.

Sandra Wiley, Zeta Sigma
Idalou, Texas

EASY 15-MINUTE SPAGHETTI

1 pound thin spaghetti
1 pound ground beef
1 (32-ounce) jar onion
  and garlic-flavor
  spaghetti sauce
1 (15-ounce) can Italian-
  style stewed tomatoes
Crushed red pepper to
  taste
Garlic powder to taste

Cook the spaghetti using the package directions. Brown the ground beef in a skillet, stirring until crumbly; drain. Add the spaghetti sauce, tomatoes, red pepper and garlic powder and mix well. Cook over medium heat just until heated through. Serve over the spaghetti. May substitute Italian sausage for the ground beef. Yield: 4 servings.

Diane Pringle, Preceptor Epsilon Theta
Pinellas Park, Florida

ALL-AT-ONCE SPAGHETTI

1 pound ground beef
1 cup chopped onion
1 tablespoon salt
1/2 teaspoon pepper
2 teaspoons parsley
1 teaspoon basil
1 teaspoon sugar
4 cups tomato sauce
3 cups water
1/2 pound spaghetti

Brown the ground beef with the onion in a stockpot, stirring until the ground beef is brown and crumbly; drain. Add the salt, pepper, parsley, basil, sugar, tomato sauce and water and mix well. Bring to a boil, stirring constantly. Break the spaghetti into halves. Add to the ground beef mixture. Simmer, covered for 20 to 25 minutes, stirring occasionally to keep spaghetti separated. Do not overcook. May garnish with Parmesan cheese. Serve with salad and garlic bread. May substitute 7 cups tomato juice for the tomato sauce and water. Yield: 4 to 6 servings.

Barbara Oestmann, Xi Gamma Nu
Alva, Oklahoma

STUFFED SHELL DINNER

Since this dish can be frozen for later use, it's a great dish to take to friends.

20 jumbo pasta shells
1 pound ground beef
2 cups shredded
  mozzarella cheese
1 (15-ounce) jar pasta
  sauce
Salt and pepper
  to taste
Parmesan cheese to
  taste

Cook the pasta shells using the package directions. Brown the ground beef in a skillet, stirring until crumbly; drain. Combine the ground beef, 1 cup of the mozzarella cheese, 1 cup of the pasta sauce, salt and pepper in a bowl and mix well. Fill each shell with a heaping spoonful of the ground beef mixture. Arrange the pasta shells in a 9-inch square baking dish. Pour the remaining pasta sauce over the pasta shells. Top with the remaining 1 cup mozzarella cheese and Parmesan cheese. Bake, covered, at 350 degrees for 30 minutes. Bake, uncovered, for 15 minutes longer or until hot and bubbly and the cheese is light brown. Yield: 5 servings.

Cheri Metzler, Zeta Xi
Omaha, Nebraska

SCOW

1 pound ground beef
1 teaspoon sugar
1 onion, chopped
2 teaspoons flour
Salt and pepper to taste
1/4 cup catsup
1/2 cup water
Hot cooked noodles or
  rice

Brown the ground beef with the sugar in a skillet, stirring until the ground beef is crumbly; drain. Add the onion. Cook over medium heat until the onion is tender, stirring frequently. Stir in the flour, salt, pepper, catsup and water. Simmer over low heat for 30 minutes. Serve over noodles or rice. Yield: 4 to 6 servings.

Gayle A. Lea
Fredericksburg, Virginia

PEGALINI

1 (8-ounce) package wide egg noodles	1 (16-ounce) can corn or green beans
1 pound ground beef	1 (8-ounce) package mozzarella cheese
1 (16-ounce) can Sloppy Joe mix	

Cook the noodles using the package directions. Brown the ground beef in a skillet, stirring until crumbly; drain. Add the Sloppy Joe mix and simmer over medium heat for 10 minutes. Stir in the corn and noodles. Spoon into a 7x11-inch baking dish. Bake at 350 degrees for 10 minutes or until heated through. Top with the cheese. Bake for 5 minutes longer or just until the cheese is melted. Serve with hot buttered French bread. Yield: 6 servings.

Melinda Ann Harden, Preceptor Gamma Zeta
Fraser, Michigan

CHICKEN AND NOODLES

3 tablespoons margarine	1 (5-ounce) can chicken
3 tablespoons flour	1/2 (12-ounce) package frozen noodles
1 (14-ounce) can chicken broth	

Melt the margarine in a skillet over medium heat. Stir in the flour until a smooth paste forms. Add the chicken broth gradually, stirring constantly. Add the chicken and noodles. Simmer over low heat for 15 to 20 minutes, stirring occasionally. Yield: 2 servings.

Mary Kay Zinn, Eta Master
Spencer, Iowa

QUICK CHICKEN TETRAZZINI

1 (10-ounce) package spaghetti	1 (4-ounce) can chopped green chiles
1 (10-ounce) can cream of chicken soup	1 (8-ounce) package Velveeta cheese, chopped
1 (5-ounce) can chicken	

Cook the spaghetti using the package directions. Combine the soup, chicken, green chiles and cheese in a large microwave-safe bowl and mix well. Microwave on High for 5 minutes or just until the cheese is melted, stirring occasionally. Add the spaghetti and mix well. Serve with garlic bread and a salad. Yield: 8 servings.

Karen Sue Todd, Laureate Rho
Stillwater, Oklahoma

HAM AND MACARONI

When my husband was a child, this was his favorite dish. Now it is my sons' favorite dish.

1 (16-ounce) package macaroni	1 (28-ounce) can tomato purée
2 cups chopped ham	8 ounces shredded Cheddar cheese
8 slices bacon, crisp-fried, crumbled	

Cook the macaroni using the package directions. Combine the macaroni, ham, bacon, tomato purée and cheese in bowl and mix well. Spoon into a 9x13-inch baking dish. Bake, tightly covered with foil, at 350 degrees for 45 minutes. Yield: 8 to 10 servings.

Patricia J. Haefner, Xi Gamma
South Williamsport, Pennsylvania

DANNY PEPPE'S PASTA

Danny Peppe is my husband's cousin. He teaches in Rome, where he met his wife. She gave this recipe to her American in-laws, and everyone loves it.

1/2 pound bacon, finely chopped	1/2 teaspoon crushed red pepper
1 large onion, chopped	4 cups cooked penne pasta
2 tablespoons olive oil	Fresh Parmesan cheese to taste
1 (15-ounce) can tomatoes, coarsely chopped	

Cook the bacon and onion in the olive oil in a skillet over medium heat for 15 to 20 minutes or just until bacon is cooked but not crisp. Add the tomatoes and red pepper and mix well. Simmer for 20 minutes over low heat, stirring frequently. Serve over the penne pasta. Sprinkle with Parmesan cheese just before serving. Yield: 3 to 4 servings.

Judy Glorioso, Eta Theta
Plant City, Florida

TANGY TUNA PASTA

This makes a wonderful weekend lunch or weeknight dinner.

1 (12-ounce) package tri-color spiral pasta	1 (8-ounce) bottle coleslaw dressing
1 (12-ounce) can water-pack tuna, drained	1/2 cup mayonnaise

Cook the pasta using the package directions. Combine the pasta, tuna, coleslaw dressing and mayonnaise in a bowl and mix well. Yield: 5 servings.

Kellie Webb, Alpha Chi
Austin, Texas

VEGETARIAN CHILI

1 (15-ounce) can kidney
  beans
1 (15-ounce) can chili
  hot beans
1 (15-ounce) can tomato
  sauce

1 (15-ounce) can garlic
  and herb-flavor
  tomato sauce

Combine the kidney beans, chili beans, tomato sauce and garlic and herb-flavor tomato sauce in a saucepan and mix well. Cook over medium heat until bubbly. Serve with graham crackers. Yield: 4 or 5 servings.

Julie Moffett, Nu Rho
Leon, Iowa

TEX-MEX BLACK BEANS

1 (10-ounce) package
  yellow rice
1 (15-ounce) can black
  beans
1/2 cup taco sauce
1 cup sour cream or
  plain yogurt, at room
  temperature

1/2 cup lightly packed,
  coarsely chopped
  fresh cilantro, or to
  taste (optional)

Cook the rice using the package directions. Combine the black beans and taco sauce in a saucepan. Cook over low heat until heated through. Spoon the rice into 4 shallow bowls. Add the black bean mixture. Top with the sour cream and cilantro. Yield: 4 servings.

Karen L. Sawyer, On Line Alpha and Xi Epsilon Kappa
Douglasville, Georgia

EGGS NEW HAMPSHIRE WITH A TOUCH OF TEXAS

12 eggs, beaten
6 ounces cream cheese,
  chopped
4 green onions, chopped

Salt and pepper to taste
12 flour tortillas
Pico de gallo to taste

Cook the eggs, cream cheese and green onions in a skillet until set, stirring constantly. Season with salt and pepper. Spoon equal amounts of the egg mixture onto each tortilla. Add desired amount of pico de gallo. Fold the tortilla to enclose. Yield: 12 servings.

Sabra Hawkings, Xi Alpha Delta Gamma
Mansfield, Texas

EGG BRUNCH CASSEROLE

12 eggs
16 ounces Monterey Jack
  cheese, shredded

16 ounces Cheddar
  cheese, shredded
1 cup salsa (optional)

Beat the eggs in a bowl. Add the Monterey Jack cheese, Cheddar cheese and salsa and mix well. Spoon into a 9x13-inch baking dish. Bake at 350 degrees for 35 minutes or until set. Yield: 12 servings.

Sharon Talley, Preceptor Zeta
Caldwell, Idaho

JALAPENO CASSEROLE

1 (16-ounce) jar
  jalapeños, drained
2/3 cup heavy cream
2 eggs

2 cups shredded
  mozzarella cheese
2 cups shredded Cheddar
  cheese

Cover the bottom of a greased 9-inch square baking dish with the jalapeños. Combine the cream and eggs and mix well. Pour over the jalapeños. Sprinkle with the mozzarella cheese and Cheddar cheese. Bake at 350 degrees for 30 minutes or until set. May substitute skim milk for the heavy cream for a low-fat version. Yield: 4 servings.

Leslie Williams, Xi Alpha Rho
Danville, Kentucky

FAT EGGS

6 eggs
1 cup milk
2 tablespoons sugar

1/2 cup flour
1/2 cup baking mix

Process the eggs and milk in a blender until smooth. Add the sugar, flour and baking mix gradually, processing constantly at high speed until smooth. Pour into an 8x11-inch baking pan sprayed with nonstick cooking spray. Bake at 425 degrees for 20 minutes or until set. Serve immediately with maple syrup. Yield: 6 servings.

Jan Angotti, Laureate Lambda
Walla Walla, Washington

Spinach Pie is a favorite of Kathleen Johnson, Laureate Alpha Xi, London, Ontario, Canada. Mix 2 packages dry thawed chopped spinach with 1/2 cup cottage cheese, 3 chopped green onions, 1/2 cup Parmesan cheese, 3 eggs, 1 tablespoon oil and dillweed. Line a 9x9-inch pan with mozzarella slices, add spinach mixture, 1/2 cup bread crumbs and additional Parmesan cheese. Bake at 400 degrees for 30 minutes.

CHEESE SOUFFLE

We serve this dish every Christmas morning.

6 eggs
2 cups milk
1 teaspoon salt
14 slices bread, cut into
   cubes

8 ounces Cheddar
   cheese, shredded
1/2 cup melted butter

Beat the eggs with the milk and salt in a bowl. Divide the bread into 4 portions. Divide the Cheddar cheese into 3 portions. Layer the bread and cheese alternately in a greased 2-quart baking dish, beginning and ending with the bread. Pour the egg mixture over the layers. Drizzle with the butter. Chill, covered, for 8 to 10 hours. Bake, uncovered, at 375 degrees for 80 minutes or until set. Serve with sausage balls, fresh fruit and danish.
Yield: 6 to 8 servings.

Doreen Wells, Xi Alpha Chi
Cooper City, Florida

CRUSTLESS SPINACH QUICHE

This quiche is a great quick dish.

1 (10-ounce) package
   frozen chopped
   spinach, thawed
1 large onion, chopped
1 tablespoon vegetable
   oil

5 eggs
12 ounces Muenster
   cheese, shredded
Salt and pepper to taste

Squeeze the spinach to remove as much liquid as possible. Sauté the onion in the oil in a skillet just until tender. Add the spinach. Cook until any excess liquid evaporates. Let stand until cool. Beat the eggs in a bowl. Add the cheese and mix well. Combine the egg mixture with the spinach mixture. Add salt and pepper and mix well. Spoon into a 9-inch pie plate, spreading evenly. Bake at 350 degrees for 40 to 45 minutes or until brown and a wooden pick inserted near the center comes out clean. Yield: 6 to 8 servings.

Nelda Mavis Wheeldon, Theta Pi
Rushville, Indiana

Gergana Orahovats, Russell, Kansas, makes Tutmanik by mixing 1 cup plain yogurt with 2 eggs, 1/4 cup oil, 8 ounces crumbled feta cheese, 2 cups sifted flour, 1 teaspoon baking soda and 1/2 teaspoon salt. Pour into a well greased 8x8-inch baking pan, sprinkle with 1 teaspoon sweet paprika and bake at 400 degrees for 20 minutes. Serve with additional yogurt and a salad.

FROSTED CAULIFLOWER

My vegetarian friends love this dish.

1 (2-pound) head
   cauliflower
1/2 cup light mayonnaise
1 teaspoon finely
   chopped onion

1 teaspoon Dijon
   mustard
3/4 cup shredded Cheddar
   cheese

Remove the base and leaves from the cauliflower. Place bottom side up in a covered microwave-safe dish. Microwave, covered, on High for 9 to 13 minutes or until the cauliflower is cooked but firm. Turn over the cauliflower. Microwave, covered, for 2 minutes. Combine the mayonnaise, onion and Dijon mustard in a bowl and mix well. Spoon over the top of the cauliflower. Sprinkle with the cheese. Microwave, covered, for 1 minute or just until the cheese melts. Serve with salad and corn bread.
Yield: 4 servings.

Marge Hefty, Laureate Alpha Epsilon
Tucson, Arizona

BROCCOLI AND SUN-DRIED TOMATO PASTA

My family enjoys this as an occasional meatless meal.

1 large bunch broccoli
1/2 cup oil-pack sun-
   dried tomatoes,
   drained
1 tablespoon chopped
   garlic

8 ounces rotelle
1/2 cup grated Parmesan
   cheese

Break the broccoli into small florets. Combine the sun-dried tomatoes and garlic in a large bowl and mix well. Cook the rotelle using the package directions, adding the broccoli during the last 2 minutes of cooking time; drain. Add the rotelle mixture to the sun-dried tomato mixture. Toss to mix. Sprinkle with the Parmesan cheese. Serve with freshly baked bread.
Yield: 2 servings.

Anne Reiners, Beta Gamma
Millersville, Maryland

Pam Morgan, Mu, Santa Monica, California, makes Cheese and Onion Enchiladas by heating a can of enchilada sauce and dipping in a tortilla. She rolls up shredded sharp Cheddar cheese and chopped onion in the tortilla and places in a lightly greased baking dish until she has made enough for the meal. Bake at 350 degrees for 20 to 30 minutes, top with black olives, sour cream and remaining sauce.

SUN-DRIED TOMATO PASTA TREAT

1 onion, chopped
3 garlic cloves
2 teaspoons basil
1 cup oil-pack sun-dried
*   tomatoes*

3 tablespoons olive oil
2 cups hot cooked pasta

Sauté the onion, garlic, basil and sun-dried tomatoes in the olive oil in a skillet until the onion is tender. Combine the onion mixture and pasta in a bowl and toss to mix. Serve warm with Caesar salad and fresh bread. Yield: 2 servings.

Eileen McQuaid, Alpha
Charlottetown, Prince Edward Island, Canada

LOW-FAT FETTUCCINI ALFREDO

1½ teaspoons butter
¼ cup light cream
*   cheese, chopped*
1⅓ cups skim milk
2 tablespoons parsley
⅛ teaspoon white
*   pepper*

⅛ teaspoon nutmeg
¾ cup freshly grated
*   Parmesan cheese*
8 ounces fettuccini,
*   cooked*

Melt the butter in a skillet over low heat. Add the cream cheese and milk. Cook until cream cheese is melted, whisking constantly until smooth. Stir in the parsley, white pepper and nutmeg. Add the Parmesan cheese gradually, stirring constantly after each addition until smooth; sauce will be thin. Pour the sauce over the fettuccini in a large serving dish. Sprinkle with additional Parmesan cheese. Yield: 4 servings.

Carol Roper
Litchfield, Illinois

SPAGHETTI SQUARES

16 ounces spaghetti,
*   cooked, drained*
4 eggs, beaten
½ cup Parmesan cheese

¼ cup parsley
2 (8-ounce) packages
*   shredded mozzarella*
*   cheese*

Combine the spaghetti, eggs, Parmesan cheese and parsley in a bowl and mix well. Layer the spaghetti mixture and mozzarella cheese ½ at a time in a greased 9x13-inch baking pan. Bake at 350 degrees for 25 to 30 minutes or until the cheese is bubbly. Let stand for 5 minutes before cutting into squares. Serve with your favorite spaghetti sauce. Serve with a salad and garlic bread. Yield: 12 servings.

Cyndi Hill, Xi Beta Alpha
Bolling Air Force Base, District of Columbia

MEXICAN PASTA

My niece loves salsa, so I created this dish for her.

16 ounces pasta ruffles,
*   cooked*
10 ounces sharp Cheddar
*   cheese, shredded*

1 (16-ounce) jar salsa
Pepper to taste

Combine the pasta, Cheddar cheese, salsa and pepper in a bowl and toss to mix. Spoon into a 9x13-inch baking pan. Bake at 375 degrees for 30 minutes or until heated through. May add 1 chopped green bell pepper if desired. Serve with Parmesan cheese. Yield: 8 servings.

Madeline O'Halloran, Alpha Chi
Crofton, Maryland

Side Dishes

CANDIED RED APPLES

¼ cup margarine
6 to 8 apples, coarsely
*   chopped*

1 (12-ounce) package red
*   hot cinnamon candies*

Melt the margarine in a large saucepan. Stir in the apples. Cook over medium-high heat for 10 minutes or until the apples are partially cooked. Stir in the candies. Cook until the candies are dissolved. Yield: 8 to 10 servings.

Rosemary Coleman, Preceptor Zeta Epsilon
Stockton, California

BOURBON CRANBERRY SAUCE

1 (12-ounce) package
*   cranberries, rinsed,*
*   drained*
1½ cups sugar

½ cup orange
*   marmalade*
¼ teaspoon cinnamon
¼ cup bourbon

Combine the cranberries, sugar, marmalade and cinnamon in a large saucepan. Cook over medium-low heat for 45 minutes or until the berries burst, stirring frequently. Remove from heat. Stir in the bourbon. Yield: 8 to 10 servings.

Julia Stinson, Zeta Alpha
Sheridan, Arizona

CHRISTMAS CRANBERRIES

3 cups sugar
Zest of 2 lemons
2 cups chopped walnuts
2 (12-ounce) packages
*   cranberries, rinsed,*
*   drained*

Juice of 2 lemons
2 cups orange
*   marmalade*

Combine the sugar, lemon zest and walnuts in a bowl. Spread the cranberries into an 11x13-inch baking dish. Top with the sugar mixture. Drizzle the lemon juice over the top. Spoon the marmalade over the prepared dish. Place the dish on a baking sheet. Bake, covered, at 350 degrees for 45 minutes. Yield: 10 to 12 servings.

Rose Cook
Cypress, Texas

ROASTED ASPARAGUS WITH BALSAMIC VINEGAR

1 pound fresh asparagus	**1½ teaspoons extra-virgin olive oil**
Salt to taste	**1 tablespoon balsamic vinegar**
Pepper to taste	

Place the asparagus in a large, shallow baking dish. Sprinkle with the salt and pepper. Drizzle the olive oil over the asparagus, tossing to coat. Bake at 500 degrees for 10 minutes or until the asparagus is tender and light brown, stirring every 2 minutes. Drizzle the vinegar over the asparagus, tossing to coat. Serve immediately. Yield: 2 servings.

Freda I. Bush, Preceptor Gamma Kappa
Chesapeake, Virginia

SPEEDY BAKED BEANS

3 slices bacon, chopped	**1 tablespoon mustard**
1 (16-ounce) can pork and beans	**1 tablespoon brown sugar**
1 tablespoon Worcestershire sauce	**1 tablespoon onion powder**

Fry the bacon in a skillet until crisp. Stir in the pork and beans, Worcestershire sauce, mustard, brown sugar and onion powder. Simmer for 10 minutes. Yield: 4 servings.

Carol Sassin, Xi Psi Beta
Beeville, Texas

HARVARD BEETS

1 (16-ounce) can sliced beets	**1 tablespoon cornstarch**
½ cup sugar	**2 tablespoons vinegar**
	2 tablespoons margarine

Drain the beets, reserving ¼ cup of the liquid. Combine the sugar and cornstarch in a saucepan. Add the vinegar, reserved liquid and margarine and mix well. Bring to a boil, stirring frequently. Cook for 5 minutes. Stir in the beets. Cook until heated through. Yield: 4 servings.

Opal H. Stallings, Preceptor Theta Eta
Washington, North Carolina

CHEESY BROCCOLI-CAULIFLOWER

2 (16-ounce) packages frozen broccoli-cauliflower mix	**1 (10-ounce) can cream of mushroom soup**
1 cup shredded Cheddar cheese	**1 cup shredded Cheddar cheese**
2 eggs	**8 butter crackers, crushed**

Combine the broccoli-cauliflower mix, 1 cup Cheddar cheese, 2 eggs and cream of mushroom soup in a bowl and mix well. Spoon into a baking dish. Top with 1 cup Cheddar cheese. Sprinkle with the crushed crackers. Bake at 350 degrees for 45 minutes. Yield: 8 servings.

Joan Griffin, Xi Alpha Omega
Story, Wyoming

PAPRIKA CABBAGE

1 small to medium head of cabbage, coarsely chopped	**2 cups grated carrots**
1 large onion, coarsely chopped	**2 tablespoons paprika**
½ cup water	**1 tablespoon onion powder**
	1 teaspoon salt
	1 teaspoon pepper

Combine the cabbage, onion and water in a large skillet. Add the carrots and mix well. Sprinkle the paprika, onion powder, salt and pepper over the top. Cook over medium heat until vegetables are tender, stirring frequently. May add sliced Polish sausage or smoked sausage. Yield: 6 to 8 servings.

Nedra Murphy, Xi Phi Iota
Victorville, California

HUNGARIAN FRIED CABBAGE AND NOODLES

1 head of cabbage, shredded	**½ cup oil or bacon drippings**
2 tablespoons salt	**1 teaspoon pepper**
1 (16-ounce) package wide egg noodles	**Salt to taste**

Combine the cabbage and 2 tablespoons salt in a bowl. Let stand for 1 hour. Cook the egg noodles in water to cover in a saucepan until tender; drain and set aside. Heat the oil in a large skillet. Add the cabbage, pepper and salt and cook over low heat for 1 hour or until tender, stirring frequently. Combine the cabbage and egg noodles in a serving dish and mix well. Yield: 6 to 8 servings.

Esther Westfall, Laureate Psi
Grand Island, New York

CHEESY CARROT CASSEROLE

This recipe, handed down by my mother, made eating cooked carrots a real treat.

1/2 cup plus 3 tablespoons butter or margarine	5 cups sliced carrots
	8 ounces Velveeta cheese, sliced
1 onion, chopped	Crushed butter crackers

Melt the butter in a skillet. Sauté the onion in the melted butter until tender. Cook the carrots in a small amount of boiling water in a saucepan until tender; drain. Alternate layers of carrots and Velveeta cheese in a 9x9-inch baking dish until all ingredients are used. Spoon the onions over the top. Sprinkle with the crushed crackers. Bake at 350 degrees for 30 minutes. Yield: 6 to 8 servings.

Sandy Huhn, Laureate Zeta Epsilon
Redwood Valley, California

YUMMY CARROTS

2 pounds carrots, sliced	2 tablespoons dry mustard
1/4 cup packed brown sugar	
2 tablespoons melted margarine	

Cook the carrots in a small amount of boiling water in a saucepan until tender-crisp; drain. Combine the brown sugar, margarine and dry mustard in a small bowl and stir until blended. Arrange the carrots in a 9x13-inch baking dish. Pour the brown sugar mixture over the carrots. Bake at 300 degrees for 1 hour. Yield: 10 servings.

Janice Jacobson, Iota Phi
Fayetteville, North Carolina

CORN PUDDING

1 (16-ounce) can whole kernel corn, drained	2 tablespoons melted butter
4 eggs, beaten	1 teaspoon salt
2 cups whipping cream	1/2 teaspoon pepper
2 tablespoons sugar	

Combine the corn, eggs, whipping cream, sugar, butter, salt and pepper in a bowl and mix well. Pour the corn mixture into a 1 1/2-quart baking dish. Place in a larger dish filled with 2 inches of water. Bake at 350 degrees for 1 hour. Yield: 6 servings.

Sharon Gladish, Xi Zeta Omega
Petersburg, Indiana

HAYSTACKS

2 (16-ounce) cans whole green beans	1/4 cup butter
	Garlic salt to taste
Bacon strips	
1/2 cup packed brown sugar	

Drain the green beans, reserving the liquid from one can. Cut each bacon strip in half. Wrap 8 to 10 green beans with each bacon slice. Secure with a wooden pick. Place the prepared green beans in a 9x13-inch baking dish. Combine the reserved liquid, brown sugar, butter and garlic salt in a saucepan. Bring to a boil, stirring frequently. Pour over the prepared green beans. Bake, covered with foil, at 350 degrees for 45 minutes. Remove the foil and bake until bacon is brown. Yield: 6 to 8 servings.

Leisa Maliska, Pi Psi
College Station, Texas

SOUTHWESTERN HOMINY

This is a great dish to serve for a brunch. It goes great with a breakfast casserole.

2 (16-ounce) cans hominy, drained	1/4 cup finely chopped onions
2 (4-ounce) cans diced green chiles	3/4 teaspoon seasoned salt
1 cup sour cream	1/4 teaspoon pepper
1 1/2 cups shredded Cheddar cheese	

Combine the ingredients in a bowl and mix well. Spoon into a greased baking dish. Bake at 350 degrees for 30 minutes. Yield: 6 to 8 servings.

Rose Ann Munn, Xi Psi Xi
League City, Texas

BAKED ONIONS

2 (10-ounce) cans cream of mushroom soup	1 (4-ounce) package potato chips, crushed
1/2 cup milk	2 cups shredded Cheddar cheese
6 onions, thinly sliced	1/2 teaspoon cayenne

Combine the soup and milk in a bowl and stir until blended. Layer the onions, crushed potato chips and Cheddar cheese, half at a time in a greased 9x13-inch baking dish. Pour the soup mixture over the top. Sprinkle with the cayenne. Bake at 350 degrees for 1 1/2 hours. Yield: 10 servings.

Van Paschall, Laureate Alpha Delta
Amarillo, Texas

BAKED ONIONS AND POTATOES

1/3 cup butter
1/4 cup honey
1/2 teaspoon salt

4 onions, sliced
4 potatoes, sliced

Combine the butter, honey and salt in a saucepan. Cook over medium heat, stirring until blended. Place the onions and potatoes in a greased 9x13-inch baking dish. Pour the butter mixture over the top. Bake at 425 degrees for 1 hour or until golden brown. Yield: 4 servings.

Sue Steward, Alpha Beta Chi
Clinton, Missouri

ITALIAN NEW POTATOES

8 to 10 new potatoes,
*   cubed*

2 tablespoons butter
1/4 cup Italian dressing

Parboil the potatoes. Melt the butter in a skillet. Add the potatoes to the melted butter. Stir in the Italian dressing. Cook over medium heat until the potatoes are crunchy, stirring frequently. Yield: 4 servings.

Alesia Talley, Alpha Delta Nu
Kimberling City, Missouri

❖ MASHED POTATOES WITH CELERY ROOT AND BLEU CHEESE

4 large russet potatoes,
*   peeled, cubed*
1 celery root, peeled,
*   cubed*
1/3 cup milk

2 tablespoons butter
1 1/3 cups crumbled bleu
*   cheese*
Salt to taste
Pepper to taste

Boil the potatoes and celery root in water to cover in a saucepan for 20 minutes or until tender; drain. Remove to a bowl. Mash the potato mixture. Beat in the milk, butter and bleu cheese until blended. Stir in the salt and pepper. Yield: 6 servings.

Mary Braganza, Xi Beta Mu
Trenton, Ontario, Canada

PARTY POTATOES

8 to 10 potatoes, peeled,
*   cubed*
8 ounces cream cheese,
*   softened, or*
1 (8-ounce) jar Cheez
*   Whiz*

1 cup sour cream
Salt to taste
Pepper to taste
Butter, cut into pieces
Paprika

Boil the potatoes in water to cover in a saucepan until tender; drain. Beat the cream cheese and sour cream in a bowl until blended. Add the potatoes gradually, beating constantly until fluffy. Stir in the salt and pepper. Spoon into a 2-quart baking dish. Dot with the butter. Sprinkle with the paprika. Bake at 325 degrees for 25 minutes. Yield: 6 to 8 servings.

Sundee Price, Iota Lambda
Indian Mound, Indiana

RED ROASTED POTATOES

3 pounds red potatoes,
*   quartered*
1 cup chopped white
*   onions*
6 tablespoons butter

Salt to taste
Pepper to taste
1 1/4 cups shredded Swiss
*   cheese*
1/2 cup chopped scallions

Boil the potatoes in water to cover in a saucepan until tender; drain. Let stand until cool. Sauté the onions in the butter in a saucepan until translucent. Arrange the potatoes in a greased 9x13-inch baking dish. Top with the onions. Sprinkle with the salt and pepper. Bake at 375 degrees for 8 minutes. Top with the Swiss cheese and scallions. Bake for 7 to 9 minutes or until cheese is melted. Yield: 6 to 8 servings.

Marjorie A. Bailey, Epsilon Master
Kittery Point, Maine

ROASTED MUSTARD POTATOES

4 tablespoons Dijon
*   mustard*
2 teaspoons paprika
1 teaspoon cumin

1 teaspoon chile powder
1/8 teaspoon cayenne
16 small red potatoes

Whisk the Dijon mustard, paprika, cumin, chile powder and cayenne in a bowl until blended. Prick the potatoes with a fork. Place the potatoes in a greased 9-inch square baking dish. Pour the mustard mixture over the potatoes. Bake at 350 degrees for 45 minutes. Yield: 4 servings.

Penny McCurdy, Alpha Alpha Zeta
Independence, Missouri

TATER TOT CASSEROLE

2 tablespoons butter or
*   margarine*
1 (10-ounce) can cream
*   of chicken soup*
1 cup sour cream

1 1/2 cups shredded
*   Cheddar cheese*
1 (32-ounce) package
*   frozen Tater Tots*

Combine the butter, cream of chicken soup, sour cream and Cheddar cheese in a saucepan. Bring to a boil, stirring until blended. Arrange the Tater Tots in a 9x13-inch baking dish. Pour the cheese mixture over the Tater Tots. Bake at 350 degrees for 30 minutes. Yield: 10 servings.

Maxine M. Morrison, Laureate Epsilon Lambda
Pasadena, Texas

TWICE-COOKED HASHED BROWNS

6 baking potatoes
1/2 cup butter or
  margarine
1 onion, chopped
1 1/2 teaspoons Italian
  seasoning
1 teaspoon seasoning
  salt
1 teaspoon pepper
1/2 teaspoon garlic
  powder

Microwave the potatoes on Medium for 30 minutes. Dice the unpeeled potatoes. Melt the butter in a large skillet. Add the potatoes, onion, Italian seasoning, seasoning salt, pepper and garlic powder and stir to mix. Sauté until the potatoes are tender and brown. Yield: 6 servings.

Jesse Bridges, Xi Alpha Nu
Florence, South Carolina

ZUCCHINI WITH BASIL

1 tablespoon flour
Pinch of salt
Pinch of pepper
3/4 pound zucchini, sliced
2 tablespoons olive oil
1 garlic clove, minced
3 tablespoons chopped
  fresh basil
2 tablespoons grated
  Parmesan cheese

Combine the flour, salt and pepper in a bowl. Add the zucchini, tossing to coat. Heat the olive oil in a skillet. Add the prepared zucchini. Cook until the zucchini is golden brown, stirring occasionally. Spoon the zucchini into an 8-inch square baking dish. Sprinkle the garlic, basil and Parmesan cheese over the top. Bake at 400 degrees for 5 minutes. Yield: 4 servings.

Linda Jean Leake, Preceptor Alpha Sigma
Beaverton, Oregon

SAUSAGE STUFFED YAMS

4 medium yams
1/4 to 1/2 pound ground
  sweet Italian sausage
1/4 cup melted butter
1 teaspoon nutmeg
1/8 teaspoon sage

Bake the yams at 400 degrees for 15 minutes. Reduce the temperature to 375 degrees and bake an additional 45 minutes or until the yams are tender. Brown the Italian sausage in a skillet, stirring until crumbly; drain. Cut the yams in half lengthwise. Scoop out the pulp from the yams, leaving the shells intact. Mash the pulp in a bowl. Add the butter, nutmeg and sage and mix well. Stir in the Italian sausage. Spoon the yam mixture into the shells. Bake at 375 degrees for 15 minutes. Yield: 4 to 6 servings.

Marie Toni Zeman, Chi Zeta
Dunnelon, Florida

CANDIED DILLS

1 (2-ounce) container
  mixed pickling spices
1 (1-gallon) jar whole
  dill pickles, drained
1 (5-pound) bag sugar
1 (17-ounce) bottle
  tarragon vinegar

Place the pickling spices in a cheese cloth bag. Slice the dill pickles. Combine the sugar and tarragon vinegar in a bowl and mix well. Place the sliced pickles in a large container. Add the sugar mixture and pickling spice bag and stir gently. Let stand for 10 to 14 days, stirring every day. Remove the pickling spice bag. Transfer the pickles to quart jars. Yield: 4 quarts.

Betty Quigley, Preceptor Zeta Gamma
Tampa, Florida

PARKER PICKLES

A gift jar with the recipe attached has started many friends and family on the road to making their own.

1 (1-gallon) jar whole
  dill pickles, drained
1 (5-pound) bag sugar
1 tablespoon celery seed
1 small bulb of garlic,
  minced

Slice the dill pickles. Layer the sliced pickles, sugar, celery seed and garlic in the gallon jar. Seal with the lid. Let stand for 24 hours, turning frequently to let the spices blend. Chill once the sugar is dissolved. May transfer to smaller containers. Yield: 1 gallon.

Phyllis Carver, Laureate Beta Eta
Lakeland, Florida

GREEN TOMATO MINCEMEAT

This will keep for up to two years.

5 cups chopped peeled
  apples
4 cups chopped green
  tomatoes
2 cups raisins
6 cups sugar
1/2 cup lemon juice
4 teaspoons cinnamon
2 teaspoons allspice
2 teaspoons ground
  cloves
2 teaspoons salt

Combine the apples, green tomatoes and raisins in a large saucepan and mix well. Stir in the sugar, lemon juice, cinnamon, allspice, ground cloves and salt. Bring to a boil. Boil slowly for 1 hour, stirring frequently. Place the green tomato mixture in quart jars. Let stand until cool. Cover with waxed paper and a lid. May add 1 tablespoon of rum to each jar. Yield: 5 quarts.

Dianne V. Benn, Laureate Beta
Victoria, British Columbia, Canada

CORN MAC

1 (15-ounce) can whole kernel corn	1 cup uncooked shell macaroni
1 (15-ounce) can cream-style corn	1/4 cup margarine, softened
1 cup cubed Velveeta cheese	

Combine the whole kernel corn, cream-style corn, Velveeta cheese, macaroni and margarine in a greased 2-quart baking dish. Bake at 350 degrees for 45 minutes to 1 hour or until macaroni is cooked, stirring frequently. Yield: 6 to 8 servings.

Bonita G. Price, Preceptor Nu
Trenton, Missouri

MAMA'S MACARONI AND CHEESE

This was my mother's specialty for picky eaters.

1 (10-ounce) package macaroni, cooked	1/2 cup milk
1 (10-ounce) can cream of chicken soup	1/2 cup shredded Cheddar cheese
1 cup shredded Cheddar cheese	

Combine the macaroni, cream of chicken soup, 1 cup Cheddar cheese and milk in a bowl and mix well. Spoon the mixture into a 2-quart baking dish. Sprinkle with 1/2 cup Cheddar cheese. Bake at 350 degrees for 10 to 15 minutes or until cheese is melted. Yield: 6 servings.

Kathy Wagner, Beta Epsilon Tau
Houston, Texas

SPINACH FILLED PASTA SHELLS

This is great to have on hand for unexpected guests.

1 (12-ounce) container cottage cheese	1 (12-ounce) package jumbo pasta shells, cooked
2 (10-ounce) packages frozen spinach, thawed	1 (48-ounce) jar spaghetti sauce
2 eggs	

Combine the cottage cheese, spinach and eggs in a bowl and mix well. Spoon the mixture into the pasta shells. Place the prepared pasta shells in a 9x13-inch baking dish. Pour the spaghetti sauce over the top. Bake at 350 degrees for 30 minutes. May store the filled pasta shells in the freezer until ready to bake. Yield: 8 servings.

Mary Fisher, Laureate Xi
Coldwater, Michigan

ELEGANT ALMOND RICE MADE SIMPLE

2 tablespoons margarine	1 (10-ounce) can chicken broth
1/2 onion, chopped	2 cups quick-cooking rice
1/2 cup almond slivers	

Melt the margarine in a skillet. Add the onion and almonds. Cook until the almonds are golden brown, stirring frequently. Pour in the chicken broth. Stir in the rice. Bring to a boil. Turn off the heat. Let stand, covered for 10 minutes. May add 1/8 teaspoon of your favorite seasoning. Yield: 8 servings.

Nita J. Chambers, Laureate Alpha Theta
Claremore, Oklahoma

BAKED SPICED RICE

3 tablespoons butter	1 teaspoon curry powder
1 cup rice	2 cups hot chicken broth
1 green onion, chopped	1 bay leaf
1 teaspoon chervil (optional)	

Melt the butter in a saucepan. Add the rice and green onion and cook until the rice is glossy, stirring continuously. Stir in the chervil and curry powder. Add the chicken broth and bay leaf. Bring the mixture to a boil. Pour into a 2-quart baking dish. Bake, covered for 15 to 20 minutes or until liquid is absorbed. Discard bay leaf. Yield: 4 servings.

Doreen Gray, Preceptor Epsilon Kappa
Yarker, Ontario, Canada

FRIED RICE

1/2 pound bacon, chicken or ham, chopped	1 (16-ounce) package frozen mixed vegetables, cooked
2 cups cooked rice	
1 egg, beaten	

Sauté the bacon in a skillet until cooked through. Remove the bacon from the skillet to a plate and set aside. Drain the pan drippings, reserving 1 to 2 tablespoons. Heat the rice in the skillet with the reserved pan drippings. Push the rice to the side of the skillet. Pour the egg into the skillet. Scramble gently just until set. Stir in the rice and vegetables. Add the cooked bacon. Cook for 5 minutes or until heated through. Yield: 4 servings.

Sarah E. Jensen, Epsilon Psi
Eagle Grove, Iowa

RICE PILAF

Armenian in origin, this recipe was given to me by my friend Louise Rask of Colorado, formerly of California.

1 cup coiled vermicelli, crumbled
1/4 cup margarine
3 cups strong chicken broth
1 cup rice
Salt to taste
Pepper to taste

Brown the vermicelli in the margarine in a skillet, stirring constantly. Do not burn the vermicelli. Spoon the vermicelli into a 3-quart baking dish. Stir in the chicken broth and rice. Sprinkle with the salt and pepper. Bake at 350 degrees for 45 minutes, stirring once. Yield: 6 servings.

Alice Clapsaddle, Laureate Beta Nu
Larned, Kansas

SPANISH RICE PRONTO

This is a favorite at potlucks.

1/2 to 1 pound ground beef
2 cups quick-cooking rice
1/2 cup sliced onion
2 cups hot water
2 (8-ounce) cans tomato sauce
1 teaspoon chile powder
1 teaspoon salt
Dash of pepper

Brown the ground beef with the rice and onion in a skillet, stirring until the ground beef is crumbly; drain. Stir in the hot water, tomato sauce, chile powder, salt and pepper. Bring the mixture to a boil. Reduce the heat and simmer for 5 minutes. May sprinkle shredded Cheddar cheese on top before serving. Yield: 6 servings.

Victoria Smith, Preceptor Gamma Iota
Marysville, Washington

SPICY SPANISH RICE

1 cup water
1 1/2 cups brown quick-cooking rice
1/3 cup salsa
1 (16-ounce) can diced tomatoes
1 green bell pepper, finely chopped
1/4 teaspoon thyme
1/4 teaspoon salt
1/8 teaspoon pepper

Combine the water, rice, salsa, tomatoes, green pepper, thyme, salt and pepper in a large nonstick skillet and mix well. Bring to a boil. Reduce the heat to low. Simmer, covered for 25 minutes or until most of the liquid is absorbed. Yield: 5 servings.

Cheryl Schmale, Xi Iota
Garden City, Kansas

Bread

CHEESE GARLIC BISCUITS

2 cups baking mix
2/3 cup milk
1/2 cup shredded Cheddar cheese
1/4 cup melted butter
1/4 teaspoon garlic powder

Combine the baking mix, milk and Cheddar cheese in a bowl and beat until a soft dough forms. Beat vigorously for 30 seconds. Drop by tablespoonfuls 2 inches apart on a greased baking sheet. Bake at 425 degrees for 8 to 10 minutes or until golden brown. Combine the butter and garlic powder in a bowl and mix well. Brush over hot biscuits. Serve warm. Yield: 12 biscuits.

Judy Reynolds, Xi Zeta Sigma
Herrin, Illinois

❖ CREAMED CORN BISCUITS

2 cups baking mix
1 (15-ounce) can cream-style corn
1/2 cup melted butter

Combine baking mix and corn in a bowl and mix well. Turn the dough out onto a lightly floured surface. Roll the dough to 1/2-inch thickness and cut with a biscuit cutter. Pour the melted butter in a baking pan. Place the biscuits in the pan, turning once to coat each side with the butter. Bake at 450 degrees for 10 to 15 minutes or until golden brown.
Yield: 12 servings.

Donna Wood, Xi Chi
Boyce, Louisiana

QUICK BISCUITS

2 cups baking mix
1/3 cup sour cream
1/3 cup sparkling water

Combine the baking mix, sour cream and sparkling water in a bowl and stir just until moistened. Knead gently 5 or 6 times on a lightly floured surface. Roll or pat the dough to 1/2-inch thickness and cut with a floured biscuit cutter. Arrange the biscuits on a lightly greased baking sheet. Bake at 400 degrees for 12 to 15 minutes or until golden brown.
Yield: 8 biscuits.

Doris Tanner, Laureate Delta Phi
St. Augustine, Florida

RED HOT BISCUITS

2¾ cups baking mix
½ teaspoon crushed red
   pepper
½ teaspoon garlic
   powder
1 cup milk
1 cup shredded Cheddar
   cheese
2 tablespoons melted
   butter
¼ teaspoon garlic
   powder

Combine the baking mix, red pepper and ½ teaspoon garlic powder in a bowl and stir with a fork. Add the milk and Cheddar cheese and stir until mixture forms a soft dough. Drop the dough by ¼ cupfuls onto a greased baking sheet. Combine the butter and ¼ teaspoon garlic powder and mix well. Brush the tops of the biscuits with the butter mixture. Bake at 425 degrees for 10 to 12 minutes or until golden brown. Yield: 12 biscuits.

Alisha Gruenloh, Xi Pi
Lamar, Colorado

SOFT COUNTRY BISCUITS

2 cups sifted flour
4 teaspoons baking
   powder
½ teaspoon salt
¼ cup shortening
⅔ cup milk

Combine the flour, baking powder and salt in a bowl. Cut in the shortening. Stir in the milk. Roll the dough into ½-inch thickness on a floured surface. Cut with a biscuit cutter. Arrange on a baking sheet. Bake at 425 degrees for 10 minutes. Yield: 8 to 10 servings.

Bonnie Adams, Xi Theta Pi
Chillicothe, Ohio

SOUTHERN BUTTERMILK BISCUITS

This is the first recipe I mastered after marrying a biscuit-loving man 40 plus years ago.

2 cups flour
1 tablespoon baking
   powder
¾ teaspoon salt
½ teaspoon baking soda
5 tablespoons chilled
   shortening
1 cup buttermilk

Sift the flour, baking powder, salt and baking soda together in a bowl. Cut in the shortening until crumbly. Add the buttermilk, stirring with a fork until a soft dough forms. Knead lightly on a floured surface. Pat the dough out to ¾-inch thickness. Cut with a biscuit cutter. Arrange on an ungreased baking sheet. Bake at 425 degrees for 12 to 15 minutes or until golden brown. Yield: 12 servings.

Jo Ann Walcher, Laureate Theta
Austin, Texas

CURRANT SCONES

5 cups flour
3 tablespoons baking
   powder
¾ cup butter, softened
1½ cups sugar
¾ cup dried currants
1½ cups milk
1 egg, beaten

Combine the flour and baking powder in a large bowl. Cut in the butter until crumbly. Stir in the sugar and currants. Add the milk gradually, stirring with a fork until a soft dough forms. Divide the dough into 4 portions and place on a floured surface. Roll into circles, ½ inch thick. Cut each circle into 8 wedges. Brush the top with the egg. Arrange on a greased baking sheet. Bake at 375 degrees for 8 to 10 minutes or until light brown. Yield: 32 servings.

Susan McCullough, Xi Gamma Phi
Prineville, Oregon

BEER BREAD

We enjoy this bread on cold winter nights with a pot of stew or soup.

3 cups self-rising flour
3 tablespoons sugar
1 (12-ounce) bottle beer

Combine the flour, sugar and beer in a bowl and mix well. Pour into a loaf pan. Bake at 350 degrees for 35 minutes. Butter the top of the loaf and bake for an additional 10 minutes. Yield: 12 servings.

Mary J. Claflin, Xi Alpha Omicron
Bronaugh, Missouri

BUTTER STICK BREAD

⅓ cup butter
2¼ cups sifted self-
   rising flour
1 cup milk
1 tablespoon sugar

Melt the butter in a 9x13-inch baking pan in the oven. Combine the flour, milk and sugar in a bowl and mix well. Knead 10 times on a floured surface. Roll out to ½-inch thick. Cut into ½x6-inch strips. Dip each strip into the melted butter. Place the strips in the baking pan. Bake at 450 degrees for 15 minutes. May top with poppyseeds. Yield: 6 to 8 servings.

Darlene Dresser, Preceptor Alpha Tau
Ft. Cobb, Oklahoma

Karla Bauer, Beta Iota, Brookings, Oregon, makes Lunch Bread by spreading a mixture of 1 cup each mayonnaise, shredded Cheddar cheese, green onions and ½ cup butter on split rolls and baking at 350 degrees for 5 minutes, then broiling until cheese melts.

MINI CHEDDAR LOAVES

3½ cups baking mix
2½ cups shredded sharp
   Cheddar cheese
2 eggs, beaten
1¼ cups milk

Combine the baking mix and Cheddar cheese in a large bowl. Add the eggs and milk, stirring just until moistened. Pour the batter into 4 greased and floured 6x3-inch loaf pans. Bake at 350 degrees for 35 to 40 minutes or until loaves test done. Serve warm. Yield: 4 loaves.

Katie Ritterskamp, Gamma Tau
Washington, Indiana

ONION-GARLIC BREAD STICKS

1 cup margarine,
   softened
1 envelope onion soup
   mix
16 slices bread, crusts
   trimmed

Combine the margarine and onion soup mix in a bowl and mix well. Spread the mixture on 1 side of each slice of bread. Cut each slice of bread into 5 strips. Arrange on a baking sheet. Bake at 375 degrees for 10 to 12 minutes or until golden brown. Remove to a wire rack to cool. Yield: 16 servings.

Lila Beth Hoffert, Preceptor Alpha Omicron
Pekin, Illinois

WORLD'S QUICKEST YEAST BREAD

Hot, fresh bread smothered in butter is a true comfort food.

5 to 6 cups flour
2 cups hot water
2 tablespoons dry yeast
2 tablespoons sugar
1 tablespoon salt

Combine 5 cups of the flour, hot water, yeast, sugar and salt in a bowl and mix to form a ball, adding additional flour if dough is sticky. Knead the dough on a floured surface for 5 minutes or until smooth. Place in a greased bowl, turning to coat the surface. Let rise, covered, for 15 minutes. Shape the dough into 2 balls. Place on a baking sheet. Cut an x in the top of each ball. Place a pan of hot water on bottom shelf of a cold oven. Place the baking sheet on the middle shelf of the oven. Bake at 400 degrees for 20 to 30 minutes or until golden brown. Yield: 25 servings.

Anne-Marie Ball, Psi Gamma Psi
Shelton, Washington

CHEESE CROUTONS

2 tablespoons shredded
   American cheese
¼ teaspoon dry mustard
2 English muffins, split,
   cubed

Combine the American cheese and dry mustard in a small bowl and mix well. Place the muffin pieces in a bowl. Spray with nonstick cooking spray to coat. Stir and spray again. Sprinkle the cheese mixture over the top of the muffin pieces, tossing to coat. Spread in an ungreased 15x10-inch baking pan. Bake at 300 degrees for 20 to 25 minutes or until crisp, stirring occasionally. Let stand until cooled completely. Store in an airtight container. Yield: 7 servings.

Patti Moore, Preceptor Gamma
Salt Lake City, Utah

PARTY ROLLS

1 cup butter, softened
1 cup sour cream
2 cups self-rising flour
   or baking mix

Cream the butter and sour cream together in a bowl. Add the flour and mix well. Spoon into petite muffin cups. Bake at 425 degrees for 15 minutes. Yield: 50 servings.

Mildred S. Mahler, Laureate Nu
Cookeville, Tennessee

SURPRISE MUFFINS

3 cups vanilla ice cream
3 cups self-rising flour

Combine the vanilla ice cream and flour in a bowl and stir with a wooden spoon just until moistened. Spoon into paper-lined muffin cups, filling the cups ¾ full. Bake at 350 degrees for 20 to 30 minutes or until muffins test done. Yield: 18 servings.

Phyllis Ann Revello, Preceptor Beta Sigma
Scottsdale, Arizona

BALLOON BUNS

This is a great recipe to make with your children. I made it with my mother when I was a little girl.

1 (5-count) can biscuits
¼ cup sugar
¾ teaspoon cinnamon
5 large marshmallows
2 tablespoons
   margarine, melted

Pat the biscuits to flatten on a floured surface. Combine the sugar and cinnamon in a small bowl. Dip the marshmallows in the margarine. Roll in the sugar mixture. Place 1 marshmallow in the center of each biscuit. Pull the biscuit around the marshmallow to cover, pressing the edges to seal. Dip the biscuits in the margarine. Roll in the sugar mixture.

Place the biscuits, sealed side down, on a baking sheet lined with waxed paper. Bake at 400 degrees for 10 minutes. Yield: 5 servings.

Brenda Shawgo, Epsilon Alpha
Canton, Illinois

CUSTARD-LIKE WAFFLES

1 cup cottage cheese	**¼ cup vegetable oil**
6 eggs	**½ cup milk**
½ cup flour, sifted	**¼ teaspoon vanilla**
¼ teaspoon salt	**extract**

Combine the cottage cheese, eggs, flour, salt, oil, milk and vanilla in a blender container; process at high speed for 1 minute. Pour ¼ cup of the batter onto a hot waffle iron. Bake until brown, using manufacturer's directions. May bake on a hot griddle until brown on both sides, turning once.
Yield: 8 waffles or 20 (4-inch) pancakes.

Pat Scharch, Beta Epsilon
Madison, Wisconsin

MONKEY BREAD

1 cup sugar	**1 cup margarine**
1 teaspoon cinnamon	**1 teaspoon cinnamon**
1 cup packed brown	**4 (10-count) cans**
sugar	**buttermilk biscuits**

Combine the sugar and cinnamon in a bowl. Heat the brown sugar, margarine and cinnamon in a saucepan until blended, stirring frequently. Cut each biscuit into 4 pieces. Dip in the sugar mixture. Arrange in a greased angel food pan. Pour the brown sugar mixture over the biscuits. Bake at 400 degrees for 30 minutes. Let stand for 5 minutes before serving.
Yield: 10 servings.

Rachel Hart, Beta Lambda
Auburn, Indiana

PUFFED POTATO PANCAKES

1 cup mashed cooked	**½ cup baking mix**
potatoes	**1 cup vegetable oil**
1 egg	

Combine the potatoes and egg in a bowl and mix well. Add the baking mix and stir until blended. Heat the oil in a skillet. Drop the potato mixture by tablespoonfuls into the hot skillet, spreading the batter with a spoon. Bake until golden brown on both sides, turning once. Yield: 4 servings.

Margaret Wallace Loftin, Beta Zeta Phi
Iowa Park, Texas

QUICK ELEPHANT EARS

1½ cups sugar	**10 (7-inch) flour**
2 teaspoons	**tortillas**
cinnamon	**Vegetable oil for frying**

Combine the sugar and cinnamon in a shallow bowl. Fry the tortillas in oil in a hot skillet for 5 seconds. Turn and fry for 10 seconds or until brown. Dip in sugar mixture, turning to coat. Serve immediately. Yield: 10 servings.

Heather Peterson, Upsilon Alpha
North Bloomfield, Ohio

STICKY BUNS

1 cup packed brown	**1 (24-count) package**
sugar	**frozen yeast rolls**
½ cup butter or	**1 (4-ounce) package**
margarine	**butterscotch pudding**
1 to 2 teaspoons	**and pie filling mix**
cinnamon	
1 cup chopped pecans or	
walnuts	

Combine the brown sugar, butter and cinnamon in a saucepan and heat until blended, stirring frequently. Sprinkle the pecans in 2 greased round baking pans. Arrange 12 of the rolls in each of the prepared baking pans. Sprinkle with the pudding mix. Pour the brown sugar mixture over the rolls. Let stand, covered, for 8 hours or until doubled in bulk. Bake at 350 degrees for 20 minutes. Invert onto a serving plate. Serve hot. Yield: 12 servings.

Wanda E. Dudley, Laureate Alpha
Albuquerque, New Mexico

SUNDAY MORNING TOAST

¼ cup butter or	**2 eggs**
margarine, softened	**1 cup shredded Cheddar**
1 garlic clove, minced	**cheese**
2 thick slices French	
bread	

Combine the butter and garlic in a bowl and mix well. Spread the butter mixture over both sides of each slice of bread. Place the bread on a baking sheet. Press each slice of bread with the back of a spoon to form an indentation. Break an egg into the indentation. Broil for 20 minutes or until egg is opaque and toast is brown. Sprinkle with the Cheddar cheese. Broil until cheese is melted. May garnish with chopped green onions or salsa. Yield: 2 servings.

Vicky McCurdy, Pi Theta
Goddard, Kansas

CRANBERRY BUTTER

This makes a really nice gift for friends and neighbors at Christmas with a homemade loaf of bread.

2 cups butter, softened
1 (16-ounce) can
  cranberry sauce
1 tablespoon grated
  dried orange peel

Combine the butter, cranberry sauce and orange peel in a mixer bowl. Beat at low speed until blended. Spoon into butter molds or shaker boxes lined with waxed paper. Chill, covered, until firm. Serve with bread or crackers. Yield: 3 cups.

Patricia Kyle Vance, Laureate Rho
Lebanon, Tennessee

HONEY BUTTER SPREAD

1 cup honey
1/2 cup butter or
  margarine, softened
1/2 cup confectioner's
  sugar
1 1/2 teaspoons cinnamon

Combine the honey, butter, confectioner's sugar and cinnamon in a mixer bowl and beat until creamy. Store, covered, in the refrigerator. Yield: 2 cups.

Dorothy Eyberg, Laureate Tau
Arispe, Iowa

PUMPKIN PECAN BUTTER

2 cups mashed cooked
  pumpkin
1 cup ground pecans
1 cup sugar
1/2 cup butter
1 tablespoon cinnamon
1 teaspoon salt

Combine the pumpkin, pecans, sugar, butter, cinnamon and salt in a saucepan. Cook over low heat for 15 to 20 minutes or until blended, stirring frequently. Store, covered, in the refrigerator for up to 2 months. Yield: 24 to 30 servings.

Ann Howell, Xi Upsilon Iota
Tyler, Texas

Desserts

APRICOT ANGEL CAKE

1 (3-ounce) package
  orange gelatin
1 cup boiling water
2 (4-ounce) jars apricot
  baby food
1 cup whipping cream,
  whipped
1 angel food cake, split
  horizontally

Dissolve the orange gelatin in the boiling water. Chill until partially set. Fold in the baby food and whipped cream. Spread the mixture between the layers of the cake. Frost the side and top of cake with the remaining apricot mixture. Chill until serving time. Yield: 12 to 14 servings.

Vera Teasdale, Kappa Master
Guelph, Ontario, Canada

EASY BLACK FOREST CAKE

5 ounces miniature
  marshmallows
1 (2-layer) package
  chocolate cake mix
1 (21-ounce) can cherry
  pie filling
Whipped topping
  (optional)

Line the bottom of a 9x13-inch cake pan with the marshmallows. Prepare the cake mix using package directions and pour on top of the marshmallows. Pour the pie filling on top of the prepared cake mix. Bake at 350 degrees for suggested time on cake mix package. Let stand until cool. Serve with whipped topping. Yield: 12 servings.

Mavis Boehmer,
Coppersands, Saskatchewan, Canada

CHERRY CAKE

1 (2-layer) package
  white cake mix
1 (21-ounce) can cherry
  pie filling
8 ounces whipped
  topping
1 to 2 cups
  confectioners' sugar

Prepare the cake mix using package directions. Pour into a 9x13-inch cake pan. Bake at 350 degrees for 30 minutes. Let stand until cool. Combine remaining ingredients in a bowl; mix well. Spread on cooled cake. Chill until serving time. Yield: 18 servings.

Jo Ann Unrein, Lambda Epsilon
Russell, Kansas

CHERRY CREAM CHEESE CAKES

1 (2-layer) package
  white cake mix
4 cups confectioners'
  sugar
16 ounces cream cheese,
  softened
2 cups whipping cream,
  whipped
2 (21-ounce) cans cherry
  pie filling

Prepare the cake mix using package directions. Pour into 2 greased 9x13-inch cake pans. Bake at 350 degrees for 20 minutes or until cake tests done. Let stand until cool. Beat the confectioners' sugar and cream cheese in a mixer bowl until light and fluffy. Fold in the whipped cream. Spread cream cheese mixture on top of each cooled cake. Top each cake with the pie filling. Chill for 4 hours or overnight. Yield: 30 servings.

Audrey Hill, Beta Chi
Independence, Iowa

CHOCOLATE FUDGE CHERRY CAKE

1 (2-layer) package
  chocolate fudge
  cake mix
11 ounces cherry pie
  filling

Prepare the cake mix using package directions. Fold in the pie filling. Pour the mixture into a 9x13-inch cake pan. Bake at 350 degrees using the time on the package or until cake tests done. Yield: 8 to 10 servings.

Joyce Keller, Preceptor Epsilon Theta
Pinellas Park, Florida

ALMOND JOY CHOCOLATE CAKE

The longer this cake chills, the better. The hard part is waiting the 2 to 3 days because we always want to "test it" right away!

16 ounces sour cream
12 ounces frozen
  coconut, thawed
2 cups sugar
1 (2-layer) package
  chocolate cake mix
1 cup sliced almonds

Combine the sour cream, coconut and sugar in a bowl and mix well. Chill, covered, for 4 hours or overnight. Prepare and bake cake mix using package directions in two 9-inch round cake pans. Let stand until cool. Cut each cake lengthwise to make 4 layers. (Dental floss works well). Place first layer on cake plate with the cut-side up; spread with coconut mixture. Sprinkle with almonds. Repeat with remaining cake layers. Frost top and sides of cake with coconut mixture and sprinkle with almonds. Chill for at least 24 hours or up to 2 to 3 days. Yield: 16 to 20 servings.

Linda C. Madden, Laureate Omicron
Elberton, Georgia

COCONUT-PECAN BUNDT CAKE

1 (2-layer) package
  yellow cake
  mix
1 (16-ounce) can
  coconut-pecan
  frosting

Prepare the cake mix using the package directions. Stir in the frosting. Pour into a greased bundt pan. Bake at 350 degrees for 45 minutes to 1 hour or until cake test done. Remove to wire rack and let stand until cool. Invert cake onto serving plate. May drizzle with a glaze of confectioners' sugar and water if desired. Yield: 12 servings.

Lois Marie McGuire, Xi Alpha Omicron
Nacogdoches, Texas

THREE-DAY COCONUT CAKE

1 (2-layer) package
  yellow cake mix
2 cups sugar
2 cups sour cream
2 cups flaked coconut
12 ounces whipped
  topping

Prepare and bake the cake mix using package directions in two 9-inch round cake pans. Let stand until cool. Cut each cake lengthwise to make 4 layers. (Dental floss works well). Combine sugar, sour cream and coconut in a bowl and mix well. Reserve 1 cup of the coconut mixture. Spread coconut mixture between each layer of cake. Combine the reserved coconut mixture with the whipped topping and mix well. Spread the whipped topping mixture on the top and sides of cake. Sprinkle with coconut if desired. Chill, covered, for 3 days. Yield: 16 servings.

Kimberly Grob, Psi Epsilon
Sesser, Illinois

WHITE COCONUT CAKE

My husband requests this cake every year for his birthday.

1 (2-layer) package
  white cake mix
1 (14-ounce) can
  sweetened condensed
  milk
1 (9-ounce) can cream of
  coconut
16 ounces whipped
  topping
1 cup flaked coconut

Prepare the cake mix using package directions. Pour into a 9x13-inch cake pan. Bake at 350 degrees for 30 to 40 minutes or until cake tests done. Combine the sweetened condensed milk and cream of coconut in a bowl and mix well. Punch holes in the top of the warm cake. Pour the cream of coconut mixture over cake. Let cake stand until cool. Spread cake with whipped topping and sprinkle with coconut. Chill until serving time. Yield 12 to 15 servings.

Keri Welsch, Iota Gamma
Kinsley, Kansas

Delores Start, Preceptor Gamma Beta, Caledonia, Michigan, mixes up a quick Mandarin Orange Cake using a lemon cake mix, 3 eggs, 1/3 cup oil and a small can of mandarin oranges and beating for 2 minutes. Bake in a 9x13-inch cake pan at 325 degrees for 30 to 35 minutes. Frosting the cooled cake is easy with a mixture of a small package of coconut instant pudding, a small can of crushed pineapple and 9 ounces of whipped topping. Keep the cake in the refrigerator.

HEATH BAR CAKE

1 (2-layer) package chocolate cake mix	8 ounces whipped topping
1 (14-ounce) can sweetened condensed milk	2 frozen Heath Bars, crushed
1 (6-ounce) package Heath Bits-o-Brickle	

Prepare and bake the cake mix using package directions in a 9x13-inch cake pan. Punch holes in the top of warm cake. Pour the sweetened condensed milk over cake. Sprinkle the Bits-o-Brickle over cake. Let cake stand until cool. Spread whipped topping over cake and sprinkle with crushed Heath Bars. Chill until serving time. Yield: 15 servings.

Christen Stoeber, Delta Sigma
Cypress, Texas

PINEAPPLE ANGEL FOOD CAKE

1 package angel food cake mix	1 (20-ounce) can crushed pineapple

Combine the cake mix and pineapple in a bowl and mix well. Pour the mixture into a greased 10-inch tube pan or a 9x13-inch cake pan. Bake at 350 degrees for 35 to 40 minutes. May add chopped nuts or flaked coconut to the cake mix and pineapple before baking. Serve topped with whipped topping and crushed pineapple. Yield: 15 servings.

LaVerne Morris, Laureate Alpha Zeta
Drumright, Oklahoma

POPPY SEED SQUASH CAKE

1 (2-layer) package yellow cake mix	2/3 cup orange juice
1 medium butternut squash, cooked, mashed	3 eggs
	1/4 cup poppy seeds

Combine the cake mix, squash, juice and eggs in a mixer bowl. Beat at low speed for 30 seconds. Beat at medium speed for 2 minutes. Blend in the poppy seeds. Pour mixture into a greased and floured bundt pan. Bake at 350 degrees for 35 to 40 minutes or until cake tests done. Let cool for 10 minutes. Serve with whipped topping. May glaze with a mixture of 1 1/2 cups confectioners' sugar and 3 tablespoons orange juice. Yield: 16 servings.

Marie Kendrick, Preceptor Beta Iota
Lockport, New York

STRAWBERRY ANGEL FOOD CAKE

1 package angel food cake mix	2 egg whites
1 (12-ounce) can strawberry soda	16 ounces whipped topping

Combine the cake mix, strawberry soda and egg whites in a mixer bowl and beat until stiff. Spoon the batter into a 10-inch tube pan and bake using package directions. Let stand until cool. Split cooled cake lengthwise into 3 or 4 layers. Spread whipped topping between the layers and on the top and sides of the cake. Chill until serving time. Serve with fresh strawberries. Yield: 16 servings.

Lois Kotas, Laureate Kappa
Milligan, Nebraska

LAYERED TOFFEE CAKE

2 cups whipping cream	1 angel food cake
1/2 cup caramel or butterscotch ice cream topping	10 to 12 Butterfinger candy bars, crushed
1/2 teaspoon vanilla extract	

Beat the whipping cream in a mixer bowl until it begins to thicken. Add the ice cream topping and vanilla gradually, beating until soft peaks form. Cut the cake horizontally into 3 layers. Place the bottom layer on a serving plate, spread with 1 cup of the cream mixture and sprinkle with 1/2 cup of the crushed candy bar. Repeat. Place the top layer on the cake and frost the top and side of the cake with the remaining cream mixture and sprinkle with remaining crushed candy bar. Chill or freeze until serving time. Yield: 12 to 14 servings.

Ladonna K. Davis, Xi Alpha Sigma
New Castle, Indiana

GOOD AND EASY CHOCOLATE ICING

1 (14-ounce) can sweetened condensed milk	1 cup chocolate chips

Combine sweetened condensed milk and chocolate chips in a microwave-safe bowl. Microwave on High, stirring at 15 second intervals until chips are melted. Yield: Enough for two 9x13-inch cakes or one 8- or 9-inch round cake.

Delona Shockey, Preceptor Xi
Palmyra, Tennessee

CHERRY BALLS

1 cup butter or
  margarine, softened
1/2 cup coconut

Confectioners' sugar
36 maraschino cherries
Graham cracker crumbs

Combine the butter and coconut in a bowl and mix well. Stir in confectioners' sugar and mix until of desired stiffness. Roll a tablespoon of the coconut mixture around each cherry. Roll each cherry ball in the graham cracker crumbs. Store in the refrigerator. Yield: 3 dozen.

*Margaret Jennings, Preceptor Gamma Alpha
Windsor, Ontario, Canada*

CHOCOLATE TRUFFLES

These truffles were brought to my house for a Christmas dinner. Each little truffle was packed in a tiny paper cup in a beautiful tin. This makes a wonderful hostess gift.

4 cups chocolate chips
1 (14-ounce) can
  sweetened condensed
  milk

2 tablespoons vanilla
  extract

Combine the chocolate chips and sweetened condensed milk in a microwave-safe bowl. Microwave on High until the chocolate chips are melted, stirring occasionally. Add the vanilla and stir until smooth. Chill until firm. Roll into 1-inch balls. May roll balls in flaked coconut, confectioners' sugar or chocolate shavings. May substitute Kahlua for the vanilla extract. Store in the refrigerator or freezer. Yield: 3 dozen.

*Marjorie Snyder, Laureate Zeta Xi
Cedar Creek, Texas*

COW PIES

2 cups milk chocolate
  chips
1 tablespoon shortening

1/2 cup raisins
1/2 cup sliced almonds

Melt the chocolate chips and shortening in a double boiler, stirring until smooth. Remove from heat and stir in the raisins and almonds. Drop by tablespoonfuls onto waxed paper. Chill until serving time. Yield: 2 dozen.

*Betty West, Laureate Omicron
Pahrump, Nevada*

DATE LOAF CANDY

My mother made this every Christmas. The recipe is probably 60 or 70 years old.

3 cups sugar
1 cup milk
1 (8-ounce) package
  chopped dates

1 tablespoon butter
1 cup chopped nuts
1 teaspoon vanilla
  extract

Combine the sugar and milk in a saucepan. Cook over medium heat until sugar is dissolved. Add the dates and butter. Cook to 234 to 240 degrees on candy thermometer, soft-ball stage. Remove from heat and stir in the nuts and vanilla. Beat until the mixture stiffens. Roll the mixture in a damp cloth. Let stand until firm. Cut into slices to serve. Yield: 24 slices.

*Evelyn A. Whitney, Beta Pi Master
Powderly, Texas*

NO-COOK DIVINITY

1 (7-ounce) package
  white frosting mix
1/3 cup light corn syrup
1 teaspoon vanilla
  extract

1/2 cup boiling water
1 (1-pound) package
  confectioners' sugar
1 cup chopped pecans

Combine the first 4 ingredients in a large mixer bowl. Beat on high speed until smooth. Add confectioners' sugar gradually, beating on low speed until thickened. Stir in pecans. Drop by teaspoonfuls onto waxed paper. Let stand for 12 hours. Store in an airtight container. Yield: 30 servings.

*Lucylee Lively, Preceptor Iota Sigma
Dallas, Texas*

CHOCOLATE BUTTER FUDGE

3 cups sugar
1 envelope unflavored
  gelatin
1 cup milk
1/2 cup light corn syrup
1 1/4 cups butter

3 (1-ounce) squares
  unsweetened
  chocolate
2 teaspoons vanilla
  extract
1 cup chopped walnuts

Combine the sugar and gelatin in a saucepan. Add the milk, syrup, butter and chocolate. Cook over medium heat until sugar completely dissolves, stirring constantly. Cook to 234 to 240 degrees on a candy thermometer, soft-ball stage. Remove from heat and let cool for 30 minutes. Add vanilla and beat until mixture thickens and loses its luster. Stir in the walnuts. Pour into a greased 9-inch square dish. Let stand until firm. Cut into squares. Yield: 3 pounds.

*Adelaide Stenehjem, Master Alpha
Williston, North Dakota*

DROPPED FUDGE

4 cups sugar
1 cup evaporated milk
5 tablespoons (heaping)
  chocolate drink mix
1/2 cup light corn syrup

1/2 cup butter or
  margarine
1/8 teaspoon salt
2 tablespoons vanilla
  extract

Combine the first 6 ingredients in a large saucepan. Cook over medium heat until the sugar dissolves, stirring constantly. Cook to 234 to 240 degrees on a candy thermometer, soft-ball stage. Remove from heat and stir in the vanilla. Set the saucepan in a sink filled with cold water. Beat until the mixture thickens and loses its luster. Drop by spoonfuls onto waxed paper. Yield: 7 dozen.

Donna Wheeler, Kappa Psi
Levelland, Texas

FAMOUS FUDGE

4 (1-ounce) squares
  unsweetened
  chocolate
3 cups sugar
1 cup milk
1 cup chunky peanut
  butter

1/2 cup chopped black
  walnuts
1 teaspoon vanilla
  extract

Combine the chocolate, sugar and milk in a large saucepan. Cook over medium heat until the mixture boils and sugar is dissolved, stirring constantly. Cook over low heat to 234 to 240 degrees on a candy thermometer, soft-ball stage. Remove from heat and stir in peanut butter, walnuts and vanilla. Stir until the peanut butter is melted. Set the saucepan in a sink filled with cold water. Beat until the mixture thickens and loses its luster. Pour into a greased 6x9-inch dish. Chill for 1 hour. Cut into squares. Yield: 3 pounds.

Shirley Sixma, Laureate Zeta
Middletown, Maryland

YUMMY CHOCOLATE FUDGE

6 tablespoons butter
1/2 cup baking cocoa
4 1/2 tablespoons milk
1 teaspoon vanilla
  extract

1 (1-pound) package
  confectioners' sugar
1 cup chopped nuts

Melt the butter in a saucepan over medium heat. Stir in the baking cocoa and milk. Add the vanilla and confectioners' sugar and stir until blended. Stir in the nuts. Pour into a foil-lined 8-inch square dish. Chill until firm. Cut into squares. Yield: 25 to 30 servings.

Sarah C. Byerly, Laureate Chi
Salisbury, North Carolina

PEANUT BUTTER FUDGE

1 (18-ounce) jar chunky
  peanut butter

1 (16-ounce) can vanilla
  frosting

Combine the peanut butter and frosting in a bowl and mix until thoroughly blended. Press the mixture into an 8x8-inch dish. Chill until firm. Cut into squares to serve. Yield: 2 pounds.

Norene M. Fossick, Alpha Master
Nashville, Tennessee

GRANDMA'S PEANUT BUTTER FUDGE

I learned many cooking tips from my husband's grandma. This was her fudge recipe, and she had to teach me about the "soft-ball" stage. It took me a while, but I finally got it! She was a wonderful cook and a great grandma.

2 cups sugar
2/3 cup sweetened
  condensed milk
1 cup marshmallow
  crème

1 cup peanut butter
1 teaspoon vanilla
  extract

Combine the sugar and sweetened condensed milk in a large saucepan. Bring to a boil, stirring constantly. Boil for 8 minutes or until 234 to 240 degrees on a candy thermometer, soft-ball stage. Remove from heat and stir in marshmallow crème, peanut butter and vanilla. Mix until well blended. Pour into a greased 8x8-inch dish. Yield: 2 to 4 dozen.

Kelli Canevit, Xi Mu Phi
Canton, Illinois

PUDDING FUDGE

1 (4-ounce) package
  chocolate pudding
  mix
2 tablespoons butter

1/4 cup milk
1 1/2 cups sifted
  confectioners' sugar
1/4 cup chopped walnuts

Combine the pudding mix, butter and milk in a saucepan. Bring to a boil and boil for 1 minute, stirring constantly. Remove from heat. Add confectioners' sugar and stir until well blended. Stir in nuts. Pour into a greased 8x8-inch dish. Let stand until firm. Cut into squares to serve. May also use butterscotch or vanilla pudding mix for variation. Yield: 1 pound.

Carmel-Beth Kemerling, Nu Sigma
Tarkio, Missouri

EASY PEANUT BRITTLE

3 cups sugar
1 cup water
1 cup light corn syrup
3½ cups raw peanuts
½ cup butter
1 tablespoon baking
soda

Combine the sugar, water and corn syrup in a saucepan. Bring to a boil and cook to 250 degrees on a candy thermometer, hard-ball stage. Add the peanuts and butter and cook to 290 degrees on a candy thermometer, soft-crack stage. Stir constantly to prevent the peanuts from sticking to the bottom of the saucepan. Stir in the baking soda. Pour mixture onto 3 greased baking sheets. Let stand until cool. Break into pieces. Yield: 3 pounds.

Louise T. Moore, Preceptor Alpha
Boise, Idaho

PEANUT BUTTER CUPS

These are delicious served cold from the refrigerator. You will be amazed at how much these taste like a popular candy from the store!

22 graham crackers,
crushed
1 (1-pound) package
confectioners' sugar
1 cup butter, melted
1 cup peanut butter
1 (1-pound) milk
chocolate candy bar,
melted

Combine the graham crackers, confectioners' sugar, butter and peanut butter in a bowl and mix well. Press into an 8x8-inch dish. Top with the melted chocolate. Let stand until cool. Cut into squares to serve. Yield: 2 pounds.

Stacy McAward, Nu Beta
Troy, Michigan

PECAN KISSES

1 egg white
3/4 cup packed brown
sugar
½ teaspoon vanilla
extract
2 cups chopped pecans

Combine the egg white, brown sugar and vanilla in a mixer bowl and beat until stiff. Stir in the pecans. Drop by teaspoonfuls onto a baking sheet. Bake at 250 degrees for 30 minutes. Turn off the oven and leave in the oven for 30 minutes. Yield: 2 dozen.

Wanda S. Amick, Laureate Mu
Lexington, South Carolina

PERFECT PEPPERMINT PATTIES

1 (1-pound) package
confectioners' sugar
3 tablespoons butter or
margarine
2 to 3 teaspoons
peppermint extract
½ teaspoon vanilla
extract
¼ cup evaporated milk
2 cups semisweet
chocolate chips
2 tablespoons
shortening

Combine the confectioners' sugar, butter, peppermint extract and vanilla in a bowl and mix well. Add the evaporated milk and mix well. Roll mixture into 1-inch balls and place on a cookie sheet lined with waxed paper. Flatten balls into ¼-inch thick patties with the bottom of a glass. Chill for 30 minutes. Combine chocolate chips and shortening in a microwave-safe bowl. Microwave on High until chocolate chips melt, stirring frequently. Dip the patties into the melted chocolate and place on the waxed paper. Let stand until firm. Yield: 5 dozen.

Yvonne Crist, Laureate Epsilon Sigma
Chamby, Pennsylvania

SIMPLE SALTED NUT BARS

Pay Day candy bars have been a favorite of mine since I was a child. The first time I tried this recipe I realized I had an entire pan full of Pay Days!

1 pound raw peanuts
1 (10-ounce) package
Reese's peanut butter
chips
1 tablespoon margarine
1 (14-ounce) can
sweetened condensed
milk
8 ounces miniature
marshmallows

Cover the bottom of a greased 9x13-inch baking dish with half of the peanuts. Combine the peanut butter chips and margarine in a saucepan. Cook over medium heat until melted, stirring frequently. Stir in the sweetened condensed milk. Add the marshmallows and stir until almost melted, remove from heat. Pour the mixture over the peanuts in the baking dish. Top with the remaining ½ pound of peanuts. Press the mixture down slightly with wet hands. Chill for 1 hour. Cut into bars. Yield: 15 to 20 servings.

Dawn C. Irish, Xi Rho Theta
Ennis, Texas

Sally Dickinson, Preceptor Alpha, Watertown, New York, makes a Super-Easy Punch by pouring equal parts of chilled white grape juice and ginger ale over a pretty ice ring.

ENGLISH TOFFEE

This is a Christmas favorite of my four children.

1 cup sugar	1 (4½-ounce) milk
1 cup butter	chocolate bar,
3 teaspoons water	chopped
1 teaspoon vanilla	½ cup finely chopped
extract	pecans

Combine the sugar, butter and water in a saucepan. Cook over high heat to 300 degrees on a candy thermometer, hard-crack stage, stirring constantly. Remove from heat and stir in the vanilla. Pour into a greased 8-inch dish. Let cool for 5 minutes. Top with the chocolate bar pieces, spreading as they melt. Sprinkle with the nuts. Let stand until firm. Break into pieces to serve. Yield: 1 pound.

Frances C. Hearn, Laureate Alpha
Scottsdale, Arizona

SIMPLE TOFFEE

1 cup butter	¼ cup water
1 cup sugar	

Combine the butter, sugar and water in a saucepan. Bring to a boil and boil for 10 minutes, stirring constantly. Pour into a greased 8-inch dish. Let stand until firm. Break into pieces to serve. Can also pull apart when slightly cool. Yield: 1 pound

Charlene Stushnoff, Epsilon
Saskatoon, Saskatchewan, Canada

TIGER BUTTER

1 pound white	1 cup semisweet
chocolate, melted	chocolate chips
½ cup peanut butter	

Combine the melted white chocolate and peanut butter in a bowl and stir until well blended. Spread the mixture on a jelly roll pan lined with waxed paper. Microwave chocolate chips in a microwave-safe bowl on Medium until melted. Pour the melted chocolate chips on top of the white chocolate mixture. Swirl with a knife. Chill until firm. Cut into squares to serve. Store in an airtight container. Yield: 2 pounds.

Shirley E. Pearce, Xi Beta Omega
Magnolia, Arkansas

TURTLE CANDY

1 (14-ounce) package	2 cups chopped pecans
caramels	1 (24-ounce) package
2½ tablespoons	chocolate bark
evaporated milk	

Combine caramels and evaporated milk in a microwave safe bowl. Microwave on High for 2 to 2½ minutes, stirring frequently. Add the pecans and mix well. Drop by teaspoonfuls onto a greased baking sheet. Freeze for 2 hours. Melt the chocolate bark in a microwave safe bowl in the microwave for 2 to 2½ minutes, stirring frequently. Dip the caramel drops in the melted chocolate bark and place on waxed paper to cool. Yield: 3 to 4 dozen

Darlene H. Broussard, Epsilon Chi
Kaplan, Louisiana

VALENTINE CANDY HEARTS

My daughters and I "invented" this recipe one year when we had left over candy canes from Christmas. It is now a Valentine tradition.

8 peppermint candy	1 (24-ounce) package
canes or 16 to 20	almond bark
peppermint disks	

Crush the peppermint very finely on waxed paper or a cutting board. Microwave 1 square of almond bark at a time in a microwave-safe bowl until melted. Stir in 2 teaspoons of crushed peppermint candy until smooth. Immediately spoon into a heart-shaped candy mold. Repeat for each square of almond bark. Let cool and remove from molds. May use a variety of candy mold shapes. Yield: 12 hearts.

Jeanne Hayden, Preceptor Upsilon
Boise, Idaho

CHEESE COOKIES

1 cup margarine,	8 ounces sharp Cheddar
softened	cheese, shredded
2 cups flour	2 cups crisp rice cereal
¼ teaspoon salt	

Combine the margarine, flour and salt in a bowl and mix well. Stir in the cheese and cereal. Roll the dough into 1-inch balls and place on baking sheets. Flatten each ball with a fork. Bake at 350 degrees for 12 to 15 minutes. Cool on wire rack. Yield: 3 dozen.

Clara Orndoff, Zeta Master
Winchester, Virginia

CHOCOLATE CHIP BUTTER COOKIES

1 cup butter	1 cup confectioners'
½ teaspoon vanilla	sugar
extract	1 cup semisweet
2 cups flour	chocolate chips

Melt the butter in a double boiler or in the microwave. Stir in the vanilla and remove from heat.

Let cool. Combine the flour and confectioners' sugar in a large bowl. Add the butter mixture and chocolate chips and mix well. The mixture will be crumbly. Roll into 1-inch balls and place 2 inches apart on cookie sheets. Flatten slightly. Bake at 375 degrees for 12 minutes or until edges are light brown. Cool on wire racks. Do not substitute margarine for butter. Yield: 4 dozen.

Jean Haynes, Preceptor Alpha Zeta
Bothell, Washington

CHOCOLATE PEANUT CLUSTERS

My mom shared this recipe with me on one of my visits back home to Midland, Texas.

2 cups peanut butter
   chips
2 cups milk chocolate
   chips

1 (12-ounce) can Spanish
   peanuts

Combine the peanut butter chips and the milk chocolate chips in a microwave safe bowl. Microwave on High for 45 seconds and stir. Repeat, stirring until chips are melted. Stir in the peanuts. Drop by spoonfuls onto waxed paper. Let stand until firm. Chill until serving time. Yield: 15 servings.

Teresa Muscovalley, Xi Gamma Beta
Beaumont, Texas

CINNAMON CREAM CHEESE BARS

2 (8-count) cans crescent
   rolls
16 ounces cream cheese,
   softened
1 cup sugar

1 egg, separated
1 teaspoon vanilla
   extract
3 tablespoons sugar
1 teaspoon cinnamon

Unroll one can of crescent roll dough onto a greased baking sheet, sealing all perforations. Beat the cream cheese, sugar, egg yolk and vanilla in a mixer bowl until creamy. Spread the mixture over crescent roll dough. Unroll the other can of crescent roll dough, sealing the perforations. Place on top of the cream cheese mixture and seal at the edges. Beat the egg white until stiff and brush over the top. Combine the sugar and cinnamon and sprinkle over the top. Bake at 350 degrees for 25 to 30 minutes. Yield: 12 servings.

Nedral Brown-Gockel, Xi Epsilon Pi
Centerville, Ohio

COCONUT DATE BARS

2 egg whites
1/8 teaspoon salt
1 cup sugar

1 1/2 cups flaked coconut
1 cup chopped dates

Combine the egg whites and salt in a mixer bowl and beat until foamy. Add the sugar 2 tablespoons at a time, beating well between each addition. Continue to beat until mixture forms peaks. Fold in the coconut and dates. Drop by spoonfuls onto cookie sheets. Bake at 350 degrees for 20 minutes. Yield: 2 dozen.

Charlotte V. Backstedt, Xi Beta Xi
El Cajon, California

ALMOND CREAM CHEESE BARS

2 (8-count) cans crescent
   rolls
16 ounces cream cheese,
   softened
1 cup sugar
1 egg, separated

1 teaspoon vanilla
   extract
3/4 cup almonds
1/2 cup sugar
1 teaspoon cinnamon

Unroll one can of crescent roll dough onto a greased baking sheet, sealing all perforations. Beat the cream cheese, sugar, egg yolk and vanilla in a mixer bowl until creamy. Spread the mixture over the crescent roll dough. Unroll the other can of crescent roll dough, sealing the perforations. Place on top of the cream cheese mixture and seal at the edges. Beat the egg white until stiff and brush over the top. Combine the almonds, sugar and cinnamon and sprinkle over the top. Bake at 350 degrees for 30 minutes. Serve warm with ice cream. Yield: 12 servings.

Laurie Lang, Epsilon Zeta
Rolla, Missouri

CREAM CHEESE CHOCOLATE CHIP BARS

This recipe was given to me by my Aunt Aris whom I greatly admire because she puts up with my Uncle Russell.

1 (18-ounce) package
   refrigerated chocolate
   chip cookie dough
8 ounces cream cheese,
   softened

1 egg
1/4 cup sugar
1 teaspoon vanilla
   extract

Slice the package of cookie dough in half. Roll out one half and press into a greased 8x8-inch dish. Combine the cream cheese, egg, sugar and vanilla in a mixer bowl and beat until creamy. Spread this mixture over the cookie dough. Roll out the other half of the cookie dough and place on top of the cream cheese mixture. Bake at 350 degrees for 30 minutes. Yield: 12 servings.

Beverly Stewart
Huntsville, Texas

BAKE-EASY COOKIES

I made these for my grandsons one time and forgot and used water instead of oil. It worked, but they were more like "cakies" instead of cookies!

1 egg	**1 (2-layer) package cake**
½ cup oil	**mix (any flavor)**

Combine the egg and oil in a mixer bowl and beat on low until blended. Add the cake mix and stir until dough thickens. Drop by spoonfuls onto a greased cookie sheet. Bake at 350 degrees for 15 to 17 minutes. Cool on wire rack. May add candy or nuts to the dough if desired. Yield: 2 dozen.

Louise Gorton, Beta Theta Master
Arlington, Texas

DOUBLE CHOCOLATE COOKIES

1 (2-layer) package	**1 cup semisweet**
pudding-recipe devil's	**chocolate chips**
food cake mix	**¾ cup chopped nuts**
½ cup oil	**(optional)**
2 eggs	

Combine the cake mix, oil and eggs in a mixer bowl and beat until well blended. Stir in the chocolate chips and nuts. Drop by teaspoonfuls 2 inches apart on a greased cookie sheet. Bake at 350 degrees for 10 to 12 minutes. Cool on wire rack. Yield: 4 to 5 dozen.

Arlene Miller, Preceptor Delta Theta
Hoopeston, Illinois

FRUIT FILLED SPICE BARS

1 (15-ounce) package	**½ cup raisins**
gingerbread mix	**½ cup diced dried**
1 cup applesauce	**apricots**
2 tablespoons water	**Confectioners' sugar**

Combine the gingerbread mix, applesauce, and water in a mixer bowl and beat for 2 minutes on medium speed. Fold in the raisins and the apricots. Pour into a greased and floured jelly roll pan. Bake at 375 degrees for 15 to 20 minutes. Let cool. Top with confectioners' sugar. Cut into squares to serve. Yield: 32 servings.

Frances Hoskins, Chi Master
Middletown, Ohio

FORGOTTEN COOKIES

2 egg whites	**1 cup chopped nuts**
¾ cup sugar	**1 cup chocolate chips**

Beat the egg whites in a mixer bowl until stiff peaks form. Add the sugar gradually. Fold in the nuts and chocolate chips. Drop by spoonfuls onto a greased cookie sheet. Place cookie sheets in an oven preheated to 350 degrees. Turn off the oven and leave the cookies in the oven for 3 hours or overnight. Yield: 2 to 3 dozen.

Nancy McDoehring, Preceptor Alpha
Lakeland, Florida

SIMPLE GINGERSNAP COOKIES

This is a Christmas Eve tradition for our family. It takes very little time and is a wonderful treat to leave for Santa!

1 (15-ounce) package	**⅓ cup shortening or oil**
gingerbread mix	**Sugar**
½ cup milk	

Combine the gingerbread mix, milk and oil in a mixer bowl and beat on high for 30 seconds. Drop by teaspoonfuls 3 inches apart on cookie sheet. Sprinkle with sugar. Bake at 375 degrees for 8 to 10 minutes. May need to adjust oven temperature and time for non-high altitude baking. Yield: 4 dozen.

Ruth Pullen, Preceptor Beta Pi
Eastlake, Colorado

GRAHAM CRACKER BROWNIES

These are a favorite of my husband, Jimmy. His grandmother sent him a batch of these every week when he was in Vietnam during the war. The recipe was handed down to me.

1 stack graham crackers,	**1 (14-ounce) can**
crushed	**sweetened condensed**
1 cup semisweet	**milk**
chocolate chips	
1 (4-ounce) can chopped	
walnuts	

Combine the crushed graham crackers, chocolate chips and walnuts in a bowl. Add the sweetened condensed milk and stir until all ingredients are well coated. Pour into a foil-lined 8x8-inch pan. Bake at 325 degrees for 30 minutes. Yield: 9 servings.

Irene Rivers, Preceptor Chi
Stillwater, Maine

GRAHAM CRACKER CRISPIES

This recipe is always a big hit. My friends are always amazed that something so good is so simple to make!

15 graham crackers	**1 cup packed brown**
1 cup butter or	**sugar**
margarine	**1 cup chopped nuts**

Line a jellyroll pan with the graham crackers. Melt the butter in a saucepan on the stove. Stir in the brown sugar. Bring to a boil, stirring constantly. Let boil for 2 minutes, stirring constantly. Remove from heat. Stir in the nuts. Pour mixture over the crackers and spread until smooth. Bake at 325 degrees for 10 minutes. Cut into squares immediately and cool on a wire rack. Yield: 2 to 3 dozen.

Frances Kucera, Laureate Omicron
Eugene, Oregon

LAST MINUTE COOKIES

1/2 cup butter, softened
1 cup sugar
1 egg
2 1/2 cups flour
1 teaspoon baking soda
1/2 teaspoon salt
1 teaspoon vanilla
* extract*
1/4 cup milk

Cream the butter and sugar in a mixer bowl until light and fluffy. Add the egg and beat well. Add the flour, baking soda, salt and vanilla and beat until thickened. Beat in the milk, gradually. Drop by teaspoonfuls onto a greased cookie sheet. Flatten with a fork dipped in sugar. Sprinkle sugar on top of cookies. Bake at 350 degrees for 6 to 8 minutes. Yield: 3 dozen.

Patricia A. Thompson, Preceptor Beta Mu
Prineville, Oregon

LEMON BUTTER THIN COOKIES

I always make these cookies for my grandnephews on special occasions like Valentines Day, Christmas, Easter and Halloween.

1 cup butter,
* softened*
1/2 cup sugar
1 to 2 tablespoons
* grated lemon peel*
2 cups flour

Cream the butter, sugar and lemon peel in a bowl until light and fluffy. Add the flour gradually, beating well. Chill, covered, for 1 hour. Divide the dough in half. Roll out the dough between 2 sheets of waxed paper. Cut the dough with cookie cutters in desired shapes. Place cookies 1-inch apart on cookie sheets. Bake at 325 degrees for 15 to 20 minutes or until light brown. Remove to wire rack. Yield: 3 dozen.

Kathleen Radcliffe
Lancaster, Pennsylvania

LEMON CRISP COOKIES

1 (2-layer) package
* lemon cake mix*
1 cup crisp rice cereal
1/2 cup butter, melted
1 egg, beaten
1 teaspoon grated lemon
* peel*

Combine the cake mix, cereal, butter, egg and lemon peel in a large mixer bowl and beat on low until well blended. Dough should be crumbly. Roll into 1-inch balls and place 2-inches apart on a cookie sheet. Bake at 350 degrees for 10 to 12 minutes. Cool on wire rack. Yield: 4 dozen.

Jodi Bokhoven, Iota Theta
Pella, Iowa

LEMON COOKIES

1 (2-layer) package
* lemon cake mix*
2 eggs, beaten
1 teaspoon vanilla or
* lemon extract*
2 cups whipped topping
Confectioners' sugar

Combine the cake mix, eggs, vanilla and whipped topping in a large mixer bowl and beat on low until well blended. Roll into teaspoon-size balls and coat with confectioners' sugar. Place 2-inches apart on greased cookie sheets. Bake at 350 degrees for 10 minutes or until light brown. Yield: 3 to 4 dozen.

Eileen Rosser, Chi Zeta
Dunnellon, Florida

ALICE'S MACAROONS

1 egg, beaten
1/2 cup sugar
1/2 teaspoon vanilla
* extract*
2 cups flaked coconut
1/8 teaspoon salt

Combine the egg, sugar, vanilla, coconut and salt in a mixer bowl and beat well. Roll into 15 small balls. Place on cookie sheet and bake at 300 degrees for 30 minutes. Let cool. Yield: 15 cookies.

Barbara Brown, Alpha Master
Victoria, British Columbia, Canada

PEANUT BUTTER BARS

1 cup margarine, melted
1 1/2 cups graham cracker
* crumbs*
1 cup peanut butter
2 cups confectioners'
* sugar*
2 cups chocolate chips,
* melted*

Combine the margarine, graham cracker crumbs, peanut butter and confectioners' sugar in a bowl and mix well. Pat the mixture into a 9x13-inch pan and chill for 30 minutes. Spread the melted chocolate chips on top. Cut into squares before the chocolate hardens. Chill until serving time. Yield: 24 servings.

Kelli Clevenger, Xi Theta Delta
Wakarusa, Kansas

CAKE MIX PEANUT BUTTER COOKIES

1 (2-layer) package
  yellow cake mix
1 cup chunky peanut
  butter

1/2 cup oil
2 eggs
2 tablespoons water

Combine the cake mix, peanut butter, oil, eggs and water in a large mixer bowl. Beat until well blended. Drop by teaspoonfuls onto cookie sheets and flatten with a fork. Bake at 350 degrees for 10 to 12 minutes. Yield: 3 to 4 dozen.

Marilyn Romsdahl, Laureate Beta Alpha
Seattle, Washington

PEANUT BUTTER CHOCOLATE CHIP COOKIES

2 eggs, slightly beaten
1 cup sugar
1 cup chunky peanut
  butter

2 cups semisweet
  chocolate chips

Combine the eggs and sugar in a bowl and mix well by hand. Stir in the peanut butter until well blended. Fold in the chocolate chips. Drop by heaping tea-spoonfuls 2 inches apart on a cookie sheet. Bake at 350 degrees for 8 to 10 minutes. Yield: 3 dozen.

Wilma Coffman, Laureate Gamma Zeta
Nevada, Missouri

PECAN POTATO CHIP COOKIES

1 cup butter or
  margarine
1/2 cup sugar
1 teaspoon vanilla
  extract

1/2 cup chopped pecans
1/2 cup crushed potato
  chips
2 cups sifted flour

Cream the butter, sugar and vanilla in a mixer bowl. Add the pecans and potato chips and mix well. Stir in the flour until the dough is thickened. Roll into tablespoon size balls. Place on a cookie sheet. Flatten balls with the bottom of a glass dipped in sugar. Bake at 350 degrees for 16 to 18 minutes or until light brown. May sprinkle colored sugar on top of cookies before baking. Yield: 3 dozen.

Dorothy Morgan, Laureate Zeta
Frederick, Maryland

SHORTBREAD COOKIES

2 cups butter
1 cup sugar

4 1/2 cups flour, sifted

Cream the butter and sugar in a mixer bowl until light and fluffy. Stir in the flour gradually. Chill for several hours. Divide the dough into 4 parts. Roll out each section into a 7-inch circle on a baking sheet. Prick deeply with a fork. Bake at 300 degrees for 30 minutes. Repeat for all sections of dough. Let cool and cut into desired shapes and sizes of cookies. Do not substitute margarine for butter.
Yield: 6 or 7 dozen.

Paula H. Osborne, Preceptor Alpha Kappa
Dacula, Georgia

SUGAR PLUMS

This is a great no-bake cookie that children can help prepare.

1 1/2 cups vanilla wafer
  crumbs
3/4 cup flaked coconut
1/2 cup frozen orange
  juice concentrate

3/4 cup confectioners'
  sugar

Combine the vanilla wafer crumbs, coconut and orange juice concentrate in a bowl and mix well. Roll into balls. Roll balls in confectioners' sugar. Store in the refrigerator. Yield: 2 dozen.

Carol J. Oneslager, Preceptor Alpha Omega
Coffeyville, Kansas

SUNDAY SCHOOL COOKIES

1 cup baking mix
1 (4-ounce) package
  instant pudding mix
  (any flavor)

1 egg, beaten
1/4 cup oil
Sugar

Combine the baking mix, pudding mix, egg and oil in a bowl and mix well. Roll into balls and roll balls in sugar. Place on a cookie sheet and flatten with the bottom of a glass dipped in sugar. Bake at 350 degrees for 10 minutes. Yield: 12 to 14 cookies.

Arlene Lander, Laureate Alpha
Marshalltown, Iowa

WHEAT FLAKE KISSES

2 cups Wheaties
1 cup flaked coconut or
  chopped nuts

2 egg whites
1 cup sugar

Combine the Wheaties and coconut in a bowl and mix well. Beat the 2 egg whites in a bowl and gradually add the sugar. Beat until soft peaks form. Fold in the Wheaties mixture. Drop by spoonfuls onto a greased cookie sheet. Bake at 350 degrees for 5 to 10 minutes. Yield: 2 dozen.

Raigh Kinsler, Alpha Epsilon
Honolulu, Hawaii

CHOCOLATE ICE CREAM PUDDING PIE

2 cups whole milk
1½ cups chocolate ice
   cream, softened
2 (4-ounce) packages
   chocolate instant
   pudding mix

1 (6-ounce) graham
   cracker pie shell

Combine the milk and ice cream in a bowl and mix well. Add the pudding mix. Beat on low speed for 1 minute or until well blended. Pour into the pie shell. Chill for 1 hour or until set. Top with whipped topping and chocolate shavings if desired.
Yield: 6 to 8 servings.

Belly Boynton
Dunnellon, Florida

COCONUT PINEAPPLE PIES

My Mother loved going to her Woman's Club meeting. She was always bringing back new recipes and she especially loved this one. I always use it to take to church functions because it is easy to make and makes 2 pies.

2 cups sugar
½ cup margarine,
   melted
1 (8-ounce) can crushed
   pineapple

4 eggs, beaten
1 cup flaked coconut
⅛ teaspoon salt
2 unbaked (9-inch) pie
   shells

Combine the sugar, margarine, pineapple, eggs, coconut and salt in a large bowl and mix well. Pour the mixture into the two pie shells. Bake at 325 degrees for 45 minutes to 1 hour.
Yield: 10 to 12 servings.

Ginger Tyler, Xi Xi
Thomaston, Georgia

NO-FAIL EGG CUSTARD PIE

1 (14-ounce) can
   sweetened condensed
   milk
1½ cups hot water
½ teaspoon vanilla
   extract

½ teaspoon salt
3 eggs, beaten
1 unbaked (9-inch) pie
   shell
Nutmeg

Combine the condensed milk, water, vanilla and salt in a bowl and mix well. Add the eggs and mix well. Pour the mixture into the pie shell and sprinkle with nutmeg. Bake at 425 degrees for 10 minutes. Reduce heat to 300 degrees and bake for 20 to 25 minutes or until pie tests done when a knife inserted in the center comes out clean. Yield: 8 servings.

Grace Pender, Xi Alpha Xi
Adamsville, Alabama

EGG NOG PIE

My mother-in-law handed down this recipe to me. It is a Christmas tradition in our family.

1 (4-ounce) package
   vanilla pudding mix
2 cups eggnog
2 teaspoons unflavored
   gelatin mix
½ teaspoon rum
   flavoring

1 cup whipping cream,
   whipped
1 baked (9-inch) pie
   shell

Combine the pudding mix, eggnog and unflavored gelatin mix in a saucepan over low heat. Cook until thickened. Remove from heat and stir in the rum flavoring. Chill until firm. Whip the chilled eggnog mixture and fold in the whipping cream. Pour into the pie shell and chill until serving time. May sprinkle with nutmeg. Yield: 6 servings.

Norma Gragg, Laureate Delta Pi
Euless, Texas

DELICIOUS HERSHEY'S PIE

6 chocolate candy bars
1 tablespoon brewed
   coffee
12 ounces whipped
   topping

1 (9-inch) graham
   cracker pie shell

Combine the chocolate bars and coffee in a microwave-safe bowl. Microwave on High for 1 minute or until the chocolate bars are melted. Let stand until cool. Stir in the whipped topping. Spoon into the pie shell and chill for 3 or more hours.
Yield: 6 to 8 servings.

Patricia A. Gillmore, Xi Omega
Murphysboro, Illinois

KEY LIME PIE

1 (14-ounce) can
   sweetened condensed
   milk
¼ to ½ cup Key lime
   juice

8 ounces whipped
   topping
1 (9-inch) graham
   cracker pie shell

Combine the sweetened condensed milk and Key lime juice in a bowl and mix well. Fold in the whipped topping and pour into the pie shell. Chill for 1 to several hours. Yield: 6 to 8 servings.

Jane Melissari, Chi Zeta
Dunnellon, Florida

LEMONADE PIE

This pie took the first prize when I took it to our neighborhood cookout contest. It freezes wonderfully, which is great for a fast, summer dessert.

1³/4 cups milk
2 (4-ounce) packages
   vanilla instant
   pudding mix
1 (6-ounce) can frozen
   lemonade
   concentrate, thawed

8 ounces whipped
   topping
1 (9-inch) graham
   cracker pie shell

Whisk the milk and pudding mix in a bowl for 30 seconds. Add the lemonade concentrate and whisk for 30 seconds or until mixture is thickened. Fold in the whipped topping and spoon into the pie shell. Chill for 4 hours. Top with lemon slices if desired. Yield: 8 servings.

Opal H. Stallings, Preceptor Alpha Theta
Washington, North Carolina

PINK LEMONADE PIE

1 (14-ounce) can
   sweetened condensed
   milk
1 (6-ounce) can frozen
   pink lemonade
   concentrate, thawed

8 ounces whipped
   topping
1 (9-inch) graham
   cracker pie shell

Combine the condensed milk and pink lemonade concentrate in a bowl and mix well. Fold in the whipped topping. Pour into the pie shell and chill. May add a drop of red food coloring for pink color if desired. Yield: 6 to 8 servings.

Janice Gibson, Xi Epsilon Epsilon
Sterling, Virginia

LEMON-LIME CHEESECAKE PIE

16 ounces cream cheese,
   softened
1 (6-ounce) can frozen
   limeade concentrate
1 (5-ounce) can
   evaporated milk

1 (4-ounce) package
   lemon instant
   pudding mix
1 (9-inch) graham
   cracker pie shell

Mix the cream cheese and limeade concentrate in a bowl. Combine the evaporated milk and pudding mix in a bowl and mix well. Add the evaporated milk mixture to the cream cheese mixture and mix well. Pour into the pie shell. Chill. Serve topped with whipped topping if desired. Yield: 6 to 8 servings.

Cheryl Schroeder, Beta Theta Psi
Bay City, Texas

MANGO PIE

3¹/2 cups peeled, sliced
   mangos
³/4 cup packed brown
   sugar
2 tablespoons tapioca

1 tablespoon margarine,
   melted
2 unbaked (9-inch) pie
   shells

Combine the mangos, brown sugar, tapioca and margarine in a bowl and mix well. Line a pie plate with 1 pie shell. Fill the pie shell with the mango mixture. Top with the other pie shell, sealing the edges with a fork and cutting vents. Bake at 425 degrees for 55 minutes or until light brown. Serve with whipped topping or vanilla ice cream. Yield: 6 to 8 servings.

Judie Fair, Xi Eta
Birmingham, Alabama

PEACH MALLOW PIE

35 large marshmallows
¹/2 cup milk
1¹/2 cups frozen sliced
   peaches, thawed
¹/8 teaspoon almond
   extract

8 ounces whipped
   topping
1 (9-inch) graham
   cracker pie shell

Combine the marshmallows and milk in a microwave-safe bowl and microwave on High for 1 to 2 minutes, stirring until smooth. Chop the peaches finely, mashing lightly with a fork. Add the peaches to the marshmallow mixture and mix well. Stir in the almond extract. Fold in the whipped topping and pour the mixture into the pie shell. Chill for 2 or more hours. Yield: 6 to 8 servings.

Mary Jo Bent, Epsilon Master
Kansas City, Missouri

PEANUT BUTTER PIE

1 (6-ounce) package
   vanilla pudding mix
3 cups milk
1 cup chunky peanut
   butter

1 (9-inch) graham
   cracker pie shell
8 ounces whipped
   topping

Combine the pudding mix and milk in a saucepan and stir to mix. Cook until mixture begins to boil, stirring constantly. Stir in the peanut butter. Remove from heat and cool for 10 minutes. Pour the mixture into the pie shell. Let cool. Top with the whipped topping and chill until serving time. Yield: 8 servings.

Penny Bell, Preceptor Psi
Galveston, Texas

NO-FAIL PEANUT BUTTER PIE

4 ounces cream cheese,
  softened
1 cup peanut butter
12 ounces whipped
  topping

1 cup confectioners'
  sugar
1 (9-inch) chocolate
  crumb pie shell

Combine the cream cheese and peanut butter in a mixer bowl and beat until smooth. Add the whipped topping and confectioners' sugar and mix well. Spoon mixture into the pie shell. Chill for 4 hours. Top with chocolate shavings. Yield: 8 servings.

Judy Amig, Xi Alpha Epsilon
Clarksville, Indiana

PINEAPPLE PIE

My mother-in-law who lives in Florida gave this recipe to me. This pie reminds me of Florida sunshine!

2 cups sour cream
1 (4-ounce) package
  instant vanilla
  pudding mix
1 tablespoon sugar

1 (8-ounce) can crushed
  pineapple
1 (9-inch) graham
  cracker pie shell

Combine the sour cream, pudding mix and sugar in a bowl and mix well. Stir in the pineapple. Pour the mixture into the pie shell and chill for 2 hours. Yield: 8 servings.

Kathy Chapman, Preceptor Gamma Beta
Rockford, Michigan

QUEBEC SUGAR PIE

1 recipe (2-crust) pie
  pastry
2 cups packed brown
  sugar

1/2 cup rolled oats
1 (5-ounce) can
  evaporated milk

Line a 9-inch pie plate with half the pastry. Combine the brown sugar and oats in a bowl. Spread the mixture evenly on the bottom of the pie shell. Roll out the other half of the pastry. Cut into 1/2-inch strips. Arrange the strips on top of the pie in a lattice design, sealing the edges. Pour the evaporated milk in the holes of the lattice design. Bake at 350 degrees for 30 to 35 minutes or until bubbly. Serve with ice cream. May also prepare using 30 small tart shells for individual pies. Yield: 8 to 10 servings.

Françoise Robertson, Xi Zeta
Calgary, Alberta, Canada

TIN ROOF PIE

1/3 cup peanut butter
1 tablespoon light corn
  syrup
1 quart vanilla ice
  cream, softened

Chocolate syrup
Salted peanuts, chopped

Combine the peanut butter and corn syrup in a bowl and blend well. Spread the mixture over the bottom and side of a 9-inch pie plate. Chill until firm. Spread the softened ice cream in the prepared pie plate and freeze until firm. Drizzle with chocolate syrup and top with peanuts before serving.
Yield: 8 to 10 servings.

Carol Johannigmeier, Laureate Mu
Ft. Collins, Colorado

CARAMEL TARTS

1 (12-ounce) package
  caramels
1/2 cup water
1/2 cup sour cream

8 ounces whipped
  topping
24 ready-made tart
  shells

Unwrap the caramels. Combine the caramels and water in a saucepan. Cook over low heat until the caramels are melted, stirring constantly. Remove from heat and let stand until cool. Fold in the sour cream and whipped topping. Spoon the caramel mixture into the tart shells. Chill or freeze until serving time. For variation: May substitute 1/4 cup Bailey's Irish Cream for 1/4 cup water if desired.
Yield: 2 dozen tarts.

Kathy Rand, Xi Alpha Pi
Madison, Wisconsin

MRS. TIPTON'S PIE CRUST

1 1/2 cups flour
2 teaspoons sugar
1/4 teaspoon salt

1/2 cup oil
1/4 cup milk

Combine the flour, sugar and salt in a bowl. Mix oil and milk together and add to the flour mixture gradually, mixing with a fork until the mixture forms a ball. Chill, wrapped in plastic wrap, for 30 minutes or longer. Roll into a 12-inch circle on a lightly floured surface. Press into the pie plate. Bake at 350 degrees for 10 to 15 minutes or until golden brown. Yield: 1 pie shell.

Mary Ann Koch, Xi Preceptor Xi
Odessa, Texas

SWEET OIL PASTRY

1¹/2 cups flour
1¹/2 teaspoons sugar
1 teaspoon salt
¹/2 cup oil
2 tablespoons milk

Sift the flour, sugar and salt into a 9-inch pie plate. Combine the oil and milk in a bowl. Pour the oil mixture over the flour mixture in the pie plate. Mix with a fork until the dry ingredients are well coated. Press out the pastry into the pie plate with the back of a spoon or your fingers. Prick the bottom of the pastry with a fork. Bake at 425 degrees for 12 to 15 minutes or until golden brown. Yield: 1 pie shell.

Carolyn Sites, Laureate Gamma Lambda
Lima, Ohio

NEVER-FAIL PIE CRUST

¹/2 cup oil
1¹/2 cups flour
2 tablespoons milk
¹/8 teaspoon salt

Pour the oil into a 9-inch pie plate. Add the flour, milk and salt. Mix well with a fork. Press into the pie plate with the back of a spoon or your fingers. Prick the bottom with a fork. Bake at 375 degrees for 20 minutes or until golden brown. Yield: 1 pie shell.

Ruth Schwarck, Laureate Gamma
Spencer, Iowa

APPLE CAKE COBBLER

2 (21-ounce) cans apple
  pie filling
Cinnamon to taste
1 (2-layer) package
  butter pecan cake mix
¹/4 cup packed brown
  sugar
¹/4 cup chopped pecans
1 cup margarine

Pour the pie filling into the bottom of a 9x13-inch baking dish. Sprinkle with cinnamon. Spread the cake mix evenly over the pie filling layer. Sprinkle with the brown sugar and pecans. Dot the top with the margarine. Bake at 350 degrees for 50 minutes. Serve warm with ice cream. Yield: 12 to 15 servings.

Rebecca J. Roberson, Laureate Theta
Aiken, South Carolina

Dianna Hawkins, Nu Sigma, Tarkio, Missouri, makes Butterfinger Dessert. Press ²/3 of a mixture of 2 cups graham cracker crumbs, 1 cup club cracker crumbs and ¹/2 cup melted butter into a 9x13-inch pan. Add 2 small packages vanilla instant pudding mix mixed with 2 cups milk and 1 quart softened vanilla ice cream. Refrigerate for 1 hour. Top with whipped topping and remaining crumbs.

OLD-FASHIONED APPLE CRUMB

2 cups flour
1 cup sugar
¹/2 cup butter, softened
¹/2 teaspoon cinnamon
¹/4 teaspoon salt
5 medium apples, peeled
  and chopped

Combine the flour, sugar, butter, cinnamon and salt in a bowl to form a crumbly mixture. Divide the mixture in half. Press half of the mixture into the bottom of an 8x8-inch dish. Bake at 350 degrees for 10 minutes. Combine the other half of the mixture with the apples. Spread the apple mixture on top of the baked layer. Bake at 350 degrees for 25 to 30 minutes. Serve with whipped topping. Yield: 4 to 6 servings.

Ruthanne Hallmark-Inscore, Preceptor Omicron Alpha
Mission Viejo, California

BERRY COBBLER

1 recipe (2-crust) pie
  pastry
1 (21-ounce) can
  blueberry pie filling
1 (21-ounce) can
  strawberry pie filling
1 (10-ounce) package
  frozen raspberries,
  thawed

Line a 9x13-inch baking dish with 1 pie pastry. Combine the blueberry pie filling, strawberry pie filling and raspberries in a bowl and mix well. Pour the mixture over the layer of pie pastry. Top with the other pie pastry, sealing the edges. Bake at 425 degrees for 10 minutes. Reduce the heat to 350 degrees and bake for 25 to 30 minutes or until golden brown. Serve warm with ice cream or whipped topping. Yield: 12 to 14 servings.

Arlene Covington, Preceptor Omega
Anthony, Texas

BOYSENBERRY COBBLER

I made this recipe on our local public television station during a Pledge Drive week because they had asked for recipes made with berries. It was later published in our local newspaper with me listed as "World Class Cook." I had my fifteen minutes of fame!

1 cup sugar
¹/4 cup shortening
1¹/2 cups flour
1 cup milk
2 teaspoons baking
  powder
¹/2 teaspoon salt
2 cups boysenberries
1 cup sugar
1 cup boiling water
Butter

Cream the sugar and shortening in a mixer bowl. Beat in the flour, milk, baking powder and salt. Pour the dough mixture into a 9x13-inch dish. Place the boysenberries in the center of the dough. Sprinkle 1 cup sugar over the boysenberries and pour boiling water over the mixture. Dot the top with butter. Bake at 350 degrees for 1 hour. Serve warm with vanilla ice cream. Yield: 10 to 12 servings.

Nanci Gruber, Laureate Delta Epsilon
Manteca, California

QUICK AND EASY PEACH COBBLER

My college roommate gave this recipe to me. We live within 5 miles of each other after 30 years.

¹/₂ cup butter or margarine, melted	*1 cup self-rising flour*
	1 cup sugar
2 (16-ounce) cans sliced peaches	*1 cup milk*
	¹/₄ teaspoon nutmeg

Pour the melted butter into a 9x13-inch baking dish. Pour the peaches over the butter. Combine the flour, sugar and milk in a mixer bowl and beat until smooth. Pour over the peaches. Sprinkle with nutmeg. Bake at 375 degrees for 45 minutes or until golden brown. Serve warm with vanilla ice cream. Yield: 8 servings.

Carol Grosbier, Preceptor Nu
Frederick, Maryland

ALMOND CREAM WITH FRUIT

1 (4-ounce) package instant French vanilla pudding mix	*1 cup whipping cream*
	¹/₂ to ³/₄ teaspoon almond extract
2¹/₂ cups milk	*3 cups assorted fruit*

Combine the pudding mix and milk in a mixer bowl and beat on low speed for 2 minutes. Combine the whipping cream and almond extract in a small mixer bowl and beat until soft peaks form. Fold the whipping cream mixture into the pudding mixture. Spoon into individual serving dishes and chill. Top with fruit before serving. Yield: 8 servings.

Kandee Graham, Laureate Alpha Kappa
Hershey, Pennsylvania

CHERRY PUDDING

2 (21-ounce) cans cherry pie filling	*1 cup chopped nuts*
	³/₄ cup butter or margarine
1 (2-layer) package yellow cake mix	

Pour the pie filling into a 9x13-inch baking dish. Combine the cake mix and nuts in a bowl and sprinkle over the pie filling. Dot with thin slices of butter. Bake at 350 degrees for 45 minutes. Serve warm with ice cream. Yield: 8 to 10 servings.

Jeanne G. Smith, Epsilon Mu
Mansfield, Louisiana

CINNAMON RAISIN BREAD PUDDING

1 (16-ounce) loaf raisin-cinnamon bread, cubed	*2 (4-ounce) packages vanilla (not instant) pudding mix*
6 cups milk	

Toss the bread cubes with 2 cups milk in a 9x13-inch baking dish. Let stand for 10 minutes. Combine the remaining milk with the pudding mix in a bowl and mix until smooth. Pour the mixture over the bread and toss lightly. Bake at 350 degrees for 1 hour or until light brown and the center tests done. Yield: 12 servings.

Gloria Scherrer, Preceptor Alpha Xi
Green Valley, Arizona

POT DU CREME AU CHOCOLAT

³/₄ cup milk	*2 tablespoons sugar*
1 cup chocolate chips	*¹/₈ teaspoon salt*
1 egg	

Scald the milk in a saucepan on the stove. Combine the milk, chocolate chips, egg, sugar and salt in a blender container. Process for 1 minute or until smooth. Pour into small individual serving dishes and chill for 3 to 4 hours. Yield: 8 servings.

Cindy Strecker, Xi Alpha Omega
Oelwein, Iowa

REAL CHOCOLATE CHIP MOUSSE

1 cup chocolate chips	*1 teaspoon vanilla extract*
1 egg	*¹/₈ teaspoon salt*
2 tablespoons sugar	*³/₄ cup milk*

Combine the chocolate chips, egg, sugar, vanilla, and salt in a blender container. Heat milk in a saucepan on the stove until almost boiling and pour into the blender container. Process until smooth. Pour into individual dessert dishes. Chill for 2 hours. Yield: 4 servings.

Hilda Hedley, Phi Master
Kingston, Ontario, Canada

FAT-FREE RICE PUDDING

I developed this recipe after my husband had a heart attack. It tastes just like regular rice pudding.

8 cups skim milk
1 cup rice
1/4 teaspoon salt
8 egg whites, beaten

1 1/4 cups sugar
2 teaspoons vanilla
   extract

Combine the milk, rice and salt in a large saucepan. Bring to a boil, stirring occasionally. Reduce heat and simmer for 20 minutes. Combine the egg whites, sugar and vanilla in a small bowl and mix well. Add to the rice mixture and bring to a boil. Remove from heat and let cool. Yield: 6 to 8 servings.

Judith A. Hadesty, Xi Delta Omega
Tamaqua, Pennsylvania

OLD-FASHIONED RICE PUDDING

1/3 cup rice
4 cups milk, scalded
1/4 teaspoon salt
1/4 cup sugar

2 tablespoons butter
Chocolate candy kisses
   (optional)

Combine the rice, milk, salt, sugar and butter in a bowl and mix well. Pour into a 7x11-inch baking dish. Bake at 300 degrees for 1 1/2 hours or until rice is tender and pudding is thick and creamy. Stir every 15 minutes with a fork, turning under the brown top and pushing the edges down. Let cool and top with chocolate candy kisses. May serve warm or cold. Yield: 5 servings.

Lucy A. Igna, Preceptor Beta Nu
Hacienda Heights, California

ORANGE TAPIOCA

This is an easy recipe that has been a family favorite for years. It can be served as a salad or a dessert.

2 (3-ounce) packages
   instant vanilla
   tapioca pudding mix
1 (3-ounce) package
   orange gelatin
3 cups boiling water

2 (11-ounce) cans
   mandarin oranges,
   drained
8 ounces whipped
   topping

Combine the tapioca pudding mix and orange gelatin mix in a bowl. Pour the boiling water over the mixture and mix well. Chill for 2 hours, stirring every 15 minutes. Fold the mandarin oranges and whipped topping into the gelatin mixture. Pour into a 9x13-inch dish and chill for 4 hours or overnight. Yield: 12 servings.

Betty L. Bishop, Xi Gamma Mu
Ontario, Oregon

CORNSTARCH VANILLA PUDDING

1 1/2 cups milk
2 eggs, beaten
1/3 cup sugar
2 tablespoons
   cornstarch

1 teaspoon vanilla
   extract

Combine the milk, eggs, sugar, cornstarch and vanilla in a bowl and mix well. Cook in a saucepan over low heat until boiling. Boil for 1 minute, stirring constantly. Pour into individual dessert dishes. Let cool. Yield: 2 servings.

Elaine Penner, Preceptor Epsilon Theta
St. Petersburg, Florida

FROZEN FRUIT DESSERT

I made this for my chapter several years ago on Valentines Day. They like it so much they expect it every year now. It is low fat, so everyone can eat it.

1/2 cup sugar
4 bananas, sliced
1 (16-ounce) can whole
   cranberry sauce

1 (20-ounce) can crushed
   pineapple, drained
16 ounces whipped
   topping

Pour the sugar over the bananas in a bowl and let stand for a few minutes. Add the cranberry sauce, pineapple and whipped topping and mix well. Spoon into paper-lined muffin tins. Freeze until firm. Yield: 30 to 40 servings.

Sondra West, Laureate Lambda
Aurora, Colorado

CHOCOLATE-GLAZED ORANGE SHERBET BALLS

1 quart orange sherbet
1/4 cup butter or
   margarine
1 cup semisweet
   chocolate chips

1/4 teaspoon grated
   orange peel
1/8 teaspoon orange
   extract

Scoop the sherbet into 1-cup-size balls and place on serving plate. Freeze. Microwave the butter on High in a microwave-safe bowl for 20 to 25 seconds or until melted. Add the chocolate chips and microwave on High for 30 to 35 seconds, stirring once. Stir in the orange peel and orange extract. Remove the sherbet balls from the freezer and drizzle with the chocolate glaze. Serve immediately. Yield: 4 servings.

Ruth Neumann, Preceptor Gamma Epsilon
DeKalb, Illinois

CRUNCHY ICE CREAM RING

This is my special dish. It is wonderful served in the early evening of a hot, summer day.

1/2 cup finely crushed vanilla wafers	2 tablespoons margarine, melted
1/2 cup finely chopped peanuts	1 quart vanilla ice cream, softened
1/4 cup packed brown sugar	

Combine the vanilla wafer crumbs, peanuts and brown sugar in a bowl. Add the melted margarine and mix well. Spread 2 cups of the ice cream in a ring mold. Sprinkle with the crumb mixture. Spread the remaining ice cream over the crumb mixture layer. Top with the remaining crumb mixture and press lightly into the ice cream. Freeze until firm. Invert onto serving plate. Yield: 8 servings.

Judi Wright, Preceptor Zeta Xi
Cedar Park, Texas

HOMEMADE VANILLA ICE CREAM

3 quarts milk	4 1/2 tablespoons vanilla extract
3 cups sugar	
3 cups whipping cream	

Combine the milk, sugar, whipping cream and vanilla in a 1 1/2 gallon ice cream freezer container. Place freezer container in ice cream bucket. Freeze using manufacturer's directions. Yield: 1 1/2 gallons.

Caroline Stuerke, Preceptor Xi
Higginsville, Missouri

ICE CREAM SUPREME

1 (3-ounce) package blackberry gelatin	3/4 cup cold water
1 cup boiling water	1/4 cup sherry
	2 cups vanilla ice cream

Dissolve the gelatin in the boiling water. Add the cold water and sherry and mix well. Add the ice cream gradually, stirring until melted. Chill until slightly thickened. Spoon into individual dessert dishes. Chill until set. Garnish with mint leaves if desired. Yield: 7 servings.

Bobbie Moody
Florence, South Carolina

INSTANT ICE CREAM

5 eggs, separated	1 teaspoon vanilla extract
2 cups heavy whipping cream, whipped	1 teaspoon orange extract
3/4 cup sugar	1/8 teaspoon salt
1/4 cup orange juice	

Beat the egg whites in a large mixer bowl until stiff peaks form. Combine the egg yolks, whipped cream, sugar, orange juice, vanilla, orange extract and salt in a blender container; process for 1 minute. Fold the mixture into the egg whites. Pour into an 8x11-inch dish and freeze. For a sugar-free variation: substitute 1 teaspoon stevia sweetener for sugar.
Yield: 10 to 12 servings.

Barbara J. Jackson, Epsilon Xi
Independence, Oregon

SUGAR-FREE HOMEMADE ICE CREAM

8 cups milk	32 packets aspartame
4 eggs	1 1/4 teaspoons vanilla extract
1 (12-ounce) can evaporated milk	

Combine the milk, eggs, evaporated milk, aspartame and vanilla in a large bowl and mix well. Pour the mixture into an ice cream freezer container. Place freezer container in ice cream bucket. Freeze using manufacturer's directions. Yield: 8 servings.

Patti Nichols, Eta Beta
Karnack, Texas

KIWI SORBET

6 kiwifruit, peeled and thinly sliced	2 tablespoons sugar

Combine the kiwifruit and sugar in a blender container; process until smooth. Freeze, stirring occasionally until thickened. Scoop into individual dessert dishes when frozen. Yield: 4 servings.

Geri Sherwin, Preceptor Gamma
Castle Rock, Washington

RAINBOW SHERBET DESSERT

18 pecan sandies cookies, crushed	1 (1-quart) carton rainbow sherbet
8 ounces whipped topping	

Combine the crushed cookies and the whipped topping in a bowl. Pat the mixture into the bottom of a 9x13-inch dish. Slice the ice cream and place the slices on the crushed cookie layer. Top with additional crushed cookies if desired. Freeze until serving time. Cut into squares to serve. Yield: 15 servings.

Shirley Grudzinski, Laureate Psi
Grand Island, Nebraska

OREO COOKIE DESSERT

1 (16-ounce) package
   Oreo cookies, crushed
1/3 cup margarine,
   melted
1/2 gallon vanilla ice
   cream, softened

1 (16-ounce) jar
   chocolate fudge
   ice cream topping
8 ounces whipped
   topping

Combine the crushed cookies and melted margarine in a bowl and mix well. Reserve one cup for the topping. Pat the mixture into the bottom of a 9x13-inch dish. Spread the ice cream on top of the cookie layer. Pour the fudge topping on top of the ice cream and spread with whipped topping. Top with the reserved crushed cookie mixture. Freeze. Yield: 18 servings.

Linda Birchard, Zeta Iota
Creston, Iowa

HOT APPLE SPICE SUNDAE TOPPING

2 tablespoons butter or
   margarine
2 tablespoons brown
   sugar

1 (21-ounce) can apple
   pie filling
1/2 teaspoon cinnamon
1/4 cup chopped walnuts

Melt the butter in a saucepan on the stove. Stir in the brown sugar, pie filling and cinnamon. Bring to a boil, stirring constantly. Remove from heat and stir in the walnuts. Serve warm over ice cream.
Yield: 8 servings.

Linda Huse, Xi Theta Gamma
Mt. Pleasant, Iowa

BROWNIE TRIFLE

1 (20-ounce) package
   fudge brownie mix
1/4 cup praline or coffee
   flavored liqueur
2 (4-ounce) packages
   instant chocolate
   mousse mix

8 Heath candy bars,
   crushed
12 ounces whipped
   topping

Prepare and bake the brownie mix using the package directions. Prick the top of warm brownies with a fork. Brush warm brownies with the liqueur. Let cool and crumble brownies. Prepare chocolate mousse mix using the package directions. Place half of the crumbled brownies in the bottom of a trifle bowl. Top with half of the mousse, half of the crushed candy bars and half of the whipped topping. Repeat. Garnish the top with shaved chocolate.
Yield: 16 to 18 servings.

Norma Gilmore, Laureate Alpha Chi
Pittsburg, Kansas

CHERRY DELIGHT

2 envelopes dry whipped
   topping mix
16 ounces cream cheese,
   softened
2 cups confectioners'
   sugar

1 teaspoon vanilla
   extract
1 angel food cake, torn
   into 1-inch pieces
2 (21-ounce) cans cherry
   pie filling

Prepare the whipped topping mix using package directions. Beat the cream cheese, confectioners' sugar and vanilla in a mixer bowl until creamy. Add the prepared whipped topping mix and mix well. Fold in the cake pieces. Pour the mixture into a 9x13-inch dish or a trifle bowl. Top with the cans of pie filling. Chill overnight. Yield: 10 to 12 servings.

Linda Burgess, Preceptor Delta Pi
Wamego, Kansas

LEMON FLUFF DESSERT

1 angel food cake, torn
   into pieces
1 (14-ounce) can
   sweetened condensed
   milk

Juice of 2 large lemons
2 cups whipping cream,
   whipped
Chopped walnuts to
   taste

Place the cake pieces in the bottom of a greased 9x13-inch dish. Combine the sweetened condensed milk and the lemon juice in a bowl and mix well. Fold in the whipped cream. Pour mixture over the cake pieces, pressing down to soak. Sprinkle with walnuts. Chill, covered. May chill overnight.
Yield: 12 to 15 servings.

Mardell Garrett, Alpha Master
Duluth, Minnesota

SHERRY SURPRISE

1 angel food cake, torn
   into pieces
3 ounces sherry
1 (4-ounce) package
   instant chocolate
   pudding mix

1 Skorr candy bar,
   crushed
12 ounces whipped
   topping

Place half of the cake pieces in the bottom of a glass bowl. Sprinkle half of the sherry on the cake pieces. Prepare the pudding mix using the package directions. Pour half of the pudding on the cake pieces. Top with half of the crushed candy bar. Repeat. Chill for 1 hour. Yield: 8 servings.

Marilyn P. Zanca, Xi Master
Cocoa Beach, Florida

Brisk Beginnings

Launch a lavish meal with appetizers
and beverages fit for a pleasure cruise.
Put *Brisk Beginnings* at the helm, and you'll
easily bring about an event that stands in
a class by itself. Smooth sailing is assured
with Tea Punch or Peach Brandy Slush,
as refreshing as the sea's summer breeze.
And you may embark remarkably with
Fruit and Brie Appetizer or Stuffed Jalapeño
Peppers, as bracing as a warm western wind.
So set a course for success and get underway
with *Brisk Beginnings*, securing fast those
favorable first impressions, shipshape
and squared away.

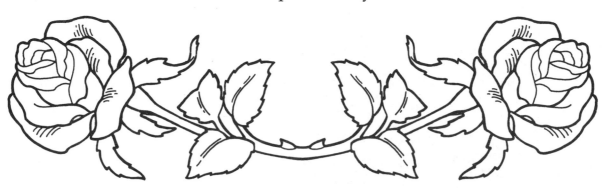

MARINATED CHEESE

Place the cream cheese in the freezer for an hour or so to make it easier to slice.

1/2 cup olive oil	1 teaspoon sugar
1/2 cup white wine	3/4 teaspoon dried basil
vinegar	1/2 teaspoon salt
1 (2-ounce) jar diced	1/2 teaspoon freshly
pimento, drained	ground pepper
3 tablespoons chopped	8 ounces (5 1/2x2x1-inch
fresh parsley	block) sharp Cheddar
3 tablespoons minced	cheese
green onions	1 (8-ounce) package
3 garlic cloves, minced	cream cheese

Combine the first 10 ingredients in a jar with a lid; cover tightly and shake vigorously. Cut the Cheddar cheese block in half lengthwise; cut crosswise into 1/4-inch slices. Prepare the cream cheese block in the same way. Arrange the Cheddar and cream cheese slices on edge in a shallow baking dish. Shake the jar of olive oil mixture again, then pour mixture over cheese slices. Chill, covered, for at least 8 hours. Remove the cheese slices to a serving platter, arranging on edge as they were arranged in the marinating dish. Spoon the remaining marinade over the cheese. Serve with assorted crackers. Yield: 16 servings.

Susie Poindexter, Theta Kappa
Bentonville, Arkansas

BAKED CHINESE SHRIMP TOAST

2 scallions, chopped	1 1/2 teaspoons dry
1 tablespoon chopped	vermouth or sherry
water chestnuts	1/2 pound medium-sized
1 1/2 teaspoons chopped	shrimp, shelled,
fresh gingerroot	deveined
1 1/2 teaspoons	8 thin slices firm-
cornstarch	textured white bread,
1 garlic clove, crushed	crusts trimmed
1/2 teaspoon salt	1/4 cup butter, softened
1/8 teaspoon sugar	2 tablespoons chopped
Dash of cayenne pepper	cilantro or parsley
1 egg white	

Combine the first 8 ingredients in a food processor container; pulse several times until well mixed. Add the egg white and vermouth. Process for 3 to 5 seconds or until egg white is slightly foamy. Add the shrimp; pulse until mixture has formed a paste but shrimp retains some texture. Lightly butter both sides of each bread slice. Spread the shrimp mixture over 1 side of each slice; cut slice diagonally into 4 triangles. Arrange the triangles shrimp side up on a baking dish. (May be made to this point, covered, and refrigerated for up to 8 hours.) Preheat the oven to 375 degrees. Bake, uncovered, for 10 minutes or just until the shrimp topping turns pink and bread is lightly toasted. Garnish with chopped cilantro or parsley and serve at once. Yield: 32 triangles.

Margaret J. McDaniel, Laureate Gamma
Anchorage, Alaska

❖ BRUSCHETTA WITH GOAT CHEESE AND TAPENADE

12 slices crusty white	4 ounces soft goat
bread	cheese or plain cream
Olive oil	cheese, softened
2 garlic cloves, halved	Tapenade

Preheat the broiler. Grill the bread slices under the broiler until both sides are golden, turning once. Brush each slice with olive oil and rub with cut side of garlic. Spread the cheese over the garlic toast and roughen cheese surface with a fork. Spoon the Tapenade over the cheese. Garnish with fresh parsley or basil. Yield: 24 appetizers.

TAPENADE

1 (4-ounce) can pitted	2 tablespoons drained
black olives, chopped	capers
2 ounces olive oil-pack	3 tablespoons chopped
sun-dried tomatoes,	fresh basil, or
chopped	1 teaspoon dried
3 to 4 tablespoons olive	Salt and pepper to taste
oil	

Combine the olives, tomatoes, olive oil, capers, basil, salt and pepper in a medium bowl. Chill, covered, for 8 to 10 hours.

Jean Jones, Beta Beta Chi
Cedar Hill, Texas

CHEESY MUSHROOM CANAPES

This quick last-minute recipe produces appetizers that are great for sorority meetings.

2 tablespoons butter	Freshly ground pepper
4 ounces fresh	to taste
mushrooms, chopped	8 slices French bread
4 teaspoons flour	2 teaspoons chopped
2 cups shredded sharp	fresh parsley
Cheddar cheese	Paprika
1 teaspoon dry mustard	
1 teaspoon	
Worcestershire sauce	

Melt the butter in a small skillet over medium-low heat. Add the mushrooms and sauté for 3 to 4 minutes. Stir in the flour. Add the cheese, mustard and Worcestershire sauce; cook until the cheese begins to melt, stirring constantly. Remove from heat and season with the pepper. Preheat broiler for 5 minutes. Toast one side of each bread slice under broiler. Spread the cheese mixture over the untoasted side of bread slices; place under broiler and heat until mixture melts. Cut into bite-size pieces. Sprinkle with chopped parsley and paprika. Garnish with parsley sprigs. Serve warm. Yield: 4 to 6 servings.

K-L Holter-Ferguson, Nu
Thompson, Manitoba, Canada

❖ CROSTINI WITH BEEF AND CAPER MAYONNAISE

24 (¹/₄- to ¹/₂-inch)
  baguette slices
2 tablespoons olive oil
¹/₂ cup mayonnaise
¹/₄ cup grated Parmesan
  cheese
2 tablespoons chopped
  fresh chives
2 to 4 tablespoons
  drained capers

¹/₄ teaspoon garlic
  powder
¹/₂ pound thinly sliced
  cooked deli roast
  beef, cut into 24
  pieces
2 Italian plum
  tomatoes, cut into
  24 thin slices

Preheat the oven to 350 degrees. Arrange the bread slices on an ungreased baking sheet; brush slices lightly with olive oil. Bake for 8 to 10 minutes or until crisp. Cool completely. Combine the mayonnaise, Parmesan cheese, chives, capers and garlic powder in a small bowl; mix well. Spread the mayonnaise mixture over the toasted bread slices. Cover each toasted bread slice with a piece of roast beef and a slice of tomato. Garnish with chopped fresh chives. Yield: 24 servings.

Judith Murrill, Preceptor Sigma
Corvallis, Montana

SPECIAL ITALIAN OLIVES

Serve these flavorful olives with a selection of other appetizers.

1 (10-ounce) jar green
  olives, drained
1 (9-ounce) can pitted
  black olives, drained
1 (4-ounce) can button
  mushrooms, drained
3 garlic cloves, minced

3 tablespoons olive oil
6 tablespoons wine
  vinegar
2 tablespoons water
1 tablespoon oil from a
  can of anchovies
  (optional)

Combine the green olives, black olives, mushrooms, garlic, olive oil, vinegar, water and anchovy oil in a medium bowl; toss to mix well. Let stand at room temperature for at least 1 hour before serving; longer is even better. Yield: 20 servings.

Margaret P. Cruickshank, Xi Iota Rho
Yucca Valley, California

FETA-FILLED CHERRY TOMATOES

2 pints cherry tomatoes
1¹/₄ cups finely crumbled
  feta cheese
1 (4-ounce) can sliced
  black olives, drained,
  finely chopped
¹/₃ cup minced green
  onions

2 tablespoons olive oil
1 tablespoon minced
  fresh parsley
¹/₂ to 1 teaspoon dried
  oregano
1 garlic clove, minced

Remove stems from the tomatoes and cut a thin slice from the top of each. Scoop out seeds and pulp and discard, leaving shells intact. Invert tomato shells on paper towels to drain. Combine the feta cheese, olives, green onions, olive oil, parsley, oregano and garlic in a bowl; mix well. Spoon the feta mixture into the tomato shells. Chill, covered, until ready to serve. Yield: 4 dozen.

Paula Foy, Lambda Rho
Troy, Michigan

BROCCOLI DIP

1 cup chopped purple
  onion
¹/₂ cup (1 stick) butter or
  margarine, melted
2 rolls garlic cheese
1 (10-ounce) can cream
  of mushroom soup

2 (4-ounce) cans
  mushroom pieces
2 (10-ounce) packages
  frozen chopped
  broccoli, cooked,
  drained

Sauté the onion in butter in a skillet over medium heat for 5 minutes or until onions are clear. Stir in the garlic cheese, soup, mushrooms and broccoli. Serve warm in a warmed serving bowl with Mexican chips. Yield: 12 to 24 servings.

Bobette Risk, Laureate Alpha Epsilon
Fayetteville, Arkansas

Charlotte Cole, Preceptor Alpha Tau, Lawton, Oklahoma, heats the liquid from a 6-ounce can of black olives with ¹/₂ teaspoon curry powder and 1 teaspoon Worcestershire sauce to marinate the olives. After a day she has Curried Olives.

GREEN CHILE-BROCCOLI DIP

1 pound lean ground beef	4 ounces Velveeta cheese
1 (10-ounce) can broccoli-cheese soup	1 teaspoon minced garlic
1 (10-ounce) can cream of chicken soup	Chopped green chiles to taste
1 (10-ounce) package frozen chopped broccoli, thawed	

Cook the ground beef in a skillet until brown and crumbly; drain. Add the canned soups, broccoli, cheese, garlic and chopped chiles. Simmer until broccoli is tender, adding enough water to make of desired consistency. Yield: 12 servings.

Honoria McClanahan, Xi Beta Iota
Gallup, New Mexico

HOT CHICKEN DIP

2 boneless, skinless chicken breasts	1/4 cup milk
Cajun seasoning to taste	2 fresh jalapeño peppers, chopped
Salt and pepper to taste	1 tablespoon lemon juice
Vegetable oil	3/4 teaspoon Tabasco sauce
1/4 cup mayonnaise	
8 ounces cream cheese, softened	

Season the chicken with Cajun seasoning, salt and pepper; brown chicken in oil in a skillet over medium-high heat. Cut the chicken into bite-size pieces. Preheat the oven to 375 degrees. Mix the mayonnaise, cream cheese, milk, jalapeño peppers, lemon juice and Tabasco sauce in a small casserole. Add the chicken pieces to the mayonnaise mixture. Bake for 20 minutes. Serve warm with tortilla chips or wheat crackers. Yield: 3 cups.

Laurie Belz, Beta Theta Upsilon
Spring, Texas

ZESTY CORN DIP

This dip is even better when prepared the day before serving.

2 (11-ounce) cans Mexicorn, drained	1 cup Hellman's mayonnaise
1 cup sour cream	1/2 jar jalapeño peppers, diced
10 ounces shredded Cheddar cheese	
1 (4-ounce) can chopped green chiles	

Combine the Mexicorn, sour cream, Cheddar cheese, green chiles, mayonnaise and jalapeño peppers in a bowl; mix well. Chill, covered, until ready to serve. Serve with corn chips. Yield: 4 cups.

Cynthia A. Guderian
North Zulch, Texas

HUMMUS

4 green onions, green part discarded	2 tablespoons olive oil
1 (16-ounce) can chick-peas, drained	1 or 2 garlic cloves
1/4 teaspoon cumin	4 to 6 dashes hot sauce
1/2 teaspoon coriander	Salt and pepper to taste
2 tablespoons lemon juice	4 to 6 tablespoons water

Combine green onions, chick-peas, cumin, coriander, lemon juice, olive oil, garlic, hot sauce, salt and pepper in a food processor container; process until smooth, adding water until mixture is of desired consistency. Serve with crackers or fresh vegetables for dipping. Yield: 10 to 12 servings.

Carrie Schmitz, Gamma Delta
Oklahoma City, Oklahoma

PUMPKIN DIP

It's fun to ask your guests to guess the secret ingredient in this dip. They almost never do! Serve with raw vegetables, crackers, or corn chips, as well as with the scooped-out bread pieces.

3/4 cup canned pumpkin	1/3 cup chopped green bell pepper
12 ounces cream cheese, softened	1/3 cup chopped red bell pepper
2 tablespoons taco seasoning mix	1 (21/4-ounce) can sliced black olives, drained
1/8 teaspoon garlic powder	1 (1-pound) round loaf Italian or pumpernickel bread
1/3 cup chopped dried beef	

Beat the pumpkin, cream cheese, taco seasoning mix and garlic powder in a mixer bowl until smooth. Stir in the dried beef, green pepper, red pepper and olives. Chill, covered, until ready to serve. Before serving, cut a 1-inch slice off the top of the bread. Scoop out the bread from inside, leaving a 1/2-inch shell; save the scooped-out bread pieces for dipping. Fill the bread shell with the cream cheese mixture. Yield: 10 servings.

Ruth King, Laureate Alpha Rho
Leon, Kansas

RHO ETA RIPPED DIP

This dip is best served with baguettes and lots of red wine!

1 pound zucchini, chopped
2 medium green bell peppers, chopped
3 tablespoons olive oil
3 tablespoons red wine vinegar
1 cup pitted black olives, coarsely chopped
1 large tomato, chopped
1 tablespoon chopped fresh parsley
2 (6-ounce) jars marinated artichoke hearts, drained, coarsely chopped
5 garlic cloves, chopped
Salt and pepper to taste
2 to 3 ounces feta cheese, crumbled (optional)

Combine the zucchini, green peppers, olive oil, vinegar, olives, tomato, parsley, artichoke hearts, garlic, salt, pepper and feta cheese in a large bowl; mix well. Yield: 4 cups.

K. Fairbanks, Rho Eta
Oroville, California

AVOCADO AND WHITE BEAN SALSA

1 (16-ounce) can white beans or pinto beans
1 firm-ripe medium avocado, chopped
1 medium tomato, chopped
1/2 medium red onion, chopped
2 tablespoons fresh lime juice
1 teaspoon olive oil
1 teaspoon garlic salt

Rinse and drain enough of the beans to measure 1/2 cup; save the remainder for another use. Combine the 1/2 cup beans, avocado, tomato and onion in a small bowl; mix well. Stir in the lime juice, olive oil and garlic salt. Serve with tortilla chips. Yield: 2 servings.

Kim Collins, Beta Sigma Phi
Springfield, Illinois

CALIFORNIA SALSA

3 pounds ripe tomatoes, chopped
1 medium bunch cilantro, chopped
2 to 3 jalapeño peppers, chopped
2 serrano peppers, chopped
3 Fresno peppers (yellow), chopped
1 medium bunch green onions, chopped
1 medium carrot, shredded
4 medium radishes, thinly sliced
1/2 cup orange juice concentrate
Juice of 1 lime
1/2 teaspoon salt
1/2 teaspoon seasoned salt
1/2 teaspoon garlic salt
1 teaspoon cumin
1 medium avocado, chopped (optional)

Combine the tomatoes, cilantro, jalapeño peppers, serrano peppers, Fresno peppers, green onions, carrot, radishes, orange juice concentrate, lime juice, salt, seasoned salt, garlic salt, cumin and avocado in a bowl. Serve with tortilla chips. Yield: 10 servings.

Pam Price, Zeta Rho
San Bernardino, California

MEXICAN PARTY SALSA

1 tablespoon vinegar
1 tablespoon sugar
2 (14-ounce) cans stewed tomatoes, mashed
1 medium bunch green onions, chopped
1/2 large white onion, chopped
4 fresh Roma tomatoes, chopped
3 ripe medium avocados, coarsely chopped
2 teaspoons Worcestershire sauce
1/2 teaspoon cayenne pepper
1/2 cup fresh cilantro, minced
1 teaspoon cumin
Salt and pepper to taste
Garlic powder to taste
1 or 2 fresh jalapeño peppers, chopped (optional)

Stir together the vinegar and sugar in a large bowl. Add the stewed tomatoes, green onions, white onion, Roma tomatoes, avocados, Worcestershire sauce, cayenne, cilantro, cumin, vinegar-sugar mixture, salt, pepper, garlic powder and jalapeño peppers; mix well. Chill for 1 hour. Serve with warm tortilla chips. Yield: 4 cups.

Jannette Caudle, Alpha Zeta
Early, Texas

SEVEN-INGREDIENT DIP

I get my best recipes from fellow educators—I knew this one was a hit when I took it to a meeting and noticed someone eating it with a fork!

1 package zesty Italian dressing mix
1 pound Monterey Jack cheese, shredded
1 (4-ounce) can chopped black olives
1 (4-ounce) can chopped green chiles
3 medium tomatoes, chopped
1 bunch green onions, chopped
1/2 medium bunch cilantro, chopped

Prepare the Italian dressing using package directions. Combine half the prepared dressing with the cheese, olives, chiles, tomatoes, green onions and cilantro in a bowl; mix well. Serve with tortilla chips. Reserve the remaining half of the prepared dressing for another use. Yield: 5 cups.

Cheryl Lind, Rho
Spearfish, South Dakota

SPINACH AND ARTICHOKE DIP

1 (10-ounce) package
   frozen chopped
   spinach, thawed
1 (6-ounce) can
   artichoke hearts,
   drained, chopped
12 ounces Monterey Jack
   cheese, shredded

12 ounces mozzarella
   cheese, shredded
1/2 cup sour cream
1/2 cup mayonnaise
2 garlic cloves, crushed
Sliced provolone cheese

Drain the spinach and squeeze dry. Combine the spinach, artichoke hearts, shredded cheese, sour cream, mayonnaise and garlic in a microwave-safe bowl. Microwave on High until hot and bubbly. Cover with provolone slices. Microwave for less than 1 minute or just until provolone begins to melt. Serve with nacho chips, salsa and sour cream. Yield: 4 cups.

Donna Lynch, Xi Beta Xi
York, Nebraska

GRANDPA'S SHRIMP DIP

1/2 cup sour cream
1/2 cup mayonnaise
8 ounces cream cheese,
   softened
1 teaspoon Tabasco
   sauce
1 small onion, finely
   chopped

1/2 teaspoon celery salt
1 to 2 tablespoons garlic
   powder
2 (4-ounce) cans small
   shrimp, drained

Combine the sour cream, mayonnaise and cream cheese in a bowl. Add the next 4 ingredients; mix well. Stir in the shrimp. Chill, covered, for 30 to 60 minutes. Serve with chips. Yield: 3 cups.

Florence Watson, Eta Omicron
Clearwater, British Columbia, Canada

SOUTHWEST SIZZLER DIP

16 ounces cream cheese,
   softened
1/4 cup fresh lime juice
1 tablespoon cumin
1 teaspoon salt
1 teaspoon black pepper
1 teaspoon cayenne
   pepper

1 (8-ounce) can whole
   kernel corn, drained
1 cup chopped walnuts
1 (4-ounce) can chopped
   green chiles
3 green onions, chopped,
   including tops

Beat the cream cheese until fluffy. Beat in the lime juice, cumin, salt, black pepper and cayenne pepper. Fold in the next 4 ingredients. Chill, covered, for 2 to 4 hours. Serve with tortilla chips. Yield: 4 cups.

Ruth Mencl
Lake Winnebago, Missouri

FRUIT AND BRIE APPETIZER

1 (8-ounce) wheel soft
   ripened Brie
1 cup low-fat granola
1 cup chopped almonds,
   toasted

1 1/4 cups fresh raspberries
1/4 cup fresh blueberries
1/4 cup chunky apricot
   preserves
1/4 cup kirsch

Slice Brie wheel horizontally into 2 layers. Place the bottom half on a serving platter and cover with 1/2 cup of the granola. Combine the almonds, raspberries, blueberries and the remaining granola in a bowl. Place the top half of the Brie over the granola-covered bottom half. Spoon the almond mixture over the top. Combine the apricot preserves and kirsch in a saucepan. Cook over medium-low heat until preserves are melted, stirring constantly. Spoon over the almond mixture. Garnish with fresh basil sprigs and serve with assorted crackers. Yield: 4 to 6 servings.

Walda Weaver, Xi Gamma Omicron
Pryor, Oklahoma

CRAB AND SHRIMP MOUSSE

Serve this popular mousse with any of your favorite crackers or with small bread cubes.

1 1/2 envelopes
   unflavored gelatin
2 tablespoons water
1 (10-ounce) can cream
   of chicken soup
8 ounces cream cheese
3/4 cup mayonnaise
1 cup finely diced celery

1 small onion, finely
   diced
2 tablespoons chopped
   fresh parsley
12 to 16 ounces fresh
   crab, cleaned
12 to 16 ounces fresh
   shrimp, cleaned

Soften the gelatin in the water. Combine the soup and softened gealtin in a saucepan; heat over medium-low heat until gelatin dissolves, stirring constantly. Add the cream cheese; heat until melted, stirring constantly. Remove from heat. Add the mayonnaise, celery, onion, parsley, crab and shrimp; stir until well mixed. Pour into an oiled 6-cup mold. Chill, covered, for several hours or until firm. Unmold onto a serving plate. Yield: 20 servings.

Mary Kay Hefty, Preceptor Zeta
Anchorage, Alaska

Louise Fleetwood, Alpha Zeta Master, Belton, Missouri, slices Monterey Jack cheese 1/4 inch thick, then into 1 1/2-inch circles or squares and arranges 3 inches apart on a nonstick baking sheet. Bake at 400 degrees for 9 to 10 minutes and remove from baking sheet to cool on a wire rack. Serve Monterey Jack Wafers with cocktails, soups or salads.

HOLIDAY TORTA

Decorate the top of this pretty holiday appetizer with a sprig of parsley and several roasted red peppers.

16 ounces light cream cheese, softened
1 (1-ounce) envelope ranch salad dressing mix
3 tablespoons minced fresh parsley
1 (6-ounce) jar marinated artichoke hearts, drained, chopped
1/3 cup canned roasted red peppers, drained, chopped

Blend the cream cheese and salad dressing mix in a small bowl. Stir together the remaining ingredients in a separate bowl. Line a 3-cup bowl with plastic wrap; layer the cream cheese mixture and vegetable mixture in the bowl, beginning and ending with a cream cheese layer. Chill, covered, for 4 hours or overnight. Invert over a serving plate. Remove the plastic wrap. Serve with crackers. Yield: 10 to 12 servings.

Dorothy Parsons, Alpha Upsilon Master
San Leandro, California

MOUSSE PATE

This pâté has a very delicate flavor. Garnish with fresh parsley and serve with melba toast, toasted baguette slices, or crisp crackers.

1/2 cup currants
1/2 cup brandy
6 slices bacon, diced
1 pound chicken livers, rinsed, patted dry
3/4 cup heavy cream
1 medium onion, chopped
1/4 cup mayonnaise
1 teaspoon dried thyme
1/8 teaspoon ground nutmeg
1/2 cup coarsely chopped walnuts
Salt and pepper to taste

Plump the currants in the brandy. Drain and reserve both the currants and brandy. Fry the bacon in a large skillet over medium heat until crisp; remove from skillet with a slotted spoon. Drain on paper towels. Fry the chicken livers in the drippings for 5 minutes or until cooked on the outside but still pink inside. Remove with a slotted spoon to a food processor. Add the brandy to the skillet and deglaze. Add the cream and boil over medium heat until reduced to 1 cup. Add the cream mixture and onion to the livers; process until smooth. Add the remaining ingredients; process until smooth. Remove to a serving bowl. Chill, covered, for several hours to overnight to blend the flavors. Yield: about 3 cups.

Bobbie Singer, Preceptor Gamma Kappa
Chesapeake, Virginia

SALMON MOUSSE

1 (15-ounce) can salmon
2 envelopes unflavored gelatin
1/2 cup water
2 tablespoons sugar
2 tablespoons lemon juice
4 teaspoons dried onion flakes
1/2 teaspoon salt
1/2 teaspoon paprika
1 1/2 cups finely chopped celery
1 cup mayonnaise

Drain the salmon, reserving the liquid; set aside. Sprinkle the gelatin over water in a small saucepan; let stand for 5 minutes. Heat over medium-low heat until gelatin is completely dissolved, stirring constantly. Add the sugar, lemon juice, onion flakes, salt, paprika and reserved salmon liquid; mix well. Chill, covered, for 1 to 3 hours or until the mixture is the consistency of syrup. Remove the round bones and skin from salmon; mash the salmon. Fold the salmon, celery and mayonnaise into the chilled gelatin mixture. Pour the mixture into an oiled 4-cup mold. Chill, covered, for 8 to 10 hours or until set. Unmold the mousse onto a serving plate. Serve with crackers or melba toast. Yield: 4 cups.

Margaret Du Basse, Preceptor Theta
Winnipeg, Manitoba, Canada

SALMON ROLL

8 ounces cream cheese, softened
2 tablespoons soft goat cheese
1 tablespoon fresh lemon juice
1 green onion, finely chopped
1 tablespoon horseradish
1/2 teaspoon cayenne pepper
1 (15-ounce) can salmon, drained
1/2 cup finely chopped pecans
2 tablespoons finely chopped fresh parsley

Combine the cream cheese, goat cheese, lemon juice, green onion, horseradish and cayenne pepper in a medium bowl; mix well. Add the salmon; stir until well mixed. Chill, covered, for 2 hours or longer. When ready to serve, combine the pecans and parsley on waxed paper. Shape the chilled salmon mixture into a cylinder about 8 inches long. Roll the cylinder in the pecan mixture until it is completely coated. Place on a serving platter and garnish with parsley sprigs. Serve with crackers. Yield: 8 servings.

Bernice Edgar, Laureate Beta Delta
South Delta, British Columbia, Canada

CINNAMON TORTILLAS WITH FRUIT SALSA

This delightful dish, light and tasty for a hot summer day, has no fat! Make with lightly sweetened fresh berries.

4 (12-inch) soft flour tortillas	1/2 cup frozen unsweetened blueberries, thawed, coarsely chopped
1 teaspoon cinnamon	
1/2 cup sugar	
1 cup frozen sliced strawberries in light syrup, thawed, slightly drained	1 large apple, peeled, cored, finely chopped
	Grated zest of 1/2 medium orange

Use a spray bottle to lightly mist the tortillas with water. Combine the cinnamon and sugar in a small bowl; sprinkle the cinnamon mixture over the misted tortillas. Cut tortillas into quarters to make 16 triangles. Arrange the triangles in a single layer on a baking sheet. Bake at 375 degrees for 4 to 8 minutes; watch closely to make sure the triangles become crisp but not too brown. Remove from oven. Combine the strawberries, blueberries, apple and orange zest in a bowl. Serve the salsa in a pretty bowl and use the triangles for dipping. Yield: 6 to 8 servings.

Cathy Janes, Alpha Omega
Port Alberni, British Columbia, Canada

BAKED EGG ROLLS

1/2 pound ground turkey breast	1 garlic clove, minced
2 cups shredded cabbage	1/4 cup sliced celery
1 (8-ounce) can sliced water chestnuts, drained	1 (14-ounce) can sliced mushrooms, drained
1 small onion, chopped	2 tablespoons soy sauce
1 (14-ounce) can bean sprouts, drained	Pinch of cayenne pepper
	16 egg roll wrappers

Cook the turkey in a large skillet until brown and crumbly. Add the remaining ingredients except egg roll wrappers and heat through, stirring frequently. Spray a baking sheet with nonstick cooking spray. Preheat the oven to 425 degrees. Spoon 1/4 cup of the turkey filling onto 1 egg roll wrapper; fold sides toward center and roll up tightly, forming an egg roll. Place seam side down on the baking sheet. Repeat procedure with the remaining filling and wrappers. Spray the egg rolls with nonstick cooking spray. Bake for 10 to 15 minutes or until light brown. Yield: 16 servings.

Julie K. Boettcher, Xi Alpha Iota
Custer, South Dakota

CRUNCHY BARBECUE MEATBALLS

This is a great dish for people who can't eat onions yet like a little crunch in a meatball—in this case, provided by the water chestnuts.

2 pounds lean ground beef	Salt and pepper to taste
1 cup soft bread crumbs	Bottle of favorite barbecue sauce
2 eggs, beaten	3/4 cup packed brown sugar
3/4 cup water	1 teaspoon lemon juice
2 (8-ounce) cans water chestnuts, drained, chopped	

Preheat the oven to 350 degrees. Combine the ground beef, bread crumbs, eggs, water, water chestnuts, salt and pepper in a large bowl. Form the ground beef mixture into small balls; arrange in a 9x13-inch baking dish. Bake for 15 minutes; drain. Combine the barbecue sauce, brown sugar and lemon juice in a medium saucepan. Heat to serving temperature over low heat until well blended, stirring frequently. Pour over cooked meatballs. Keep the meatballs warm in a slow oven until ready to serve. Yield: 8 servings.

Linda Boland, Preceptor Alpha Zeta
Montgomery, Alabama

MEXICAN BARS

2 (8-count) packages refrigerated crescent rolls	1 1/2 cups shredded Cheddar cheese
8 ounces sour cream	1/2 cup chopped green onions
2 tablespoons taco seasoning	1/2 cup chopped green bell pepper
1 (16-ounce) can refried beans	1 cup chopped tomatoes
	1/2 cup sliced olives
	Salsa (optional)

Preheat the oven to 375 degrees. Spread the crescent roll dough over the bottom of an 11x17-inch baking pan, pressing perforations to seal. Bake for 14 to 19 minutes, or until golden brown. Let stand until cool. Combine the sour cream and taco seasoning. Layer the refried beans, sour cream mixture, cheese, green onions, green pepper, tomatoes and olives over the baked crescent roll dough. Cover the dish with aluminum foil and let stand for about 1 hour. Remove foil; cover with salsa. Cut into squares and serve. Yield: 6 dozen.

Tonya Fillmore, Xi Alpha Eta
Fruitland, Idaho

ITALIAN PINWHEELS

1/2 cup shredded mozzarella cheese	*1 egg yolk*
1/2 cup chopped pepperoni	*1 (8-count) package refrigerated crescent rolls*
1/4 teaspoon dried oregano	*1 egg white, beaten*

Preheat the oven to 375 degrees. Combine the cheese, pepperoni, oregano and egg yolk in a medium bowl; mix well. Separate the dough into 4 rectangles; press perforated lines to seal. Spread 3 tablespoons of the pepperoni mixture over each rectangle. Beginning at the short side, roll up each rectangle like a jelly roll, pinching edges to seal. Cut each roll into 6 slices. Arrange slices cut side down on an ungreased baking sheet. Brush with beaten egg white. Bake for 12 to 15 minutes. Serve warm. Yield: 2 dozen.

Verna Bunten, Preceptor Alpha
Council Bluffs, Iowa

STUFFED MUSHROOMS

This appetizer is excellent anytime, but especially when served with an Italian meal.

1 pound large fresh mushrooms	*1 (26-ounce) jar spaghetti sauce*
2 small onions or 1 large onion, chopped	*2 tablespoons oregano*
1/2 cup (1 stick) butter, melted	*8 ounces mozzarella cheese or provolone, sliced*
1 (6-ounce) package stuffing mix	

Preheat the oven to 325 degrees. Spray a large baking pan with nonstick cooking spray. Wash the mushrooms and remove stems. Chop the mushroom stems. Sauté stems with the onions in the butter in a skillet over medium-low heat for 5 minutes. Prepare the stuffing using package directions. Add the onion mixture to the stuffing mixture; mix well. Arrange the large mushroom caps in the baking pan. Spoon the stuffing mixture into the mushrooms. Spoon the spaghetti sauce over the stuffed mushrooms. Sprinkle with the oregano. Bake for 15 to 20 minutes or until tops begin to brown. Cover each stuffed mushroom with a small square of cheese and bake for 5 minutes longer. Yield: 12 to 16 servings.

Sharon Hatker, Preceptor Gamma
Key West, Florida

AVOCADO-STUFFED MUSHROOMS

You can stir Worcestershire sauce into the avocado mixture before stuffing the mushrooms, or sprinkle grated Parmesan cheese over the mushrooms for final 3 minutes of baking time.

1/2 pound large fresh mushrooms	*2 tablespoons minced onion*
2 teaspoons lemon juice	*Dash of Tabasco sauce*
6 saltines, crushed	*Garlic salt and pepper to taste*
1 ripe medium avocado, mashed	

Preheat the oven to 350 degrees. Remove the mushroom stems; finely chop enough of the stems to measure 1/2 cup. Combine the lemon juice, crackers, avocado, onion, Tabasco sauce, garlic salt, pepper and chopped mushroom stems in a medium bowl. Spray a baking sheet with nonstick cooking spray. Arrange the mushroom caps on the baking sheet. Spoon the avocado mixture into each mushroom cap. Bake for 10 minutes. Yield: 8 to 12 appetizers.

Kathy Cook, Xi Omega Nu
Needville, Texas

❖ STUFFED JALAPENO PEPPERS

Always use plastic gloves when working with jalapeño peppers.

1 pound (about 20 to 25) fresh jalapeño peppers	*8 ounces cream cheese, softened*
1 pound bulk Italian sausage	*3/4 cup freshly grated Parmesan cheese*

Preheat oven to 350 degrees. Trim the stems from peppers and cut in half lengthwise; remove the veins and seeds. Cook the sausage in a large skillet until brown and crumbly, stirring frequently; drain well. Combine the cooked sausage with the cream cheese and Parmesan cheese in a medium bowl; fill the pepper halves with the sausage mixture. Arrange the stuffed peppers in a single layer in a 9x13-inch baking dish. Bake for 20 minutes. Broil for 2 to 3 minutes or until tops are brown. Serve hot.
Yield: 40 to 50 appetizers.

Janet Hamilton, Xi Zeta Epsilon
Kalamazoo, Michigan

Betty Schaertl, Xi Omicron Lambda, Del Rio, Texas, spreads soda crackers with pimento cheese and adds pineapple chunks and parsley to make Can't Pass Up Do-Dads.

SMOKED SALMON TARTS

4 unbaked (9-inch) pie
   shells
1½ cups half-and-half
4 eggs, beaten
4 ounces smoked
   salmon, chopped
½ cup shredded
   Monterey Jack cheese

¼ cup chopped green
   onions
½ teaspoon dillweed
¼ teaspoon salt
⅛ teaspoon pepper

Preheat the oven to 375 degrees. Grease miniature muffin cups. Cut each pie shell into 12 to 14 circles with a 2½-inch round cookie cutter. Press the dough circles into the muffin cups; trim off excess pastry. Combine the half-and-half and eggs in a medium bowl; beat with a wire whisk until well blended. Stir in the salmon, cheese, green onions, dillweed, salt and pepper. Spoon 1 tablespoon of the salmon mixture into each pastry cup. Bake for 25 to 30 minutes or until set. Remove tarts from the muffin cups to cool on wire racks. May be frozen in airtight containers for up to 2 weeks. Thaw at room temperature, place on a baking sheet, cover lightly with foil, and bake at 375 degrees for 5 to 10 minutes. Yield: 4 dozen.

Patience Flynn, Preceptor Alpha Psi
Midlothian, Virginia

CHAFING DISH SHRIMP

1 (10-ounce) can cream
   of celery soup
1 (10-ounce) can cream
   of mushroom soup
8 ounces cream cheese
½ cup chopped green
   bell pepper

1 cup chopped celery
1 cup mayonnaise
24 to 32 ounces shrimp,
   cleaned, cooked
Tabasco sauce to taste
Pastry shells

Combine soups and cream cheese in the top of a large double boiler. Heat over boiling water until cream cheese has melted, stirring occasionally. Add the green pepper, celery, mayonnaise, shrimp and Tabasco sauce. Heat until the shrimp are heated through, stirring constantly. Serve from a chafing dish into pastry shells. Yield: 12 to 15 servings.

Frances Reynolds, Delta Kappa
Ellisville, Mississippi

Evelyn Stewart, Chi Zeta, Dunnellon, Florida, makes Herbed Puff Pastry Bites by brushing the pastry with olive oil, sprinkling with fresh or dried basil, rosemary, thyme, chives and Parmesan cheese, cutting into bite-size pieces and baking at 400 degrees for 10 to 12 minutes.

WONDERFUL WON TONS

1 pound hot sausage
½ cup chopped red bell
   pepper
½ cup chopped green
   onions
1 cup prepared ranch
   salad dressing

1½ cups shredded sharp
   Cheddar cheese
1½ cups shredded
   Monterey Jack cheese
1 (12-ounce) package
   won ton wrappers

Preheat the oven to 350 degrees. Grease miniature muffin cups. Cook the sausage in a skillet until brown and crumbly; drain. Add the red pepper and onions. Cook until the vegetables are tender. Remove from heat; stir in the salad dressing and cheeses. Set aside. Press the won ton wrappers into the greased muffin cups. Bake for 2 to 3 minutes. Remove the won ton cups to a nonstick baking sheet. Spoon a small amount of the sausage mixture into each won ton cup. Bake for 5 to 10 minutes or until cheese melts. Yield: 50 appetizers.

Terri Carman, Mu Tau
Augusta, Kansas

CUCUMBER APRICOT SANDWICHES

1 large cucumber, peeled,
   halved lengthwise
4 ounces Neufchâtel
   cheese, softened
2 tablespoons chopped
   fresh basil
⅛ teaspoon salt
   (optional)

8 slices firm-textured
   whole wheat bread
2 large apricots or 1
   nectarine, thinly
   sliced
¼ cup alfalfa sprouts
¼ cup arugula leaves or
   cilantro sprigs

Scoop the seeds out of the cucumber halves; thinly slice the cucumbers and set aside. Combine the Neufchâtel cheese, basil and salt in a small bowl; mix well. Spread about 1 tablespoon of the cheese mixture over each slice of bread. Cover 4 of the bread slices with the cucumber slices, fruit slices, sprouts and arugula; top with the remaining bread. Cut each sandwich in half, diagonally. Serve immediately or chill, covered, for 2 hours before serving. Yield: 4 servings.

Daphene D. Miller, Laureate Delta Beta
Princeton, Missouri

Mary W. Gist, Preceptor Epsilon Delta, Independence, Missouri, sandwiches crab meat between brussels sprout halves, serves with a wooden pick and marinates overnight in Italian dressing for Marinated Brussels Sprouts.

MINI MONTE CRISTO SANDWICHES

These miniature appetizers are great when served with chips and pickle spears.

2 tablespoons butter or
  margarine, softened
2 tablespoons prepared
  mustard
8 slices white bread
4 slices Swiss cheese
4 slices cooked ham
3 eggs
1/2 cup milk
1 envelope golden onion
  soup mix
1/4 cup butter or
  margarine

Blend 2 tablespoons butter and mustard in a bowl; spread mixture evenly over each bread slice. Cover 4 of the bread slices with cheese slices. Cover the cheese slices with ham slices, and then with the remaining slice of bread, buttered side down. Cut each sandwich into 4 triangles. Beat the eggs, milk and soup mix in a bowl until well blended. Dip the sandwiches in the egg mixture to coat well. Melt 1/4 cup butter in a large skillet. Add the coated sandwiches to the skillet; cook over medium heat, turning once, until brown on both sides. Yield: 16 appetizers.

Karon Parrish, Xi Beta Delta
Monticello, Arkansas

DOUBLE-FILLED PARTY SANDWICHES

Try this fun sandwich that has almost-impossible-to-guess ingredients. The sandwiches can be prepared a day before serving. Cover with waxed paper, then a slightly dampened lightweight kitchen towel, and store in the refrigerator.

Cheese and Orange
  Filling
18 slices oatmeal bread,
  crusts trimmed
Tomato-Curry Orange
  Butter

Spread Cheese and Orange Filling over 9 of the bread slices; spread Tomato-Curry Orange Butter over the remaining 9 bread slices. Place spread sides of slices together, cheese filling against tomato filling. Cut sandwiches in quarters. Yield: 36 party sandwiches.

CHEESE AND ORANGE FILLING

1 (11-ounce) can
  mandarin oranges,
  drained
8 ounces cream cheese,
  softened
1/2 cup finely chopped
  walnuts, toasted
1/2 teaspoon ground
  cinnamon

Press the orange segments between paper towels to remove excess moisture. Combine the orange segments, cream cheese, walnuts and cinnamon in a small bowl; blend well.

TOMATO-CURRY ORANGE BUTTER

1/2 cup (1 stick) butter,
  softened
1/4 teaspoon curry
  powder
1/4 teaspoon grated
  orange rind
1/4 teaspoon catsup
1/8 teaspoon salt

Combine the butter, curry powder, orange rind, catsup and salt in a small bowl; blend well.

Norma Newmeister, Preceptor Lambda
Cedar Rapids, Iowa

CARAMEL-COATED CHEX MIX

Leftover Chex Mix may be frozen for later use.

2 cups Rice Chex
2 cups Wheat Chex
2 cups Corn Chex
1 cup pecans
1/4 cup raisins
3/4 cup (1 1/2 sticks) butter
3/4 cup packed brown
  sugar

Preheat the oven to 350 degrees. Grease a 9x13-inch baking dish. Place the Chex cereals, pecans and raisins in the baking dish; set aside. Place the butter and brown sugar in a small saucepan over medium-low heat; cook, stirring constantly, until thick and clear. Pour the brown sugar mixture over the cereals, pecans and raisins; mix well. Bake for 30 minutes, stirring twice. Cool completely. Yield: 20 servings.

Kathryn Seifert, Xi Beta Xi
Hartland, Wisconsin

GOOF-PROOF CARAMEL CORN

1 cup (2 sticks)
  margarine
2 cups packed brown
  sugar
1/2 cup light corn syrup
1/8 teaspoon cream of
  tartar
1 teaspoon baking soda
5 quarts plain popped
  corn

Preheat the oven to 200 degrees. Spray 2 (12x18-inch) shallow baking pans with nonstick cooking spray. Melt the margarine in a 3-quart saucepan over medium heat. Add the brown sugar, corn syrup and cream of tartar; bring to a boil. Boil for 5 minutes, stirring constantly. Remove from heat. Stir in the baking soda. Pour the brown sugar mixture over the popcorn in a large bowl. Stir quickly to coat the popcorn. Spread the mixture in the 2 baking pans and place them on the bottom and middle oven racks. Bake for 30 minutes. Stir the mixture in both pans, then exchange positions of pans. Bake for 30 minutes longer. Cool completely; break into pieces. Store in airtight containers or sealable plastic bags. Yield: 5 quarts.

Lori Murphy, Xi Upsilon
Salem, Oregon

FROZEN ALEXANDERS

The mixture may be frozen until firm and served as a delicious dessert.

6 ounces 80 proof vodka
3 ounces crème de cacao
3 ounces chocolate
  syrup
1 ounce evaporated milk

1/2 gallon ice cream
Whipped cream
  (optional)
Nutmeg (optional)

Combine the vodka, crème de cacao, chocolate syrup and evaporated milk in a blender container. Add enough ice cream so the blender container is as full as instructions allow. Process at high speed until smooth. Freeze for an hour or so until thickened. Spoon into cocktail glasses. Top with whipped cream and sprinkle with nutmeg if desired.
Yield: 10 servings.

Susan Mercer, Xi Beta Gamma
Overland Park, Kansas

GRANDMA ERB'S CHRISTMAS PUNCH

My grandmother makes this wonderful punch every Christmas.

1 (12-ounce) can frozen
  orange juice
  concentrate
1/2 cup amaretto

1/2 cup 80 proof Southern
  Comfort
1/2 cup sloe gin

Prepare the orange juice using directions on can. Pour into a punch bowl. Stir in the amaretto, Southern Comfort and sloe gin and add a block of ice. Yield: 1 quart.

Stephanie Strand, Beta Phi
Challis, Idaho

PARTY PUNCH

1 (12-ounce) can frozen
  orange juice
  concentrate
1 (12-ounce) can frozen
  pink lemonade
  concentrate
1 (12-ounce) can frozen
  fruit punch
  concentrate

Orange sherbet
Cantaloupe balls, frozen
Melon balls, frozen
3 (2-liter) bottles lemon-
  lime soda

Combine orange juice, lemonade and fruit punch concentrates in a large punch bowl. Add ice, sherbet, cantaloupe, melon and Sprite. Yield: 50 servings.

Tamme Garmendia, Alpha Rho
Mountain Home, Idaho

TEA PUNCH

For this punch, make ice cubes from lemon-lime soda with a maraschino cherry and a splash of cherry juice in each cube.

2 cups strong black tea
1 cup honey
2 1/2 cups fresh orange
  juice
2 (32-ounce) bottles
  cranberry juice
  cocktail

1 cup fresh lemon juice
2 quarts lemon-lime
  soda
1 pint dark rum
Ice cubes

Combine tea, honey, orange juice, cranberry juice and lemon juice in a large container. Chill, covered, until serving time. Pour tea mixture into a large punch bowl. Stir in lemon-lime soda, rum and ice cubes.
Yield: 35 servings.

Mary Louise Eayrs, Delta Master
Kalispell, Montana

PEACH BRANDY SLUSH

6 cups water
4 green tea bags
1 1/2 cups sugar
1 (12-ounce) can frozen
  lemonade
  concentrate, thawed

1 (12-ounce) can frozen
  orange juice
  concentrate, thawed
2 cups mild peach
  brandy
2 liters lemon-lime soda

Bring 2 cups of the water to a boil in a saucepan; remove from heat. Steep for 5 minutes. Combine the sugar, lemonade and orange juice concentrates in a large container; mix well. Stir in the tea, the remaining 4 cups of water and the brandy; mix well. Chill until serving time. Pour equal amounts of the tea mixture and the lemon-lime soda over ice in a blender container; process until slushy.
Yield: 36 servings.

Judy Miller, Xi Iota Pi
Palm Harbor, Florida

MULLED WINE

1 cup sugar
1/2 cup water
1/2 lemon, sliced
2 dozen whole cloves

2 sticks cinnamon
1 quart red wine
1 quart citrus juice

Combine the sugar, water, lemon, cloves and cinnamon sticks in a heavy saucepan; bring to a boil. Boil for 5 minutes; cool and strain the resulting syrup. Combine the syrup, wine and fruit juice in a kettle over medium heat. Serve hot with pineapple chunks and additional lemon slices. Yield: 15 servings.

Carolyn H. Waters, Xi Psi
Crestview, Florida

Simple Soups
& Salads

Salad has long held the time-honored
position of the last course in Euro-style
cuisine. And in a similar traditional sense,
both soup and salad have served to
merely whet the appetite for the New World
palate. But in this enlightened era of light
eateries, neither soup nor salad is simply
a side dish anymore. And they don't
dent the budget. Healthfully gratifying and
ultimately satisfying, a hearty soup or
wholesome salad truly does stand alone
as a complement or an entrée,
whether solo or *à deux*.

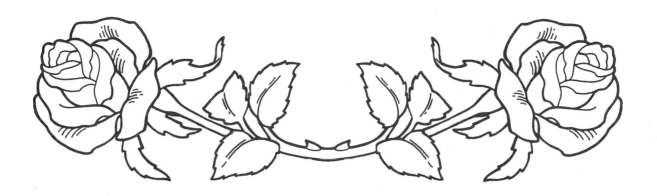

MICROWAVE THREE-BEAN SOUP

1 pound lean ground
 beef
1/2 teaspoon onion
 powder
2 cups tomato juice
1 tablespoon grated
 Parmesan cheese
1 teaspoon sugar
1/2 teaspoon chili
 powder
1/4 teaspoon dried
 parsley flakes
2 (15-ounce) cans three-
 bean salad

Crumble the ground beef into a 3-quart microwave-safe dish. Stir in the onion powder. Microwave, loosely covered, on High for 3 minutes. Stir in the tomato juice, Parmesan cheese, sugar, chili powder and parsley. Microwave for 1 minute. Stir in the undrained three-bean salad. Microwave, covered with a vented lid, for 30 minutes or until thickened and bubbly. Let stand, covered, for 10 minutes before serving. Yield: 6 servings.

Iva Jean Duntz, Preceptor Xi
Higginsville, Missouri

WONDERFUL BLACK BEAN SOUP

This soup was first served to me at our monthly stitching group on a very cold day. It is wonderful with a salad and nice crusty bread.

1 tablespoon olive oil
1 onion, chopped
1 garlic clove, minced
2 carrots, chopped
1 to 2 ribs celery,
 chopped
2 teaspoons chili
 powder
1 teaspoon cumin
4 cups vegetable or
 chicken stock
1 (7-ounce) can corn,
 beans or peas,
 drained
1 (28-ounce) can black
 beans, drained,
 rinsed
1 (10-ounce) can stewed
 tomatoes
Salt and pepper
 to taste

Heat the oil in a Dutch oven over medium heat. Sauté the onion and garlic for 3 to 4 minutes or just until translucent. Stir in the carrots and celery. Cook for 2 to 3 minutes or until vegetables start to soften. Add the chili powder and cumin. Cook for 1 minute, stirring constantly. Stir in the vegetable broth, corn, half the black beans and half the tomatoes. Combine the remaining black beans and tomatoes in a food processor container; process until smooth. Stir the processed bean mixture into soup mixture. Cook until heated through. Yield: 4 to 6 servings.

Carolyn Goldie, Iota Kappa
Brampton, Ontario, Canada

HUNGARIAN CREAMED GREEN BEAN SOUP

1 pound fresh green
 beans, or 1 (20-ounce)
 bag frozen green
 beans
1 potato, finely chopped
Salt to taste
3 to 4 tablespoons flour
2 cups sour cream
2 to 3 cups milk
2 quarts water
1 tablespoon vinegar
2 tablespoons
 Hungarian paprika

Place the beans and potato in salted water to cover in a kettle over medium heat. Cook for 15 to 20 minutes or until tender. Combine the flour with a small amount of water in a medium bowl; stir until smooth. Stir in the sour cream and milk; mix well. Add the sour cream mixture and water to the beans. Stir in the vinegar and paprika. Bring just to the boiling point, stirring constantly. Serve hot.
Yield: 4 servings.

Sweetie Wilson, Xi Beta Epsilon
Sewell, New Jersey

BEEF AND BARLEY SOUP

If you love hearty soups, you'll want to try this one. It is exceptionally good.

6 ounces lean beef, cubed
2 garlic cloves, crushed
2 teaspoons olive oil
1 large onion, chopped
2 carrots, thinly sliced
2 turnips, chopped
2 leeks (white part),
 diced
1/2 cup barley
2 cups beef broth
1/2 teaspoon thyme
1/2 teaspoon pepper
1 tablespoon lemon
 juice

Brown the beef with the garlic in the olive oil in a skillet over medium heat, stirring frequently. Stir in the onion, carrots, turnips, leeks, barley, beef broth, thyme and pepper. Simmer for 40 minutes or until the vegetables are tender, stirring occasionally. Stir in the lemon juice just before serving. Yield: 6 servings.

Vickie Thomas, Preceptor Tau
Weiser, Idaho

Katherine Meyer, Preceptor Iota Sigma, Lewisville, Texas, makes Bodacious Black Bean Soup by sautéing 1/2 cup each carrots, onion and celery and 2 garlic cloves, adding a can of tomatoes and green chiles, 2 cans of ranch-style beans and 1 can of chicken broth and simmering for 10 minutes. Purée in batches, reheat and serve with sour cream or yogurt and warm tortillas.

❖ SUPERMARKET BOUILLABAISSE

This is a wonderfully adaptable soup since you can add or subtract any kind of seafood. When adding different kinds of fish, be sure the cooked fish is firm enough to stay in chunks. When I served it for my daughter's birthday dinner, she said she didn't like fish soup but she ended up eating two bowlsful.

1 (15-ounce) can spaghetti sauce with mushrooms	1 large garlic clove
1 pound potatoes, peeled, cubed	1/2 teaspoon each thyme, oregano, basil and rosemary
1 1/2 pounds halibut, tuna or snapper, cut into 2-inch pieces	1/2 teaspoon crushed hot chiles
1 medium onion, chopped	1 (6-ounce) can chopped clams
1 small green bell pepper, seeded, chopped	1 (3-ounce) jar oysters
	1 (12-ounce) can beer
	1 cup water
2 ribs celery, diced	3/4 cup shrimp, or 1 (4-ounce) can cooked shrimp
2 tablespoons chopped parsley	Salt and pepper to taste
	Lemon wedges

Pour 1/3 of the spaghetti sauce into a 4- to 5-quart kettle. Place even layers of the potatoes and fish over the sauce. Add layers of half the onion, half the green pepper, half the celery and half the parsley. Add half the remaining spaghetti sauce. Add the garlic, thyme, oregano, basil, rosemary and chiles. Cover with the remaining onion, green pepper, celery and parsley. Add the clams and oysters. Add the beer and water. Place the kettle over medium heat; bring to a boil. Reduce heat; simmer, covered, about 20 minutes or until potatoes are tender. Stir in the shrimp, salt and pepper. Serve with lemon wedges to squeeze over individual portions. Yield: 6 to 8 servings.

*Alice Summers, Preceptor Beta Beta
Portland, Oregon*

CABBAGE SOUP

6 tablespoons butter	2 tablespoons sugar
4 pounds cabbage, shredded	1/2 teaspoon pepper
2 onions, chopped	2 tablespoons lemon juice
2 tablespoons flour	2 tablespoons salt
6 cups water	1 teaspoon caraway seeds
4 chicken bouillon cubes	
1 quart tomatoes	

Melt the butter in a kettle. Add the cabbage and onions and sauté for 15 minutes. Sprinkle the flour over the cabbage mixture; stir well. Add the water

gradually, stirring constantly. Bring to a boil. Stir in the bouillon cubes, tomatoes, sugar, pepper, lemon juice, salt and caraway seeds. Reduce heat and simmer, covered, over low heat for about 1 hour. Yield: 6 servings.

*Blanche Warren, Beta Master
Greensboro, North Carolina*

CABBAGE AND POTATO SOUP

Serve with crackers, hush puppies, or crusty bread.

5 (14-ounce) cans chicken broth	1 tablespoon minced garlic
4 potatoes, peeled, cubed	Salt and pepper to taste
1/2 to 1 head cabbage, chopped	1/2 pound Polish sausage, sliced
1 (14-ounce) can small English peas	1/2 cup (1 stick) butter
1 onion, chopped	1/2 cup heavy cream

Combine the chicken broth, potatoes, cabbage, peas, onion, garlic, salt and pepper in a large kettle over medium heat. Simmer for 15 minutes or just until vegetables are tender, stirring occasionally. Add the Polish sausage. Simmer about 1 hour longer. Just before serving, add the butter and cream. Simmer for 10 minutes longer, stirring occasionally, making sure the mixture does not boil. Yield: 6 to 8 servings.

*Gwenette Jacobson, Xi Beta Omega
Magnolia, Arkansas*

CARROT CHEESE SOUP

For a heartier soup, you may add 1 cup cooked elbow macaroni and 2 cups chopped cooked chicken.

4 carrots, grated	8 chicken bouillon cubes
1 onion, finely chopped	1 (16-ounce) jar Cheez Whiz
1/4 cup (1/2 stick) margarine	1/2 teaspoon liquid smoke
1/2 cup flour	1 pint half-and-half
2 1/2 quarts water	

Sauté the carrots and onion in the margarine in a skillet over medium heat for 5 to 10 minutes or until tender. Stir in the flour and cook until golden brown and a roux forms, stirring constantly. Combine the water and bouillon cubes in a saucepan over high heat. Bring to a boil, stirring constantly to dissolve bouillon cubes. Pour the hot broth into the roux gradually and whisk until well mixed. Bring just to a boil; remove from heat. Stir in the Cheez Whiz, half-and-half and liquid smoke. Heat to serving temperature, stirring frequently. Yield: 6 to 8 servings.

*Dorothy A. Kramer, Gamma Master
Omaha, Nebraska*

LOW-CALORIE CARROT SOUP

4 tablespoons butter or
  margarine
1 small onion, chopped
1 garlic clove, chopped
1 teaspoon ground
  cumin or ginger
10 medium carrots,
  peeled, chopped
2 potatoes, peeled,
  chopped

4 cups chicken broth
1/2 teaspoon salt
1/8 teaspoon freshly
  ground pepper
2 cups (about) 2% milk
2 tablespoons cooking
  sherry
Minced parsley

Melt the butter in a large saucepan over medium-low heat. Sauté the onion and garlic until tender. Stir in the cumin, carrots and potatoes. Cook, stirring constantly, for 3 minutes. Stir in the broth, salt and pepper. Bring just to a boil. Reduce heat and simmer, covered, for about 20 minutes or until vegetables are tender. Cool slightly. Place the mixture in the container of a food processor or blender; process until smooth. Add enough of the milk gradually to make of the desired consistency. Return soup to the saucepan and heat gently until heated through. Stir in the sherry. Pour the soup into heated bowls. Garnish with parsley. Yield: 6 servings.

Shirley J. McInnis, Mu Zeta
Tillsonburg, Ontario, Canada

CALIFORNIA CHEESE SOUP

Our chapter enjoyed this soup when we had each member bring an ingredient. We put it together, held our business meeting, and then enjoyed a meal together.

4 cups water
2 chicken bouillon cubes
1 cup diced celery
2 1/2 cups diced, peeled
  potatoes
1 (16-ounce) package
  frozen California
  Blend vegetables

1 cup diced carrots
1/2 cup diced onion
  (optional)
2 (10-ounce) cans cream
  of chicken soup
16 ounces Velveeta
  cheese, cubed

Bring the water to a boil in a 5-quart kettle over medium-high heat. Stir in the bouillon cubes, celery, potatoes, frozen vegetables, carrots and onion. Reduce heat and simmer, covered, for about 30 minutes or until all vegetables are tender. Stir in the soup and cheese. Cook until the soup is heated through and cheese is melted. Yield: 8 to 10 servings.

Rochelle Borszich, Xi Beta
Huron, South Dakota

CHEESY HAM AND HASH BROWN SOUP

1 (2-pound) package
  frozen hash brown
  potatoes, thawed
4 cups water
1 large onion, chopped
4 teaspoons chicken
  bouillon granules
1/2 teaspoon celery seeds
1/4 teaspoon pepper
1 (15-ounce) can Fiesta
  corn or Mexicorn

1 (10-ounce) can cream
  of chicken soup
1 (10-ounce) can cream
  of celery soup
2 (10-ounce) cans
  Cheddar cheese soup
1 quart milk
2 cups cubed cooked
  ham
1/2 teaspoon garlic salt

Combine the hash brown potatoes, water, onion, chicken bouillon, celery seeds and pepper in a large Dutch oven or soup kettle over medium heat. Bring just to a boil. Reduce heat; simmer, covered, for 20 minutes or until onion is soft. Add the Fiesta corn, soups, milk, ham and garlic salt; stir until well mixed. Simmer for 10 minutes longer or until heated through. Yield: 12 to 16 servings.

Michelle A. Doyle, Xi Omega
Worland, Wyoming

COMFORTING CHICKEN NOODLE SOUP

2 quarts water
8 chicken bouillon cubes
6 1/2 cups uncooked wide
  egg noodles
2 (10-ounce) cans cream
  of chicken soup

3 cups chopped cooked
  chicken
1 cup sour cream
Minced fresh parsley

Bring the water and bouillon to a boil in a large saucepan over medium heat; stir until bouillon cubes are dissolved. Stir in the noodles. Cook uncovered for about 10 minutes or until noodles are tender. Do not drain. Stir in the soup and chicken. Cook until heated through. Remove from heat. Stir in the sour cream and sprinkle with the parsley.
Yield: 10 to 12 servings.

Diane Mallinson, Iota Chi
O'Fallon, Missouri

Lora Jane McPherson, Xi Beta Alpha, Artesia, New Mexico, makes Extra-Hot Quick Soup with a pound of browned ground beef, 3 cans minestrone, 1 can each of whole kernel corn, tomatoes and green chiles and ranch-style beans. Great before or after cold weather football games.

CHRISTMAS SOUP

This makes a beautiful soup for the holidays because of its red and green colors in a white base. Serve with toasted garlic breadsticks.

1 medium potato, diced
1 medium bunch green
   onions, sliced
1 (10-ounce) can low-fat
   cream of mushroom
   soup
1 soup can skim milk
1/4 cup fresh parsley,
   finely chopped, or
   2 tablespoons dry
   parsley flakes

1/4 cup chopped canned
   roasted red peppers,
   drained
1 (11-ounce) can Shoe
   Peg white corn
4 ounces Swiss cheese,
   diced
Freshly ground pepper
   to taste

Place the potato and green onions in a large kettle; add enough water to cover the potatoes. Bring to a boil. Reduce heat, and cook slowly until tender. Combine the soup and milk in a small bowl; mix well. Add the soup mixture to the potatoes and onions. Stir in the parsley, roasted peppers and corn. Bring to a simmer. Add the cheese and stir until melted. Do not boil mixture. Serve each bowl of soup with a sprinkle of pepper. Yield: 4 servings.

Billie H. Ware, Kappa Master
Clovis, New Mexico

CLAM CHOWDER

1/2 pound (or more)
   bacon, chopped,
   crisp-fried
1 large onion, chopped
3 to 4 ribs celery,
   chopped
1/2 green bell pepper,
   chopped
2 (4-ounce) cans tiny
   clams

1/2 to 1 quart milk
Grated carrot
2 tablespoons
   margarine, softened
2 tablespoons (or more)
   flour
Salt and pepper to taste

Cook the bacon in a skillet and drain on paper towels, reserving the drippings. Sauté the onion, celery and green pepper in the bacon drippings over medium-low heat until tender. Drain the vegetables on paper towels. Combine the clams, milk, carrot, bacon and sautéed vegetables in a large saucepan. Bring to a simmer. Blend the margarine and flour in a bowl to form a paste. Stir the paste into the simmering soup and cook until thickened, stirring constantly. Add salt and pepper.
Yield: 4 to 8 servings.

Sharon Jarvis, Laureate Beta Omicron
Quesnel, British Columbia, Canada

HOMESTYLE CORN CHOWDER

My daughter used this recipe for a cooking project and won a blue ribbon.

3 slices bacon, chopped
1 onion, diced
4 medium potatoes,
   peeled, diced
1 cup chicken stock
1 cup milk

1 (16-ounce) can cream-
   style corn
1/4 teaspoon fresh
   rosemary
1/2 teaspoon thyme
Salt and pepper to taste

Cook the bacon in a large saucepan. Remove the bacon and drain on paper towels; reserve the drippings. Add the onion to bacon drippings and cook, stirring frequently, over medium-low heat, for 5 to 10 minutes or until tender. Add the potatoes and chicken stock to the skillet. Bring to a boil; boil for 15 minutes or until potatoes are tender. Add the milk, corn, rosemary, thyme, salt and pepper. Heat through, reducing heat so mixture does not boil. Serve hot. Garnish with the bacon.
Yield: 4 to 6 servings.

Hilda Hiner, Laureate Epsilon Beta
Riverview, Florida

MEXICAN CORN CHOWDER

1 1/2 pounds boneless
   skinless chicken
1/2 cup chopped onion
1 to 2 garlic cloves,
   minced
3 tablespoons margarine
2 chicken bouillon cubes
1 cup hot water
1 teaspoon ground
   cumin
4 potatoes, peeled,
   chopped

2 cups half-and-half
2 cups shredded
   Monterey Jack cheese
1 (17-ounce) can cream-
   style corn
1 (4-ounce) can green
   chiles
1/4 to 1 teaspoon
   Tabasco sauce
1 tomato, chopped

Rinse the chicken and pat dry. Cut into bite-size pieces. Brown the chicken with the onion and garlic in the margarine in a Dutch oven over medium heat. Dissolve the bouillon cubes in the hot water. Stir the bouillon, cumin and potatoes into the chicken mixture. Bring to a boil. Reduce heat. Simmer, covered, for 5 minutes. Stir in the half-and-half, cheese, corn, chiles and Tabasco sauce. Cook, stirring constantly, over low heat until the cheese is melted. Stir in the tomato and serve immediately. Garnish with cilantro if desired. Yield: 4 to 8 servings.

Hennie Harris, Laureate Beta Eta
Plains, Kansas

CREAMY CRAB CHOWDER

This chowder is so smooth and rich it can be used as a main dish . . . and leftovers just get better. I use half-and-half instead of milk or cream.

1 (16-ounce) package
  California-mixed
  frozen vegetables,
  thawed
2 cups water
6 green onions, chopped
4 cups chicken stock

6 cups milk or cream
1/4 cup cornstarch
12 ounces cream cheese,
  cubed, softened
1 (16-ounce) package
  crab meat

Combine the vegetables, water, onions and stock in a large saucepan over medium-high heat; bring to a boil. Reduce heat. Simmer, covered, for 10 minutes or until vegetables are tender. Mash the vegetables in the saucepan, or remove to a bowl to mash. Stir in the milk. Cook over low heat, stirring frequently, until thickened and bubbly. Add the cream cheese. Bring to a boil. Heat, stirring frequently, until cream cheese melts. Stir in the crab meat. Serve warm. Yield: 8 servings.

"Al" Smit-Briggs, Xi Kappa Upsilon
Cameron, Missouri

HOT FRUIT SOUP

Hot Fruit Soup is a wonderful brunch item with egg casseroles.

4 (20-ounce) cans
  pineapple chunks
4 (15-ounce) cans pear
  halves
4 (15-ounce) cans peach
  slices
2 (17-ounce) cans
  apricot halves
1 cup (2 sticks) butter

1 1/2 cups packed light
  brown sugar
Cinnamon to taste
1 teaspoon each curry,
  cloves and ginger
1 cup chopped walnuts
  or pecans
1 (7-ounce) bag coconut
1 cup raisins

Combine the undrained pineapple, pears, peaches and apricots in a large saucepan or kettle over low heat. Melt the butter in a small saucepan over medium-low heat. Stir in the brown sugar, cinnamon, curry, cloves and ginger. Pour the butter mixture over the pineapple mixture. Stir in the raisins. Bring to a boil. Stir in the walnuts and coconut just before serving. Yield: 10 servings.

Beverly Becker, Preceptor Delta Eta
Grand Prairie, Texas

PATTY'S GAZPACHO DREAM SOUP

Try a grilled fish entrée with this wonderful cold soup to make a complete meal.

1 cup chopped celery
1 cup chopped green bell
  pepper
1 cup chopped onion
1 cup thinly sliced
  cucumbers
2 cups chopped
  tomatoes
2 (10-ounce) cans
  tomato soup
3 cups vegetable juice
  cocktail

2 soup cans water
2 tablespoons wine
  vinegar
2 tablespoons Italian
  dressing
2 garlic cloves, minced
1/2 teaspoon salt
1/4 teaspoon pepper
8 dashes Tabasco sauce
2 dashes Worcestershire
  sauce

Combine the ingredients in a large bowl. Chill, covered, for 4 hours. Serve with sour cream and croutons. Yield: 8 to 10 servings.

Patricia A. Harper, Xi Epsilon Iota
Roswell, Georgia

PORTUGUESE KALE SOUP

1 cup dried navy beans
1 pound kale, torn
3 medium onions,
  chopped
1 pound linguiça or
  kielbasa sausage,
  cut up

3 tablespoons vinegar
11 cups water
4 or 5 potatoes, peeled,
  chopped
Salt, pepper and
  seasoned salt to taste

Soak the beans in water to cover for 8 to 10 hours or overnight. Drain and rinse. Combine beans, kale, onions, sausage, vinegar and 10 cups water in a large kettle. Simmer for 2 1/2 to 3 hours. Add the potatoes and the remaining cup of water. Simmer for 20 minutes longer or until potatoes are tender. Season with salt, pepper and seasoned salt. Yield: 6 to 8 servings.

Juanita W. Gray, Xi Omicron
Bluefield, West Virginia

TWENTY-MINUTE MINESTRONE

1 carrot, diced
1 small onion, chopped
1 rib celery, chopped
3 tablespoons water
4 cups chicken broth
1 medium potato, diced
1/2 cup uncooked elbow
  macaroni

1 tomato, diced
1/2 cup shredded cabbage
1 tablespoon chopped
  parsley
1/2 teaspoon basil
Salt and pepper to taste
6 tablespoons grated
  Parmesan cheese

Combine the carrot, onion, celery and water in a microwave-safe container. Microwave, loosely covered, on High for 6 minutes. Bring the chicken broth to a boil in a large kettle. Stir in the carrot mixture, potato, macaroni, tomato, cabbage, parsley, basil, salt and pepper. Reduce heat; simmer for 20 minutes or until potato is tender. Sprinkle a tablespoon of Parmesan cheese over each serving. Yield: 6 servings.

Arlene Haldeman, Omicron Master
Granite City, Illinois

CREAM OF FRESH MUSHROOM SOUP

1/4 cup (1/2 stick) butter or margarine	*Cayenne pepper to taste*
2 tablespoons chopped onion	*3 cups chicken broth*
1/2 cup flour	*8 ounces fresh mushrooms, cleaned, sliced lengthwise*
1/2 teaspoon salt	*2 cups milk, scalded*
1/8 teaspoon pepper	*2 tablespoons dry sherry*

Melt the butter in a saucepan. Sauté the onion over medium heat for a few minutes or until crisp-tender. Combine the flour and seasonings. Stir flour mixture into onions; mix well. Add the chicken broth gradually, stirring constantly. Bring to a boil. Cook for 1 minute, stirring constantly. Stir in the mushrooms. Simmer, covered, for 30 minutes, stirring occasionally. Stir in the milk. Cook, uncovered, over low heat for 5 to 10 minutes. Stir in the sherry just before serving. Garnish with parsley. Yield: 6 servings.

Patty Ragan, Xi Alpha Delta
Eugene, Oregon

MUSHROOM TOMATO PASTA SOUP

2 tablespoons butter or margarine	*1/2 teaspoon dried tarragon or basil leaves*
1 medium onion, chopped	*3/4 cup pasta shells, macaroni or orzo*
2 cups sliced mushrooms	
1 (28-ounce) can stewed tomatoes	*2 cups spinach, torn into bite-size pieces*
1 (10-ounce) can chicken broth	*1/4 cup shredded Swiss cheese*
1 soup can water	

Melt the butter in a large saucepan over medium-low heat. Sauté the onion and mushrooms for 2 minutes. Add the tomatoes, chicken broth, water and tarragon. Bring to a boil. Stir in the pasta. Reduce heat and simmer, uncovered, for 10 minutes or until pasta is tender. Stir in the spinach and heat for 1 minute or just until spinach is wilted. Serve immediately in bowls. Sprinkle each serving with Swiss cheese. Yield: 4 or 5 servings.

Marilyn Hatton, Iota Phi
Port Elgin, Ontario, Canada

SLOW-COOKER FRENCH ONION SOUP

4 large onions, peeled	*6 bouillon cubes*
6 cups water	*Garlic melba toast*
2 cups white Zinfandel wine	*3 ounces shredded Parmesan cheese*

Slice the onions into 1/4-inch slices; separate the rings. Combine the onion rings, water, wine and bouillon cubes in a slow cooker. Cook on High for about 3 to 4 hours, or until onions are tender; or cook on Low for 8 to 10 hours. Ladle into broiler-safe soup mugs or bowls. Cover each serving with 2 or 3 melba toasts and some Parmesan cheese. Broil for 2 to 3 minutes or until melted and bubbly. Yield: 8 servings.

Sharon Van Winkle, Xi Alpha Omega
Casper, Wyoming

ONION WINE SOUP

1/4 cup (1/2 stick) butter	*1 tablespoon vinegar*
5 large onions, chopped	*2 teaspoons sugar*
5 cups beef broth	*1 cup light cream*
1/2 cup celery leaves	*1 tablespoon minced parsley*
1 large potato, sliced	
1 cup dry white wine	*Salt and pepper to taste*

Melt the butter in a large saucepan over medium-low heat. Stir in the onions. Add the broth, celery leaves and potato. Bring to a boil. Reduce heat and simmer, covered, for 30 minutes or until potato is very tender. Purée the mixture in a blender. Return mixture to saucepan and stir in the wine, vinegar and sugar. Bring to a boil. Reduce heat and simmer for 5 minutes. Stir in remaining ingredients. Heat through but do not allow to come to a boil. Yield: 6 to 8 servings.

Virginia Arnold, Preceptor Laureate
Mt. Airy, Maryland

QUICK CREAM OF PEANUT SOUP

1/4 cup minced onion	*1 (10-ounce) can cream of celery soup*
1 tablespoon butter	
1/2 cup peanut butter	*2 soup cans milk*
1 (10-ounce) can cream of chicken soup	

Sauté the onion in the butter in a saucepan over medium-low heat until onion is tender but not brown. Stir in the peanut butter. Heat, stirring constantly, until peanut butter is smooth. Add the soups and milk. Heat, stirring constantly; bring just to a boil. Add more milk if soup becomes too thick. Garnish with chopped peanuts. Yield: 4 to 6 servings.

Saundra L. Nobbe, Theta Nu
Batesville, Indiana

SPICY FOUR-PEPPER SOUP

3 medium red bell peppers	3 garlic cloves, chopped
1 small yellow bell pepper	1 (14-ounce) can chicken broth
4 small cherry peppers	1/2 teaspoon chopped fresh basil
3 jalapeño peppers	

Halve, core and seed the red peppers, yellow pepper, cherry peppers and jalapeño peppers. Combine peppers in a microwave-safe bowl. Microwave, loosely covered, on High for 6 minutes or until tender. Place in a blender container; purée for 2 minutes. Combine pepper purée, garlic and chicken broth in a large saucepan. Bring to a boil, stirring occasionally. Reduce heat and simmer for 15 to 20 minutes. Sprinkle with basil before serving. Yield: 4 servings.

Toni Sweeney, Preceptor Beta
Kearney, Nebraska

STUFFED GREEN PEPPER SOUP

2 pounds ground beef	1 (28-ounce) can diced tomatoes
2 cups cooked rice	1/4 cup packed brown sugar
2 to 3 cups water	
1 1/2 green bell peppers, chopped	2 or 3 packets instant beef bouillon
1 (28-ounce) can tomato sauce	Salt and pepper to taste

Brown the ground beef in a skillet, stirring until crumbly; drain. Combine the ground beef, rice, water, green peppers, tomato sauce, diced tomatoes, brown sugar, beef bouillon, salt and pepper in a 3- to 4-quart saucepan. Cook over medium heat, stirring occasionally, for 45 minutes or until green peppers are tender. Add more water if you prefer a thinner soup. Yield: 8 to 10 servings.

Sonja Shanton, Beta Delta
Niles, Michigan

PIZZA SOUP

2 (14-ounce) cans Italian-style stewed tomatoes	1 teaspoon oregano
	8 ounces sliced pepperoni, cut into halves
2 cups beef broth	
1 small onion, chopped	1/2 (24-ounce) package small round cheese ravioli
1 (4-ounce) can sliced mushrooms	
1/2 green bell pepper, chopped	1 cup shredded mozzarella cheese
1 (4-ounce) can sliced black olives, drained	

Combine the tomatoes, beef broth and onion in a stockpot over medium heat. Stir in the mushrooms, green pepper, olives and oregano. Simmer tomato mixture for 10 minutes, then bring to a boil. Stir in the pepperoni and ravioli. Cook for 5 minutes longer. Sprinkle cheese over each serving. Yield: 4 servings.

Linda Gonzales, Preceptor Gamma Kappa
Virginia Beach, Virginia

POTATO AND BACON CHOWDER

1 pound bacon, chopped	1 cup sour cream
1 cup chopped onion	1 3/4 cups milk
2 cups frozen hash brown potatoes, thawed	1/2 teaspoon salt
	Dash of pepper
1 cup water	2 tablespoons parsley flakes
1 (10-ounce) can cream of chicken soup	

Fry the bacon in a skillet until crisp. Add the onion and sauté for 2 to 3 minutes. Pour off some of the fat. Combine the bacon, onion, potatoes and water in a 3-quart saucepan; bring to a boil. Reduce heat and simmer, covered, for 15 minutes. Stir in the soup and sour cream. Add the milk, salt, pepper and parsley flakes gradually. Heat to serving temperature; do not boil. Yield: 10 servings.

Cheryl Beachler, Lambda Master
Cedar Rapids, Iowa

CAJUN POTATO SOUP

This is my husband's favorite soup year-round. It is especially good served with French bread.

1/2 cup (1 stick) butter	6 cups chicken stock
2 cups chopped onions	10 potatoes, diced
2 bunches scallions, chopped	1 tablespoon seasoned salt
1 cup diced smoked sausage	1/2 teaspoon white pepper

Melt the butter in a large kettle over medium-low heat. Sauté the onions and half the scallions for about 5 minutes or until tender. Add the sausage. Sauté for 3 minutes longer. Stir in the chicken broth, potatoes, seasoned salt and white pepper. Simmer for about 45 minutes or until potatoes are tender but still retain some texture. Stir in the remaining scallions.
Yield: 8 to 10 servings.

Marcia Jackson, Epsilon Pi
Searcy, Arkansas

PUMPKIN SOUP

1/4 cup (1/2 stick) margarine or butter	1/4 teaspoon ground nutmeg
1 medium onion, chopped	1/4 teaspoon white pepper
1 (16-ounce) can pumpkin pie filling	1/4 teaspoon ground ginger
4 cups chicken broth	1 bay leaf
1 teaspoon salt	1 cup half-and-half
1/2 teaspoon curry powder	

Melt the butter in a kettle and sauté the onion until soft. Add the pumpkin pie filling, chicken broth, salt, curry powder, nutmeg, white pepper, ginger and bay leaf; stir to combine. Bring to a boil. Reduce heat and simmer uncovered, stirring occasionally, for 15 minutes. Remove the bay leaf. Place the mixture in a blender or food processor container; process until smooth. (At this point the mixture may be refrigerated for up to 2 days or frozen for later use). Return the mixture to the kettle. Stir in the half-and-half. Cook over medium heat, stirring occasionally, until heated through. Adjust the seasonings. Garnish each cup of soup with a bit of sour cream and cilantro if desired. Yield: 6 to 8 servings.

Mary Barnett, Xi Alpha Beta Lambda
Austin, Texas

REUBEN SOUP

4 ounces bacon, finely chopped	1/2 teaspoon caraway seeds
1 cup chopped onion	2 cups diced cooked corned beef
1 garlic clove, minced	
1 (16-ounce) can sauerkraut, drained	4 slices pumpernickel bread
6 cups chicken stock	1/4 cup (1/2 stick) butter, melted
2 teaspoons dry mustard	
3 cups diced cooked potatoes	1/4 cup shredded Swiss cheese

Fry the bacon in a kettle until crisp. Pour off some of the fat. Add the onion and garlic. Sauté for 5 minutes or until tender. Stir in the sauerkraut, chicken broth, mustard, potatoes, caraway seeds and corned beef. Heat through. Preheat the oven to 400 degrees. Cut the bread into 1/2-inch squares. Arrange the bread squares on a baking sheet. Drizzle with butter. Bake for 10 minutes. Ladle the soup into bowls. Sprinkle each serving with a teaspoon of shredded cheese and several pumpernickel croutons. Yield: 12 servings.

Patricia Nicely
Roanoke, Virginia

WILD RICE SOUP

1 (6-ounce) package long grain and wild rice	1 teaspoon curry powder
1/4 cup (1/2 stick) butter	1 teaspoon dry mustard
1/2 cup chopped celery	1 teaspoon chervil
2 onions, chopped	1/2 teaspoon pepper
1/2 cup flour	2 cups cream
6 cups chicken broth	1 (4-ounce) can chopped mushrooms
1/2 teaspoon salt	

Prepare the rice using package directions. Melt the butter in an 8-quart kettle. Sauté the celery and onions in the butter until soft. Stir in the flour. Add the chicken broth slowly, stirring until well blended. Stir in the remaining ingredients. Cook until heated through. Yield: 8 to 10 servings.

Margaret Bruin, Xi Gamma Tau
Fort Wayne, Indiana

CREAMY WILD RICE AND MUSHROOM SOUP

1 (6-ounce) package quick-cooking long grain and wild rice	2 cups chopped cooked chicken
4 cups chicken broth	1/4 cup flour
1 cup (2 sticks) plus 2 tablespoons margarine	2 cups half-and-half
	1 cup sliced fresh mushrooms
3 large carrots, chopped	1/2 cup dry sherry
3 ribs celery, chopped	1 teaspoon lemon juice
2 tablespoons onion flakes	1/4 teaspoon garlic pepper
	1/2 teaspoon salt

Prepare the rice using package directions, replacing the water with 2 1/3 cups of the chicken broth. Melt 4 tablespoons of the margarine in skillet and sauté the carrots and celery for 3 or 4 minutes. Stir in the onion flakes. Cook, covered, over low heat for 5 minutes. Stir the carrot mixture into the rice. Melt 5 tablespoons of the margarine in a medium saucepan. Whisk in the flour. Add the remaining chicken broth. Cook over medium-low heat, stirring constantly, until thickened. Stir in the half-and-half. Bring to a boil. Reduce heat and simmer for 10 minutes. Melt 1 tablespoon of the margarine in a skillet. Sauté the mushrooms for 5 minutes. Stir in the sherry and lemon juice. Simmer, covered, for 5 minutes. Stir the sautéed mushrooms into the half-and-half mixture. Add the garlic pepper and salt. Simmer for 30 to 40 minutes, or cook in a slow cooker on Low for 2 hours. Yield: 8 to 10 servings.

Jerilyn Strohecker, Zeta Upsilon
Lena, Illinois

SANTA FE SOUP

2 pounds ground beef
1 large onion, chopped
1 (15-ounce) can pinto
   beans
1 (15-ounce) can black
   beans
1 (15-ounce) can red
   beans
1 (15-ounce) can tomato
   wedges
1 (10-ounce) can
   tomatoes with green
   chiles
2 (15-ounce) cans white
   corn
2 envelopes taco
   seasoning mix
2 envelopes ranch salad
   dressing mix

Brown the ground beef with the onion in a skillet, stirring until the ground beef is crumbly; drain. Combine the ground beef mixture, pinto beans, black beans, red beans, tomato wedges, tomatoes with green chiles, white corn, taco seasoning mix and ranch dressing mix in a large stockpot. Simmer for about 1 hour, adding 2 to 3 cups water if soup is too thick. Garnish each serving with corn chips, shredded Cheddar cheese, sour cream and chopped green onions. Yield: 12 to 15 servings.

Esther Singer, Omicron Psi
Clinton, Missouri

SAUERKRAUT SOUP

Enjoy this soup on a cold, rainy day. It can be served over noodles if desired.

1/4 cup (1/2 stick) butter
2 onions, chopped
1 rib celery, chopped
2 pounds lean short ribs
1 1/2 pounds sauerkraut
10 cups beef broth
Pinch of thyme
1 bay leaf
Salt and pepper to taste
5 to 10 garlic cloves (or
   to taste)

Melt the butter in a large kettle and sauté the onions until soft. Add the celery and short ribs; brown the short ribs slightly. Stir in the sauerkraut, beef broth, thyme, bay leaf, salt, pepper and garlic. Bring to a boil. Reduce heat and simmer, partially covered, for 2 hours. Discard the bay leaf. Yield: 6 to 8 servings.

Linda Van De Grift, Preceptor Gamma Tau
Vancouver, Washington

Susan MacLeod, Xi Omega Nu, Rosenberg, Texas, makes 9 cans of vegetables and 4 cans of beef broth into Super-Easy Vegetable Soup. Combine the broth with 1 can each drained carrots, corn, green beans, kidney beans, pinto beans, undrained zucchini in tomato sauce and drained whole potatoes that have been cut up. Add 2 cans diced tomatoes with basil and oregano and heat to serving temperature.

SAUSAGE CHOWDER

2 pounds sausage
1 large onion, chopped
3 cups canned tomatoes
3 cups cooked pinto
   beans
4 cups water
2 bay leaves
1/2 teaspoon salt
1/4 teaspoon thyme
1/4 teaspoon garlic salt
1/4 teaspoon pepper
1 cup chopped peeled
   potato
1 cup chopped green bell
   pepper

Brown the sausage with the onion in a skillet, stirring until the sausage is crumbly; drain. Combine the sausage mixture, tomatoes, pinto beans, water, bay leaves and the remaining seasonings in a stockpot. Simmer, covered, for 1 hour. Add the potato and green pepper. Simmer, covered, for 20 to 30 minutes or until vegetables are tender, stirring occasionally. Remove and discard bay leaves. Ladle chowder into soup bowls. Serve with corn bread. Yield: 8 servings.

Jonnie Boggs, Laureate Alpha Delta
Amarillo, Texas

ITALIAN SAUSAGE SOUP

Serve this hearty, flavorful soup with garlic bread and a salad.

1 pound bulk Italian
   sausage
1 (16-ounce) can Italian
   stewed tomatoes
1 (8-ounce) can tomato
   sauce
4 cups (or more) water
2 tablespoons crushed
   beef bouillon cube or
   granules
2 tablespoons sugar
1 1/2 cups sliced carrots
1 cup chopped onion
1 cup (or more) chopped
   zucchini
1/4 cup minced parsley
1 tablespoon Italian
   seasoning

Brown the sausage in a skillet, stirring until crumbly; drain. Combine the sausage, tomatoes, tomato sauce, water, bouillon cube, sugar, carrots, onion, zucchini, parsley and Italian seasoning in a large kettle. Simmer for 45 minutes or until vegetables are tender. Ladle into bowls. Sprinkle with Romano cheese if desired. Yield: 8 to 10 servings.

Maurigeanne Byrd, Chi Master
Colorado Springs, Colorado

Frances J. Rowan, Xi Nu Theta, Pasadena, Texas, cooks potatoes for soup by scrubbing 5 medium russets, piercing with a fork, placing in a white plastic grocery bag (the kind from the checkout); tie the bag in a double knot and microwave on High for 10 minutes. Be careful cutting open the very hot bag.

CHARLEY'S FISH CHOWDER

This favorite recipe from Charlie's Crab in Troy, Michigan, is great for Lent or elegant dinner parties.

¼ cup olive oil	6 cups water
3 medium garlic cloves, crushed	1 pound boneless pollack or turbot
¼ cup finely chopped onion	6 cups clamato juice or clam juice
Dash each oregano, basil and thyme	Salt and pepper to taste
6 tablespoons finely chopped celery	2 tablespoons finely chopped parsley
¾ cup stewed tomatoes, finely chopped	

Heat the olive oil in a large kettle until very hot. Sauté the garlic for a few minutes or until it is golden brown, being careful not to burn it. Add the onion and sauté for a minute or two. Add the oregano, basil and thyme. Sauté for a minute longer. Add the celery. Sauté for 3 minutes or until translucent. Stir in the tomatoes. Simmer for 20 to 25 minutes, stirring occasionally to prevent sticking. Add the water and pollack. Cook, uncovered, over high heat for 15 minutes. Add the clamato juice, salt and pepper. Simmer, covered, for 20 minutes longer, stirring frequently with a wire whisk to break up the fish and blend the flavors. Sprinkle with parsley before serving. Yield: 6 to 8 servings.

Jennifer Voight, Nu Beta
Troy, Michigan

SEAFOOD CHOWDER

6 to 8 potatoes, peeled, diced	2 (7-ounce) cans chopped clams
Salt to taste	2 cups crab meat
2 cups coffee cream	1 cup baby scallops
1 cup shredded Cheddar cheese	1 onion, chopped
1 cup shredded mozzarella cheese	½ cup chopped celery
	½ cup water

Cook potatoes in salted water to cover for 20 minutes or until tender. Combine the coffee cream and cheeses in a large kettle. Cook over medium-low heat until the cheeses are melted, stirring constantly. Stir in 1 can drained clams and 1 can undrained clams, crab meat, scallops, onion, celery and water. Simmer over low heat until heated through. Yield: 8 servings.

Nancy Carter, Preceptor Epsilon
Miramichi, New Brunswick, Canada

SHRIMP AND CORN SOUP

3 tablespoons vegetable oil	1 (10-ounce) can tomatoes with green chiles
3 tablespoons flour	
1 (17-ounce) can cream-style corn	1 onion, chopped
	Salt and pepper to taste
1 (16-ounce) can whole kernel corn	1 pound shrimp, peeled, deveined
3 potatoes, cubed	

Combine the oil and flour in a large kettle over medium heat. Cook until flour mixture is light brown, stirring constantly. Add the cream-style corn, kernel corn, potatoes, tomatoes with green chiles, onion, salt and pepper. Stir in enough water to make of the desired consistency. Simmer for 45 minutes. Stir in the shrimp. Simmer for 20 minutes longer. Yield: 8 servings.

Brenda Tauzin, Xi Chi
Pineville, Louisiana

HEARTY SPINACH SOUP

I created this thick soup recipe many years ago after being served a very thin, watery spinach soup. This is better!

1 (40-ounce) can chicken broth	2 tablespoons onion flakes
1 (10-ounce) can cream of celery soup	2 teaspoons parsley
	1 cup rice
½ soup can milk	1 (10-ounce) package frozen chopped spinach
1 teaspoon salt	
⅛ teaspoon pepper	

Combine the chicken broth, soup, milk, salt, pepper, onion flakes and parsley in a large kettle. Bring to a boil. Stir in the rice. Cook over medium-low heat, stirring often, for 15 to 20 minutes or until tender. Add the spinach. Simmer for 5 to 10 minutes, breaking up the spinach with a spoon. Yield: 10 servings.

Jan Abraham, Laureate Theta Omega
San Jose, California

Linda Austin, Nu Omega, Burlington, Kansas, makes Lucky Day New Years Soup by sautéing ½ cup each chopped onion, green pepper and celery in 2 tablespoons margarine. Add 1 can of chicken broth, 1 teaspoon sugar and 1 cup diced ham and simmer. Add 1 package of prepared long grain and wild rice mix and 1 can of black-eyed peas. Simmer for 30 minutes and serve with corn bread.

GARLIC AND SPINACH SOUP

When my husband and I were both ill with terrible colds, we ate this soup—the next day we both felt much better. Now we call it the "Cold Killer."

1 medium or large onion, chopped	2 to 5 garlic cloves, peeled
2 medium potatoes, peeled, cut into bite-size pieces	1¹/₂ to 2 tablespoons butter
3 cups water	3 tablespoons flour
2 teaspoons salt	1¹/₂ cups hot skim milk
1 pound fresh spinach, cleaned, stems removed	White pepper to taste Nutmeg to taste

Combine the onion, potatoes, water and salt in a large kettle. Bring to a boil. Reduce heat and simmer, covered, for 20 minutes or until potatoes are tender. Stir in the spinach and garlic. Remove from heat. Melt the butter in a small saucepan over low heat. Add the flour. Cook, stirring constantly, for 5 minutes. Add the skim milk slowly, stirring constantly and cooking for about 10 minutes or until thick and smooth. Purée the potato mixture in a blender or food processor. Return the mixture to the kettle. Stir in the flour mixture. Add the white pepper. Serve hot. Sprinkle a little nutmeg over each serving. Yield: 4 to 6 servings.

Lonnie Gloria Wishart, Beta Omicron
Prince Rupert, British Columbia, Canada

TACO SOUP

3 large chicken breasts	1 (15-ounce) can tomato sauce
1 (14-ounce) can chicken broth	1 (16-ounce) can Mexican stewed tomatoes, chopped
2 cups water	
1 teaspoon chopped garlic	1 (14-ounce) can green chiles, chopped
1 large onion, chopped	
3 (16-ounce) cans Mexican chili beans	1 envelope taco seasoning mix
1 (16-ounce) can whole kernel corn	1 envelope ranch salad dressing mix

Rinse chicken and pat dry. Combine the chicken, broth, water, garlic and onion in a large Dutch oven over medium heat. Cook for 20 to 30 minutes or until chicken is tender. Remove the chicken. Add the chili beans, corn, tomato sauce, tomatoes, chiles, taco seasoning mix and ranch salad dressing mix; stir until seasonings are dissolved. Simmer over low heat for 15 minutes. Shred the chicken into strips or chunks; stir into the soup and simmer for 30 minutes longer.

Serve with toppings such as shredded cheese, lettuce, tomatoes, sour cream, tortilla chips and avocado slices. Yield: 6 to 8 servings.

Joyce Loveless, Xi Beta Rho
Rome, Georgia

TAMALE SOUP

Serve Tamale Soup with Mexican corn bread or tortilla chips.

4 cups beef broth	1 small onion, chopped
1 (16-ounce) can whole kernel corn	3 tablespoons chili powder
1 (15-ounce) can hominy	1 teaspoon cumin
1 (15-ounce) can pinto beans, drained	¹/₄ teaspoon garlic powder
1 (10-ounce) can tomatoes with green chiles	1 (28-ounce) can tamales

Combine the beef broth, corn, hominy, beans, tomatoes with green chiles, onion, chili powder, cumin and garlic powder in a large kettle. Simmer for 45 minutes or until onion is tender. Stir in the tamales and heat through. Yield: 6 to 8 servings.

Sandy Derichsweiler, Xi Gamma Rho
Anadarko, Oklahoma

TORTELLINI AND SAUSAGE SOUP

1 pound sweet Italian turkey sausage, casings removed	¹/₂ cup chopped parsley
	1 bay leaf
1 cup chopped onion	¹/₂ cup sliced zucchini (optional)
2 (14-ounce) cans chopped tomatoes	1 package cheese tortellini
3 cups chicken broth	
1 cup fresh green beans, cut into 2-inch pieces	¹/₂ teaspoon garlic powder
1 cup sliced carrots	¹/₂ teaspoon oregano
1 cup sliced celery	Parmesan cheese to taste

Brown the sausage with the onion in a skillet, stirring until the sausage is crumbly; drain. Stir in the tomatoes, chicken broth, green beans, carrots, celery, parsley and bay leaf. Simmer, partially covered, for about 20 minutes or until vegetables are tender. Stir in the zucchini, tortellini, garlic powder and oregano. Simmer for 10 minutes longer, or until pasta is tender but not overcooked. Discard the bay leaf. Sprinkle each serving with Parmesan cheese. Serve with crusty sourdough or French bread and a green salad. Yield: 6 servings.

Joan A. Greene, Preceptor Nu Beta
San Diego, California

TORTILLA SOUP FOR A BUSY DAY

You'll be glad you have this recipe when you don't have much time to prepare a dinner for unexpected guests. Keep the ingredients on hand for such occasions.

1 tablespoon olive oil	1 (16-ounce) can stewed
1/2 cup chopped onion	tomatoes
1 garlic clove, minced	1 (12-ounce) can whole
3 medium zucchini,	kernel corn
sliced	1 teaspoon cumin
2 (14-ounce) cans	1/2 teaspoon pepper
chicken broth	Tortilla chips
1 (15-ounce) can tomato	1/2 cup shredded
sauce	Monterey Jack cheese

Heat the olive oil in a large kettle and sauté the onion and garlic for 3 or 4 minutes or until onion is soft. Add the next 7 ingredients; stir well. Bring to a boil. Reduce heat and simmer, covered, for 15 to 20 minutes or until zucchini is tender. Crush a few tortilla chips in each bowl. Spoon the soup over the chips. Sprinkle with a little cheese. Yield: 8 to 10 servings.

Sally Klekotta, Laureate Alpha Delta
Amarillo, Texas

TURKEY CHOWDER

Our family's tradition is that we make this chowder from the leftover turkey we had for our Christmas meal; we enjoy it on Boxing Day with friends and family.

3 large potatoes, peeled,	1 (12-ounce) can
diced	evaporated milk
Salt to taste	1 1/2 teaspoons ginger
1/3 cup butter or	1 teaspoon chervil
margarine	Salt and pepper to taste
3 cups diced celery	1/4 cup chopped parsley
1 1/2 cups chopped onions	2 cups chopped cooked
12 cups turkey broth	turkey
2 (14-ounce) cans cream-	
style corn	

Cook potatoes in lightly salted water in a large saucepan for 20 minutes or until tender. Drain, reserving the cooking water. Mash the potatoes. Melt the butter in a large kettle. Sauté the celery and onions for 5 minutes or until tender but not brown. Stir in the turkey broth, mashed potatoes, potato water, corn, evaporated milk, ginger and chervil. Simmer for 20 minutes. Add salt and pepper. Stir in the parsley and turkey. Simmer for 5 minutes or until turkey is heated through. Yield: 12 servings.

Darlene Bennett, Lambda Delta
Amherstburg, Ontario, Canada

GREEK-STYLE VEGETABLE BEEF PASTA SOUP

1 tablespoon margarine	2 (14-ounce) cans diced
or butter	tomatoes
1 pound lean stir-fry	10 1/2 cups water
beef	2 medium zucchini,
1 teaspoon basil	quartered
1 teaspoon oregano	2 carrots, thinly sliced
1 medium onion,	8 ounces orzo or other
chopped	small pasta
1 teaspoon garlic salt	Salt and pepper to taste

Melt the margarine in a stockpot over medium-high heat. Add the beef, basil, oregano, onion and garlic salt. Sauté for 5 to 10 minutes or until beef is lightly browned. Add the tomatoes and water. Bring to a boil. Reduce heat and simmer for 1 hour. Stir in the zucchini and carrots. Simmer for 45 minutes longer or until carrots are tender. Stir in the pasta. Simmer for 15 minutes longer. Add salt and pepper to taste. Yield: 8 servings.

Mary Ellen Tellgren, Theta
APO AE 209009-1700, Germany

BEEFY VEGETABLE SOUP WITH MUSHROOMS

1 tablespoon vegetable	1 tablespoon caraway
oil	seeds
1 1/2 pounds beef, cubed	Paprika to taste
1 cup chopped onions	1/4 teaspoon pepper
2 tablespoons flour	2 cups each chopped
3 quarts water	carrots, celery,
1 1/2 pounds beef soup	potatoes, cabbage
bones	1 pound fresh
1 (28-ounce) can	mushrooms, sliced
tomatoes	2 tablespoons (about)
5 teaspoons salt	butter

Heat the oil in a 6- to 8-quart kettle. Brown the beef. Remove the beef from the kettle. Add the onions and toss in the hot oil, cooking until slightly brown. Remove kettle from heat. Whisk in the flour; blend well. Add the water, soup bones, tomatoes, salt, caraway seeds, paprika and pepper. Simmer for 1 1/2 to 2 hours. Remove the bones from the soup. Stir in the carrots, celery, potatoes and cabbage. Simmer for 20 to 30 minutes or until tender. Brown the mushrooms in butter in a skillet and stir into the soup. Yield: 4 1/2 quarts.

Joyce B. DeCrocker, Xi Zeta Epsilon
Kalamazoo, Michigan

VEGETABLE CHEESE SOUP

1 (32-ounce) package
    frozen hash brown
    potatoes, thawed
1 (16-ounce) package
    frozen mixed
    vegetables, thawed
1 (8-ounce) package
    frozen chopped
    broccoli, thawed

1 medium onion, diced
6 cups water
6 chicken bouillon cubes
2 (10-ounce) cans cream
    of mushroom soup
2 cups milk
1 pound Velveeta cheese,
    cubed

Combine the hash brown potatoes, mixed vegetables, broccoli, onion, water and bouillon cubes in a slow cooker. Cook on High for 30 minutes. Stir in the soup, milk and Velveeta cheese. Turn heat to Low and cook for about 1 hour. Yield: 8 to 10 servings.

Jody Farmer, Preceptor Delta Sigma
Bedford, Texas

✤ GOLDEN VEGETABLE SOUP

1/4 cup (1/2 stick) butter
    or margarine
1 cup chopped onion
1 cup chopped celery
3/4 cup chopped carrot
1 1/4 cups chopped
    potatoes
1 cup sliced yellow wax
    beans or green beans

1 garlic clove, peeled
3 cups chicken broth
1/4 teaspoon marjoram
1/4 teaspoon tarragon
1/8 teaspoon dillweed
1/2 cup milk
Salt and pepper to taste

Melt the butter in a large saucepan over low heat. Add the onion, celery, carrot, potatoes, beans and garlic. Cook over low heat, stirring occasionally, for 20 to 25 minutes or until tender, not brown. Stir in the chicken broth, marjoram, tarragon and dillweed. Bring to a boil. Reduce heat and simmer, uncovered, for 30 minutes or until vegetables are tender. Pour the hot soup carefully into the container of a blender or food processor; process until smooth. Return the soup to the saucepan. Stir in the milk. Add salt and pepper. Heat to serving temperature. Serve hot, garnished with a dollop of sour cream.
Yield: 4 to 6 servings.

Shirley Day, Kappa Master
Guelph, Ontario, Canada

Shawna Peterson, Gamma Pi, Wellsville, New York, cooks 8 potatoes, peeled and diced in water to cover with a chopped onion, adds 2 cans drained whole kernel corn, 2 cans cream of mushroom soup and 4 soup cans milk with 1 pound of crisp crumbled bacon and seasonings. Thicken with a blend of 1/4 cup flour and bacon drippings for Creamy Corn Chowder.

VICHYSSOISE

This soup can be served hot or cold. If you like the taste of garlic, add a minced garlic clove or two before serving.

1/4 cup (1/2 stick) butter
6 leeks, white part only,
    minced
4 cups chicken broth or
    water with 4 chicken
    bouillon cubes
4 medium potatoes,
    sliced

3 ribs celery
White pepper, cayenne
    pepper and salt to
    taste
2 cups crème fraîche or
    heavy cream
4 tablespoons chopped
    parsley or chives

Melt the butter in a skillet over low heat. Sauté the leeks slowly. The leeks must remain white and limp; do not brown. Stir in the chicken broth and potatoes. Simmer, covered, over very low heat for 30 minutes or until vegetables are tender. Purée the soup in a blender container. Return the soup to the skillet and add the white pepper, cayenne pepper and salt. Stir in the crème fraîche just before serving. Garnish with the chopped parsley or chives. Yield: 8 to 10 servings.

Judy Sharp, Preceptor Gamma Epsilon
Rochelle, Illinois

QUICK WEDDING SOUP

When my nephew was about 3 years old, he asked what was in the soup. I told him "chicken, noodles and meatballs." He said, "What's the green stuff?"

1 pound ground beef
1 cup Italian flavored
    bread crumbs
1/2 cup milk
2 envelopes dry noodle
    and chicken broth
    soup mix

9 cups water
1 tablespoon butter
1 (9-ounce) package
    frozen chopped
    spinach, thawed
2 eggs, beaten

Preheat the oven to 350 degrees. Combine the ground beef, bread crumbs and milk in a medium bowl and mix well. Shape the ground beef mixture into marble-sized meatballs. Arrange the meatballs in a single layer on baking sheets. Bake for 20 to 30 minutes or until browned and cooked through. Drain the meatballs. Combine the soup mix, water and butter in a kettle over medium heat; bring to a simmer. Add the spinach and cooked meatballs. Simmer for 30 minutes. Just before serving, stir the eggs in slowly. Yield: 10 servings.

Rosemarie Thompson, Laureate Epsilon Gamma
Altoona, Pennsylvania

APRICOT SALAD

2 (17-ounce) cans apricots	2 tablespoons lemon juice
2 tablespoons flour	8 ounces longhorn cheese, shredded
1 cup sugar	
2 eggs, beaten	1 cup pecans, chopped

Drain the apricots, reserving the liquid from one of the cans. Combine the flour and sugar in a bowl. Combine the flour mixture with the eggs, lemon juice and apricot juice in a heavy saucepan over medium heat. Cook until thickened, stirring constantly. Layer half the apricots, half the longhorn cheese and half the pecans in a glass dish. Pour half the apricot juice mixture over the pecan layer. Add layers of the remaining apricots, cheese, pecans and apricot juice mixture. Chill, covered, until ready to serve. Yield: 6 to 8 servings.

Glenda Shugart, Preceptor Zeta Upsilon
Mesquite, Texas

CANTALOUPE AND BACON SALAD

1 large cantaloupe	1 tablespoon minced onion
8 ounces bacon, crisp-fried, crumbled	1 tablespoon Dijon mustard
1/3 cup honey	
1/4 cup red wine vinegar	1 teaspoon salt
2 tablespoons poppy seeds	3/4 cup vegetable oil

Cut cantaloupe into bite-size pieces; place in a salad bowl. Sprinkle a layer of the bacon over the cantaloupe. Combine the remaining ingredients in a bowl; blend well. Pour over the bacon. Toss and serve. Yield: 8 servings.

Michel Olds, Mu
Norman, Oklahoma

CASHEW AND ORANGE SALAD

4 tablespoons sugar	1/2 cup unsalted cashews
3 tablespoons olive oil	2 tablespoons water
3 tablespoons water	1 head leaf lettuce
1 tablespoon chopped parsley	1/2 head romaine lettuce
	1 cup chopped celery
2 tablespoons red wine vinegar	2 green onions, chopped
Dash of Tabasco sauce	1 1/3 cups mandarin orange sections or peeled orange slices, chopped
3 tablespoons brown sugar	

Combine the sugar, olive oil, 3 tablespoons water, parsley, red wine vinegar and Tabasco sauce in a lidded jar; shake well to mix. Chill until serving time. Combine the brown sugar, cashews and 2 table-spoons water in a small saucepan. Cook over medium heat until the sugar is dissolved and cashews are coated, stirring constantly. Spread the cashews on waxed paper to cool. Combine the leaf lettuce, romaine lettuce, celery and green onion in a large salad bowl. Shake the red wine dressing vigorously and pour over the salad. Add the cashews and oranges; toss gently. Yield: 6 to 8 servings.

Edith Stone, Xi Gamma Alpha
Paris, Ontario, Canada

CREAM CHEESE AND TOMATO SOUP SALAD

This is a hearty salad that is great for carry-in potluck dinners. Serve in lettuce cups or over chips.

1 (10-ounce) can tomato soup	1/2 cup chopped celery
	1/2 cup chopped onion
1 1/2 soup cans water	1/2 cup chopped green bell pepper
2 (3-ounce) packages lemon gelatin	
	1/2 cup mayonnaise
8 ounces cream cheese, softened	1/2 cup chopped walnuts or pecans
1/2 cup chopped olives	

Combine the tomato soup and water in a medium saucepan over medium heat; bring to a boil. Remove from heat. Stir the gelatin into the hot tomato soup mixture. Stir in the cream cheese; blend well. Cool slightly. Add the olives, celery, onion, green pepper, mayonnaise and walnuts; mix well. Chill, covered, until serving time. Yield: 8 servings.

Winifred Olds, Laureate Beta Iota
Okemos, Michigan

FROZEN MINT SALAD

2 (20-ounce) cans crushed pineapple	2 envelopes whipped topping mix
1 (10-ounce) package miniature marshmallows	1 (7-ounce) package butter mints, crushed
	1 teaspoon pineapple flavoring
1 (3-ounce) package lime gelatin	

Mix the pineapple, marshmallows and gelatin in a medium bowl. Chill, covered, for 8 to 10 hours, stirring occasionally. Prepare the whipped topping mix using package directions. Stir the whipped topping, butter mints and pineapple flavoring into the pineapple mixture. Pour into a freezer container. Freeze. Remove from freezer at serving time; cut into squares. Yield: 12 or more servings.

Jean M. Erickson, Preceptor
Ada, Oklahoma

ORANGE CREAM FRUIT SALAD

I have served this special salad at all our holiday dinners.

1 (20-ounce) can
  pineapple chunks,
  drained
1 (11-ounce) can
  mandarin oranges,
  drained
2 medium apples,
  chopped
1 (16-ounce) can peach
  slices, drained

3 medium bananas,
  sliced
1½ cups milk
1 (4-ounce) package
  vanilla instant
  pudding mix
⅓ cup thawed orange
  juice concentrate
¾ cup sour cream

Combine the pineapple chunks, mandarin oranges, apples, peaches and bananas in a large bowl. Combine the milk, vanilla pudding mix and orange juice concentrate in a small bowl; beat for 1 to 2 minutes or until well blended. Beat in the sour cream. Fold into the pineapple mixture. Chill, covered, for 3 to 10 hours. Yield: 10 to 12 servings.

Joyce Snavely, Laureate Omega
Redmond, Washington

VELVET PINEAPPLE SALAD

1 (3-ounce) package
  lemon gelatin
4 cups boiling water
1 (16-ounce) package
  marshmallows
1 (8-ounce) can crushed
  pineapple, drained
½ cup mayonnaise-type
  salad dressing

3 ounces cream cheese,
  softened
½ cup whipping cream,
  whipped
2 (3-ounce) packages
  raspberry gelatin

Dissolve the lemon gelatin in 1 cup boiling water in a large bowl. Add the marshmallows to 1 cup boiling water in a small bowl and stir until melted. Stir the marshmallow mixture into the lemon gelatin mixture. Allow the mixture to cool. Combine the pineapple, salad dressing, cream cheese and whipped cream in a medium bowl. Add the pineapple mixture to the lemon gelatin mixture; mix well. Pour into a 9x13-inch dish. Chill, covered, for 2 to 3 hours or until set. Dissolve the raspberry gelatin in the remaining 2 cups boiling water in a bowl. Chill for 1 to 2 hours or until syrupy. Pour over the marshmallow mixture. Chill for 1 to 3 hours longer or until set. Cut into squares. Yield: 8 to 10 servings.

Barbara Garton, Iota Lambda
Buffalo, Missouri

WINTER FRUIT SALAD WITH POPPY SEED DRESSING

½ cup sugar
⅓ cup lemon juice
2 teaspoons finely
  chopped onion
1 teaspoon Dijon
  mustard
½ teaspoon salt
⅔ cup vegetable oil
1 tablespoon poppy
  seeds

1 large head romaine
  lettuce, torn
1 cup shredded Swiss
  cheese
1 cup cashews
¼ cup sweetened dried
  cranberries
1 apple, chopped
1 pear, chopped

Combine the sugar, lemon juice, onion, mustard and salt in the container of a food processor or blender; process until smooth. Add the oil in a slow, steady stream while the machine is running; process until thick and smooth. Add the poppy seeds; process for a few seconds to mix. Toss together the lettuce, Swiss cheese, cashews, cranberries, apple and pear in a large salad bowl. Pour the poppy seed dressing over the salad; toss to coat. Yield: 12 servings.

Sue Brown, Preceptor Epsilon Lambda
Rolla, Missouri

CRAB LOUIS OVER AVOCADO

A favorite for a special celebration dinner. Serve with white wine.

4 small Boston lettuce
  leaves
1 avocado, peeled,
  pitted, sliced

1 cup cooked crab meat
½ cup Sauce Louis
4 to 6 walnuts, halved

Place the lettuce leaves on 2 salad plates. Arrange the avocado slices in a fan shape over the lettuce; top with the crab meat. Pour the Sauce Louis over the crab meat. Garnish with walnuts. Yield: 2 servings.

SAUCE LOUIS

1 cup mayonnaise
¼ cup half-and-half
¼ cup chili sauce
1 teaspoon
  Worcestershire sauce

3 or 4 green onions,
  thinly sliced
1½ tablespoons fresh
  lemon juice

Combine the mayonnaise, half-and-half, chili sauce, Worcestershire sauce, green onions and lemon juice in a large lidded jar; shake well to blend.

Marilyn Finucan, Lambda Lambda
Brechin, Ontario, Canada

HEARTS OF PALM AND SHRIMP SALAD

1/2 cup olive oil	2 (14-ounce) cans hearts
1/4 cup red wine vinegar	of palm, drained,
1/4 cup water	halved lengthwise
1 tablespoon sugar	1 1/2 pounds large shrimp,
2 teaspoons lemon juice	cooked, peeled,
1 teaspoon Dijon	deveined
mustard	6 slices bacon, cooked,
1 teaspoon	drained, chopped
Worcestershire sauce	1 red onion, sliced
3/4 teaspoon garlic salt	(optional)
1/4 teaspoon freshly	Lettuce
ground black pepper	

Combine the olive oil, vinegar, water, sugar, lemon juice, mustard, Worcestershire sauce, garlic salt and pepper in a small bowl; whisk until well blended. Place the hearts of palm, shrimp, bacon and onion in a 1-gallon sealable plastic bag. Add the dressing and seal the bag. Chill for 8 to 10 hours to allow flavors to blend. To serve, remove the shrimp and hearts of palm and arrange them over lettuce on individual serving plates. Pour the dressing over each salad. Garnish with parsley. Yield: about 10 servings.

Margie Kelarek, Laureate Eta Beta
Hilltop Lakes, Texas

CREAMY TUNA SALAD

1 envelope unflavored	Salt to taste
gelatin	Dash of cayenne pepper
1/4 cup cold water	6 to 8 ounces cream
1 (3-ounce) package	cheese, softened
lemon gelatin	1 cup cottage cheese
1 cup hot water	1 cup finely chopped
2 teaspoons tarragon	celery
vinegar	1 cup flaked tuna fish
1 (10-ounce) can tomato	3/4 cup mayonnaise
soup	

Dissolve the gelatin in the cold water in a bowl. Dissolve the lemon gelatin in the hot water in a separate bowl. Combine the vinegar, tomato soup, salt, cayenne pepper, cream cheese, cottage cheese, celery and tuna in a large bowl; mix well. Stir in the dissolved gelatin mixtures and mayonnaise; mix well. Pour into a 5x9-inch glass dish. Chill, covered, until set. Cut in squares when ready to serve. Yield: 6 to 8 servings.

Georgine Wasley, Preceptor Nu Delta
Nevada City, California

TUNA CAESAR WRAPS

4 cups bite-size pieces	1/2 cup Caesar croutons
romaine lettuce	1/4 cup grated Parmesan
1/3 cup creamy Caesar	cheese
salad dressing	4 (9- to 10-inch) flour
1 (12-ounce) can tuna in	tortillas
spring water, drained	

Combine the lettuce and salad dressing in a large bowl; toss to coat. Add the tuna, croutons and Parmesan cheese; toss to combine. Spoon some of the salad mixture along one of the edges of each tortilla. Roll up each tortilla, beginning at edge near salad mixture. Seal each end with a bit of Caesar dressing. Cut tortillas in half to serve. Yield: 4 servings.

Beth Bubonovich, Xi Theta Alpha
Uniontown, Pennsylvania

❖ GRILLED CHICKEN, PORTOBELLO MUSHROOM AND SPINACH SALAD

I didn't know I could get so excited about entering a contest. I won First Place at our county fair with this recipe. Then our local TV station asked me to demonstrate making it on TV!

2 portobello mushroom	2 teaspoons lemon juice
caps	1/4 teaspoon grated
2 skinless chicken	lemon zest
breasts	1 teaspoon salt
Dash of lemon pepper	6 cups spinach leaves,
1/4 cup pine nuts	washed, dried
3 tablespoons red wine	1/4 cup thinly sliced red
vinegar	onion
1 teaspoon sugar	3 tablespoons crumbled
1/3 cup olive oil	feta cheese

Prepare medium-hot coals (350 to 400 degrees) in a barbecue grill. Grill the portobello mushroom caps, for 5 minutes or until grill marks show on both sides, turning once. Slice mushroom caps diagonally. Rinse chicken and pat dry. Place chicken on the grill. Sprinkle lemon pepper over the chicken. Grill for 25 minutes or until juices run clear. Toast the pine nuts in a dry skillet over medium heat until slightly browned. Cool. Whisk together the red wine vinegar, sugar, olive oil, lemon juice, lemon zest and salt in a bowl. Arrange spinach leaves on salad plates. Slice chicken diagonally; place over spinach. Sprinkle the pine nuts, onion and feta cheese over the chicken. Surround chicken with mushroom slices. Serve with the red wine vinegar dressing. Yield: 2 to 4 servings.

Patricia Kelley Lahey, Xi Alpha Iota
Rochester, Minnesota

CHICKEN VERONICA

Serve on a hot summer evening with cold fresh fruit garnished with raspberry purée.

2 cups cooked rice
1 cup seedless green or
  red grapes, halved
1/2 cup sliced celery
1/4 cup sliced green
  onions
2 cups cubed cooked
  chicken, cooled

1/2 cup sour cream
1/2 cup mayonnaise
1 teaspoon dry mustard
1 teaspoon celery salt
2 tablespoons
  chardonnay or
  chablis
1/4 cup slivered almonds

Combine the rice, grapes, celery, green onions and chicken in a medium bowl. Chill, covered, for 8 to 10 hours to blend the flavors. When ready to serve, place the sour cream, mayonnaise, mustard, celery salt and chardonnay in a food processor or blender container; process until smooth. Stir into the rice mixture. Serve over lettuce. Sprinkle with almonds. Yield: 4 to 6 servings.

Rita Rosen, Preceptor Epsilon Sigma
Danville, California

MAMA'S CHICKEN SALAD

My college roommates were always waiting at the door in anticipation of my return with a bowl of Mama's Chicken Salad. Twenty-five years later, this chicken salad is still a hit with my friends and family. I salt the chicken before cooking it.

4 cups chopped cooked
  chicken breasts
1 cup chopped celery
2 teaspoons grated
  onion
1 teaspoon (or more)
  salt

1/2 teaspoon pepper
1 teaspoon monosodium
  glutamate
2 teaspoons lemon juice
2/3 cup chopped pecans
1 cup (or more)
  mayonnaise

Combine the chicken, celery, onion, salt, pepper, monosodium glutamate, lemon juice, pecans and mayonnaise in a large bowl; mix lightly but thoroughly. Yield: 6 servings.

Dianne Fair, Laureate Alpha Delta
Cleveland, Tennessee

Ann Cazer, Xi Alpha Iota, Custer, South Dakota, makes a mixture of 3 cups chopped cooked chicken, 1/2 cup each diced celery, chopped onion, green pepper, sliced black olives, mandarin oranges, pineapple chunks and grapes with a dressing of 2 cups mayonnase-type salad dressing and 1 tablespoon mustard into a luscious Chow Mein Salad with the noodles added just before serving.

MANGO CHUTNEY CHICKEN SALAD

1 cup mayonnaise
1 cup sour cream
1/2 cup mango chutney
1/4 cup minced green
  onions

1/4 cup chopped cilantro
1 teaspoon salt
6 cups chopped cooked
  chicken
Toasted pecans

Combine the mayonnaise, sour cream, chutney, green onions, cilantro and salt in a large bowl; mix well. Add the chicken; toss gently to combine. Marinate, covered, in the refrigerator for 2 to 24 hours. Sprinkle with toasted pecans at serving time. Yield: 6 to 8 servings.

Betty Erickson, Preceptor Psi
Diamond Bar, California

ORIENTAL CHICKEN SALAD

2 cups water
1 package oriental
  ramen noodle soup
  mix
1 rib celery, chopped
1 carrot, chopped

1 1/2 cups chopped cooked
  chicken breasts
1/4 cup mayonnaise
2 teaspoons soy sauce
1 teaspoon lemon juice
1/4 cup chopped onion

Bring the water to a boil in a medium saucepan. Break up the noodles; stir into the boiling water. Cook for 3 minutes. Drain and set aside to cool. Mix the soup's seasoning packet with the remaining ingredients in a medium bowl. Fold in the noodles. Chill, covered, for 2 to 10 hours. Yield: 6 to 8 servings.

Vineta Mickie Reass, Xi Nu
Winter Haven, Florida

WILD RICE CHICKEN SALAD

2 boneless skinless
  chicken breasts
1 1/2 cups apple juice
1 cup mayonnaise
1/2 teaspoon seasoned
  salt
1/4 teaspoon cinnamon
3 cups cooked wild rice

1 1/2 cups green grapes,
  halved
1 cup chopped apple
1 cup chopped celery
3/4 cup slivered almonds
1/2 cup sliced water
  chestnuts

Rinse chicken and pat dry. Place the chicken with the apple juice in a medium saucepan. Simmer for about 20 minutes or until chicken is tender. Drain. Cut chicken into bite-size pieces. Combine the mayonnaise, seasoned salt and cinnamon in a lidded jar; shake well. Combine the chicken, wild rice, grapes, apple, celery, almonds and water chestnuts in a medium bowl; stir in the mayonnaise dressing. Chill, covered, until ready to serve. Yield: 4 to 6 servings.

Irene Johnson, Preceptor Tau
Silver Bay, Minnesota

LITTLE KING'S SALAD

To make this a serve-yourself salad, toss together everything except the roll pieces and dressing. Each person will make his or her own salad as desired. We named this recipe after our favorite restaurant in Yankton, South Dakota, The Little King, which features a similar recipe.

3 tomatoes, chopped	1/4 pound salami, cut
1 head lettuce, chopped	into thin strips
1 onion, chopped	3/4 cup vegetable oil
6 ounces Swiss cheese,	1/4 cup tarragon vinegar
cut in julienne strips	2 teaspoons oregano
6 ounces Cheddar	1/4 teaspoon pepper
cheese, cut in julienne	1 teaspoon salt
strips	1/4 teaspoon garlic
1/4 pound ham, cut into	powder
thin strips	3 poppy seed rolls

Combine the tomatoes, lettuce, onion, Swiss cheese, Cheddar cheese, ham and salami in a large bowl. Combine the oil, vinegar, oregano, pepper, salt and garlic powder in a lidded jar; shake vigorously to blend. Tear the rolls into walnut-size pieces; stir into the tomato mixture. Pour the dressing over the salad; toss to combine. Yield: 4 to 6 servings.

Patricia A. Lipp
Olathe, Kansas

MEAT AND POTATO SALAD

1 pound smoked	2 tablespoons
sausage, cut into	mayonnaise
1/2-inch slices	2 teaspoons Dijon
1 pound small red	mustard
potatoes, cut into	1 teaspoon sugar
1/2-inch cubes	1/2 teaspoon salt
1 1/2 cups chicken broth	1 large green bell pepper,
1/2 cup sour cream	chopped
2 tablespoons cider	1/2 cup chopped red
vinegar	onion

Place the sausage, potatoes and chicken broth in a 10-inch skillet over medium-high heat. Bring to a boil. Reduce heat and simmer, covered, for 10 minutes or until potatoes are tender. Drain. Cool for about 5 minutes. Combine the sour cream, vinegar, mayonnaise, mustard, sugar and salt in a 2-quart bowl. Add the sausage mixture, green pepper and onion; toss to coat. Serve warm. Yield: 6 to 8 servings.

Vera Jean Hamilton, Gamma Tau
Washington, Indiana

CRAB MEAT AND PASTA SALAD

Serve with French bread, fresh fruit, and iced tea. A wonderful variation of this tasty salad is to make it without the pasta and stuff avocado halves with the mixture.

1 pound mock crab meat	1/2 cup chopped black
1/4 cup chopped green	olives
onions	Garlic powder to taste
1/4 to 1/2 cup chopped	1 teaspoon fresh lemon
celery	juice
1 cup mayonnaise	1 teaspoon parsley
2 cups shredded Colby,	flakes
Swiss or mozzarella	1 to 1 1/2 cups cooked
cheese	pasta

Combine the crab meat, green onions, celery, mayonnaise, Colby cheese, olives, garlic powder, lemon juice, parsley and pasta in a large bowl. Serve over a lettuce leaf. Garnish with fresh strawberries or orange slices. Yield: 6 to 8 servings.

Sylvia Poupard, Preceptor Epsilon Omicron
Merced, California

CUCUMBER PASTA SALAD

16 ounces rotini	2 teaspoons pepper
8 ounces shell noodles	2 teaspoons parsley
1 1/4 cups cider vinegar	flakes
3/4 cup vegetable oil	1 or 2 onions, chopped
3/4 cup sugar	1 or 2 cucumbers,
2 teaspoons garlic salt	chopped

Prepare the rotini and shell noodles using package directions. Cool. Combine the vinegar, oil, sugar, garlic salt, pepper and parsley flakes in a small bowl; blend well. Combine rotini, shell noodles, vinegar dressing, onions and cucumbers in a large bowl; mix well. Serve at room temperature or chilled. Yield: 10 to 12 servings.

Lianne Forsey, Xi Gamma Omega
Fort Smith, Arkansas

Doris M. Gunn, Preceptor Gamma Beta, Grand Rapids, Michigan, mixes up shrimp, seashell macaroni, hard-cooked eggs, torn lettuce, chopped tomatoes, onion, dill pickles, celery, fresh mushrooms, pineapple and shredded Cheddar cheese. She adds a dressing of half ranch and half mayonnaise-type salad dressing with a splash of lemon juice and 1 teaspoon of sugar. What else could she call it except Everything But the Kitchen Sink Salad?

SPIRAL PASTA SALAD

For a heartier luncheon salad, add crab meat, cooked chicken, or tuna.

8 ounces spiral noodles	2/3 cup sliced carrots
1 cup chopped celery	12 cherry tomatoes
1/2 cup each chopped red and green bell peppers	1 teaspoon salt
	1/2 teaspoon pepper
1 cup broccoli florets	1 teaspoon Dijon mustard
1 cup cauliflower, broken up	1/2 cup olive oil
	1/2 cup vegetable oil
1 (4-ounce) can sliced black olives, drained	1/2 cup red wine vinegar
	1 1/2 teaspoons oregano
1/2 small red onion, chopped	2 green onions, chopped
	1 1/2 teaspoons parsley

Cook the noodles using package directions; drain. Place the noodles, celery, red and green peppers, broccoli, cauliflower, olives, red onion, carrots and tomatoes in a large bowl; toss to combine. Combine the salt, pepper, mustard, olive oil, vegetable oil, vinegar, oregano, green onions and parsley in a bowl; blend well. Pour the vinegar dressing over the salad. Marinate, covered, for 3 to 10 hours.
Yield: 6 to 8 servings.

Beverly A. Raze, Preceptor Alpha Nu
Ontario, Oregon

SEAFOOD PASTA SALAD

8 ounces bow tie pasta	1 1/2 cups frozen peas, thawed
1 cucumber, peeled, seeded, chopped	1 pound large cooked shrimp, peeled, deveined
3 large tomatoes, chopped	
5 green onions, chopped	2 to 3 king crab legs, shelled, cut into bite-size pieces
1/2 red bell pepper, chopped	
1/2 (12-ounce) can hearts of palm, sliced into 1/2-inch pieces	Fresh dill
	Garlic salt
1 (2-ounce) can sliced black olives, drained	

Cook pasta using package directions. Drain and rinse with cold water. Cool. Place the pasta, cucumber, tomatoes, green onions, red pepper, hearts of palm, olives, peas, shrimp and crab meat in a large bowl; toss to combine. Season with dill and garlic salt. Chill, covered, until ready to serve. Serve with assorted favorite salad dressings on the side.
Yield: 6 to 8 servings.

Barbara Rodgers, Preceptor Beta Iota
Colorado Springs, Colorado

BEAN SALAD

This flavorful salad will keep well refrigerated for 8 to 10 days. It is also a delicious side dish for beef, pork or poultry.

1 (16-ounce) can kidney beans, drained, rinsed	1 small red onion, chopped
1 (16-ounce) can wax beans, drained	1 green bell pepper, chopped
1 (16-ounce) can cut green beans, drained	3/4 cup sugar
	1/2 teaspoon pepper
3 ribs celery, thinly sliced	2/3 cup vinegar
	1/2 cup vegetable oil
1 small white or yellow onion, chopped	1 teaspoon salt

Combine the kidney beans, wax beans and green beans in a medium bowl. Combine the celery, onions and green pepper in a separate bowl; stir in the sugar, pepper, vinegar, oil and salt; mix well. Pour onion mixture over bean mixture; toss lightly. Chill, covered, for 8 to 10 hours. Yield: 6 to 8 servings.

Minnie K. Stapleton, Xi Alpha Tau
Morristown, Tennessee

CAULIFLOWER AVOCADO SALAD

4 cups chopped cauliflower	2 tablespoons lemon juice
4 avocados, chopped	Salt and pepper to taste
1/4 cup olive oil	1 teaspoon paprika
3/4 cup mayonnaise	

Place the cauliflower and avocados in a bowl. Combine the olive oil, mayonnaise and lemon juice in a separate bowl; blend well. Pour the olive oil mixture over the cauliflower mixture; mix well. Season with salt and pepper. Sprinkle paprika over the top. Marinate, covered, for 3 to 10 hours.
Yield: 10 servings.

Bonnee Blue Pierson, Xi Gamma Omicron
Pryor, Oklahoma

Valerie R. Valdez-Fitzgibbons, Laureate Alpha Eta, Lakewood, Colorado, serves a Beet and Pear Salad of canned Bartlett pear halves, sliced lengthwise with a can of sliced beets and 1/2 cup thinly sliced red onion with a dressing of 2 tablespoons oil, 1 tablespoon each white wine vinegar and pear syrup. Toss with 1/3 cup crumbled bleu cheese before serving.

CALIFORNIA SLAW

1 (8-ounce) can crushed pineapple	1 avocado, cubed
4 cups shredded cabbage	1 cup sour cream
1/4 cup chopped green bell pepper	2 tablespoons mayonnaise
2 tablespoons chopped green onions	1 teaspoon soy sauce
	1/2 teaspoon ginger

Drain the pineapple, reserving 3 tablespoons of the juice. Combine the pineapple, cabbage, green pepper and green onions in a large bowl. Fold avocado into cabbage mixture. Combine the sour cream, mayonnaise, soy sauce, ginger and the 3 tablespoons pineapple syrup in a small bowl; blend well. Pour over cabbage mixture; toss gently.
Yield: 6 to 8 servings.

Mildred Burns, Alpha Master
Alamosa, Colorado

MARINATED CARROT SALAD

I have successfully kept this salad for two weeks in the refrigerator. Serve with meat, potatoes, bread, and dessert.

2 pounds carrots, peeled, sliced	1 (10-ounce) can tomato soup
Salt to taste	1 cup sugar
1 head cauliflower, sliced	1 teaspoon dry mustard
1 large onion, sliced	1 cup vinegar
1 green bell pepper, chopped	1 teaspoon salt
	3/4 cup vegetable oil

Cook carrots in salted water to cover in a medium saucepan until crisp-tender; drain. Combine the carrots, cauliflower, onion and green pepper in a large bowl. Combine the tomato soup, sugar, mustard, vinegar, salt and vegetable oil in a medium bowl; blend well. Pour over vegetable mixture. Toss gently. Chill, covered, for 3 to 10 hours.
Yield: 8 to 10 servings.

Kay Weakland, Laureate Kappa
Beatrice, Nebraska

CORN AND PEANUT SALAD

1 (16-ounce) package frozen yellow corn	6 tablespoons peanut oil
1 small red onion, finely chopped	2 tablespoons cider vinegar
1 tablespoon chopped Italian flat-leaf parsley	1 cup salted dry-roasted peanuts

Rinse the corn in hot water until thawed; drain well. Place in a bowl. Stir in the onion and parsley.

Combine the oil and vinegar in a small bowl; blend well. Stir the vinegar mixture into the corn mixture; mix well. Chill, covered, for 4 to 6 hours. Just before serving (no more than 1 hour ahead), add the peanuts. Toss and serve. Yield: 6 servings.

MaryAnn Evans, Preceptor Epsilon Phi
Castro Valley, California

MARIA'S ITALIAN SALAD

2 garlic cloves, crushed	1/2 cup diced mozzarella cheese
2 tablespoons cider vinegar	2 green onions, chopped
1 teaspoon Dijon mustard	3 tomatoes, cut into wedges
1/2 cup olive oil	1 (4-ounce) can green or black sliced olives
Salt and pepper to taste	1 red onion, thinly sliced
1 avocado, cubed	1 head leaf lettuce, chopped
1 (14-ounce) can artichoke hearts	

Whisk together the garlic, vinegar, mustard, olive oil, salt and pepper in a large salad bowl. Layer the avocado, artichoke hearts, mozzarella cheese, green onions, tomatoes and olives in the bowl. Do not mix. Place the chopped lettuce over the layers. Chill, covered, until ready to serve. Toss salad and serve.
Yield: 12 servings.

Carole Tanney, Preceptor Epsilon Sigma
Stittsville, Ontario, Canada

ITALIAN OLIVE SALAD

4 cups pimento-stuffed green olives	2 teaspoons oregano
2 cups black or Greek olives	2 tablespoons parsley
6 garlic cloves, chopped or pressed	1 teaspoon salt
3/4 cup chopped celery	1/2 teaspoon black pepper
	4 ounces olive oil

Drain the green and black olives; mix together in a large bowl. Stir in the garlic, celery, oregano, parsley, salt and pepper. Pour the olive oil over the olive mixture; mix well. Marinate, covered, for 8 to 10 hours or overnight. Yield: 8 to 10 servings.

Sheila Clark, Preceptor Chi
Old Town, Maine

Verna Howard, Zeta Zeta Advisor, Pine, Arizona, makes a Salad Relish by mixing chopped cucumber, fresh tomatoes, celery, green onions and grated carrots and adding Italian dressing.

ROASTED RED PEPPERS WITH RED GRAPES

2 large red bell peppers	6 to 8 chopped fresh
15 to 20 seedless red	basil leaves
grapes, halved	1/4 cup chopped fresh
1/4 teaspoon salt	parsley
1/2 teaspoon (about)	1 garlic clove, minced
pepper	

Preheat broiler for 5 minutes. Place red peppers on a rack on a baking pan. Broil peppers 4 to 6 inches from heat until all sides are blackened, turning occasionally. Cool. Peel black skin off peppers, seed and cut into strips. Arrange the pepper strips and grape halves on a serving platter. Combine the salt, pepper, basil, parsley and garlic in a bowl; sprinkle over pepper strips and grapes. Chill, covered, if desired. Yield: 4 servings.

L. Robin LaFerrara, Kappa Kappa
Slidell, Louisiana

ZESTY POTATO SALAD

8 medium potatoes	1/2 teaspoon salt
1 1/2 cups mayonnaise	1 cup fresh parsley,
1 cup sour cream	finely chopped
1 1/2 teaspoons	2 medium onions, finely
horseradish	chopped
1 teaspoon celery seeds	Salt to taste

Boil the potatoes in their skins in a stockpot for 20 to 30 minutes or until tender. Cool and remove skins. Combine the mayonnaise, sour cream, horseradish, celery seeds and salt in a bowl; blend well. Combine the parsley and onions in a separate bowl; mix well. Cut the potatoes horizontally into 1/2-inch slices. Layer half the potato slices in the bottom of a large bowl; salt the layer. Layer half the mayonnaise mixture over the potatoes. Sprinkle with parsley mixture. Repeat the layers. Chill, covered, for 8 to 10 hours. Yield: 8 to 10 servings.

Julie Cowgur, Xi Alpha Zeta
Bentonville, Arkansas

SPINACH SALAD

1 (10-ounce) package	1/3 cup sugar
fresh spinach, cleaned	1 cup vegetable oil
3 hard-cooked eggs,	1/3 cup vinegar
sliced	1/2 teaspoon salt
3 slices bacon, crisp-	1/2 teaspoon pepper
fried, crumbled	1 medium onion,
1 red onion, cut into	chopped
rings	1 teaspoon dry mustard
1/2 to 1 cup herb-	1 teaspoon celery salt
seasoned stuffing mix	

Combine the spinach, eggs, bacon, red onion rings and stuffing mix in a large salad bowl. Chill, covered, until serving time. Combine the sugar, oil, vinegar, salt, pepper, onion, mustard and celery salt in a blender container; blend until smooth. Pour the dressing over the salad at serving time; toss gently. Sprinkle a little extra stuffing mix over the top if desired. Yield: 6 to 8 servings.

Rose Andersen, Iota Iota
Blairsville, Georgia

SPINACH AND STRAWBERRY SALAD

The almonds can be toasted by baking for 5 minutes or until browned in a 350-degree oven, or by microwaving on High for 2 to 4 minutes, stirring nuts every minute or so.

1 (10-ounce) package	2 tablespoons cider
fresh spinach, cleaned	vinegar
2 tablespoons sugar	1 tablespoon balsamic
2 tablespoons sesame	vinegar
seeds	1 tablespoon raspberry
1 tablespoon poppy seeds	or red wine vinegar
1 green onion, chopped	1 quart fresh
1/2 cup olive oil	strawberries, cleaned
1 teaspoon	1/2 cup toasted almonds
Worcestershire sauce	

Remove stems from the spinach and tear into bite-size pieces; place in a large salad bowl. Combine the sugar, sesame seeds, poppy seeds, green onion, olive oil, Worcestershire sauce, cider vinegar, balsamic vinegar and raspberry vinegar in a lidded jar; shake vigorously to blend. Chill, covered, until ready to use. Slice the strawberries no more than 10 minutes before serving time. Add the strawberries and almonds to the spinach. Pour the vinegar dressing over the salad; toss and serve. Yield: 8 to 10 servings.

Rose Hawley, Xi Epsilon Kappa
Orleans, Ontario, Canada

PEA AND NUT SALAD

1 (16-ounce) package	2 cups chopped celery
frozen peas, thawed	8 slices bacon, crisp-
1 cup cashew halves	fried, crumbled
1/2 cup chopped green	1 cup sour cream
onions	Salt and pepper to taste

Combine the peas, cashews, green onions, celery and bacon in a large bowl. Add the sour cream; toss to coat well. Add salt and pepper. Chill, covered, for 3 to 4 hours before serving. Yield: 8 servings.

Olive Ross, Gamma Master
Des Moines, Iowa

Entertaining Entrées

Spectacular entrées don't have to take
all day, whether you're planning a large
party or merely making a meal.
We've gathered scrumptious recipes with
a wide variety of primary ingredients
including meats, pastas, and even veggies.
Spice up the showiest soirée with
Chili Rellenos, or spruce up your simplest
supper with Broccoli Bleu Cheese Fettucini.
Truly tantalizing and time-saving,
each entrée offers the practical simplicity
that you deserve. These marvelous
main dishes almost make themselves!

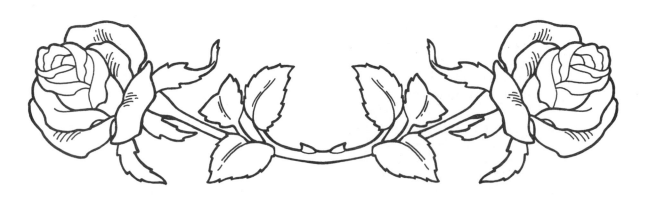

ROAST BEEF PROVENCALE

6½ pounds boneless beef ribeye	½ cup (1 stick) butter or margarine, melted
2 cups fresh white bread crumbs	2 tablespoons meat drippings
½ cup chopped parsley	3 tablespoons flour
2 garlic cloves, crushed	1 (10-ounce) can condensed beef broth
2 teaspoons salt	
½ teaspoon pepper	¼ teaspoon salt
¼ cup Dijon mustard	Dash of pepper

Preheat the oven to 325 degrees. Wipe the roast with damp paper towels. Place in an open roasting pan. Combine the bread crumbs, parsley, garlic, 2 teaspoons salt and ½ teaspoon pepper in a bowl. Spread the mustard over the roast. Pat the crumb mixture firmly into the mustard. Drizzle with butter. Insert a meat thermometer into center of roast. Roast, uncovered, for 2 to 2¼ hours or until meat thermometer registers 140 degrees if you want rare beef; for medium beef, roast for 2¼ to 3 hours or until thermometer registers 160 degrees. Let roast stand for 20 minutes, for easier carving. Remove roast and pour off the drippings; return 2 tablespoons of the drippings to the pan. Stir in the flour; blend until smooth. Brown the flour over low heat, stirring constantly to loosen brown bits left in pan. Add enough water to the beef broth to make 2 cups. Stir broth slowly into the flour mixture. Add ¼ teaspoon salt and a dash of pepper. Bring to a boil, stirring; cook and stir until smooth and bubbly. Yield: 12 servings.

Elayne Bernier, Preceptor Pi
Burley, Idaho

SWEET-AND-SOUR BRISKET

3 onions, sliced	1½ cups packed brown sugar
4 garlic cloves, minced	
1 (7- to 10-pound) brisket	1 cup white vinegar
	2 cups pineapple juice
1 tablespoon Cajun seasoning	2 cups catsup

Preheat the oven to 350 degrees. Spray a large baking pan with nonstick cooking spray. Layer the onions and garlic in the pan. Rub the brisket with Cajun seasoning. Place over the onions, fat side up. Combine the brown sugar, vinegar, pineapple juice and catsup; mix well. Pour over the brisket. Bake, covered, for 4 to 4½ hours or until tender. Yield: 15 to 20 servings.

Carol A. Schaubhut, Preceptor Alpha Beta
Terrytown, Louisiana

BEER POT ROAST

I use my cast-iron Dutch oven to prepare this dish. Try serving the drippings as a dip for bread. Another idea is to quarter potatoes and add them to the pan 30 to 40 minutes before meat is done. Both ideas are delicious!

1 (3- to 4-pound) chuck roast	½ cup chili sauce
	¼ cup water
1 medium onion, sliced	1 (12-ounce) can beer
2 ribs celery, chopped	

Preheat the oven to 325 degrees. Place the roast in a medium-size roasting pan. Cover roast with onion and celery. Season with salt and pepper. Combine the chili sauce and water; pour over the roast. Bake, covered, for 1 hour. Pour the beer over the roast. Bake, covered, for 3 to 4 hours longer or until fork tender. Yield: 6 to 8 servings.

Yvonne Mann, Laureate Rho
Merrill, Wisconsin

YUMMY SPICY BURRITOS

1 (6-pound) chuck roast	2 medium jalapeño peppers, chopped (optional)
1 cup water	
2 (4-ounce) cans chopped green chiles	
	2 (16-ounce) jars medium salsa
1 teaspoon pepper	
2 garlic cloves, minced	Burrito-size tortillas

Cook the beef, water, green chiles, pepper, garlic and jalapeño peppers on Low in a slow cooker for 8 to 10 hours. Place the cooked ingredients in a large bowl; chill for several hours or until fat rises to the top. Remove the fat. Remove the beef and shred. Return the beef and other cooked ingredients to the slow cooker. Stir in the salsa. Cook 1 to 2 hours longer to blend the flavors. Spoon over burritos; fold and enjoy. Add salt and pepper to taste.
Yield: 8 or more servings.

Althea M. Wise, Xi Beta Lambda
Mesa, Arizona

FREDA'S FILET MIGNON WITH BLEU CHEESE

2 (6-ounce or larger) filet mignons	¼ cup brandy
	1 teaspoon fresh rosemary, or ½ teaspoon dry
Salt and pepper to taste	
2 tablespoons (or less) melted butter	
	½ cup crumbled bleu cheese
1 (10-ounce) can beef broth	

Rub the filets with salt and pepper. Cook them in the butter in a skillet over medium-high heat for about 4 minutes on each side or until meat is done to taste. Remove the filets to a serving platter. Cover the filets loosely with foil while preparing the sauce. Pour the beef broth, brandy and rosemary into the skillet. Boil, scraping up browned bits, for about 5 minutes or until mixture is reduced to ⅓ cup. Sprinkle the bleu cheese over the filets. Spoon the sauce over the bleu cheese. Serve immediately. Yield: 2 servings.

Freda I. Bush, Preceptor Gamma Kappa
Chesapeake, Virginia

PEPPERY STEAKS WITH WINE SAUCE

2 tablespoons grainy Dijon mustard	2 shallots or scallions, minced
4 trimmed boneless beef ribeye steaks, ½ inch thick	½ teaspoon thyme
	¼ cup dry red wine
2 teaspoons cracked black pepper	½ cup canned low-sodium beef broth
1 tablespoon olive oil	Fresh thyme (optional)

Spread the mustard over both sides of each steak. Press the cracked pepper into the mustard. Heat the olive oil in a large heavy skillet over high heat. Add the steaks. Cook for 5 to 6 minutes for rare or until steaks are cooked to taste. Remove steaks to a platter. Cover loosely with foil while making the sauce. Discard fat left in skillet; reduce heat to medium-high. Add the shallots and thyme; cook for 30 seconds, stirring constantly. Add the wine; cook for 1 minute longer. Add the beef broth. Bring to a boil, stirring to loosen browned bits. Stir in juices from the platter; cook for 3 minutes or until sauce is reduced by half. Spoon the sauce over the steaks. Garnish with thyme. Yield: 4 servings.

Christine A. Stevenson, Beta Chi
Independence, Iowa

SLOW-COOKER PEPPER STEAK

Anyone can prepare a delicious dinner with this easy recipe.

1 to 2 pounds beef round steak	¼ teaspoon ground ginger
2 tablespoons vegetable oil	1 (16-ounce) can tomatoes
¼ cup soy sauce	2 large green bell peppers, cut into strips
1 cup chopped onion	
1 garlic clove, minced	
1 teaspoon sugar	½ cup cold water
½ teaspoon salt	2 tablespoons cornstarch
¼ teaspoon pepper	

Cut the beef into bite-size pieces. Brown in the oil in a heavy skillet over medium-high heat. Remove beef to a slow cooker. Combine the soy sauce, onion, garlic, sugar, salt, pepper and ginger; blend well. Pour over the beef. Cook on Low for 5 to 6 hours or until meat is tender. Add the tomatoes and green peppers. Cook for 1 hour longer. Blend the water and cornstarch to make a paste; stir into the liquid in the slow cooker. Cook on High for 30 minutes or until thickened. Yield: 6 to 8 servings.

Olava Lee, Laureate Psi
Albuquerque, New Mexico

GREEN CHILE STEW

Serve this spicy stew with hot flour tortillas.

1½ pounds sirloin steak, cubed	3 garlic cloves, crushed
	½ teaspoon oregano
Flour	1 cup fresh salsa
¼ cup vegetable oil	2 (4-ounce) cans green chiles
1 cup dark Mexican beer	
2 cups beef broth	1 (14-ounce) can pinto beans
1 cup minced onion	
1 bay leaf	Salt and pepper to taste
½ teaspoon crushed cumin	

Dredge the steak in the flour. Heat the oil in a Dutch oven. Add the meat; sear over high heat until browned. Reduce heat. Stir in the beer, beef broth, onion and bay leaf. Cook, uncovered, over low heat for 1 hour. Stir in the cumin, garlic, oregano, salsa, green chiles, beans, salt and pepper. Cook for 30 minutes longer. Remove bay leaf. Yield: 4 to 6 servings.

Rena Heinz, Preceptor Iota Omicron
San Angelo, Texas

ESTAFADO (SPANISH STEW)

Serve this stew over cooked rice or noodles.

¼ cup olive oil	½ cup tomato sauce
1 large onion, chopped	1 cup red wine
1 garlic clove, chopped	1 bay leaf
1½ pounds stew beef, cut in bite-size pieces	1 (7-ounce) can green chile salsa
3 tablespoons vinegar	

Heat the olive oil in a Dutch oven; sauté the onion and garlic until onion is clear. Add the meat, vinegar, tomato sauce, wine, bay leaf and salsa; stir well to combine. Cook, covered, for 2½ hours or until meat is done. Remove the bay leaf. Yield: 6 to 8 servings.

Lillian Hermann, Laureate Alpha Iota
Roswell, New Mexico

EXOTIC FIVE-HOUR STEW

This is a great recipe for a crowd: you can easily double it and put it in a large baking dish. I have successfully substituted venison for the beef.

2 pounds (or less)
   boneless chuck, cut
   into 1¹/₂-inch cubes
1 (16-ounce) can
   tomatoes
1 (1¹/₂- or 2-pound)
   package frozen stew
   vegetables, or fresh
   vegetables
3 tablespoons quick-
   cooking tapioca

1 tablespoon sugar
1 (5-ounce) can sliced
   water chestnuts,
   drained
1 tablespoon (or less)
   salt
¹/₄ teaspoon pepper
¹/₄ cup red wine

Preheat the oven to 250 degrees. Place the meat, tomatoes, vegetables, tapioca, sugar, water chestnuts, salt, pepper and wine in a 3-quart baking dish; stir gently to combine. Bake, covered, for 5 hours. Yield: 5 to 6 servings.

Mary Anne Rehbock, Laureate Gamma
Bothell, Washington

SWEET-AND-SOUR STEW

3 tablespoons flour
1¹/₄ teaspoons salt
Dash of pepper
1¹/₂ pounds beef stew
   meat, cut into 1-inch
   cubes
2 tablespoons butter or
   margarine
¹/₂ cup catsup
¹/₄ cup packed brown
   sugar

¹/₄ cup red wine vinegar
1 tablespoon
   Worcestershire sauce
1 cup water
¹/₄ teaspoon salt
12 small boiling onions,
   peeled
4 large carrots, cut into
   1-inch chunks
Chopped parsley

Combine the flour, 1¹/₄ teaspoons salt and pepper. Dredge the meat in the flour mixture; shake to remove excess. Melt the butter in a heavy skillet over medium-high heat. Brown the floured beef on all sides; drain. Combine the catsup, brown sugar, vinegar, Worcestershire sauce, water and ¹/₄ teaspoon salt in a medium bowl; mix well. Add the catsup mixture and the onions to the browned meat. Simmer, covered, for 1 hour and 15 minutes, stirring occasionally. Add the carrots. Simmer for 40 minutes longer, or until meat and vegetables are tender. Sprinkle with parsley. Yield: 4 to 6 servings.

Joanne Taylor
Port St. Lucie, Florida

BARBECUED HAMBURGERS

After you fry the hamburger patties and make the sauce, you can put all in a slow cooker and cook on Low for several hours or until dinnertime.

2¹/₂ to 3 pounds ground
   chuck
1 envelope onion soup
   mix
¹/₂ cup bread crumbs
1 egg
1 teaspoon minced
   garlic
1 large onion, sliced
1 green bell pepper, cut
   into strips

1 (8-ounce) can tomato
   sauce
¹/₂ cup packed brown
   sugar
1 tablespoon sweet
   relish
1 tablespoon vinegar
1 tablespoon
   Worcestershire sauce

Combine the ground chuck, onion soup mix, bread crumbs and egg in a medium bowl; mix lightly. Form into patties. Fry in a heavy skillet over medium heat for about 15 minutes on each side. Remove patties from skillet; drain most of the drippings. Add the garlic, onion and green pepper to the remaining drippings in the skillet; sauté until tender. Add the tomato sauce and about ¹/₂ cup water. Stir in the brown sugar, sweet relish, vinegar and Worcestershire sauce. Return the patties to the skillet. Simmer for about 45 minutes, or until sauce is thick and bubbly. Yield: 10 to 12 servings.

Ida Senic, Xi Eta Eta
Jeannette, Pennsylvania

CILANTRO BURGERS

10 stalks fresh cilantro,
   chopped
2 tomatoes, chopped
2 pounds ground beef
2 tablespoons soy sauce
1 green bell pepper,
   chopped

Bread crumbs from
   2 slices bread
¹/₂ onion, chopped
2 eggs
1 tablespoon garlic
   powder
1 teaspoon pepper

Combine the cilantro, tomatoes, ground beef, soy sauce, green pepper, bread crumbs, onion, eggs, garlic powder and pepper; mix lightly and form into patties. Preheat the grill or broiler. Place the patties on the grill or on the rack in a broiler pan and cook until cooked through, turning as necessary. May cook the patties in a heavy skillet by searing on both sides in a preheated skillet and continuing to cook and turn until cooked through, pouring off drippings as necessary. Yield: 8 servings.

Wendi Peters, Upsilon PI
Navasota, Texas

MOM'S WORLD-FAMOUS BURRITOS

1 pound ground beef	1 (15-ounce) can refried
1 (28-ounce) can whole	beans
tomatoes, chopped	10 flour tortillas
1 (10-ounce) can	3 cups shredded Cheddar
tomatoes with green	cheese
chiles, chopped	

Brown the ground beef in a skillet, stirring until crumbly; drain. Combine the ground beef, tomatoes and tomatoes with green chiles in the skillet over medium heat. Heat until bubbly. Place the refried beans in a small saucepan over medium-low heat until heated through. Offer 1 or 2 warm tortillas for each serving. Spoon 2 to 3 tablespoons refried beans in the center of each tortilla. Cover beans with 2 to 3 tablespoons beef mixture. Sprinkle cheese over filling. Roll each tortilla and cover with additional beef mixture and cheese. Yield: 5 to 8 servings.

Diana Bentley, Preceptor Xi Alpha
Houston, Texas

PUMPKIN CHILI

1 pound lean ground	1 (32-ounce) can
beef	chopped tomatoes
1 (16-ounce) can	1 (15-ounce) can French-
pumpkin	style green beans
1 tablespoon onion	Salt and pepper to taste
flakes	
1 envelope chili	
seasoning mix	

Brown the ground beef in a skillet, stirring until crumbly; drain. Stir in the pumpkin, onion flakes, chili seasoning mix and tomatoes. Simmer for 1 hour. Stir in the green beans, salt and pepper. Simmer for 30 minutes longer. Yield: 8 servings.

R. Jeen Davis, Preceptor Laureate Rho
Harrison, Arkansas

ITALIAN ENCHILADAS

Serve with garlic bread and fresh corn.

1 pound ground beef	1 tablespoon oregano
1 small onion, chopped	1 tablespoon sweet basil
1 tablespoon cumin	1 teaspoon garlic
1 teaspoon red pepper	powder
1 teaspoon black pepper	4 cups shredded
1/2 teaspoon salt	mozzarella cheese
1 (15-ounce) can tomato	10 flour tortillas
sauce	

Brown the ground beef with the onion, cumin, red pepper, black pepper and salt in a skillet, stirring until the ground beef is crumbly; drain. Combine the tomato sauce, oregano, sweet basil and garlic powder in a small bowl; mix well. Preheat the oven to 350 degrees. Grease the bottom of a 9x12-inch baking pan. Layer 1/3 cup beef mixture, 1 tablespoon tomato sauce mixture and a spoonful of mozzarella cheese in the center of each tortilla. Roll up the tortillas and place them side-by-side in the baking dish. Drizzle the remaining sauce over the tortillas. Sprinkle with the remaining cheese. Bake for about 20 minutes or until cheese is melted and lightly browned.
Yield: 6 to 8 servings.

Lara F. Miller, Rho
Riverton, Wyoming

SOUR CREAM ENCHILADAS

2 pounds ground beef	2 cups sour cream
1 large white onion,	1 (4-ounce) can chopped
chopped	green chiles
1 tablespoon garlic	12 flour tortillas
powder	4 cups shredded Cheddar
Salt and pepper to taste	cheese
2 (10-ounce) cans cream	
of chicken soup	

Brown the ground beef with the onion, garlic powder, salt and pepper in a skillet, stirring until the ground beef is crumbly; drain. Combine the cream of chicken soup, sour cream and green chiles in a medium bowl; blend well. Preheat the oven to 350 degrees. Spread half the sour cream mixture over the bottom of a 9x13-inch baking dish. Spoon 2 rounded tablespoons of beef mixture over the center of each tortilla. Sprinkle with a tablespoon of Cheddar cheese. Roll up the tortillas and arrange them side by side, seam side down over the sour cream mixture in the baking dish. Spoon the rest of the sour cream mixture over the tortillas. Sprinkle with any remaining beef mixture and cheese. Bake, uncovered, for 30 to 45 minutes or until cheese is melted and lightly browned. Yield: 6 to 8 servings.

Charlotte Santangelo, Xi Alpha Upsilon
Independence, Missouri

Lori Stover, Kappa Upsilon, Colby, Kansas, makes a Slow-Cooker Roast with Olives by combining a 2- to 3-pound chuck roast, a jar of green olives and 2 cups tomato juice and cooking on Low for 10 to 12 hours. Thicken the juices to serve as gravy if desired.

✤ WHISKEY-GLAZED CORNED BEEF

1 (6- to 7-pound) corned beef	2 tablespoons corned beef broth
3/4 cup blended whiskey	1 teaspoon prepared mustard
2 garlic cloves	Large head white cabbage, cut into 12 wedges
2 bay leaves	
4 whole cloves	
4 white peppercorns	
1/4 cup orange juice	Boiled new potatoes tossed with fresh parsley
3/4 cup packed brown sugar	

Place the corned beef in a large saucepan in water to cover. Add 1/2 cup of the whiskey, garlic, bay leaves, cloves and peppercorns. Bring to a boil. Reduce heat and simmer, covered, for 3 to 4 hours or until tender. Remove the corned beef to a roasting pan. Cut the outer fat in a cross-hatch pattern. Strain the corned beef broth and return to the saucepan. Preheat the oven to 400 degrees. Combine the orange juice, brown sugar, 2 tablespoons of the corned beef broth, mustard and the remaining 1/4 cup whiskey in a small saucepan over low heat. Heat, stirring until well blended. Pour over the corned beef. Bake for 30 minutes, basting every 10 minutes. Add the cabbage to the corned beef broth in the saucepan. Simmer for 10 minutes or until tender. Serve the glazed corned beef with cabbage and potatoes.
Yield: 6 to 8 servings.

Naomi E. Champa, Preceptor Beta Epsilon
Westlake, Ohio

MOUSSAKA

This lovely dish tastes even better when made a day ahead and reheated before serving.

2 medium eggplant, peeled, cut into 1/2-inch slices	1/4 teaspoon cinnamon
	Salt and pepper to taste
	6 tablespoons flour
1 cup (2 sticks) butter	4 cups milk
3 onions, finely chopped	4 eggs, well beaten
2 pounds ground lamb	Nutmeg
3 tablespoons tomato paste	2 cups ricotta cheese
	1 cup fine bread crumbs
1 cup red wine	1 cup freshly grated Parmesan cheese
1/2 cup chopped parsley	

Preheat the oven to 375 degrees. Brown the eggplant in 1/4 cup of the butter in a skillet. Melt another 1/4 cup of butter in a large skillet and sauté the onions for 2 to 3 minutes. Cook the ground lamb with the onions in the skillet over medium heat, stirring until the ground lamb is crumbly. Stir in the tomato paste, wine, parsley, cinnamon, salt and pepper. Simmer until the liquid is absorbed. Remove from heat. Let cool. Melt the remaining 1/2 cup butter in a saucepan. Stir in the flour. Add the milk gradually and cook until thickened, stirring constantly. Remove from heat. Let cool. Stir in the eggs, nutmeg, ricotta cheese, salt and pepper. Grease an 11x16-inch baking pan and sprinkle with 1/4 cup of the bread crumbs. Layer the eggplant slices and lamb mixture in the prepared pan, 1/2 at a time, sprinkling each layer with Parmesan cheese and bread crumbs. Pour the ricotta cheese mixture over the lamb mixture. Bake for 1 hour or until golden brown. Yield: 10 servings.

Norma Schnackenberg, Laureate Eta Eta
Yucca Valley, California

PORK TENDERLOIN WITH HOMESTYLE POTATOES

Another cup of apple juice may be substituted for the cup of white wine.

1 yellow bell pepper	2 tablespoons olive oil
1 red bell pepper	Salt and pepper to taste
1 orange bell pepper	2 teaspoons freshly chopped rosemary
3 green medium zucchini	
2 yellow medium zucchini	1 cup white wine
	1 cup apple juice
3 small onions, peeled	1 teaspoon red currant jelly
2 (10-ounce) pork tenderloins	

Preheat the oven to 350 degrees. Wash the bell peppers and zucchini and cut into 1-inch pieces. Cut the onion vertically into 8 sections. Brown the pork tenderloins in the olive oil in a skillet over medium heat, turning so they brown on all sides. Remove to a large baking dish. Sprinkle with salt, pepper and rosemary. Place the vegetables in the skillet with the pork drippings and sauté over medium heat for about 5 minutes or until tender-crisp. Arrange the vegetables around the pork. Pour the wine over the pork and vegetables. Bake, uncovered, for 25 minutes or until juices are no longer pink. Pour the pan juices into a skillet. Stir in the apple juice. Bring to a boil. Boil until reduced by half, stirring occasionally. Stir in the currant jelly and simmer for another minute. Slice the pork into thin slices and arrange on a serving plate. Cover with the currant jelly sauce and garnish with the vegetables. Serve with Homestyle Potatoes.
Yield: 8 servings.

HOMESTYLE POTATOES

1½ pounds red potatoes,
  unpeeled
⅓ cup heavy cream
2 tablespoons Dijon
  mustard

¼ cup freshly chopped
  mint or parsley
Salt and freshly ground
  pepper to taste

Place potatoes in a kettle with cold salted water to cover. Bring to a boil. Boil for 10 minutes or just until tender. Drain well. Slice potatoes thinly and return to the kettle. Combine the cream and mustard in a small bowl; blend well. Stir mustard mixture into potatoes. Simmer over low heat for about 10 minutes or until sauce is slightly thickened and partially absorbed by potatoes. Stir in the mint. Season with salt and pepper.

Anna Hanlon
Ottawa, Ontario, Canada

GRILLED PORK TENDERLOIN

½ cup peanut oil
⅓ cup soy sauce
¼ cup red wine vinegar
3 tablespoons lemon
  juice
2 tablespoons
  Worcestershire sauce
1 garlic clove, crushed

1 tablespoon chopped
  fresh parsley
1 tablespoon dry
  mustard
1½ teaspoons pepper
2 (¾- to 1-pound) pork
  tenderloins

Combine the peanut oil, soy sauce, vinegar, lemon juice, Worcestershire sauce, garlic, parsley, mustard and pepper in a heavy-duty sealable bag. Place tenderloins in the mixture, turning to coat. Seal bag and place on a shallow dish. Chill for 4 hours, turning occasionally. Prepare charcoal for grilling or preheat a gas grill. Remove the tenderloins from marinade and grill for 12 to 14 minutes or until done, turning once. Yield: 6 servings.

Jenny Smith, Xi Gamma Epsilon
Gallipolis, Ohio

PECAN-CRUSTED PORK ROAST WITH BOURBON GRAVY

1 (5-pound) boneless
  pork roast
Salt to taste
¼ teaspoon ground
  pepper

3 tablespoons Dijon
  mustard
¾ cup chopped pecans
¼ cup soft bread crumbs

Preheat the oven to 425 degrees. Place the roast in a large roasting pan and season with salt and pepper. Spread the mustard evenly over the roast. Combine the pecans and bread crumbs in a small bowl. Pat pecan mixture over the mustard. Cover loosely with foil and roast for 1½ to 2 hours. Remove the foil. Roast for 10 minutes longer, or until a meat thermometer registers 150 degrees. Remove the roast from the pan. Cover loosely with foil and let stand while Bourbon Gravy is made. Yield: 6 to 8 servings.

BOURBON GRAVY

2 tablespoons unsalted
  butter
2 tablespoons flour

1½ cups chicken broth
¼ cup bourbon

Drain the fat from the roasting pan. Add butter to pan and place over low heat. Scrape the bottom of the pan to loosen bits. Stir in the flour and whisk vigorously for 2 minutes. Turn heat to medium. Stir in the chicken broth and bourbon. Cook, stirring constantly, until thickened.

Arlene Urbain, Mu Sigma
Plantation, Florida

DIXIE PORK CHOPS

3 tablespoons
  shortening
8 center-cut pork chops
½ teaspoon salt
½ teaspoon sage
4 tart apples, cored,
  sliced in rings

¼ cup packed brown
  sugar
2 tablespoons flour
½ cup water
1 tablespoon vinegar
½ cup seedless raisins

Heat the shortening and brown the chops in a heavy skillet. Arrange chops in a 9x13-inch baking dish. Sprinkle salt and sage over the chops. Cover with apple rings. Sprinkle the brown sugar over the apple rings. Stir the flour into the shortening in the skillet over medium heat; whisk until smooth. Stir in the water and vinegar gradually; cook until thick and smooth, stirring constantly. Stir in the raisins. Pour the flour mixture over the chops. Bake, uncovered, at 350 degrees for 1 hour. Yield: 8 servings.

Deanie Strehlow, Laureate Omicron
Eugene, Oregon

Laura Ross Wingfield, Xi Beta Kappa, Kansas City, Missouri, prepares Hash Brown Dinner Casserole by cooking a pound of ground beef with 1 onion until crumbly and mixing in a can of any cream soup. Spread in a baking pan and add a layer of hash browns mixed with 1 onion, a can of cream soup, 1 cup milk, 2 cups sour cream and 2 to 3 cups sharp Cheddar cheese. Bake at 350 degrees for 30 minutes. Top with 3 cups crushed cornflakes mixed with ½ cup melted margarine and bake for 30 minutes longer.

LOW-SODIUM PORK CHOPS

4 pork chops
1 teaspoon unsalted
   margarine or butter
1/2 medium onion, sliced
1 (15-ounce) can no-salt
   tomatoes
1 (6-ounce) can tomato
   paste

Pepper
Italian seasoning
1/2 to 1 teaspoon sugar
1 tablespoon vinegar
2 small zucchini, sliced
1/2 cup uncooked rice

Brown the chops in the margarine in a heavy skillet. Remove the chops. Sauté the onion until translucent. Return the chops to the skillet. Place the tomatoes, tomato paste, pepper, Italian seasoning, sugar and vinegar in the container of a blender or food processor; blend until smooth. Pour the tomato purée over the chops. Add the zucchini and rice. Simmer, covered, for about 1 hour or until chops test done. Add water if sauce becomes too thick. Yield: 4 servings.

Judy Funke, Zeta Sigma
Fairfield Bay, Arkansas

MARTINI SAUERKRAUT

1/4 cup (1/2 stick) butter
1/2 large onion, chopped
1 tart apple, chopped
1 (16-ounce) can
   sauerkraut
1 cup dry white wine
Dash of hot pepper
   sauce
1/2 teaspoon
   Worcestershire sauce

1/2 cup gin
1/2 pound carrots, cut
   into 2-inch pieces
3 potatoes, quartered
1 pound pork chops,
   browned
1 teaspoon chopped
   parsley
1/2 teaspoon seasoned
   salt

Melt the butter in a Dutch oven or large, heavy skillet and sauté the onion until tender. Stir in the apple, sauerkraut, wine, hot pepper sauce, Worcestershire sauce and gin. Simmer for 30 to 45 minutes. Cook the carrots and potatoes in a small amount of water in a large saucepan until tender. Preheat the oven to 350 degrees. Layer the sauerkraut mixture, pork chops and vegetables in a 2-quart baking dish. Sprinkle with parsley and seasoned salt. Bake, covered, for 35 to 45 minutes or until chops test done.
Yield: 4 to 6 servings.

Mary Ellen Grossman, Preceptor Gamma Eta
Lawrenceburg, Indiana

Linda Hoyer, Chi Zeta, Dunnellon, Florida, makes a Sausage Roll by sealing perforations of a can of crescent rolls, spreading with 8 ounces cream cheese, sprinkling with 1 pound browned sausage, rolling as for a jelly roll and baking for 12 to 15 minutes.

❖ ASPARAGUS PUFF RING

3/4 cup water
6 tablespoons butter
3/4 cup flour
1/2 teaspoon salt
3 eggs
1/4 cup grated Parmesan
   cheese
1 pound fresh
   asparagus, cut into
   1-inch pieces
1/4 cup chopped onion

2 tablespoons butter
2 tablespoons flour
1/2 teaspoon salt
1/4 teaspoon pepper
11/2 cups milk
1/2 cup shredded Cheddar
   cheese
2 tablespoons grated
   Parmesan cheese
2 cups chopped ham

Preheat the oven to 400 degrees. Bring the water and 6 tablespoons butter to a boil in a saucepan over medium heat. Add 3/4 cup flour and 1/2 teaspoon salt; stir until a smooth ball forms. Remove from heat and let stand for 5 minutes. Add the eggs 1 at a time, beating well after each addition. Stir in 3 tablespoons Parmesan cheese. Drop quarter-cupfuls of dough to form a ring as large as possible inside a greased 10x10-inch quiche pan. Sprinkle with 1 tablespoon Parmesan cheese. Bake for 35 minutes. Cook the asparagus in simmering water for 3 to 4 minutes or until tender-crisp; drain. Sauté the onion in 2 tablespoons butter in a skillet until tender. Stir in 2 tablespoons flour, 1/2 teaspoon salt and pepper. Add the milk gradually. Bring to a boil over medium heat, stirring constantly. Reduce heat to medium-low; stir in cheeses until melted. Stir in the ham and asparagus. Spoon into the pastry ring. Serve immediately. Yield: 6 servings.

Connie Nygren, Lambda Chi
Danville, Pennsylvania

FARMER'S CASSEROLE

The dish may be covered and refrigerated just after the egg mixture is added, for several hours or overnight. Increase the baking time to 55 to 60 minutes if prepared this way.

3 cups frozen shredded
   hash brown potatoes,
   thawed
1/4 cup shredded
   Monterey Jack cheese
   with jalapeño
   peppers or shredded
   Cheddar cheese
1 cup chopped fully
   cooked ham or
   Canadian bacon

1/4 cup sliced green
   onions
4 eggs, beaten, or 1 cup
   frozen egg substitute
1 (12-ounce) can
   evaporated milk or
   evaporated skim milk
1/4 teaspoon pepper
1/8 teaspoon salt

Preheat the oven to 350 degrees. Layer the potatoes evenly in the bottom of a greased 2-quart square baking dish. Layer the cheese, ham and green onions over the potatoes. Combine the eggs, evaporated milk, pepper and salt in a medium bowl; mix well. Pour the egg mixture over the potatoes and cheese in the dish. Bake, uncovered, for 40 to 45 minutes or until center appears set. Let stand 5 minutes before serving. Yield: 6 servings.

Valerie Rankin, Preceptor Epsilon Theta
Pinellas Park, Florida

HAM AND CHEESE PUFF

2 (1-pound) loaves Italian bread	1 medium onion, chopped
6 cups chopped cooked ham	16 eggs
	7 cups milk
1½ pounds Monterey Jack cheese, cubed	½ cup prepared mustard
¼ cup (½ stick) butter or margarine	

Cut the bread into 1-inch cubes. Mix the bread, ham and cheese in a large bowl. Spread the bread mixture in 2 greased 9x13x2-inch baking pans. Melt the butter in a skillet and sauté the onion until tender. Remove onion to a large bowl. Stir in the eggs, milk and mustard; mix well. Pour carefully over the pans of bread mixture. Chill, covered, for 8 to 10 hours. Remove from the refrigerator 30 minutes before baking. Preheat the oven to 350 degrees. Bake, uncovered, for 55 to 65 minutes, or until a knife inserted in the center comes out clean. Serve immediately.
Yield: 24 to 30 servings.

Faye A. Magers, Laureate Beta Upsilon
Chester, Illinois

SWEET-AND-SOUR HAM AND YAMS

2 (16-ounce) cans yams, drained	1 cup green bell pepper strips
¼ cup plus 2 tablespoons margarine	3 cups pineapple chunks, drained
½ teaspoon salt	¼ cup packed brown sugar
¼ teaspoon pepper	2 tablespoons cornstarch
⅛ teaspoon nutmeg	1½ cups pineapple juice
Milk	¼ cup vinegar
4 cups cooked ham, cubed	

Mash the yams in a medium mixer bowl. Add 2 tablespoons of the margarine, salt, pepper, nutmeg and enough milk to moisten. Beat on high speed for 2 minutes. Melt the remaining ¼ cup margarine in a

skillet and sauté the ham until lightly browned. Add the green pepper and pineapple chunks; sauté for 2 minutes. Combine the brown sugar and cornstarch; stir sugar mixture into ham mixture. Stir in the pineapple juice and vinegar. Cook until thickened and clear, stirring constantly. Pour into a shallow baking dish. Arrange scoops of the yam mixture over the top, using an ice cream scoop. Bake at 400 degrees for 25 minutes or until bubbly. Yield: 8 servings.

Marie M. Bray, Laureate Gamma Nu
Orlando, Florida

SWEDISH HAM LOAF

2 pounds ground ham	1 (10-ounce) can tomato soup
1½ pounds ground beef	
½ pound pork sausage	1½ cups packed brown sugar
2 cups crushed graham crackers	1 tablespoon dry mustard
2 eggs	½ cup vinegar
1½ cups milk	

Preheat the oven to 350 degrees. Combine the first 6 ingredients in a large bowl; mix well. Pat into a large loaf and place in a roasting pan. Combine the tomato soup, brown sugar, mustard and vinegar in a small bowl; mix well. Pour over the loaf. Bake, covered, for 1 hour, basting once or twice. Uncover and bake for 15 minutes longer. Yield: 16 to 20 servings.

Carol Miller, Laureate Beta Phi
Council Bluffs, Iowa

EASTER BRUNCH EGGS

12 thin slices Canadian bacon	½ teaspoon salt
	½ teaspoon pepper
3 (4-ounce) packages shredded Swiss cheese	⅓ cup grated Parmesan cheese
12 eggs	1 teaspoon paprika
1 cup half-and-half	¼ cup chopped parsley
¼ cup white wine (optional)	English muffins

Preheat the oven to 425 degrees. Arrange the Canadian bacon in a single layer in a lightly greased 9x13-inch baking dish. Sprinkle the Swiss cheese over the bacon. Pour eggs over evenly. Pour a mixture of half-and-half and wine over the eggs. Season with salt and pepper. Bake for 10 minutes. Sprinkle with the Parmesan cheese and paprika. Bake for 10 minutes longer or until set. Remove from the oven. Sprinkle with the parsley. Let stand 10 minutes. Serve over toasted English muffins. Yield: 8 to 10 servings.

Deborah A. Miller, Xi Beta Sigma
Hutchinson, Kansas

ROYAL BREAKFAST

1½ cups French bread cubes	12 cherry tomatoes, sliced into halves
½ pound cooked sausage or ham, cubed	8 ounces Cheddar cheese, shredded
1 (8-ounce) package frozen chopped spinach, thawed, drained	8 eggs
	1 cup milk
	1 teaspoon dried mustard
	¼ teaspoon pepper

Line a buttered 9x13x2-inch baking dish with bread cubes. Layer the sausage, spinach, tomatoes and Cheddar cheese over the bread. Whisk together the eggs, milk, mustard and pepper. Pour the egg mixture over the cheese layer. Chill, covered, for at least 1 hour and up to 10 hours. Bake, uncovered, at 350 degrees for 30 to 40 minutes or until lightly browned. Yield: 8 to 10 servings.

Glenna Priday, Preceptor Beta Sigma
Sikeston, Missouri

SCRAMBLED EGG MUFFINS

Serve with hash brown potatoes and a fresh fruit cup.

½ pound bulk pork sausage	½ teaspoon salt
12 eggs	¼ teaspoon pepper
½ cup chopped onion	¼ teaspoon garlic powder
¼ cup chopped green bell pepper	½ cup shredded Cheddar cheese

Preheat the oven to 350 degrees. Brown the sausage in a skillet, stirring until crumbly; drain. Beat the eggs well in a large bowl. Add the onion, green pepper, salt, pepper and garlic powder; mix well. Stir in the sausage and Cheddar cheese. Spoon about ⅓ cup of mixture into each of 12 greased muffin cups. Bake for 20 to 25 minutes or until a knife inserted in the center comes out clean. Yield: 12 servings.

Jenni McConnell, Epsilon Omega
Dalton, Nebraska

SOUTHWEST STEW

½ pound Polish sausage, cut up	1 each green and red bell pepper, chopped
1 (15-ounce) can black beans	1½ teaspoons chili powder
1 cup picante sauce	1 teaspoon cumin
1 large onion, chopped	Hot cooked rice
1 (8-ounce) can tomato sauce	Shredded cheese (optional)
1 cup frozen corn, thawed	Sour cream (optional)

Combine the sausage, beans, picante sauce, onion, tomato sauce, corn, green pepper, red pepper, chili powder and cumin in a large kettle. Bring to a boil. Reduce heat and simmer for about 30 minutes. Serve over hot rice. Garnish with cheese and sour cream if desired. Yield: 4 servings.

Mary Torrence, Iota Eta
Louisburg, Kansas

HONEY CURRY CHICKEN

¼ cup honey	1 (3-pound) chicken, cut up
1 tablespoon curry powder	1 medium onion, thinly sliced
1 teaspoon salt	2 tablespoons butter or margarine
¾ teaspoon ground ginger	¾ cup dry white wine
½ teaspoon pepper	

Preheat the oven to 400 degrees. Combine the honey and curry powder; blend well. Combine the salt, ginger and pepper. Rub the salt mixture over the chicken pieces. Layer the onion slices in the bottom of a well-greased 9x13-inch baking pan. Place the chicken pieces over the onions, skin side up. Dot with the butter. Pour the wine over the chicken. Bake for about 50 minutes, basting several times with the honey mixture during the last 20 minutes. Yield: 4 servings.

Anita Hanson, Delta Sigma
Boulder, Colorado

CARIBBEAN CHICKEN BREASTS

½ teaspoon coriander	¼ cup fresh lemon juice
¼ teaspoon ground ginger	3 tablespoons fresh orange juice
½ teaspoon cumin	3 tablespoons fresh lime juice
⅛ teaspoon cayenne pepper	⅓ cup mango chutney with jalapeños
4 boneless skinless chicken breast halves	Cilantro sprigs
1 tablespoon vegetable oil	Red chile peppers

Combine the coriander, ginger, cumin and cayenne in a small bowl. Rub the coriander mixture over the chicken. Heat the oil in a nonstick skillet over medium heat. Cook the chicken in the oil for 10 to 15 minutes or until the chicken is fork-tender, turning occasionally. Remove the chicken to a serving platter and keep warm by covering loosely with foil. Place the lemon juice, orange juice, lime juice and chutney in the skillet; stir well. Bring to a boil. Cook, stirring, for about 2 minutes or until mixture begins to thicken. Pour over the chicken. Garnish with cilantro and red chile peppers. Yield: 4 servings.

T-Ann Kerschner, Laureate Alpha Tau
McPherson, Kansas

CHICKEN BERBERE

Berberé is an Ethiopian spice mixture. Unused berberé can be kept in an airtight container for later use.

1 teaspoon ground ginger	1 tablespoon vegetable oil
3 tablespoons cayenne pepper	1 medium onion, chopped
1/4 teaspoon ground cloves	2 garlic cloves, minced
1/2 teaspoon cinnamon	1 tablespoon tomato paste
1 pound skinless chicken breasts	1/2 cup water
1 tablespoon butter	Salt and pepper to taste

Combine the ginger, cayenne pepper, cloves and cinnamon to make the berberé; blend well. Rinse the chicken and pat dry. Cut into bite-size pieces. Heat the butter and oil in a skillet and sauté the onion and garlic for a few minutes or until translucent. Sprinkle in 1/4 teaspoon or more of the berberé (use caution: the berberé is hot). Stir well. Add the tomato paste and the chicken, stirring to coat. Stir in the water. Simmer, covered, for 15 to 20 minutes or until chicken is no longer pink. Add salt and pepper. Place chicken on a serving platter. Drizzle the sauce over chicken. Garnish with slices of hard-cooked egg. Yield: 3 to 4 servings.

Donnette Hancock, Preceptor Eta
Coaldale, Alberta, Canada

CHICKEN BREASTS IN LEMON CREAM SAUCE

This chicken is best when served with egg noodles.

3 boneless skinless whole chicken breasts	2 tablespoons lemon juice
1/2 teaspoon salt	2 teaspoons cornstarch
1/4 teaspoon pepper	1 cup heavy cream
1/2 cup (1 stick) butter	1/2 cup grated Parmesan cheese
2 tablespoons dry sherry	
1 tablespoon grated lemon zest	

Rinse the chicken and pat dry; season with salt and pepper. Melt the butter in a skillet over medium heat and sauté the chicken for 12 minutes. Remove the chicken to an ungreased 9x13-inch baking dish. Stir the sherry, lemon zest and lemon juice into the butter remaining in the skillet. Whisk the cornstarch into the cream until incorporated. Add the cornstarch mixture slowly to the sherry mixture; bring to a boil. Cook for 1 minute, stirring constantly, until thickened. Pour the sherry sauce over the chicken. Sprinkle with the Parmesan cheese. Preheat the broiler. Broil for about 2 minutes or until golden brown. Yield: 6 servings.

Lisa Barta, Xi Epsilon Eta
Clearwater, British Columbia, Canada

CHICKEN CHILI

3 large boneless skinless chicken breasts	2 teaspoons garlic powder
2 tablespoons olive oil	2 teaspoons cumin
1 large onion, chopped	1 teaspoon oregano
2 cups chicken broth	1/2 teaspoon ground red pepper
2 (4-ounce) cans diced green chiles, undrained	4 (16-ounce) cans light or white beans, undrained
1 (4-ounce) can mushrooms, drained	4 green onions, chopped

Rinse the chicken and pat dry. Cut into bite-size pieces. Heat the olive oil in a skillet and sauté the chicken and onion for 5 minutes. Stir in the chicken broth, green chiles, mushrooms, garlic powder, cumin, oregano and red pepper. Simmer for 15 minutes. Stir in the beans; simmer for 5 minutes longer. Serve hot. Garnish with green onions.
Yield: 8 servings.

Cheryl A. Romeo, Xi Epsilon Upsilon
Moneta, Virginia

CHICKEN PICATTA

2 cups fresh bread crumbs	4 large chicken breasts
1/2 cup grated Parmesan cheese	1/2 cup melted butter
	1 teaspoon garlic salt
Freshly chopped parsley	1/3 cup melted butter
	2 teaspoons lemon juice

Preheat the oven to 325 degrees. Combine the bread crumbs, Parmesan cheese and parsley in a shallow bowl. Dip the chicken in the 1/2 cup butter, then in the bread crumbs to coat. Arrange on a baking sheet. Drizzle the rest of the 1/2 cup butter over the chicken. Bake for 40 minutes. Combine garlic salt, 1/3 cup butter and lemon juice in a bowl; mix well. Remove the chicken to a serving platter. Drizzle the lemon juice mixture over the chicken. Yield: 4 servings.

Judy Milner, Iota
Kokomo, Indiana

CHICKEN PAPRIKA

This recipe takes only about 45 minutes from start to finish.

2 pounds boneless
skinless chicken
breasts
4 tablespoons flour
2 teaspoons salt
6 tablespoons paprika
1/4 cup vegetable oil
Salt and pepper to taste
2 tablespoons butter or
margarine

1 large onion, finely
chopped
2 garlic cloves, crushed
2 teaspoons chopped
parsley
2 (14-ounce) cans
chicken broth
1 (6-ounce) can tomato
paste
Buttered noodles

Rinse the chicken and pat dry. Cut into bite-size pieces. Combine the flour, salt and 2 teaspoons of the paprika. Coat the chicken with the flour mixture. Heat the oil in a wok or a 10- or 12-inch skillet. Stir-fry the chicken pieces for 5 to 10 minutes or until golden. Remove the chicken. Add the butter to the wok; sauté the onion and garlic over low heat until soft and golden. Add the parsley, chicken broth, tomato paste and the remaining paprika; stir briefly. Return the chicken to the wok. Simmer, covered, for about 15 minutes or until chicken is tender. Serve over hot buttered noodles. Yield: 4 to 6 servings.

Kathleen A. Funk, Xi Alpha Psi
Sunbury, Pennsylvania

GUILTLESS CHICKEN BREASTS

6 boneless skinless
chicken breast
halves
1 1/2 cups light Italian
salad dressing
1 (14-ounce) can
artichoke hearts,
drained

1 (4-ounce) can sliced
mushrooms, drained
1 or 2 medium fresh
tomatoes, cut up
1/2 envelope onion soup
mix
1/2 cup white wine
(optional)

Rinse the chicken and pat dry. Marinate the chicken in 1 cup of the Italian dressing in a covered container in the refrigerator for 2 hours. Preheat the oven to 350 degrees. Arrange the chicken in a 9x12-inch baking pan with the marinade. Layer the artichoke hearts, mushrooms and fresh tomatoes over the chicken. Sprinkle the dried onion soup mix over the top. Drizzle with the remaining 1/2 cup Italian salad dressing and the wine. Bake, uncovered, for 1 hour. Serve over pasta or rice. Yield: 4 to 6 servings.

Marie Louise Greve, Beta Master
New Orleans, Louisiana

JADE EMPRESS CHICKEN

1/2 to 1 1/2 tablespoons
soy sauce
1 teaspoon grated
gingerroot
3 garlic cloves, chopped,
or 1/2 teaspoon garlic
powder
2 small boneless
skinless chicken
breast halves, cut
into 1-inch cubes
1/2 cup defatted chicken
broth

1 1/2 cups sliced fresh
mushrooms
1 1/2 cups sliced celery
1 cup coarsely chopped
onions
1 large green bell pepper,
cut into chunks
1 (8-ounce) can
unsweetened juice-
packed pineapple
tidbits
1 tablespoon arrowroot
3/4 cup sliced green onions

Combine the soy sauce, ginger and garlic in a shallow bowl. Spread the chicken cubes over the soy sauce mixture and chill, covered, for 2 to 10 hours. Bring the chicken broth to a boil in a large skillet or Dutch oven over medium-high heat. Stir in the mushrooms. Cook, stirring, for 2 minutes. Stir in the celery, onions and green pepper. Cook, stirring for 2 minutes longer. Stir in the chicken mixture. Cook, stirring, for about 2 minutes or until chicken is opaque. Drain the pineapple, reserving the juice. Add enough water to measure 3/4 cup. Blend the pineapple juice with the arrowroot. Stir into the chicken mixture. Cook until thickened, stirring constantly. Add the pineapple and 1/2 cup of the green onions. Serve over hot brown rice. Garnish with the remaining green onions. Yield: 4 servings.

Pat King, Xi Epsilon Epsilon
Albra, Iowa

LEMON GREEK CHICKEN

4 split bone-in chicken
breast halves (about
2 1/2 to 3 pounds)
2 teaspoons grated
lemon zest
1/4 cup lemon juice
2 tablespoons olive oil
4 large garlic cloves,
crushed
2 to 3 teaspoons dried
oregano leaves

3/4 teaspoon salt
1/8 teaspoon pepper
2 medium baking
potatoes
1 medium red bell
pepper, cut into
1-inch pieces
1 medium red onion, cut
into wedges
8 ounces fresh whole
mushrooms

Preheat the oven to 400 degrees. Rinse the chicken and pat dry. Combine the lemon zest, lemon juice and olive oil in a medium bowl. Stir in the garlic, oregano, salt and pepper. Cut each potato lengthwise into 8 wedges. Arrange in a 9x13-inch baking pan. Add the red bell pepper, onion, mushrooms and half the lemon juice mixture; toss to coat. Arrange the

chicken breast halves over the vegetables. Brush with the remaining lemon juice mixture. Bake for 1 hour or until chicken is no longer pink in center, brushing chicken and vegetables with the pan juices once or twice after 30 minutes of baking time.
Yield: 4 servings.

Michele Balthrop, Beta Zeta Theta
Ft. Worth, Texas

MEXICAN-STYLE CHICKEN KIEV

8 boneless skinless chicken breast halves	*2 teaspoons chili powder*
2 (4-ounce) cans whole green chiles, drained	*1/2 teaspoon garlic salt*
4 ounces Monterey Jack cheese	*1/2 teaspoon cumin*
1/2 cup dry bread crumbs	*1/4 teaspoon pepper*
1/4 cup grated Parmesan cheese	*2 tablespoons melted margarine*

Preheat the oven to 400 degrees. Rinse the chicken and pat dry. Flatten to 1/4-inch thickness. Remove the seeds from the chiles and cut each into 8 pieces. Cut the Monterey Jack cheese into 8 (2 1/2 x 1/2-inch) sticks. Place 1 cheese stick and 1 chile piece over the center of each chicken breast. Fold over the short sides and roll up along the long sides to enclose the filling. Secure with a toothpick if necessary. Combine the bread crumbs, Parmesan cheese, chili powder, garlic salt, cumin and pepper in a shallow bowl. Dip the rolled chicken in the margarine. Roll in the bread crumb mixture. Place seam side down in a greased 9x13x2-inch baking dish. Bake for 25 to 30 minutes or until chicken tests done. Yield: 8 servings.

Shirley Fitch, Preceptor Rho
Flagstaff, Arizona

MOROCCAN CHICKEN

4 boneless skinless chicken breasts	*1/4 teaspoon ground cinnamon*
1/3 cup water	*1/4 teaspoon ground ginger*
1 cup chopped peeled eggplant	*1/4 teaspoon ground turmeric*
1/2 cup chopped onion	
1/2 green bell pepper, chopped	*1/4 teaspoon salt*
1 (14-ounce) can stewed tomatoes	*1/4 teaspoon pepper*
	Dash of ground cloves
1 (8-ounce) can tomato sauce	

Rinse the chicken and pat dry. Spray a 10-inch non-stick skillet with nonstick cooking spray. Preheat the skillet for a few minutes over medium heat. Cook the chicken in the skillet, turning occasionally, for 15 to 20 minutes or until chicken is no longer pink. Remove the chicken; keep warm. Add the water, eggplant, onion and green pepper to the skillet. Bring to a boil. Reduce heat to medium and cook, covered, for about 10 minutes or until vegetables are tender; drain. Stir in the remaining ingredients. Bring to a boil. Reduce heat and simmer, uncovered, for 10 minutes. Add the chicken and heat through.
Yield: 4 servings.

Barbara Dixon, Preceptor Tau
Courtenay, British Columbia, Canada

SWEET-AND-SOUR CHICKEN

4 to 6 chicken breasts	*1/4 cup water*
1 cup Russian salad dressing	*1 (8- or 15-ounce) can pineapple tidbits*
1 cup apricot preserves	*1 green bell pepper, sliced*
1 envelope onion soup mix	

Preheat the oven to 350 degrees. Wash the chicken and pat dry. Arrange the chicken in a greased 9x13-inch baking dish. Combine the salad dressing, preserves, onion soup mix and water; mix well. Pour over the chicken. Bake, covered, for 1 hour. Add the pineapple and green pepper. Bake, uncovered, for 30 minutes longer. Yield: 4 to 6 servings.

Sheri Anderson, Lambda Omega
Weatherford, Oklahoma

ZESTY POTATO CHICKEN BAKE

1 pound boneless skinless chicken breasts	*1 large red bell pepper, cut into 1/2-inch squares*
1/2 cup red wine vinegar	*1 pound mushrooms, sliced*
1/4 cup olive oil or vegetable oil	*2 garlic cloves, sliced*
2 pounds small red potatoes, quartered	*1 cup chopped fresh parsley*
1 yellow onion, cut into 1/2-inch chunks	*Salt and pepper to taste*

Preheat the oven to 350 degrees. Wash the chicken and pat dry. Cut into 1-inch cubes. Place the chicken, red wine vinegar and olive oil in a large container. Add the next 6 ingredients to the container, 1 at a time as vegetable is chopped. Toss ingredients with each addition to blend the flavors. Arrange the chicken mixture in an 11x13-inch baking dish. Bake for 45 minutes to 1 hour or until potatoes and chicken test done. Yield: 5 to 6 servings.

Darlene Johnson, Laureate Psi
Altus, Oklahoma

LOW-FAT CHICKEN ENCHILADAS

Serve with rice, beans, and chips.

2 tablespoons light margarine	2 cups no-salt-added chicken broth
1/2 cup chopped onion	1 cup shredded mozzarella cheese
4 garlic cloves, minced	
1/4 teaspoon pepper	2 cups chopped cooked chicken or turkey
3 tablespoons flour	
8 ounces fat-free sour cream	8 (6-inch) flour tortillas

Melt the margarine in a skillet over medium heat and sauté the onion, garlic and pepper until onion is tender. Stir the flour into the sour cream; blend well. Add the flour mixture to the onion mixture. Stir in the chicken broth. Cook, stirring, until thickened and bubbly. Remove from heat. Stir in 1/2 cup of the cheese. Preheat the oven to 350 degrees. Combine the chopped chicken and 1/2 cup of the chicken broth sauce in a medium bowl to make the filling. Place about 1/4 cup filling over each tortilla; roll up. Arrange the rolls seam side down in a lightly greased 8x12-inch shallow baking dish. Drizzle the remaining chicken broth sauce over the rolls. Bake, covered, for about 35 minutes or until heated through. Serve with sliced olives, chopped tomatoes and sliced green onions. Yield: 4 servings.

Shelly Naccarato, Rho Kappa
Andover, Kansas

MICROWAVE CAN-OPENER ENCHILADAS

1 (10-ounce) can cream of chicken soup	2 (5-ounce) cans chunk chicken, drained, flaked
1 (8-ounce) can cream-style corn, partially drained	1/2 cup sour cream
	1/4 cup milk
1/2 cup sliced green onions	12 (6-inch) flour tortillas
1 tablespoon chili powder	1 1/2 cups shredded Cheddar cheese

Combine the cream of chicken soup, corn, green onions and chili powder in a microwave-safe bowl. Microwave, uncovered, on High for 4 minutes, stirring after 2 minutes. Stir in the chicken, sour cream and milk. Spread about 1 1/4 cups of the chicken mixture over the bottom of a microwave-safe 7 1/2x12x2-inch pan. Cut a slit in the package of tortillas and Microwave on High for 1 minute or until tortillas are hot. Place 1/4 cup of the chicken mixture and 1 tablespoon of the cheese over each tortilla. Roll up tortillas and place seam side down over the chicken mixture in the baking dish. Microwave, uncovered, on High for 6 to 8 minutes or until heated through. Sprinkle remaining cheese over the tortillas and Microwave for 1 minute or until cheese melts. Garnish with green pepper rings and ripe olives if desired. Yield: 6 servings.

Ursula Ericson, Delta Mu Gamma
Hemet, California

STUFFED BLUEBERRY DUCK

I won First Prize with this original recipe in the Blueberry Cook Contest at the 1987 Blueberry Festival in Poplarville, Mississippi.

2 tablespoons shortening	1/2 teaspoon salt
	1/2 teaspoon pepper
1 tablespoon chopped onion	1 large duck
	2 tablespoons butter
1/2 cup chopped celery	1/2 cup honey
2 cups fresh blueberries	2 tablespoons fresh lemon juice
1 cup water	
4 cups Italian-style bread crumbs	2 tablespoons cornstarch
1 tablespoon chopped parsley	2 tablespoons orange juice

Melt the shortening in a skillet and sauté the onion and celery until translucent. Stir in 1 cup of the blueberries, water, bread crumbs, parsley, salt and pepper. Preheat the oven to 400 degrees. Clean the duck. Rub inside and out with butter. Stuff with the blueberry stuffing. Place duck breast down with 1/2 cup water in a large roasting pan. Roast, covered, for about 10 minutes or until lightly browned. Pour off the excess fat. Turn duck breast side up. Reduce oven heat to 350 degrees. Roast, covered, for 1 hour longer, or until duck is well done. Combine the honey, lemon juice, the remaining cup of blueberries, cornstarch and orange juice in a small saucepan; heat, stirring well. Spoon the blueberry glaze over the duck at serving time. Yield: 4 servings.

Lilitha Bonvillian, Xi Alpha Delta
Metairie, Louisiana

Bobbie Moody, Eta, Florence, South Carolina, makes Chicken Salad Pie by mixing 2 cups chopped cooked chicken, 3/4 cup shredded Cheddar cheese, 1/2 cup each chopped celery, drained crushed pineapple, chopped pecans, mayonnaise and 1/2 teaspoon paprika. Spoon into a baked pie shell and spread with mixture of 1/4 cup mayonnaise and 1/2 cup whipped topping. Garnish with carrots and chill until serving time.

PHEASANT DELUXE

This was my mother's recipe for a delicious alternative to pan-frying during pheasant season in Kansas. Serve with crescent rolls and a gelatin salad.

1 fresh pheasant
3 eggs, beaten
1 (10-ounce) can cream
   of mushroom soup
1 onion, chopped
1/2 teaspoon pepper
1/2 teaspoon salt
1 1/2 cups chopped celery

1 1/2 cups cubed Velveeta
   cheese, or 1 1/2 cups
   shredded Cheddar
   cheese
4 to 5 cups crushed
   butter crackers
3 cups chicken broth

Clean the pheasant. Simmer in a kettle in salted water to cover for 30 to 40 minutes or until cooked through and tender. Remove meat from bones. Preheat the oven to 350 degrees. Combine the eggs, cream of mushroom soup, onion, pepper, salt, celery, Velveeta cheese, butter crackers and chicken broth in a large bowl. Stir in the pheasant meat. Spread the mixture over the bottom of a 9x12-inch baking dish. Bake for 1 hour, or until browned on top.
Yield: 10 to 12 servings.

Barbara L. Albers, Mu Epsilon
Colby, Kansas

❖ ARTICHOKE TURKEY CASSEROLE

1/2 cup chopped carrot
1/2 cup chopped red bell
   pepper
1/4 cup sliced green
   onions
3 tablespoons water
1 (10-ounce) can
   reduced-fat, reduced-
   sodium cream of
   chicken soup
1 (9-ounce) package
   frozen artichoke
   hearts, rinsed,
   chopped
1 1/2 cups chopped cooked
   turkey or chicken

1 cup cooked wild rice
   and/or long grain rice
1/2 cup shredded
   mozzarella cheese
1/2 cup nonfat milk
2 tablespoons dry sherry
   or milk
2 tablespoons bacon
   bits, or 2 slices
   bacon, crisp-cooked,
   crumbled
3 tablespoons grated
   Parmesan cheese

Preheat the oven to 350 degrees. Cook the carrot, red bell pepper and green onions in the water in a large skillet until tender-crisp. Remove from heat. Stir in the next 8 ingredients; mix well. Spread in a 2-quart rectangular baking dish. Sprinkle with Parmesan cheese. Bake, covered, for 20 minutes. Bake, uncovered, for 20 minutes longer or until bubbly.
Yield: 6 servings.

Idella Allen, Laureate Alpha Mu
Joseph, Oregon

ZUCCHINI TURKEY CASSEROLE

1 pound ground turkey
1 1/2 cups tomato sauce
1/4 cup red wine
4 medium zucchini,
   thinly sliced
1 teaspoon oregano
1/2 teaspoon basil

1 teaspoon garlic salt
1 3/4 cups shredded
   mozzarella cheese
1/4 cup grated Parmesan
   cheese
1/4 cup seasoned bread
   crumbs

Brown the ground turkey in a skillet, stirring until crumbly; drain. Combine the tomato sauce, wine, zucchini, oregano, basil and garlic salt in a medium bowl. Stir the zucchini mixture into the turkey and simmer for about 10 minutes. Preheat the oven to 350 degrees. Layer the turkey mixture and mozzarella cheese in a 1 1/2-quart baking dish. Sprinkle with Parmesan cheese and bread crumbs. Bake, uncovered, for 10 to 15 minutes or until cheese melts.
Yield: 4 servings.

Nancy Wahl, Epsilon Master
Cinnaminson, New Jersey

HALIBUT PARMESAN

1/2 cup grated Parmesan
   cheese
3 tablespoons
   mayonnaise
1/4 cup (1/2 stick) butter,
   softened
3 tablespoons chopped
   green onions
1/2 teaspoon salt

1/2 teaspoon prepared
   mustard
Dash of Tabasco sauce
2 pounds halibut fillets
   or other mild white
   fish
3 tablespoons lemon
   juice

Preheat the broiler. Combine the Parmesan cheese, mayonnaise, butter, green onions, salt, mustard and Tabasco sauce in a small bowl; blend well. Arrange the fillets in a single layer over the bottom of a buttered 9x13-inch baking pan. Sprinkle lemon juice over the fillets. Broil 4 inches from heat source for 5 to 8 minutes or until almost done. Remove from heat. Spread the mayonnaise mixture over the fillets. Broil for 2 to 3 minutes longer until browned.
Yield: 6 servings.

Heide Massetti, Laureate Sigma
Norfolk, Virginia

Jaylene Roberts, Delta Upsilon, Othello, Washington, makes Tuna Burgers. Mix 1 can drained tuna, 1 egg, 1/2 cup Italian bread crumbs, 1/3 cup chopped onion, 1/4 cup chopped celery and mayonnaise and season with salt, pepper, dillweed and Worcestershire sauce. Shape into patties, brown in a skillet sprayed with non-stick spray and serve on buns with lettuce and tomato.

HALIBUT VERONIQUE

½ package dried
   mushroom soup mix
1 cup sour cream
1 tablespoon lemon
   juice
½ cup dry white wine
   (chardonnay)
1 teaspoon salt
½ teaspoon pepper

Dash each of basil,
   thyme and marjoram
½ cup bleached
   almonds, slivered
1 cup seedless red or
   green grapes
4 pounds halibut fillets
2 tablespoons butter

Combine the mushroom soup mix, sour cream, lemon juice, wine, salt, pepper, basil, thyme and marjoram in a 2- or 4-quart saucepan over medium-low heat. Heat through, stirring until smooth. Add almonds and grapes to the sour cream mixture. Brown all sides of the halibut fillets lightly in the butter in a large skillet over medium-low heat. Drizzle half the sour cream mixture over the fish. Simmer, covered, for 15 minutes or until fish flakes when pierced with a fork. Serve with the remaining sour cream mixture as a sauce. Add rice and a good white wine. Yield: 6 to 8 servings.

Heather Corral, Alpha Eta
Tucson, Arizona

RUM RUNNER GROUPER

Serve with fresh fruit salad, asparagus spears, yellow squash, and crescent rolls, add island decorations on the table, and have your guests dress in island attire for an island party!

½ cup (1 stick) butter
1 tablespoon olive oil
Salt and pepper to taste
1½ pounds fresh grouper
¼ cup flour
1 tablespoon white wine
1 tablespoon lemon
   juice

2 to 3 tablespoons
   capers
1 (4-ounce) can sliced
   mushrooms
1 (14-ounce) can diced
   tomatoes
Green onions, diced

Melt the butter in a skillet over medium heat. Stir in the olive oil. Salt and pepper the grouper and dust it lightly with the flour. Brown the grouper lightly in the butter mixture. Add the wine, lemon juice, capers, mushrooms, tomatoes and green onions. Simmer over low heat, stirring to keep from sticking, for 10 to 15 minutes or until fish is flaky. Yield: 6 to 8 servings.

Marjorie Dorman, Laureate Epsilon Beta
Valrico, Florida

CRANBERRY-GLAZED SALMON

1 cup whole cranberry
   sauce
¼ cup honey
⅛ cup light soy sauce
2 garlic cloves, minced

1 tablespoon minced
   gingerroot
¼ teaspoon pepper
4 skinless salmon fillets,
   about 1½ pounds

Preheat the oven to 350 degrees. Combine the cranberry sauce, honey, soy sauce, garlic, gingerroot and pepper in a medium bowl; blend well. Arrange the salmon fillets in a single layer in a lightly greased baking pan. Spoon the cranberry mixture evenly over the fillets. Bake for about 10 minutes or until salmon flakes when tested with a fork. Yield: 4 servings.

Barbara Miller, Preceptor Beta Omicron
Schaumburg, Illinois

GRILLED SALMON WITH PINEAPPLE SALSA

This is a low-fat dish that will evoke memories of South Sea islands. Serve with a mixed green salad, sautéed asparagus, and steamed new potatoes with a touch of dill.

½ teaspoon lime juice
1½ teaspoons lemon
   juice
1 teaspoon minced
   shallots
1 teaspoon minced
   garlic
¼ teaspoon cracked
   black peppercorns
1½ pounds salmon
   fillets
2 tablespoons unsalted
   butter
2 teaspoons minced
   shallots
1 teaspoon minced
   jalapeño pepper

2 teaspoons minced
   gingerroot
¾ pound chopped fresh
   pineapple
¼ cup chopped fresh
   papaya
¾ cup fresh orange juice
1½ teaspoons chopped
   mint
1½ teaspoons chopped
   basil
½ teaspoon chopped
   cilantro
½ teaspoon curry
   powder

Combine the first 5 ingredients in a small bowl; mix well. Marinate the salmon in the lime juice mixture in a covered container in the refrigerator for 3 to 10 hours. Melt the butter in a skillet over medium heat and sauté 2 teaspoons shallots, jalapeño pepper and gingerroot for 3 minutes. Stir in the pineapple, papaya, orange juice, mint, basil, cilantro and curry powder. Warm gently over low heat. Do not allow to come to a simmer. Grill the salmon. Serve with the warm pineapple salsa. Yield: 4 to 5 servings.

Elizabeth Ebbing, Laureate Gamma Lambda
Lima, Ohio

CLAM WHIFFLE

12 ounces soda crackers,
   crumbled
1 cup milk
1/4 cup (1/2 stick) melted
   butter
1 (6-ounce) can minced
   clams, drained
2 tablespoons chopped
   onion

1 tablespoon chopped
   green bell pepper
   (optional)
1/4 teaspoon
   Worcestershire sauce
Dash of salt and pepper
2 eggs, beaten

Preheat the oven to 350 degrees. Soak the crumbled crackers in the milk in a medium bowl for a few minutes. Stir in the butter, clams, onion, green pepper, Worcestershire sauce, salt, pepper and eggs, in that order. Pour into a greased 2-quart baking dish. Bake for 45 minutes. Yield: 4 to 6 servings.

Margaret Sims, Delta Theta
Hooperton, Illinois

QUICK MOCK CRAB CASSEROLE

1 small bunch fresh
   broccoli, cut into
   bite-size pieces
1 (10-ounce) can cream
   of mushroom soup
1/2 cup milk

1 pound imitation crab
   meat, shredded
1/2 small onion, sautéed
   (optional)
1/2 cup sliced fresh
   mushrooms

Microwave the broccoli on High with 1/4 cup water in a loosely-covered microwave-safe dish for 4 minutes. Drain. Combine the cream of mushroom soup and milk in a small bowl; blend well. Toss crab meat with the broccoli, onion and mushrooms in a medium bowl. Pour the cream of mushroom soup mixture over the broccoli mixture. Microwave on High for 4 to 5 minutes or until hot. Yield: 6 servings.

Jan Freauf, Xi Beta Beta
Lincoln, Nebraska

CRAB OMELET

6 eggs, beaten
1 cup flaked crab meat
2 tablespoons soy sauce
1 teaspoon salt
1/4 teaspoon pepper
3 tablespoons
   cornstarch
1/4 cup vegetable oil

1 cup chopped bamboo
   shoots
1/2 cup chopped onion
1/2 cup sliced celery
1 tablespoon catsup
1 teaspoon sherry
1/2 cup water
Fresh parsley

Combine the eggs, crab meat, 1 tablespoon of the soy sauce, salt, pepper and 1 tablespoon of the cornstarch in a large bowl; mix well. Heat 2 tablespoons of the oil in a skillet over medium heat and sauté the bam-boo shoots, onion and celery for 1 minute. Remove from heat. Let cool. Stir the vegetable mixture into the egg mixture; mix well. Heat the remaining 2 tablespoons oil in the skillet. Pour 2 tablespoons of the egg mixture in the skillet and fry until golden brown to make an individual omelet. Add more oil if needed to make remaining omelets. Combine the remaining 2 tablespoons cornstarch, remaining 1 tablespoon soy sauce, catsup, sherry and water in a small saucepan over medium heat. Bring to a boil. Reduce heat and simmer, stirring constantly, for 5 to 10 minutes or until thickened. Pour the sherry sauce over the individual omelets. Garnish with fresh parsley. Yield: 4 to 6 servings.

Roberta T. White, Eta Master
Las Cruces, New Mexico

THAI SHRIMP AND SCALLOPS

This dish can be prepared ahead of time up to the point of adding shrimp and scallops.

1 medium lemon
1 tablespoon vegetable
   oil
1/2 cup chopped onion
6 garlic cloves, minced
1/4 cup finely chopped
   gingerroot
1 tablespoon flour
3/4 cup light coconut
   milk
1/4 cup white wine
1/4 teaspoon crushed red
   pepper flakes

1 1/2 pounds extra-large
   shrimp, peeled,
   deveined
1/2 pound large scallops
1/3 cup freshly chopped
   parsley
1/3 cup freshly chopped
   cilantro
3 green onions, finely
   chopped

Grate the zest and squeeze the juice from the lemon; set aside. Heat the oil in a large nonstick saucepan over medium heat and sauté the onion, garlic and gingerroot for about 5 minutes or until tender. Sprinkle with the flour; stir to combine. Stir in the coconut milk, wine, lemon zest, lemon juice and red pepper flakes. Bring to a simmer, stirring constantly. Stir in the shrimp and scallops. Simmer, covered, stirring occasionally, for 5 to 10 minutes or until shrimp are pink and scallops opaque. Stir in the parsley and cilantro. Sprinkle with the green onions. Serve over rice, Thai jasmine rice if possible, accompanied by green beans. Yield: 4 to 6 servings.

Tina Bowers, Xi Beta Mu
Trenton, Ontario, Canada

Pastas

BRING 'EM HOME CASSEROLE

For a fantastic crowd pleaser, simply double this recipe.

1½ pounds ground beef
1 medium onion,
   chopped
1 medium green bell
   pepper, chopped
1½ teaspoons garlic
   powder
½ cup chopped celery
1 (4-ounce) can
   mushroom stems and
   pieces
1 tablespoon pimentos

1 tablespoon
   Worcestershire sauce
1 (10-ounce) can tomato
   soup
½ cup picante sauce
1 cup medium egg
   noodles, cooked,
   drained
Salt and pepper to taste
1 cup shredded Cheddar
   cheese

Preheat the oven to 350 degrees. Brown the ground beef in a large skillet with the onion, green pepper and garlic powder, stirring until ground beef is crumbly; drain. Add the remaining ingredients except cheese; mix well. Simmer for 5 minutes. Pour into a greased 9x13x2-inch baking dish. Bake for 40 to 45 minutes or until hot and bubbly. Sprinkle the cheese over the top or mix it into the beef mixture just before serving. Yield: 10 to 12 servings.

Gloria Kostelnik, Xi Upsilon Epsilon
Hallettsville, Texas

CHEESY TACO CASSEROLE

1 (8-ounce) package
   elbow macaroni
1 pound ground beef
1 envelope taco
   seasoning mix
1 (15-ounce) can tomato
   sauce
¼ cup milk

2½ cups shredded sharp
   Cheddar cheese
1 (3-ounce) can French-
   fried onions
1 cup shredded lettuce
1 tomato, chopped
1 cup crushed taco chips

Cook the macaroni using package directions; drain. Brown the ground beef in a large skillet, stirring until crumbly; drain. Stir in the taco seasoning and tomato sauce. Simmer, uncovered, for 5 minutes. Combine the hot macaroni with milk and 2 cups of the Cheddar cheese. Layer half the macaroni mixture and half the ground beef mixture in a greased 3-quart baking dish. Sprinkle the French-fried onions over the ground beef layer. Layer the remaining macaroni mixture and ground beef mixture over the French-fried onion layer. Bake at 375 degrees for 20 minutes or until bubbly. Top with the shredded lettuce, tomatoes, taco chips and the remaining ½ cup cheese. Serve immediately. Yield: 6 to 8 servings.

Brenda Parezo, Beta
Clive, Iowa

SLOW-COOKER PIZZA

1 (16-ounce) package egg
   noodles
1 pound ground beef
1 onion, chopped
1 (3½-ounce) package
   sliced pepperoni
1 (14-ounce) jar
   spaghetti sauce

1 (14-ounce) jar pizza
   sauce
1 (8-ounce) package
   shredded mozzarella
   cheese
1 (8 ounce) package
   shredded Cheddar
   cheese

Cook the noodles using package directions. Brown the ground beef with the onion in a skillet, stirring until ground beef is crumbly; drain. Grease all inside surfaces of a slow cooker. Layer the noodles, ground beef mixture, pepperoni, spaghetti sauce, pizza sauce, mozzarella cheese and Cheddar cheese in the order listed, ½ at a time. Cook on High for 1 hour, or on Low for 6 to 8 hours. Yield: 6 or more servings.

Dana A. Lewis, Chi Theta
Paris, Illinois

PASTITSIO (MACARONI AND MEAT CASSEROLE)

Serve with bread, wine, and a Greek salad.

1 large onion, chopped
1 cup (2 sticks) butter,
   melted
2½ pounds lean ground
   beef
2 teaspoons salt
1 teaspoon pepper
1 tablespoon dried
   parsley
1 (8-ounce) can tomato
   sauce

1½ teaspoons cinnamon
Dash of sugar
1 (16-ounce) package
   elbow macaroni
Cream Sauce
2½ cups grated
   Parmesan cheese
8 slices American cheese

Preheat the oven to 350 degrees. Sauté the onion in ½ cup of the butter in a large saucepan over medium heat for 5 minutes or until tender. Brown the ground beef in a skillet, stirring until crumbly; drain. Stir the ground beef, salt, pepper, parsley, tomato sauce, cinnamon and sugar into the sautéed onion. Simmer for 30 minutes or until liquid is absorbed. Cook the macaroni in boiling salted water with a spoonful of olive oil for a little less time than specified in package directions, or until almost done. Rinse. Drain. Combine with the remaining ½ cup butter in a large bowl. Stir in a small amount of Cream Sauce. Sprinkle 2 tablespoons of the Parmesan cheese over the bottom of a greased 11x14-inch baking pan. Layer half the macaroni mixture in the pan. Sprinkle with ⅔ cup of the Parmesan cheese. Cover with the ground beef mixture. Arrange the American cheese slices over the ground beef layer. Layer the remaining macaroni mixture and another ⅔ cup Parmesan cheese over the American cheese. Sprinkle with cinnamon. Cover with the remaining Cream Sauce. Sprinkle with any remaining Parmesan cheese. Yield: 24 servings.

CREAM SAUCE

1 cup (2 sticks) butter
½ cup flour
5 cups warm milk
6 eggs

1 teaspoon salt
¼ teaspoon pepper
¼ teaspoon nutmeg

Melt the butter in a saucepan over medium-low heat. Whisk in the flour. Add the milk gradually, cooking until thickened, stirring constantly. Add the eggs 1 at a time, stirring well after each addition. Cook until thickened, stirring constantly. Stir in the salt, pepper and nutmeg.

Sharon Michailidis, Preceptor Rho
Sioux Falls, South Dakota

LASAGNA

You may substitute cottage cheese or ricotta cheese for one of the cheese layers if desired.

1½ pounds ground beef
1 (32-ounce) jar
   spaghetti sauce
1 (8-ounce) package
   lasagna noodles

2 (8-ounce) packages
   shredded mozzarella
   cheese
1 (8-count) package
   crescent rolls

Preheat the oven to 350 degrees. Brown the ground beef in a skillet, stirring until crumbly; drain. Stir in the spaghetti sauce. Bring to a simmer. Prepare the lasagna noodles using package directions; drain. Cover the bottom of a 9x13-inch baking pan with half the noodles. Layer half the ground beef mixture, half the mozzarella cheese, the remaining lasagna noodles, the remaining ground beef mixture and the remaining mozzarella cheese over the noodles. Spread crescent roll dough over the top. Bake for 7 to 10 minutes or until golden brown. May substitute mozzarella and Cheddar cheese combination for the mozzarella cheese. Yield: 15 to 16 servings.

Tami Mann, Iota Delta
Oskaloosa, Iowa

Helen Schoenrock, Lambda Master, Fairbury, Nebraska, makes Speedy Skillet Lasagna with a pound of ground beef cooked, drained and mixed with a jar of spaghetti sauce, 2½ cups water and 8 ounces pasta. Simmer for 15 minutes and sprinkle with 1 cup mozzarella cheese.

CREAMY GROUND BEEF CASSEROLE

I usually prepare this dinner in two baking dishes so I can freeze one for later use.

2 pounds ground beef	1/4 cup cottage cheese
1 teaspoon garlic salt	1 cup sour cream
1 (15-ounce) can tomato sauce	3 green onions, finely chopped
1 (16-ounce) package thin noodles	1/2 cup shredded sharp Cheddar cheese
8 ounces cream cheese, softened	

Brown the ground beef in a skillet, stirring until crumbly; drain. Stir in the garlic salt and tomato sauce. Simmer for 15 minutes. Cook the noodles according to package directions; drain. Combine the cream cheese, cottage cheese, sour cream and green onions in a medium bowl; mix well. Layer the noodles, cream cheese mixture and ground beef mixture in a greased 2- to 3-quart baking dish. Sprinkle the Cheddar cheese over the top. Yield: 10 to 12 servings.

Brenda J. Broome, Preceptor Zeta Gamma
Tampa, Florida

❖ SALSA MAC AND CHEESE

1 pound ground beef	1 (8-ounce) package elbow macaroni
1 envelope taco seasoning mix	1 1/2 to 2 cups shredded Cheddar cheese
2 cups chunky salsa	
2 cups water	

Brown the ground beef in a large skillet, stirring until crumbly; drain. Stir in the taco seasoning mix, salsa and water; mix well. Bring to a boil. Stir in the macaroni. Reduce the heat and simmer, covered, for 8 to 10 minutes or until macaroni is tender. Stir in the Cheddar cheese. Heat, stirring, until cheese is melted. Yield: 6 to 8 servings.

Grace Durham, Xi Mu Omega
Miami, Florida

SPAGHETTI AND MEATBALLS

Make lasagna with the leftovers by slicing the meatballs to layer with the pasta and cheese.

Herbed Spaghetti Sauce	3 teaspoons parsley flakes
3/4 pound ground beef	1 teaspoon sweet basil
3/4 pound pork sausage	1 teaspoon pepper
1 cup bread crumbs	1 teaspoon garlic powder
3/4 cup shredded aged Swiss cheese	1 tablespoon salt
3 eggs, beaten	

Start preparing Herbed Spaghetti Sauce. Combine the ground beef, sausage, bread crumbs, Swiss cheese, eggs, parsley flakes, basil, pepper, garlic powder and salt in a large bowl; mix well. Roll into balls. Brown the meatballs evenly in a large skillet over medium heat. Stir meatballs into Herbed Spaghetti Sauce for the last hour of cooking time. Serve over spaghetti or fettuccini. Sprinkle with Parmesan cheese. Yield: 6 to 8 servings.

HERBED SPAGHETTI SAUCE

2 (29-ounce) cans tomatoes, cut up	1 teaspoon pepper
2 (8-ounce) cans tomato sauce	1 teaspoon sweet basil
	2 teaspoons parsley
2 (6-ounce) cans tomato paste	1/2 teaspoon garlic powder
1 tablespoon salt	3 cups water

Combine the canned tomatoes, tomato sauce, tomato paste, salt, pepper, basil, parsley, garlic powder and water in a large kettle. Simmer for 1 hour, stirring occasionally. Cover and simmer for 1 hour longer.

Maryanne Bernet, Lambda Master
Coldwater, Michigan

GRANDMA'S SPECIAL SPAGHETTI SAUCE

Enjoy this special sauce over your favorite pasta. Leftovers can be frozen.

1 1/2 to 2 pounds ground beef	1 quart canned tomatoes
1 cup chopped celery	1 teaspoon salt
4 medium onions, chopped	1 teaspoon chili powder
	1/2 teaspoon Tabasco sauce
1 cup (2 sticks) butter	2 teaspoons Worcestershire sauce
2 (8-ounce) cans tomato purée	1 bay leaf
2 (6-ounce) cans tomato paste	1/2 cup sugar (or to taste)

Brown the ground beef in a medium skillet, stirring until crumbly; drain. Combine the ground beef, celery, onions, butter, tomato purée, tomato paste, canned tomatoes, salt, chili powder, Tabasco sauce, Worcestershire sauce, bay leaf and sugar in a large kettle. Cook over medium heat, stirring occasionally, for about 3 hours or until desired thickness. Yield: 15 or more servings.

Pamela D. Cochran, Xi Alpha Omega
Washington, West Virginia

REUBEN CASSEROLE

This flavorful meal can be prepared and refrigerated, then baked an hour before serving time.

1 (8-ounce) package
    noodles
1 (28-ounce) can
    sauerkraut, drained
2 (10-ounce) cans cream
    of chicken soup
1 teaspoon dry mustard

½ cup mayonnaise
½ cup chopped onion
1 (12-ounce) can corned
    beef, thinly sliced
2 cups shredded Swiss
    cheese
½ cup rye bread crumbs

Cook the noodles using package directions; drain. Preheat the oven to 350 degrees. Layer the sauerkraut and noodles over the bottom of a greased 9x13-inch baking dish. Combine the cream of chicken soup, mustard and mayonnaise in a small bowl; mix well. Spread the soup mixture evenly over the noodle layer. Layer the onion, corned beef and Swiss cheese over the soup layer. Sprinkle the bread crumbs over the top. Cover with foil and bake for 1 hour. Yield: 6 to 8 servings.

Faith A. Wallace, Laureate Epsilon Eta
Monessen, Pennsylvania

❖ ALMOND CHICKEN CHARDONNAY

Fresh mushrooms can be used instead of the mushroom soup. Just increase the cream and milk by ½ cup each.

2 tablespoons butter
6 to 8 boneless skinless
    chicken breasts,
    chopped
4 green onions with
    tops, chopped
6 garlic cloves, crushed
1 (10-ounce) can cream
    of mushroom soup
2 cups chardonnay

1 cup heavy cream
1 cup milk
¼ cup chopped fresh
    basil leaves
Salt and pepper to taste
1 pound angel hair
    pasta or noodles,
    cooked
½ to 1 cup sliced
    almonds

Melt the butter in a large skillet over medium-low heat and sauté the chicken until golden. Add the green onions, garlic and cream of mushroom soup; cook for 3 minutes, stirring constantly. Stir in the chardonnay. Simmer mixture over medium-high heat for about 10 minutes or until reduced by half. Stir in the heavy cream, milk, basil, salt and pepper. Simmer for about 5 minutes or until sauce thickens slightly, stirring frequently. Serve over pasta or noodles. Sprinkle with almonds. Yield: 6 to 8 servings.

Doreen Stever, Xi Tau Theta
Oakdale, California

BBQ CHICKEN PASTA

1 pound boneless
    skinless chicken
    breasts
3 tablespoons vegetable
    oil
1 medium onion,
    julienned

1 green or red bell
    pepper, julienned
1½ cups (or less)
    barbecue sauce
½ cup (or less) water
¾ pound cooked
    fettuccini or linguini

Cut the chicken into bite-size pieces. Heat the oil in a skillet over medium-low heat and sauté the chicken for about 5 minutes or until cooked through. Remove the chicken. Add the onion and green pepper to the skillet and sauté until tender-crisp. Stir in enough barbecue sauce and water until desired consistency. Simmer, uncovered, for 10 minutes. Serve over fettuccini or linguini. Yield: 6 servings.

Linda M. Knutson, Laureate Lambda
Polson, Montana

CAJUN CHICKEN PASTA

The uncooked chicken will slice more easily if first arranged in a single layer on a plate or baking sheet and placed in the freezer, covered, for about an hour.

1 (8-ounce) package bow
    tie pasta
4 boneless skinless
    chicken breasts
2 tablespoons Creole
    seasoning
2 tablespoons butter
1 (8-ounce) package
    fresh mushrooms,
    sliced

1 bunch green onions
    with tops, thinly
    sliced
1 teaspoon each basil,
    lemon pepper and
    garlic powder
2 to 4 cups heavy cream
2 (8-ounce) packages
    grated fresh
    Parmesan cheese

Cook the pasta using package directions; drain. Cut the chicken into thin strips. Combine chicken and Creole seasoning in a sealable plastic bag. Seal and toss to coat chicken. Melt the butter in a large skillet over medium heat and sauté coated chicken until tender. Add the mushrooms and onions. Cook for 2 to 3 minutes, stirring constantly. Reduce the heat. Stir in the basil, lemon pepper, garlic powder and enough cream to make sauce of the desired consistency. Adjust seasonings. Heat through. Place the cooked pasta in a large serving bowl. Pour 1 package of the Parmesan cheese over the pasta. Pour the chicken mixture over the top. Stir. Serve with the remaining Parmesan cheese. Yield: 4 to 6 servings.

Candace Allen, Beta Sigma
Versailles, Kentucky

CHICKEN AND BROCCOLI ALFREDO

1 pound boneless
    skinless chicken
    breasts
6 ounces uncooked
    fettuccini
1 cup fresh or frozen
    broccoli florets
2 teaspoons butter or
    margarine

1 (10-ounce) can cream
    of mushroom soup
1/2 cup milk
1/2 cup grated Parmesan
    cheese
1/4 teaspoon freshly
    ground pepper

Cut the chicken into bite-size pieces. Cook the fettuccini using package directions, adding broccoli for the last 4 minutes of cooking time; drain. Melt the butter in a large skillet over medium-high heat and sauté the chicken for 10 to 15 minutes or until browned. Reduce the heat to medium. Stir in the fettuccini mixture, cream of mushroom soup, milk, Parmesan cheese and pepper. Cook for 3 to 4 minutes or until heated through, stirring frequently. Yield: 4 servings.

Sherri Smith, Delta Chi
Blue Springs, Missouri

CHICKEN AND CHEESE TORTELLINI

1 pound boneless
    skinless chicken
    breasts
Fresh basil sprigs or 1
    teaspoon dried basil
2 cups frozen tortellini,
    cooked
1/2 cup chopped green
    onions

1/4 cup chopped green
    bell pepper
1/4 cup grated Parmesan
    cheese
1/3 cup Italian dressing
1/2 cup shredded Cheddar
    or Swiss cheese

Place the chicken and basil in a kettle. Bring to a boil. Reduce heat and simmer, loosely covered, for 30 minutes or until chicken is cooked through and tender. Cut into bite-size pieces. Combine the tortellini, green onions and green pepper in a large bowl. Stir in the chicken, Parmesan cheese, Italian dressing and Cheddar cheese. Chill, covered, for 2 to 10 hours. Yield: 6 to 8 servings.

Tammy McCoy, Kappa Delta
Flora, Illinois

Carolyn Eberts, Laureate Delta Zeta, Bethlehem, Pennsylvania, makes Night Before Macaroni Casserole by mixing 2 cups uncooked macaroni with 2 cups chopped cooked chicken, 2 cans cream of mushroom soup, 2 cups milk, 2 cups shredded Cheddar cheese, 1/4 cup chopped onion and chopped green pepper and mushroom pieces. Refrigerate overnight and bake at 350 degrees for 1 hour.

CHICKEN AND ZUCCHINI IN DIJON SAUCE

3/4 pound boneless
    skinless chicken
    breasts
1/2 cup low-fat yogurt
2 tablespoons Dijon
    mustard
1/4 teaspoon dried
    tarragon
1 garlic clove, minced

1 medium carrot, cut
    into thin strips
2 medium zucchini, cut
    into thin strips
1 tablespoon vegetable
    oil
2 cups hot cooked
    noodles

Cut the chicken into bite-size pieces. Combine the yogurt, mustard and tarragon in a small bowl; blend well. Spray a large skillet with nonstick cooking spray and heat over medium-high heat. Stir-fry the garlic and carrot for 1 minute. Add the zucchini and stir-fry for 3 minutes longer or until tender-crisp. Remove vegetables from skillet. Add the vegetable oil to the hot skillet and stir-fry the chicken for 2 to 3 minutes or until no longer pink. Return vegetables to skillet. Toss to coat with the juices. Cook for 1 minute, stirring constantly. Serve over noodles. Yield: 4 servings.

Sandra E. Moody, Delta Master
Indian Trail, North Carolina

CHICKEN WITH LINGUINI

My best friend shared this recipe with me. My daughter suggested adding the chicken broth to make more sauce without using more butter.

1 pound boneless
    skinless chicken
    breasts
1 cup bread crumbs
1/2 teaspoon salt
1/2 teaspoon pepper
1 egg, beaten
1/2 cup vegetable oil
1 (16-ounce) package
    linguini

1/2 cup plus
    2 tablespoons butter
1 (14-ounce) can chicken
    broth
1 tablespoon lemon
    juice
3 garlic cloves, crushed
1/2 teaspoon each salt
    and pepper
1/2 cup parsley

Cut the chicken into half-inch pieces. Combine the bread crumbs, salt and pepper in a shallow bowl. Dip the chicken pieces in the egg. Roll in the bread crumb mixture. Arrange the crumbed chicken pieces on a plate or on waxed paper. Heat the oil in a large skillet and sauté the coated chicken pieces for 30 seconds or until crumbs are golden brown. Drain the chicken over paper towels. Discard the excess oil and wipe out the skillet. Cook the linguini according to package directions. Melt the 1/2 cup butter in the skillet over medium-low heat while the pasta is cooking.

Stir in the chicken, chicken broth, lemon juice, garlic, salt and pepper; stir to coat. Drain the cooked pasta and toss with the 2 tablespoons butter. Arrange on a heated platter. Spoon the chicken mixture over the pasta. Sprinkle with the parsley. Garnish with lemon wedges. Yield: 4 to 6 servings.

Donna M. Straub, Xi Zeta Psi
Stroudsburg, Pennsylvania

OVEN CHICKEN AND NOODLES

Use your favorite herbs to flavor this chicken dish. I like to use parsley, basil, thyme, garlic, and poultry seasoning.

1 roasting hen
2 (12-ounce) packages frozen home-style egg noodles, thawed
3 large sweet potatoes, peeled, cut into thirds
3 large carrots, cut into 1-inch cubes
1 small onion, chopped
1/2 medium green bell pepper, chopped
2 ribs celery, cut into 1-inch cubes
2 (4-ounce) cans sliced mushrooms
2 (14-ounce) cans chicken broth
Salt and pepper to taste
Herbs to flavor

Preheat the oven to 250 to 300 degrees. Place the hen in a large roasting pan. Add the egg noodles, sweet potatoes, carrots, onion, green pepper, celery, mushrooms, chicken broth, salt, pepper and herbs. Cook, covered, for 6 to 8 hours. Check occasionally to make sure there is plenty of liquid; the noodles are better in liquid. Yield: 6 to 8 servings.

Pamela Thomas, Preceptor Pi
Sturgis, South Dakota

RED PEPPER PASTA PRIMAVERA

1 cup fresh basil, or 1 cup fresh parsley plus 1 tablespoon dried basil
1 medium red bell pepper, chopped
1/2 cup reduced-calorie salad dressing or mayonnaise
2 tablespoons grated Parmesan cheese
1 tablespoon lemon juice
1/2 teaspoon salt
1/8 teaspoon cayenne pepper
Black pepper to taste
1 (8-ounce) package fettuccini or linguini
2 large carrots, julienned
1 medium onion, cut into wedges
1 medium zucchini and/or yellow squash, julienned
10 ounces chopped cooked chicken or turkey

Combine the basil, red bell pepper, salad dressing, Parmesan cheese, lemon juice, salt, cayenne pepper and black pepper in a food processor or blender container; process until smooth to make a pesto sauce. Cook the fettuccini in a large amount of boiling water in a large stockpot for 6 minutes. Add the carrots and onion. Boil for 2 minutes longer. Add the zucchini. Boil for 2 minutes longer. Drain the fettuccini and vegetables. Return the fettuccini mixture to the stockpot over low heat and toss well with the pesto and chicken to coat and heat through. Yield: 6 servings.

Sherry Givens, Delta Mu
Murfreesboro, Tennessee

SPICY CHICKEN AND FETTUCCINI

2 boneless skinless chicken breast halves
1 (9-ounce) package fresh plain or spinach fettuccini
1 to 2 tablespoons olive oil
1/2 cup chopped onion
1/2 cup chopped mushrooms
1 tablespoon flour
1 (14-ounce) can diced tomatoes with crushed red peppers and basil
1 (10-ounce) can tomatoes with green chiles
1/2 cup shredded hot pepper Monterey Jack cheese

Cut the chicken into strips. Cook the fettuccini using package directions; drain. Return to the saucepan and cover loosely to keep warm. Heat the olive oil in a skillet over medium-high heat and sauté the chicken, onion and mushrooms for about 5 minutes or until chicken is no longer pink and vegetables are tender. Sprinkle the flour over the chicken mixture. Cook for 1 minute longer, stirring constantly. Stir in the undrained cans of tomatoes. Bring to a boil. Reduce heat to low. Simmer, covered, for 5 to 10 minutes or until sauce is thickened. Arrange the cooked fettuccini on a serving platter. Spoon the chicken mixture over the fettuccini. Sprinkle with Monterey Jack cheese. Yield: 4 servings.

Christine Shire, Gamma Lambda
Mexico, Missouri

Jeanne Alsmeyer, Laureate Zeta Mu, Houston, Texas, makes Baked Chicken Spaghetti. She stir-fries 2 pounds marinated chicken for fajitas, adds 1 pound frozen stir-fry pepper mix and a package of frozen baby peas. Cook for 10 minutes, add a family-size can cream of mushroom soup, a can of tomatoes and green chiles and a large bottle of cheese whiz. Toss with a pound of cooked spaghetti and bake at 300 degrees for 30 minutes.

CHEESE HAM CASSEROLE

Instead of baking, you may choose to microwave this dish on High for 8 to 10 minutes or until heated through.

2 cups chopped fresh
  broccoli
1½ cups uncooked
  corkscrew noodles
½ cup mayonnaise-type
  salad dressing
1½ cups shredded sharp
  Cheddar cheese

1½ cups chopped cooked
  ham
½ cup chopped red or
  green bell pepper
¼ cup milk
¾ cup seasoned
  croutons

Preheat the oven to 350 degrees. Cook the broccoli in salted water to cover for about 5 minutes; drain. Cook the noodles according to package directions; drain. Combine the salad dressing, 1 cup of the Cheddar cheese, ham, bell pepper and milk in a medium bowl. Pour into a 1½-quart baking dish. Sprinkle with the croutons and the remaining ½ cup cheese. Bake for 30 minutes. Yield: 4 to 6 servings.

Marcia Nestler, Preceptor Delta Delta
Eldridge, Iowa

BASIC ITALIAN SAUCE

This sauce can be frozen and later microwaved for easy dinners. I remember that the best was when my mom would let me dip bread into the sauce before dinner.

½ cup vegetable oil
3 pounds Italian
  sausage
3 garlic cloves, finely
  chopped
6 (6-ounce) cans tomato
  paste
1 (46-ounce) can tomato
  juice

1 tablespoon chopped
  parsley
2 teaspoons salt
½ teaspoon pepper
½ cup sugar
½ cup grated Romano
  cheese
Water

Heat the oil in a 6-quart stockpot over medium heat and brown the sausage with the garlic, stirring until sausage is crumbly; drain. Stir in the tomato paste, tomato juice, parsley, salt, pepper and sugar. Simmer over low heat for 3 to 4 hours, stirring occasionally, spooning off the grease as it rises to the top. Just before serving, stir in the Romano cheese. Stir in water at any time to make desired consistency. Yield: 15 servings.

Kristine Miller, Xi Theta Sigma
Lenexa, Kansas

POLISH REUBEN CASSEROLE

2 (10-ounce) cans cream
  of mushroom soup
1⅓ cups milk
½ cup chopped onion
1 tablespoon prepared
  mustard
2 (16-ounce) cans
  sauerkraut, rinsed,
  drained
1 (8-ounce) package
  medium noodles

1½ pounds Polish
  sausage, cut into ½-
  inch pieces
2 cups shredded Swiss
  cheese
¾ cup whole wheat
  bread crumbs
2 tablespoons melted
  butter

Preheat the oven to 350 degrees. Combine the soup, milk, onion and mustard in a medium bowl; blend well. Spread the sauerkraut over the bottom of a greased 9x13-inch baking dish. Layer the uncooked noodles, soup mixture, sausage and Swiss cheese over the sauerkraut. Combine the bread crumbs and butter. Sprinkle the crumb mixture over the top. Cover pan tightly with foil. Bake for 1 hour or until noodles are tender. Yield: 8 to 10 servings.

Barbara Kennedy, Laureate Lambda
Fort Pierce, Florida

SAUSAGE FETTUCCINI

1 pound sweet Italian
  sausage
1 garlic clove or
  ½ teaspoon minced
  garlic

¼ cup (½ stick) butter
1 cup sliced fresh
  mushrooms
1 purple onion, diced
Fettuccini

Brown the sausage with the garlic in a skillet, stirring until sausage is crumbly; drain. Add the butter, mushrooms and onion; cook for 4 to 5 minutes or until mushrooms begin to soften, stirring constantly. Cook the fettuccini according to package directions. Spoon the sausage mixture over the fettuccini. Yield: 4 servings.

Terrie Hutton, Beta Iota
Brookings, Oregon

Tina M. Tortis, Xi Beta Eta, Weirton, West Virginia, makes Polish Lasagna by sautéing a large chopped onion in a cup of margarine and mixing in a large can of rinsed sauerkraut. Prepare 2 packages of instant mashed potatoes and add 2 cups shredded Cheddar cheese. Alternate layers of sauerkraut mixture, cooked lasagna noodles and potato mixture and top with additional cheese. Bake at 325 degrees for 1 hour.

CRAWFISH FETTUCCINI

1 (16-ounce) package fettuccini	1½ pounds shrimp or crawfish, cooked, shelled
¾ cup (1½ sticks) margarine	1 cup half-and-half
2 medium onions, chopped	8 ounces Velveeta cheese, cut into 1-inch cubes
2 ribs celery, chopped	3 garlic cloves, minced
1 green bell pepper, chopped	1 teaspoon Tabasco sauce
¼ cup chopped green onions	¼ cup grated Parmesan cheese
1 tablespoon flour	Salt and pepper to taste
¼ cup chopped parsley	

Cook the fettuccini according to package directions; drain. Melt the margarine in a large saucepan over medium heat and cook the onions, celery, green pepper and green onions, stirring occasionally, for about 5 minutes or until tender. Stir in the flour, mixing well. Stir in the parsley and shrimp. Simmer for 5 minutes. Stir in the half-and-half, Velveeta cheese, garlic and Tabasco sauce. Bring almost to a simmer. Reduce heat to low and cook for 5 minutes. Toss the half-and-half mixture with the warm fettuccini in a warmed bowl. Sprinkle with Parmesan cheese, salt and pepper. Yield: 8 servings.

Donna S. Russell, Preceptor Epsilon Lambda
Alvin, Texas

HERBED SHRIMP AND PASTA

4 ounces uncooked angel hair pasta	¼ cup chopped chopped fresh parsley
½ cup butter	¼ cup chopped dillweed or ½ teaspoon dried dillweed
1 pound fresh medium shrimp, peeled, deveined	¼ teaspoon salt
2 garlic cloves, minced	⅛ teaspoon pepper
1 cup half-and-half	

Cook the pasta according to package directions; drain. Cover loosely with foil to keep warm while preparing the sauce. Melt the butter in a heavy skillet over medium-high heat and sauté the shrimp and garlic for 3 to 5 minutes or until shrimp is cooked through. Remove shrimp from skillet. Stir the half-and-half into the garlic and butter in the skillet. Bring to a boil, stirring constantly. Add the shrimp, parsley, dillweed, salt and pepper, stirring until blended. Serve over angel hair pasta. Yield: 4 servings.

Debbie Monk, Xi Mega Nu
Rosenburg, Texas

PAD THAI NOODLES

This great Asian dish, which I learned to make in a cooking class in Bangkok, Thailand, looks difficult but is actually quite easy. Dried shrimp, fish sauce, and rice stick noodles can be purchased at an Asian market. I use Bangkok Elephant brand rice noodles. Try substituting chicken for the prawns.

8 ounces rice stick noodles	3 tablespoons sugar
¼ cup vegetable oil	2 handfuls bean sprouts
2 garlic cloves, minced	2 eggs, scrambled, drained over paper towels
10 large prawns, peeled, deveined	
1 tablespoon dried shrimp	3 tablespoons crushed peanuts
1 cup (about) finely cubed bean curd	2 tablespoons chopped shallots
3 tablespoons lemon juice	2 tablespoons chopped fresh coriander leaves
3 tablespoons fish sauce	Hot pepper flakes to taste

Soak the noodles in warm water for at least 15 minutes; drain over paper towels. Heat the oil in a wok. Stir-fry the garlic gently until golden. Increase the heat. Add the prawns and dried shrimp. Stir-fry until prawns are no longer pink. Reduce the heat. Add the bean curd, lemon juice, fish sauce and sugar, stirring until sugar is dissolved. Stir in the soaked noodles, most of the bean sprouts, eggs, most of the peanuts, shallots and most of the coriander. Serve on a large platter. Sprinkle with hot pepper flakes and the remaining bean sprouts, peanuts and coriander. Garnish with lemon slices. Yield: 8 to 10 servings.

Alice McClure, Xi Sigma
Vancouver, Washington

Betty P. Shinall, Preceptor Laureate Rho, Harrison, Arkansas, prepares Shrimp and Vermicelli by sautéing 1 cup chopped onion, 1 cup chopped celery and ½ cup chopped green pepper in ¾ cup butter in a large skillet. Add 1 can cream of mushroom soup and 1 can tomato soup, ⅔ cup water and 1 pound peeled cooked shrimp and heat through. Alternate layers of 12 ounces cooked vermicelli, the shrimp sauce and 3 cups shredded Cheddar cheese. Sprinkle evenly with 1 cup Parmesan cheese and add a light sprinkle of cayenne pepper. Bake at 325 degrees for 1 hour.

SEASHORE FETTUCCINI

This dish is also wonderful with crab meat or scallops.

1 (16-ounce) package
  fettuccini
1/2 cup (1 stick) butter or
  margarine
1 small onion, diced
12 ounces fresh or frozen
  whole or broken
  shrimp, thawed
1/4 teaspoon dried basil

1/8 teaspoon crushed red
  pepper
1/2 teaspoon salt
Pinch of pepper
1 (8-ounce) can tomato
  sauce
1 cup sour cream
1/2 cup grated Parmesan
  cheese

Cook pasta according to package directions; drain. Place in a large bowl and cover loosely to keep warm while preparing the sauce. Melt the butter in a large skillet over medium-low heat and sauté the onion, shrimp, basil, red pepper, salt and pepper for about 20 minutes. Stir in the tomato sauce and sour cream. Bring to a boil. Reduce heat and simmer for about 3 minutes or until sauce is creamy. Add shrimp sauce and parmesan cheese to the pasta; toss to combine. Yield: 4 to 5 servings.

Barbara Stalfort, Laureate Phi
Sun City West, Arizona

SHRIMP AND ARTICHOKE LINGUINI

1 (8-ounce) package
  linguini
1/4 cup olive oil
1 pound medium shrimp,
  peeled, deveined
3 garlic cloves, minced
1/2 teaspoon dried
  crushed red pepper
  flakes

1 (14-ounce) can
  artichoke hearts,
  drained, quartered
1/2 cup ripe olives, sliced
1/4 cup fresh lemon juice
1/8 teaspoon salt
1/8 teaspoon pepper
1/2 cup grated Parmesan
  cheese

Cook the linguini according to package directions; drain. Cover loosely to keep warm while preparing the sauce. Heat the olive oil in a large heavy-bottomed skillet over medium-high heat and sauté the shrimp, garlic and red pepper for 5 minutes or until shrimp turn pink. Stir in the artichoke hearts, olives, lemon juice, salt and pepper. Add to the pasta; toss to combine. Sprinkle with Parmesan cheese. Yield: 3 to 4 servings.

Diane M. Sherman, Preceptor Xi Kappa
Marble Falls, Texas

SHRIMP PASTA

4 3/4 cups water
1 1/2 pounds fresh medium
  shrimp, unpeeled
1 (8-ounce) package
  fresh thin spaghetti
1/3 cup butter
1/3 cup flour
2/3 cup chicken broth
2/3 cup heavy cream
3/4 cup shredded Swiss
  cheese

2 1/2 tablespoons dry
  sherry
1/2 teaspoon salt
1/8 teaspoon ground
  white pepper
2 tablespoons grated
  Parmesan cheese
2 tablespoons slivered
  almonds

Bring the water to a boil in a kettle. Add the shrimp and cook for 3 to 5 minutes or until shrimp turn pink. Rinse with cold water; drain well. Chill, covered, for at least 1 hour. Peel and devein. Preheat the oven to 350 degrees. Cook the spaghetti according to package directions; drain. Melt the butter in a large saucepan over low heat. Stir in the flour. Cook for 1 minute, stirring constantly. Stir in the chicken broth and cream gradually. Cook over low heat until thickened, stirring constantly. Stir in the next 4 ingredients. Remove from heat. Stir in the shrimp and spaghetti. Spoon the shrimp mixture into a greased 2-quart baking dish. Sprinkle with Parmesan cheese and almonds. Bake, uncovered, for 25 minutes or until heated through. Broil 6 inches from heat for 5 minutes or until top is light brown. Yield: 6 servings.

Northa Turner, Laureate Beta Pi
Bellevue, Washington

SHRIMP SCAMPI WITH PASTA

3 garlic cloves, chopped
1 tablespoon chopped
  fresh parsley
1/8 teaspoon freshly
  ground black pepper
1/2 cup olive oil
1 pound medium shrimp,
  peeled, deveined

1 (16-ounce) package
  linguini or favorite
  pasta
1/4 cup butter
1/4 to 1/3 cup white wine
  or to taste

Blend the garlic, parsley, pepper and olive oil to make a marinade. Marinate the shrimp, covered, in the refrigerator for 3 to 4 hours. Cook the linguini according to package directions. Rinse and drain well. Melt the butter in a large heavy skillet over medium-low heat. Place the shrimp with the marinade in the skillet and cook for 2 to 3 minutes or until shrimp turn pink. Stir in white wine and serve over pasta. Garnish with chopped parsley and freshly ground black pepper. Yield: 4 servings.

Judy Freeman, Pi Master
Rosston, Arkansas

SPAGHETTI CON I CALAMARI (SPAGHETTI WITH SQUID)

5 tablespoons olive oil	Salt and pepper to taste
1 clove garlic, finely chopped	2/3 cup dry white wine
1/2 green or red chile pepper, seeded, chopped	1 (14-ounce) can tomatoes
3 anchovy fillets, chopped	12 ounces uncooked spaghetti
1 1/2 pounds squid, cut into rings	Small bunch fresh parsley, finely chopped

Heat the olive oil in a large saucepan and sauté the garlic gently until soft but not brown. Add the chile pepper, anchovies and squid. Cook, stirring, until the squid becomes opaque. Season with salt and pepper. Add the wine and boil briskly to evaporate. Stir in the tomatoes. Simmer gently, covered, for about 40 minutes or until squid is tender. Add water if necessary to reach desired consistency. Taste and adjust seasoning. Cook pasta for a little less time than package directions specify; drain. Turn the pasta into a serving dish. Toss with the squid sauce and parsley. Serve at once. Yield: 4 to 5 servings.

Margaret Lucas, Xi Epsilon Lambda
Salmon Arm, British Columbia, Canada

BROCCOLI PASTA

4 boneless skinless chicken breast halves	1 tablespoon freshly chopped basil, or 1 teaspoon dried
1/4 cup olive oil	1/4 cup white wine
2 garlic cloves, minced	3/4 cup chicken broth
2 cups broccoli florets	1 tablespoon butter
1 cup oil-packed sun-dried tomatoes, chopped	1 (8-ounce) package bow tie pasta

Cut the chicken into bite-size pieces. Heat the olive oil in a skillet over medium heat and sauté the chicken and garlic until chicken is no longer pink. Stir in the broccoli and sauté until tender-crisp. Stir in the sun-dried tomatoes, basil, wine, chicken broth and butter. Simmer, covered, for 5 minutes. Cook the pasta using the package directions just until tender. Drain well and combine with the sauce in a large bowl. Toss and serve immediately.
Yield: 4 to 6 servings.

Stefanie Brietzke, Preceptor Beta Nu
Dansville, New York

❖ BROCCOLI BLEU CHEESE FETTUCCINI

1 bunch broccoli	Freshly ground pepper to taste
1/2 cup (1 stick) butter	3/4 pound fresh fettuccini, cooked
4 large garlic cloves, chopped	1/4 pound bleu cheese, crumbled
2 green onions, finely chopped	1/4 cup freshly grated Parmesan cheese
3/4 cup heavy cream	
Salt to taste	

Trim the coarse stems from the broccoli and discard. Sliver the remaining stems and separate the florets into bite-size pieces. Steam the broccoli in a steamer basket over boiling water just until tender. Drain well; chop into smaller pieces if desired and set aside. Melt the butter in a large skillet over medium-low heat and sauté the garlic, green onions and broccoli for 3 minutes. Stir in the cream, salt and pepper. Simmer gently for 5 to 10 minutes or until the sauce thickens slightly, stirring constantly. Place the cream mixture and the pasta in a large warm serving bowl; toss to combine. Add the bleu cheese and toss to distribute evenly. Add the Parmesan cheese. Toss again. Serve immediately with additional Parmesan cheese and freshly ground pepper. Yield: 4 servings.

Susan Niepoetter, Gamma Iota
Centralia, Illinois

CHILI SPAGHETTI

1 (48-ounce) can tomato juice, or 1 (15-ounce) jar spaghetti sauce and 1 (6-ounce) can tomato paste	1 teaspoon pepper
	1 tablespoon salt
	1 1/2 tablespoons vinegar
	2 tablespoons chili powder
1 cup water	1/8 teaspoon garlic powder
1 teaspoon cinnamon	
1 teaspoon allspice	1 large onion, minced
1 teaspoon cumin	2 pounds lean ground beef
5 bay leaves	

Combine the tomato juice, water, cinnamon, allspice, cumin, bay leaves, pepper, salt, vinegar, chili powder and garlic powder in a large skillet over medium-low heat. Stir in the uncooked ground beef. Cook, uncovered, over medium-low heat for at least 2 hours, stirring occasionally. Remove bay leaves. Serve over pasta. Garnish with shredded sharp Cheddar cheese and chopped onions. Yield: 6 to 8 servings.

Sue Hamlin, Epsilon Rho
Pelham, Alabama

PARTY PASTA

1 (16-ounce) package
jumbo macaroni
shells
1 pound Italian sausage,
or ¹/₂ pound sausage
and ¹/₂ pound ground
beef
1 (32-ounce) jar
spaghetti sauce
1 (14-ounce) jar
spaghetti sauce
1 (8-ounce) can leaf
spinach, drained

2 eggs
2 cups (8 ounces)
shredded mozzarella
cheese
1 (15-ounce) carton
ricotta cheese
1 teaspoon onion salt
¹/₂ teaspoon garlic
powder
¹/₄ teaspoon nutmeg
2 tablespoons grated
Parmesan cheese

Cook the macaroni shells using package directions; drain and rinse. Arrange shells in a layer over waxed paper or foil. Brown the sausage in a large skillet, stirring until crumbly; drain. Stir the spaghetti sauce into the sausage. Simmer for 15 minutes. Press out the excess moisture from the spinach; chop. Beat the eggs in a large bowl. Add the spinach and the next 6 ingredients; mix well. Preheat the oven to 350 degrees. Pour half the sausage mixture over the bottom of a 9x13-inch baking dish. Stuff each macaroni shell with 1¹/₂ tablespoons of the remaining sausage mixture. Arrange shells in a single layer in the prepared dish. Pour the remaining sausage mixture over the shells. Sprinkle with Parmesan cheese. Bake for 30 to 35 minutes or until hot and bubbly.
Yield: 6 to 10 servings.

Barbara S. Smith, Preceptor Gamma Sigma
Miamisburg, Ohio

COTTAGE CHEESE AND NOODLE CASSEROLE

1 (8-ounce) package egg
noodles
2 tablespoons butter
2 cups cottage cheese
1 cup sour cream

2 tablespoons chopped
green onions
¹/₂ teaspoon salt
3 eggs, well beaten
Buttered bread crumbs

Preheat the oven to 350 degrees. Cook the noodles using package directions; drain. Toss with butter. Combine the cottage cheese, sour cream, green onions and salt in a large bowl; mix well. Stir in the eggs. Layer ¹/₃ of the noodles, half the egg mixture, ¹/₃ of the noodles, the remaining half the egg mixture and the remaining ¹/₃ of the noodles in a 1¹/₂-quart baking dish. Sprinkle with buttered bread crumbs. Bake for 45 minutes. Yield: 4 servings.

Waldine Garrett, Alpha Zeta Master
North Kansas City, Missouri

HOMEMADE MAC AND CHEESE

Children love this macaroni and cheese.

1 (8-ounce) package
elbow macaroni
1 tablespoon margarine
3 tablespoons flour
1 teaspoon salt
1 cup (or more) milk

2 cups (8 ounces)
shredded longhorn
cheese
2 cups (8 ounces)
shredded Cheddar
cheese

Cook the macaroni using package directions; drain. Spread macaroni over the bottom of a greased 9x12-inch baking dish. Preheat the oven to 350 degrees. Combine the margarine, flour and salt in a large microwave-safe bowl. Microwave on High, loosely covered, for 1 minute. Whisk in the milk. Microwave 1 minute at a time, whisking well after each minute, for 3 minutes longer or until mixture thickens. Stir in the longhorn cheese and Cheddar cheese, reserving ¹/₄ cup of the Cheddar. Microwave the cheese mixture for 30 seconds or until cheese is melted. Pour the cheese mixture over the cooked macaroni. Stir well, adding more milk if desired. Sprinkle with the reserved ¹/₄ cup of Cheddar cheese. Bake, uncovered, for 25 minutes. Yield: 12 servings.

Iris Puffenberger, Lambda
Cumberland, Maryland

MEXICAN LASAGNA

1 (15-ounce) can pinto
beans, drained, rinsed
1 (14-ounce) can diced
crushed tomatoes
¹/₄ cup chopped cilantro
1 garlic clove, minced
1 (4-ounce) can chopped
green chiles

2 cups frozen corn
kernels, thawed
2 scallions, minced
¹/₂ teaspoon cumin
¹/₂ teaspoon oregano
8 corn tortillas
1¹/₂ cups shredded
Monterey Jack cheese

Preheat the oven to 400 degrees. Combine the beans, tomatoes, cilantro, garlic, green chiles, corn, scallions, cumin and oregano in a large bowl; mix well. Line an oiled 2-quart baking dish with 4 tortillas, overlapping if necessary. Layer half the bean mixture over the tortillas. Sprinkle with half the cheese. Repeat the layers with the remaining tortillas, bean mixture and cheese. Bake for 12 to 15 minutes or until cheese is bubbly. Let stand for 1 or 2 minutes. Cut into squares. Garnish each serving with a dollop of yogurt or sour cream if desired. Yield: 6 servings.

Billie M. Lepere, Preceptor Theta Xi
San Ramon, California

SPINACH LASAGNA

This lasagna becomes a delicious vegetarian meal when made without the sausage.

1 (16-ounce) package lasagna noodles	1 (8-ounce) can tomato sauce
1 (10-ounce) package frozen spinach, thawed	1 (6-ounce) can tomato paste
1 (15-ounce) carton ricotta cheese	1 (8-ounce) can water
1 egg	1 (6-ounce) can water
1 pound Italian sausage (optional)	1 (4-ounce) can mushrooms
1 medium onion, chopped	1 tablespoon garlic salt
1 (15-ounce) can tomatoes	2 tablespoons Italian seasoning or to taste
	4 cups shredded mozzarella cheese

Cook the noodles using package directions until almost done; drain. Combine the spinach, ricotta cheese and egg in a medium bowl; mix well. Brown the sausage with the onion in a medium skillet, stirring until sausage is crumbly; drain. Stir in the tomatoes, tomato sauce, tomato paste, water, mushrooms, garlic salt and Italian seasoning. Simmer, uncovered, for about 30 minutes. Spread a thin layer of tomato mixture over the bottom of a 9x13-inch baking dish. Sprinkle with a little of the mozzarella cheese. Layer the noodles, spinach mixture, tomato mixture and mozzarella cheese 1/2 at a time over the first layer. Bake, uncovered, for 45 minutes.
Yield: 8 servings.

Lorraine Pello, Xi Beta Phi
Arvada, Colorado

FRESH TOMATO TOSS

Chopped cooked chicken breasts can be added to this recipe if desired.

1 (12-ounce) package medium noodles	1/4 cup sliced green onions
1/3 cup melted margarine	2/3 cup grated Parmesan cheese
1 teaspoon salt	
1/4 teaspoon pepper	1 (14-ounce) can tomatoes with garlic and basil
2 tablespoons chopped fresh basil	

Cook the noodles using package directions; drain. Melt the margarine in a kettle. Add the noodles, salt, pepper, basil and green onions; stir. Add the Parmesan cheese; stir. Add the tomatoes. Toss and serve. Yield: 6 servings.

Janet Lones, Iota Phi
Fayetteville, North Carolina

QUICK AND EASY SOUTHERN YUPPIE FETTUCCINI ALFREDO

This recipe was an adventurous experiment that has become my favorite pasta. You may substitute 1 teaspoon of broken dried rosemary for the fresh rosemary.

8 to 12 ounces dried or fresh fettuccini noodles	1 (17-ounce) jar Five Brothers Alfredo Sauce
1 teaspoon olive oil	1/2 cup sherry (optional)
2 teaspoons chopped fresh whole rosemary leaves	1/4 cup pine nuts
	6 to 10 ounces frozen cut okra, thawed
1/4 teaspoon salt	

Bring 1 1/2 quarts of water to a boil in a large kettle over high heat. Add the noodles, olive oil, rosemary and salt. Cook until noodles are tender, using package directions; drain. Rinse with fresh boiling water to remove excess starch. Combine the Alfredo Sauce and sherry in a medium microwave-safe bowl. Stir in the pine nuts and okra; mix well. Microwave on Medium-High for 10 minutes. Pour over the cooked noodles on individual plates and serve.
Yield: 4 servings.

Robbie Bryan, Preceptor Zeta Epsilon
Stockton, California

HEARTY VEGETABLE AND TORTELLINI SOUP

3 cups quartered mushrooms	3 cups stewed tomatoes
1 cup chopped onions	2 cups chicken or beef broth
1 cup chopped carrots	2 tablespoons chopped fresh parsley
1 cup chopped zucchini	
1 tablespoon vegetable oil	2 tablespoons chopped basil or dill
2 small garlic cloves, minced	56 frozen cheese or ricotta-filled tortellini
4 cups fresh spinach	

Combine the mushrooms, onions, carrots, zucchini, oil and garlic in a 4-quart microwave-safe bowl. Microwave, loosely covered, on High for 6 minutes, stirring once. Stir in the spinach, tomatoes, chicken broth, parsley and basil. Microwave for 6 minutes, stirring once. Stir in the tortellini. Microwave for 6 minutes longer. Stir. Let stand for 5 minutes. Stir just before serving. Yield: 4 servings.

Barbara J. Wiscarson, Preceptor Beta Lambda
Cottage Grove, Oregon

Vegetarian Dishes

MEATLESS LENTIL CHILI

Try using this chile on pizzas, in tacos, or as a dip.

2½ cups lentils, rinsed
5 cups water
1 envelope dry onion
    soup mix
1 (16-ounce) can
    tomatoes or tomato
    sauce
1½ teaspoons chili
    powder
½ teaspoon cumin

Combine the lentils and water in a large saucepan. Bring to a boil. Stir in the onion soup mix. Reduce heat and simmer for 30 minutes. Stir in the tomatoes, chili powder and cumin. Simmer for 30 minutes longer. Garnish each serving with shredded cheese. Yield: 6 to 8 servings.

Lois Chandler, Preceptor Alpha
Council Bluffs, Iowa

Fran McClintock, Preceptor Alpha, Edmond, Oklahoma, makes Spanish Macaroni with a prepared package of macaroni and cheese dinner mixed with onion and green pepper sautéed in vegetable oil, a can of tomatoes and green chiles, ½ to 1 cup milk and topped with shredded Cheddar cheese. Bake at 350 degrees for 20 minutes.

POTATO BROCCOLI CHILI

This is a low-calorie chili.

¼ cup vegetable broth
1 cup chopped yellow
    squash
½ cup chopped green
    bell pepper
½ cup chopped red
    onion
3 medium potatoes,
    diced
1½ cups broccoli florets
1 tablespoon chili
    powder
Pinch of cayenne pepper
3½ cups chopped fresh
    or stewed tomatoes
2 cups frozen or canned
    corn kernels
12 ounces non-alcoholic
    beer
¼ cup tomato paste
2½ cups canned pinto
    beans, drained

Heat the broth in a large heavy kettle over medium heat. Add the squash, green pepper and onion. Cook, stirring, for 10 minutes or until tender. Stir in the potatoes, broccoli, chili powder, cayenne pepper, tomatoes, corn, beer and tomato paste. Bring to a boil. Reduce heat to low and simmer, covered, for 25 minutes. Stir in the beans. Simmer for 15 minutes longer. Yield: 6 servings.

Gwen Ulibarri, Laureate Zeta Chi
Livermore, California

VEGETABLE CHILI

2 tablespoons vegetable oil	1/4 teaspoon ground red pepper
2 carrots, chopped	1 (28-ounce) can tomatoes
2 ribs celery, chopped	1 1/2 cups frozen corn
1 onion, chopped	1 1/2 cups water or beer
1 pound red potatoes	1/4 cup tomato paste
1 small bunch broccoli	1 (15-ounce) can pinto beans
3 tablespoons chili powder	

Heat the oil in a large skillet over medium heat and sauté the carrots, celery and onion for about 15 minutes or until onion is golden. Cut the potatoes and broccoli into bite-size pieces. Add to the skillet with the chili powder, red pepper, tomatoes, corn, water, tomato paste and beans. Bring to a boil. Reduce heat to low and simmer, covered for 25 to 30 minutes or until vegetables are tender, stirring occasionally. Serve with corn bread. Yield: 6 servings.

Eddie Cox, Preceptor Delta Gamma
Camarillo, California

ALMOND RAREBIT

This was a famous recipe used in the Tearoom of Halle's Department store in Cleveland, Ohio, in the late 19th century.

1/4 cup butter	1 tablespoon Worcestershire sauce
1/4 cup flour	2 cups shredded sharp Cheddar cheese
1/2 teaspoon dry mustard	
1 teaspoon salt	
1/4 teaspoon paprika	10 slices melba toast
1 cup milk	Toasted unbuttered unsalted blanched almonds
1 cup cream	
Drop of Tabasco sauce	

Melt the butter in the top of a double boiler over simmering water. Stir in the flour, mustard, salt and paprika. Add the milk and cream gradually, cooking and stirring until thickened and smooth. Stir in the Tabasco sauce, Worcestershire sauce and Cheddar cheese, stirring until lumps disappear. Arrange the melba toast in a criss-cross fashion on a serving plate. Pour the cheese mixture over the melba toast. Sprinkle generously with almonds. Yield: 5 servings.

Jean R. Izant, Laureate Alpha Phi
Cleveland Heights, Ohio

BEANS AND BARLEY

You may use four 15-ounce cans of pinto beans, rinsed and drained, instead of the dried beans. This soup is good with flour tortillas, corn bread, or homemade bread.

1 onion, chopped	2 vegetable bouillon cubes
2 garlic cloves, minced	4 cups water
1 green bell pepper, chopped	2 cups dried pinto beans, soaked overnight
1 cup pearl barley	
2 (15-ounce) cans diced tomatoes	1 (4-ounce) can green chiles
1 teaspoon cumin	
1 teaspoon salt	

Sauté the onion, garlic and green pepper in a small amount of oil in a kettle over medium heat for about 5 minutes. Add the barley, tomatoes, cumin, salt, bouillon cubes and water. Bring to a boil. Reduce heat and simmer, partially covered, for about 1 hour or until barley is soft, adding hot water as needed to prevent barley from sticking to the bottom of the kettle. Cook the pinto beans in a pressure cooker for 6 minutes; drain. Add the beans to the barley mixture when barley is cooked. Stir in the green chiles. Heat through. Yield: 10 servings.

Cheryl Mason, Xi Beta Upsilon
Angel Fire, New Mexico

MOROCCAN BULGUR AND LENTILS

Serve with pita bread and yogurt. We enjoy a variety of meatless meals, and bulgur is a nice change from rice. May add cooked lamb or pork.

2 tablespoons butter	1 (14-ounce) can chicken or vegetable broth
1/4 cup blanched sliced almonds	1/4 teaspoon cinnamon
1/2 cup uncooked bulgur	1/8 teaspoon ground cayenne pepper
1/4 cup dry lentils, rinsed	
1/4 cup chopped onion	1/3 cup chopped dried apricots
1 garlic clove, chopped	

Melt the butter in a large skillet over medium heat and sauté the almonds for 1 or 2 minutes or until browned. Remove almonds with a slotted spoon. Add the bulgur, lentils, onion and garlic to the skillet and sauté for 2 to 3 minutes. Add the chicken broth, cinnamon and cayenne pepper. Bring to a boil. Reduce heat and simmer, covered, for 20 to 30 minutes or until liquid is absorbed. Stir in the almonds and apricots. Yield: 6 servings.

Kathleen Meehan, Xi Beta Pi
Renton, Washington

CHILI RELLENOS

Be sure not to omit the long chilling period! It is essential. This makes a good breakfast during holiday gatherings.

8 slices bread, crusts removed, buttered	2 cups milk
4 cups (16 ounces) shredded Monterey Jack cheese	2 teaspoons salt
	2 teaspoons paprika
	1 teaspoon oregano
4 cups (16 ounces) shredded sharp Cheddar cheese	1/2 teaspoon pepper
	1/2 teaspoon garlic powder
6 eggs, beaten until frothy	1/4 teaspoon dry mustard
	1 (4-ounce) can green chiles

Spray a 9x11 1/2x1 1/2-inch baking dish with nonstick cooking spray. Line with the bread slices. Cover the bread with layers of Monterey Jack cheese and Cheddar cheese. Combine the eggs, milk, salt, paprika, oregano, pepper, garlic powder, mustard and green chiles; mix well. Pour the egg mixture over the cheese. Chill, covered, for 8 to 10 hours. Preheat the oven to 350 degrees. Bake for 50 to 55 minutes or until set and lightly browned. Let stand for 10 minutes before serving. Yield: 12 servings.

Clara Leonard-Bowen, Alpha Upsilon
Danville, Kentucky

EGG SALAD CASSEROLE

1 cup uncooked white rice	1 cup mayonnaise
1 cup chopped celery	1/2 cup milk
2 tablespoons chopped parsley	1/4 teaspoon salt
1/2 cup coarsely chopped walnuts	6 hard-cooked eggs, sliced
1 cup (4 ounces) shredded sharp Cheddar cheese	2 cups potato chips, crushed

Cook the rice using package directions. Combine the rice, celery, parsley, walnuts, Cheddar cheese, mayonnaise, milk and salt in a large bowl; mix well. Stir in the eggs; mix lightly. Spread in a 9x9-inch baking dish. Sprinkle with potato chips. Bake at 350 degrees for 25 minutes or until set and golden brown. Yield: 4 to 6 servings.

Lorraine L. Kirkpatrick, Preceptor Gamma Delta
Barstow, California

EGGPLANT ROLLATINI

2 pounds eggplant, trimmed, peeled	Flour
	Vegetable oil for frying
1 cup grated Romano cheese	1 cup minced spinach
	1 egg
1 1/2 cups shredded mozzarella cheese	1 (15-ounce) carton ricotta cheese
4 eggs	1 (28-ounce) jar spaghetti sauce
1/4 cup water	
Salt and pepper to taste	

Slice the eggplant lengthwise into 1/8-inch slices. Combine 1/4 cup of the Romano cheese, the mozzarella cheese, 3 of the eggs, water, salt and pepper in a shallow bowl. Dip each eggplant slice in flour. Shake off excess flour and dip in egg mixture. Fry in the oil until brown, beginning with 1/4 cup oil, adding more when necessary. Drain on paper towels. Preheat the oven to 325 degrees. Combine the spinach, the remaining 3/4 cup Romano cheese, the remaining egg, ricotta cheese, salt and pepper. Place 2 tablespoons of the spinach mixture over the small end of each eggplant slice. Roll tightly, enclosing filling. Spread 1 cup of spaghetti sauce over the bottom of a 9x13-inch baking pan. Arrange the eggplant rolls, seam side down, over the sauce. Drizzle the remaining spaghetti sauce over the eggplant rolls. Bake for 45 minutes or until hot and bubbly. Yield: 4 to 6 servings.

Gail M. Plache, Preceptor Beta Gamma
Scottsdale, Arizona

❖ LEEK AND BRIE QUICHE

Serve this excellent quiche for a Sunday brunch.

1 1/2 tablespoons olive oil	4 large eggs, beaten
2 large leeks, white and pale green parts only, finely chopped	1 1/4 cups heavy cream
	3/4 teaspoon salt
1 small onion, chopped	1/4 teaspoon black pepper
1 sheet frozen puff pastry, thawed	1/4 teaspoon nutmeg
8 ounces Brie cheese, rind removed, cut into small pieces	

Preheat the oven to 425 degrees. Heat 1/2 tablespoon of the olive oil in a heavy skillet over medium-low heat and sauté the leeks and onions for about 7 minutes or until light golden and tender. Cool. Roll out the pastry on a lightly floured surface, forming a 12-inch square. Line a 9-inch glass pie pan with the pastry. Trim to fit. Crimp the edges. Arrange the leek mixture over the pastry. Layer half the Brie over the leek mixture. Combine the eggs, cream, salt, pepper and nutmeg in a medium bowl; whisk to blend well. Stir in the remaining Brie. Pour the cream mixture over the leek mixture. Bake for 15 minutes. Reduce oven heat to 350 degrees. Bake for 15 minutes longer or until deep golden brown and filling moves only slightly when dish is shaken. Cool on a wire rack. Yield: 6 to 8 servings.

Ruth Martinez, Xi Alpha Gamma Xi
Wichita Falls, Texas

ANGEL HAIR VEGETABLE PRIMAVERA

Serve with a fresh garden salad.

1/4 cup (1/2 stick) butter	1/2 cup grated Romano
2 medium carrots,	cheese
peeled, sliced	1/4 teaspoon salt
4 broccoli spears,	1/2 teaspoon pepper
blanched	1 teaspoon fresh
1/2 head cauliflower,	chopped parsley
blanched	1 (16-ounce) package
10 ounces mushrooms,	angel hair pasta,
sliced	cooked
1 1/2 quarts heavy cream	
1/2 cup grated Parmesan	
cheese	

Melt the butter in a large heavy saucepan over medium heat and sauté the carrots, broccoli, cauliflower and mushrooms for 3 minutes. Stir in the cream. Cook over high heat for about 5 minutes or until cream is reduced by half, stirring occasionally with a wooden spoon. Stir in the next 5 ingredients. Remove from heat. Add the pasta. Toss until evenly coated and serve. Yield: 4 servings.

Dianna Maffucci, Preceptor Beta Gamma
Slingerlands, New York

PASTA WITH FETA AND MINT

1 (16-ounce) package	2 tablespoons olive oil
penne	1 tablespoon fresh
1 cup crumbled feta	lemon juice
cheese	Pinch of pepper
1 (6-ounce) can black	1/2 package baby spinach
olives, sliced	leaves, uncooked
1/4 cup chopped fresh	
mint leaves	

Cook penne using package directions; drain. Mix the feta cheese, olives, mint, olive oil, lemon juice and pepper in a large bowl. Add the spinach and penne. Toss and serve. Yield: 6 to 8 servings.

Kathleen J. Shafer, Beta Zeta
Mifflinburg, Pennsylvania

RED POTATO CRUST PIZZA

1 pound red potatoes,	1 cup ricotta cheese
thinly sliced	1/4 cup grated Parmesan
1 egg white, lightly	cheese
beaten	1/2 teaspoon sage
1/2 teaspoon salt	1 cup shredded
1/2 teaspoon pepper	mozzarella cheese
1 onion, chopped	
1 garlic clove, minced	
1 (10-ounce) package	
frozen chopped	
spinach, thawed,	
squeezed dry	

Position the oven rack in lower third of oven. Preheat the oven to 500 degrees. Spray a large baking sheet, or a 12-inch-round pizza pan, with nonstick cooking spray. Combine the potatoes, egg white, 1/4 teaspoon of the salt and 1/4 teaspoon of the pepper in a large bowl; mix well. Arrange the potato mixture, over the baking sheet, overlapping the slices in a circle to form a potato shell. Bake for about 15 minutes or until potatoes are tender. Cool slightly. Run a large spatula under the potato crust to loosen from pan. Preheat a nonstick skillet over medium-low heat, or heat 1 tablespoon vegetable oil in a regular skillet. Sauté the onion and garlic for about 5 minutes or until onion is tender. Stir in the spinach and remaining 1/4 teaspoon salt. Combine the ricotta cheese, Parmesan cheese, sage and remaining 1/4 teaspoon pepper in a medium bowl; mix well. Spread the ricotta mixture over the potato crust. Cover with the spinach mixture. Sprinkle with mozzarella cheese. Bake for 8 to 10 minutes or until heated through; cheese should melt. Let stand for 5 minutes before serving. Yield: 6 servings.

Tracey Roberts, Theta Rho
Mt. Juliet, Tennessee

Linda Wichelmann, Tau Beta, Santa Cruz, California, makes Easy Cheesy Pasta and Veggies by cutting 2 carrots and a large red or green bell pepper into bite-size pieces and mixing in a cup of broccoli florets. Cook 1 1/2 cups rotini according to package directions, adding the veggies for the last 5 minutes. Drain well. Heat 1 can cream of celery soup, 1/2 cup milk and 1 tablespoon mustard in a saucepan over medium heat, stirring occasionally. Add 1/2 cup shredded Cheddar cheese and heat until the cheese melts, stirring constantly. Toss the sauce with the pasta and vegetables.

VEGETARIAN PIZZA

½ teaspoon sugar
½ cup warm water
½ envelope dry yeast
½ tablespoon vegetable
  oil
½ teaspoon salt
1½ cups whole wheat
  flour
1 (6-ounce) can tomato
  paste

2 garlic cloves, chopped
1 teaspoon oregano
1 teaspoon basil
½ teaspoon Tabasco
  sauce
Fresh vegetables such as
  zucchini, onion,
  tomato and olives
1½ cups shredded
  mozzarella cheese

Preheat the oven to 450 degrees. Dissolve the sugar in warm water in a small bowl. Sprinkle with the yeast. Let stand for 10 minutes. Combine the yeast mixture, oil, salt and flour in the container of a food processor; process for a few minutes or until mixture forms a ball. Place dough in a greased bowl. Cover with a tea towel. Let rise in a warm place for 20 minutes. Roll out dough to fit a round pizza pan. Let rise for 30 minutes longer. Combine the tomato paste, garlic, oregano, basil and Tabasco sauce in a small bowl; blend well. Spread the tomato paste mixture over the pizza dough, leaving a half-inch border. Layer the vegetables over the tomato paste mixture. Sprinkle the mozzarella cheese over the top. Bake for 16 minutes or until crust is done and cheese begins to brown. Remove pizza from pan and let stand on a wire rack for 5 minutes. Cut and serve.
Yield: 4 servings.

Diana Wong, Theta Xi
Kamloops, British Columbia, Canada

❖ RISOTTO MAGNIFICO

This tasty risotto makes a great meatless meal . . . or stir in 1 cup chopped cooked chicken breast if desired. Serve with a green salad with light vinaigrette dressing, crusty bread, and your favorite wine.

3 cups vegetable broth
½ pound fresh
  asparagus, ends
  trimmed, cut into
  1-inch pieces
1 cup dry white wine
¼ teaspoon saffron
  threads
1½ tablespoons olive oil
1 cup arborio rice or
  medium-grain white
  rice, uncooked

1 cup frozen petit peas,
  thawed
⅓ cup grated Parmesan
  cheese
½ to 1 cup sautéed wild
  mushrooms
  (optional)

Pour the broth into a heavy saucepan over medium-high heat. Bring to a boil. Reduce heat. Stir in the asparagus and simmer for about 2 minutes or until tender-crisp. Remove asparagus from the broth with a slotted spoon and place in a small bowl. Add the wine and saffron to the broth. Bring to a simmer. Heat the olive oil in another saucepan over medium heat and sauté the rice for 2 minutes or until translucent. Add the broth mixture to the rice, reserving ¼ cup of the hot broth. Simmer rice, uncovered, for about 20 minutes or until creamy but firm to the bite, stirring occasionally. Stir in the asparagus, petit peas and Parmesan cheese. Add reserved ¼ cup broth if risotto seems dry. Stir in wild mushrooms.
Yield: 2 servings.

Nan Rutkowski, Preceptor Alpha Alpha
Minneapolis, Minnesota

PORTOBELLO MUSHROOM RISOTTO

2 teaspoons olive oil
1 large onion, chopped
1 (6-ounce) package
  portobello
  mushrooms, sliced
1 teaspoon bottled
  minced garlic

1 (14-ounce) can fat-free
  beef broth
¾ cup quick-cooking
  barley
2 tablespoons half-and-
  half
Salt and pepper to taste

Heat the oil in a 12-inch nonstick skillet over medium-low heat. Sauté the onion for 1 or 2 minutes. Turn heat to medium-high. Add the mushrooms and sauté for 1 minute. Add the garlic, beef broth and barley; stir well. Bring to a boil. Simmer, covered, for 10 to 12 minutes or until barley is tender, stirring occasionally. Remove from heat. Stir in half-and-half, salt and pepper. Serve immediately. Yield: 4 servings.

Bette Wilkens, Laureate Phi
Wilton, Wisconsin

❖ SPINACH AND FONTINA STUFFED PORTOBELLOS

4 to 6 medium or large
  portobello
  mushrooms
¼ cup olive oil
1 (10-ounce) package
  frozen chopped
  spinach, thawed,
  squeezed dry
⅓ cup chunky tomato
  sauce

½ cup sliced green
  onions
⅓ cup oil-packed sun-
  dried tomatoes,
  drained, chopped
¼ teaspoon crushed red
  pepper
¾ cup shredded fontina
  cheese

Preheat the oven to 375 degrees. Remove stems from the portobello mushrooms and save for another use. Brush both sides of mushrooms lightly with olive oil. Arrange mushrooms in a 9x13x2-inch baking pan. Bake for 10 minutes, turning once. Combine the spinach and tomato sauce in a small bowl; mix well. Combine the green onions, sun-dried tomatoes and red pepper in another small bowl; mix well. Remove mushrooms from oven. Make sure each is gill side up in the baking pan. Divide the spinach mixture evenly among the mushroom caps, spreading portion over each cap. Layer equal portions of the sun-dried tomato mixture over the spinach mixture. Sprinkle with fontina cheese. Return to oven for 5 to 8 minutes or until heated through and cheese begins to melt. Serve with additional tomato sauce if desired. Yield: 3 to 4 servings.

Juanita Lunn, Preceptor Theta Rho
Eustis, Florida

MUSHROOM TOFU MELT

Serve with pita bread, whole wheat bread, or a baked potato.

2 tablespoons olive oil	2 tablespoons tamari
1 garlic clove, chopped	soy sauce
4 medium mushrooms,	1 cup shredded sharp
sliced	Cheddar cheese
1/2 pound extra-firm	4 whole wheat pita
tofu, sliced 1/2 inch	breads
thick	1 tomato, thinly sliced

Heat the oil in a medium skillet and sauté the garlic and mushrooms for 5 to 10 minutes or until lightly brown. Add the tofu. Drizzle soy sauce over tofu until all pieces are brown. Sprinkle the Cheddar cheese over the tofu. Heat until cheese is melted. Line pita bread with tomato slices. Fill with the mushrooms, tofu and cheese. Yield: 4 servings.

Susan Thomas-Mancke, Xi Delta Iota
Oneonta, New York

"EGGLESS" SALAD

If you like egg salad but don't want the cholesterol, try this salad on a bed of lettuce or as a sandwich spread.

1 pound firm tofu	2 tablespoons honey
3/4 cup chopped celery	mustard
1/2 cup chopped scallions	1/4 teaspoon garlic
1/2 cup shredded carrot	powder
1/2 cup mayonnaise	

Crumble the tofu into a large bowl. Add the celery, scallions, carrot, mayonnaise, honey mustard and garlic powder; blend well. Yield: 4 servings.

Ione Fitzgerald, Lambda Lambda
Redford, Michigan

GARDEN DELIGHT VEGETABLE QUESADILLAS

1 large onion	2 tablespoons (about)
1 zucchini	vegetable oil
2 yellow squash	1 (10-count) package
1/2 green bell pepper	flour tortillas
1/2 yellow bell pepper	3 cups shredded Cheddar
1/2 red bell pepper	cheese
1 (12-ounce) jar sweet	1 cup sour cream
and hot peppers	1 (12-ounce) jar salsa

Cut the onion, zucchini and yellow squash into bite-size chunks. Cut the green, yellow and red bell peppers into strips. Drain and slice the sweet and hot peppers. Heat the oil in a large skillet. Add the vegetables. Cook just until the vegetables are tender-crisp, stirring gently occasionally. Pour the vegetables into a large bowl and set aside. Heat the tortillas in the microwave for about 45 seconds or until heated through. Return the skillet to the heat. Brush the skillet lightly with additional oil. Place a tortilla in the skillet. Spoon on enough vegetables to cover the tortilla, using a slotted spoon. Sprinkle with cheese and top with another tortilla. Cook until the quesadilla is golden brown and crisp on the bottom and the cheese has partially melted. Turn the quesadilla over using a turner on both the top and bottom to hold securely. Cook until the cheese has melted completely. Place on a plate and cut into wedges. Serve hot with sour cream and salsa. Repeat with the remaining tortillas, vegetables and cheese. Yield: 5 servings.

Yvonne Dionne, Xi Alpha Omega
Jacksonville, North Carolina

Barbara Sneddon, Xi Delta Xi, Long Beach, California, makes Portobello Burgers by brushing mushroom caps with olive oil and grilling for about 5 minutes on each side. Fill the caps with chopped roasted red peppers and add a slice of Swiss cheese. Grill until the cheese melts and place on buttered toasted buns. Sprinkle with salt and pepper and watercress leaves.

VEGETABLE GRAIN COMBO

*1 to 2 tablespoons
    canola oil*
*1/2 cup chopped green
    onions*
*1/2 cup chopped red bell
    peppers*
*1/2 cup carrots, cut in
    julienne*
*1/2 cup uncooked brown
    rice*
*1 (14-ounce) can chicken
    broth*

1/2 cup uncooked lentils
*1 tablespoon
    Worcestershire sauce*
*1 (15-ounce) can black-
    eyed peas, drained*
*1/4 teaspoon garlic
    powder*
1/4 teaspoon thyme
*1/4 teaspoon chili
    powder*
Salt and pepper to taste

Heat the oil in a large skillet over medium-low heat and sauté the next 3 ingredients for 3 to 4 minutes or until tender. Stir in the brown rice, chicken broth, lentils, Worcestershire sauce, black-eyed peas, garlic powder, thyme, chili powder, salt and pepper. Bring to a boil. Reduce heat to low. Simmer, covered, for 20 to 30 minutes or until vegetables are tender and liquid is absorbed. Yield: 4 servings.

*Stephanie Becker, Preceptor Alpha Nu
Pratt, Kansas*

CRUSTLESS VEGETABLE PIE

1/4 cup vegetable oil
*1 medium eggplant,
    peeled, cubed*
*2 medium zucchini,
    cubed*
1 large onion, chopped
*4 medium tomatoes,
    peeled, chopped*
3 eggs

*3/4 cup grated Parmesan
    cheese*
*1 tablespoon chopped
    parsley*
1/2 teaspoon basil
1/2 teaspoon oregano
Salt and pepper to taste
*4 ounces mozzarella
    cheese, thinly sliced*

Heat the oil in a large skillet over medium-low heat and sauté the eggplant, zucchini and onion for about 10 minutes or until tender. Add the tomatoes. Simmer, covered, for 20 to 25 minutes or until mixture is soft. Remove mixture to a large bowl. Cool. Preheat the oven to 350 degrees. Combine the eggs, 1/4 cup Parmesan cheese, parsley, basil and oregano in a medium bowl; beat well. Stir egg mixture into eggplant with salt and pepper. Pour half the vegetable mixture into a greased 10-inch pie plate. Sprinkle with 1/4 cup of the Parmesan cheese. Cover with layers of the remaining vegetable mixture, remaining Parmesan cheese and mozzarella cheese. Bake for 40 to 45 minutes or until set and cheese is golden brown. Yield: 5 to 6 servings.

*Mary Gamble, Xi Beta Tau
Huntsville, Alabama*

ZUCCHINI TORTE

This is sometimes referred to as "I can't believe this is zucchini!"

*2 cups thinly sliced
    zucchini*
2 eggs, beaten
*1/2 cup buttermilk
    baking mix*
*1/2 cup shredded sharp
    Cheddar cheese*
*1 tablespoon chopped
    fresh parsley or
    parsley flakes*

1/4 cup vegetable oil
1 garlic clove, minced
*1/2 cup finely chopped
    onion*
Salt to taste
Pepper to taste
*1 (4-ounce) can sliced
    mushrooms*
1 tomato, sliced
Parmesan cheese

Preheat the oven to 325 degrees. Combine the first 10 ingredients in a large bowl. Spread in a lightly greased 2-quart baking dish. Layer the mushrooms and tomato slices over the zucchini mixture. Sprinkle generously with Parmesan cheese. Bake for 45 minutes. Yield: 4 servings.

*Louise McCook, Xi Epsilon Lambda
Blind Bay, British Columbia, Canada*

ITALIAN ZUCCHINI CRESCENT PIE

1/4 to 1/2 cup margarine
*4 cups thinly sliced
    zucchini*
1 cup chopped onion
*1/2 cup chopped parsley,
    or 2 teaspoons dried*
1/2 teaspoon salt
1/2 teaspoon pepper
*1/4 teaspoon garlic
    powder*

1/4 teaspoon basil
1/4 teaspoon oregano
2 eggs, beaten
*2 cups shredded
    mozzarella or
    muenster cheese*
*1 (8-count) package
    crescent rolls*
*Prepared mustard to
    taste*

Preheat the oven to 375 degrees. Melt the margarine in a skillet over medium-low heat and sauté the zucchini and onion for about 10 minutes or until tender-crisp. Remove from heat. Stir in the parsley, salt, pepper, garlic, basil and oregano; mix well. Combine the eggs and mozzarella cheese in a large bowl; mix well. Stir in the zucchini mixture. Separate the crescent roll dough into triangles. Arrange the triangles in an ungreased pie plate, pressing over the bottom and sides to form a shell. Spread lightly with a small amount of mustard. Pour the zucchini mixture into the shell. Bake for 18 to 20 minutes or until center is set, covering with foil for the last 10 minutes of baking time. Let stand for 10 minutes before serving. Yield: 6 servings.

*Frances Wilson, Preceptor Epsilon Sigma
Almonte, Ontario, Canada*

Swift Side Dishes

Remember watching the old black and
white TV classics, when "Samantha"
magically manifested a family meal with a
wriggle of her nose? And "Jeannie" packed
the perfect picnic in the blink of an eye?
Glued to the screen, we wondered in awe
at their "powers." So now we know about
stop-camera action, but the mere mortal
chef still craves immediate gratification.
Create your own sense of enchanting
ease in the kitchen with the many breads
and sides in *Swift Side Dishes*—
they simply *do* appear in a snap.

CHUCK WAGON BEANS

6 slices bacon
1 green bell pepper,
   chopped
1 medium onion, chopped
1 (15-ounce) can kidney
   beans, drained
1 (15-ounce) can pinto
   beans, drained
1 (15-ounce) can navy
   beans, drained

1 (15-ounce) can lima
   beans
1 (15-ounce) can green
   beans
1 (15-ounce) can pork
   and beans
1/2 (6-ounce) jar chili
   sauce
2 cups packed brown
   sugar

Cut each bacon slice into 4 pieces. Microwave on High over paper towels for 1 to 3 minutes or until almost crisp. Combine the bacon, green pepper, onion, kidney beans, pinto beans, navy beans, lima beans, green beans, pork and beans, chili sauce and brown sugar in a slow cooker or large Dutch oven; mix well. Cook on Low or over low heat for 8 hours, stirring once or twice. Yield: 28 to 30 servings.

Nancy K. Ruzinsky, Laureate Gamma Sigma
Abilene, Texas

GREEN BEANS IN SWISS CHEESE SAUCE

This dish may be made ahead and chilled, covered, until baking time. If taken from the refrigerator, bake for longer than 30 minutes.

1 1/2 pounds fresh green
   beans, trimmed
1/4 cup butter or
   margarine
1/4 cup chopped onion
1/2 pound fresh
   mushrooms, sliced
3 tablespoons flour
1 teaspoon salt

1/8 teaspoon pepper
1/8 teaspoon thyme
1/8 teaspoon marjoram
1 cup milk
1/3 cup sherry or
   additional milk
1 cup shredded Swiss
   cheese

Preheat the oven to 400 degrees. Cut the green beans into 2-inch lengths. Cook in boiling salted water to cover in a saucepan over medium heat for about 15 minutes or until tender-crisp; drain. Melt the butter in a skillet over medium heat. Sauté the onions and mushrooms for about 6 minutes or until tender. Stir in the flour, salt, pepper, thyme and marjoram. Stir the milk in gradually. Bring to a boil. Cook, stirring, until thickened. Remove from heat. Stir in the sherry, half the Swiss cheese and the green beans. Place in a 1 1/2-quart shallow baking dish. Sprinkle with the remaining 1/2 cup cheese. Bake, uncovered, for about 30 minutes or until heated through. Yield: 6 servings.

Maryann Eldridge, Xi Chi Pi
Kernville, California

GREEK GREEN BEANS

1 1/4 cups low-sodium
   chicken broth
2 garlic cloves
1 1/4 pounds fresh green
   beans, trimmed
1 teaspoon cornstarch
1 tablespoon water
1 tablespoon chopped
   fresh oregano
1 1/2 teaspoons fresh
   lemon juice

2 teaspoons olive oil
1/2 teaspoon Dijon
   mustard
1/4 teaspoon salt
1/8 teaspoon pepper
1/4 cup crumbled feta
   cheese
English lavender flowers
   (optional)

Combine the chicken broth and garlic in a skillet over medium-high heat. Bring to a boil. Add the green beans. Reduce heat and simmer, covered, for 15 minutes or until beans are tender-crisp. Drain green beans, reserving 1/4 cup of the broth mixture and 1 garlic clove. Discard remaining broth and garlic clove. Return reserved broth and garlic to the skillet; mash well with a fork. Combine the cornstarch and water in a small bowl, stirring to blend. Stir in the oregano, lemon juice, olive oil, mustard, salt and pepper. Cook over medium heat for 3 minutes, stirring constantly. Return green beans to the skillet. Cook until heated through, stirring constantly. Spoon into a serving bowl and sprinkle with feta cheese. Garnish with lavender flowers. Yield: 4 servings.

Sonia K. Grim, Master Theta
Dallastown, Pennsylvania

ST. JOSEPH DAY GREEN BEAN CASSEROLE

2 (28-ounce) cans cut
   green beans, drained,
   rinsed
Pepper to taste
Garlic salt to taste
1 cup grated Parmesan
   or Romano cheese
1/3 cup olive oil
   (or more)

1 cup Italian bread
   crumbs
1 (14-ounce) can
   artichoke hearts,
   drained, sliced
1 (2-ounce) can sliced
   black olives
1/3 cup water

Preheat the oven to 350 degrees. Combine the green beans, pepper and garlic salt in a large oven-safe bowl; stir. Stir in the Parmesan cheese, olive oil, bread crumbs, artichoke hearts and olives; mix well, adding more olive oil if mixture is too dry. Pour water around edges of green bean mixture. Cover tightly with aluminum foil and bake for about 30 minutes. Yield: 10 to 12 servings.

Mary L. Hill, Laureate Omega
Kirkland, Washington

BAKED RED BEAN SALAD

1 (16-ounce) can red or
   kidney beans, drained
1 cup thinly sliced celery
1/3 cup chopped sweet
   pickles
1/4 cup finely chopped
   onion
1 cup diced sharp
   Cheddar cheese

1/2 cup mayonnaise or
   salad dressing
1/2 teaspoon salt
1/2 teaspoon chili
   powder
1/2 teaspoon
   Worcestershire sauce
1 cup coarsely crushed
   corn chips

Preheat the oven to 450 degrees. Combine the beans with the celery, pickles, onion and Cheddar cheese. Blend the mayonnaise, salt, chili powder and Worcestershire sauce in a small bowl. Add the mayonnaise mixture to the bean mixture; toss lightly. Place in a 1-quart baking dish. Sprinkle with the corn chips. Bake for 10 minutes. Yield: 4 to 8 servings.

Norma Smith, Alpha Delta Upsilon
Shell Knob, Missouri

SAUCY BRUSSELS SPROUTS

2 pints fresh brussels
   sprouts
2 tablespoons butter or
   margarine
1/2 cup chopped onions
1 tablespoon flour
1 teaspoon salt

1 tablespoon brown
   sugar
1/2 teaspoon dry mustard
1/2 cup milk
1 cup sour cream
1 tablespoon chopped
   parsley

Rinse and trim brussel sprouts. Cut into halves. Cook, covered, in a small amount of boiling salted water in a medium saucepan for 10 to 15 minutes or until tender; drain. Melt the butter in a medium saucepan over medium heat and sauté the onions until tender but not brown. Add the flour, salt, brown sugar and mustard, stirring until blended. Stir in the milk. Cook, stirring, until mixture thickens and bubbles. Reduce heat and stir in the sour cream. Add the brussels sprouts and parsley, stirring gently to combine. Heat through. Yield: 8 servings.

Mary Roberson, Preceptor Xi Omega
Sacramento, California

Rose Lawson, Laureate Epsilon Phi, Temple, Texas, prepares Beets in Orange Sauce by combining 1 1/2 tablespoons cornstarch and 1 tablespoon cold water in a saucepan over medium heat. Stir in 1/2 cup orange juice, 1/4 cup butter, 2 tablespoons grated orange zest, 2 tablespoons lemon juice and 1/4 teaspoon salt. Cook until thickened and clear, stirring constantly. Stir in 3 cups sliced cooked beets. Cook until heated through.

CABBAGE CASSEROLE

5 cups chopped cabbage
2 tablespoons butter
2 tablespoons flour
1/2 teaspoon salt
1/8 teaspoon pepper
1 1/4 cups milk
1/4 cup chopped onion

1/2 cup chopped yellow
   bell pepper
1/2 cup shredded Cheddar
   cheese
4 cups crumbled corn
   bread

Preheat the oven to 375 degrees. Cook the cabbage, covered, in a small amount of lightly salted boiling water in a medium saucepan for 5 minutes. Remove the cabbage to a bowl; drain. Add the butter to the saucepan, heating until melted. Stir in the flour, salt and pepper. Add the milk all at once. Cook over medium heat until thickened and bubbly, stirring constantly. Add the onion, bell pepper and Cheddar cheese. Heat, stirring, until cheese is melted. Remove from heat. Spread 3 cups of the corn bread in a 2-quart casserole. Layer the cabbage, cheese mixture and remaining cornbread over the top. Bake, uncovered, for 30 to 35 minutes or until heated through. Yield: 8 servings.

Claudia M. Long, Kappa Kappa
Meriden, Kansas

NANA'S RED CABBAGE

3 pounds red cabbage,
   cored, shredded
2/3 cup red wine vinegar
1/4 cup sugar
2 teaspoons salt
2 tablespoons bacon
   drippings
2 or 3 Granny Smith
   apples, peeled, cored,
   sliced

2 cups chopped red
   onions
1 large bay leaf
1 small onion, stuck
   with 4 whole cloves
1 cup hot water
1/4 cup red wine
   (optional)

Place the red cabbage in a large bowl. Sprinkle with the vinegar, sugar and salt; mix well. Let stand, covered, at room temperature for approximately 20 minutes. Heat the bacon drippings in a large kettle over medium heat and sauté the apples and red onions for about 5 minutes or until onions are translucent. Stir in the red cabbage, bay leaf and whole onion; mix well. Do not drain the cabbage. Add the hot water. Bring to a boil. Reduce heat and simmer, covered, for 1 to 1 1/2 hours, stirring occasionally. Stir in the wine just before serving; remove the bay leaf and whole onion. Yield: 8 to 12 servings.

Marlene Morwick, Laureate Beta
Boulder City, New York

CELERY CASSEROLE

3 cups chopped celery
1 (10-ounce) can cream
    of chicken soup
1 (4-ounce) can water
    chestnuts, sliced
1/4 cup chopped pimentos
30 butter crackers,
    crumbled
1/2 cup (1 stick)
    margarine, melted
1/2 cup sliced almonds

Preheat the oven to 350 degrees. Place celery and water to cover in a medium saucepan. Bring to a boil. Reduce heat and simmer, covered, for 7 minutes; drain. Combine the celery, cream of chicken soup, water chestnuts and pimentos in a medium bowl; mix well. Pour the celery mixture into a greased 2 1/2-quart baking dish. Combine the butter crackers and margarine. Layer the cracker mixture over the celery mixture. Sprinkle with the almonds. Bake for 30 minutes. Yield: 4 to 6 servings.

Sandra A. Lawson, Zeta
Hendersonville, Tennessee

BUCKEYE CORN PUDDING

2 tablespoons flour
2 tablespoons sugar
1 teaspoon salt
3 eggs, beaten
2 cups milk
2 cups fresh corn kernels
1 tablespoon butter

Preheat the oven to 350 degrees. Combine the flour, sugar and salt in a large bowl. Add the eggs; mix well. Stir in the milk and corn. Pour into a well-buttered 1 1/2-quart baking dish. Dot with butter. Bake for about 45 minutes or until firm custard forms. Yield: 6 to 8 servings.

Ginny Tawzer, Laureate Mu
Lexington, South Carolina

CREAMY CHEDDAR CORN BREAD

The substitution of pancake mix for cornmeal makes this bread especially moist and delicious. Do not use the "complete" type of pancake mix.

1 (15-ounce) can whole
    kernel corn, drained
1 (15-ounce) can cream-
    style corn
8 ounces cream cheese,
    softened
2 eggs, beaten
1 cup pancake mix
1/4 cup sugar
1 cup shredded mild
    Cheddar cheese

Preheat the oven to 350 degrees. Combine the ingredients in a large bowl; mix well. Pour into a greased 9x13-inch baking dish. Bake for 45 minutes or until firm. Yield: 12 to 15 servings.

Julie Echelmeier, Tau Epsilon
Corder, Missouri

SOUTHWESTERN HOMINY

2 (17-ounce) cans
    hominy, drained
1 (8-ounce) can chopped
    green chiles
1/4 cup finely grated
    onions
1 cup sour cream
1 1/2 cups shredded
    Cheddar cheese
3/4 teaspoon seasoned
    salt
1/4 teaspoon pepper

Preheat the oven to 350 degrees. Combine the hominy, green chiles, onions, sour cream, Cheddar cheese, seasoned salt and pepper in a large bowl; mix well. Pour into a greased 1 1/2-quart baking dish. Bake for 30 to 35 minutes or until hot and bubbly. Yield: 4 to 6 servings.

Rose Ann Munn, Xi Psi Xi
League City, Texas

BAKED MUSHROOMS

1 pound fresh
    mushrooms, cleaned,
    quartered
1/3 cup melted butter
1 tablespoon chopped
    parsley
1 tablespoon minced
    onion
1 1/2 tablespoons flour
1 teaspoon salt
1 tablespoon Dijon
    mustard
Pinch of cayenne pepper
Pinch of nutmeg
1 cup heavy cream

Preheat the oven to 375 degrees. Arrange the mushrooms evenly in a 1 1/2-quart glass baking dish. Combine the butter, parsley, onion, flour, salt, mustard, cayenne pepper and nutmeg in a medium bowl; mix well. Drizzle the butter mixture over the mushrooms. Pour 1/2 cup of the cream over the butter mixture; stir well. Bake uncovered for 30 minutes, stirring frequently. Drizzle the remaining 1/2 cup cream over the ingredients. Bake for 30 minutes longer. Yield: 4 to 6 servings.

Wanda Long, Alpha Xi Master
Fresno, California

VIDALIA ONION CASSEROLE

1/2 cup (1 stick) butter
4 Vidalia onions, cut
    into 1/4-inch slices
20 saltine crackers,
    crushed
1 (10-ounce) can cream
    of mushroom soup
2 eggs, beaten
1/2 to 3/4 cup milk
1 cup shredded Cheddar
    cheese

Preheat the oven to 350 degrees. Melt the butter in a large skillet over medium-low heat and sauté the onions for 5 to 10 minutes or until clear and tender. Set aside 5 tablespoons of the cracker crumbs. Layer the remaining cracker crumbs, cream of mushroom soup and onion mixture in a buttered 1½-quart baking dish. Pour the eggs over the onion mixture. Add enough milk to cover. Sprinkle with the Cheddar cheese and reserved 5 tablespoons cracker crumbs. Bake for 30 minutes or until hot and bubbly. Yield: 4 to 6 servings.

Herberta G. Moore, Preceptor Alpha Xi
Brentwood, Tennessee

CONFETTI SCALLOPED POTATOES

½ cup (1 stick) butter or | *1 cup shredded Cheddar*
margarine | *cheese*
1/2 cup chopped onion | *1 small green bell*
1 (16-ounce) package | *pepper, cut into strips*
frozen hash brown | *2 tablespoons chopped*
potatoes | *pimentos*
1 (10-ounce) can cream | *Salt and pepper to taste*
of mushroom soup | *1 cup cheese cracker*
1 (10-ounce) soup can | *crumbs*
milk

Preheat the oven to 375 degrees. Melt the butter in a medium skillet over medium heat and sauté the onion until tender. Stir in the potatoes, cream of mushroom soup and milk. Add the Cheddar cheese, green pepper, pimentos, salt, pepper and ½ cup of the cracker crumbs; mix well. Pour into a shallow 1½-quart baking dish. Sprinkle with remaining ½ cup cracker crumbs. Bake for 35 to 40 minutes or until hot and bubbly. Yield: 6 to 8 servings.

Donna Hoxie, Preceptor Delta
Lincoln, Nebraska

CHEESY POTATOES

1 (32-ounce) package | *8 ounces shredded*
frozen hash brown | *mozzarella cheese*
potatoes, thawed | *8 ounces shredded*
2 cups half-and-half | *Cheddar cheese*
¼ cup plus 2
tablespoons (¾ stick)
margarine, melted

Preheat the oven to 350 degrees. Arrange the potatoes evenly in a buttered 9x13-inch baking dish. Combine the half-and-half and margarine in a small bowl; blend well. Pour the butter mixture over the potatoes. Layer the mozzarella cheese and Cheddar cheese over the potatoes. Cover tightly with foil and bake for 30 minutes. Uncover and bake for 30 minutes longer. Yield: 12 to 15 servings.

Linda Dubke, Xi Alpha Phi
Fairmont, Minnesota

❖ HORSERADISH POTATOES

1 (16-ounce) package | *8 ounces cream cheese,*
instant mashed | *softened*
potatoes | *1 (5-ounce) jar*
¾ cup (1½ sticks) | *horseradish*
margarine, softened | *¼ to ½ cup shredded*
3½ cups milk | *Cheddar cheese*
1½ cups sour cream

Preheat the oven to 350 degrees. Prepare entire package of instant mashed potatoes using the margarine and milk. Combine the potatoes, sour cream, cream cheese and horseradish in a large mixer bowl. Beat at medium speed for 2 to 3 minutes or until blended. Spread evenly in a lightly greased 9x13-inch baking dish. Sprinkle with Cheddar cheese. Bake for 30 minutes. Yield: 6 to 8 servings.

Pamela Osborn, Iota
Rapid City, South Dakota

PISTOL PACKIN' POTATO STICKS

This recipe is delicious substituting onions for potatoes. Cut 2 large onions into slices of the desired thickness. Separate into rings and proceed as described.

1 bag frozen steak fries | *½ cup club soda*
1 cup self-rising flour | *⅓ cup minced jalapeño*
⅓ cup self-rising | *peppers*
cornmeal | *1 teaspoon chili powder*
1 egg | *1 teaspoon seasoned*
½ cup sweetened | *salt*
condensed milk | *Oil for deep-frying*

Combine the flour, cornmeal, egg, condensed milk, club soda, jalapeño peppers, chili powder and seasoned salt; blend well to form a rather thick batter, adding more club soda if necessary to achieve desired consistency. Dip frozen steak fries into batter to coat well. Deep-fry 2 or 3 at a time in hot oil. Yield: 4 to 6 servings.

Shelly Allison, Nu Kappa
Guthrie, Oklahoma

Suzanne Harris, Alpha Omega, Camarillo, California, makes Screaming Mashed Potatoes by peeling and chopping a large potato for each person and boiling until tender. After draining well, she adds a packet of dry ranch dressing mix and enough sour cream, whipping cream and butter to mash the potatoes to the desired consistency and adds salt and pepper to taste.

POTATO PIZZA CASSEROLE

4 cups sliced raw potatoes	1 (15-ounce) can tomato sauce
1 pound ground beef	1 teaspoon oregano
1/2 cup chopped onions	1/2 teaspoon sugar
1 (10-ounce) can Cheddar cheese soup	1 cup shredded mozzarella cheese
1/2 cup milk	

Preheat the oven to 375 degrees. Spread the potato slices evenly in a greased 9x13-inch baking pan (preheat oven to 325 if using a glass baking dish). Brown the ground beef with the onions in a skillet, stirring until ground beef is crumbly; drain. Combine the cheese soup and milk in a small bowl; mix well. Add the soup mixture to the skillet; mix well. Pour the ground beef mixture evenly over the sliced potatoes. Combine the tomato sauce, oregano and sugar in a small bowl; mix well. Pour the tomato sauce mixture evenly over the ground beef mixture. Bake uncovered for 1 hour. Sprinkle with mozzarella cheese. Bake for 15 minutes longer. Yield: 5 servings.

Jackie Burns, Preceptor Gamma Eta
Hamilton, Ontario, Canada

PUMPKIN CASSEROLE

Serve warm as a side dish or cold as a dessert.

1/2 cup (1 stick) margarine	1/2 teaspoon salt
2 eggs, well beaten	1/2 teaspoon baking soda
1 (15-ounce) can pumpkin	1/2 cup flour
1 cup sugar	1 teaspoon vanilla extract
1 cup evaporated milk	1 teaspoon cinnamon or to taste

Preheat the oven to 350 degrees. Melt the margarine in a 1 1/2- to 2-quart baking dish in the oven while preparing other ingredients. Combine the eggs and pumpkin in a large bowl. Add the sugar, evaporated milk, salt, baking soda, flour, vanilla extract and cinnamon 1 ingredient at a time, beating well after each addition with a wire whisk. Remove the hot baking dish from the oven, being careful not to burn yourself, and being careful to place the hot dish on a dry surface. Pour the pumpkin mixture into the baking dish. Bake for 1 hour or until knife inserted in center comes out clean. Surface will be golden brown and center will fall when removed from oven. Yield: 4 to 6 servings.

Ruth Clark Smith, Preceptor Gamma Rho
Bourbonnais, Illinois

FIREHOUSE SAUERKRAUT

1 (2-pound) package sauerkraut, rinsed, drained	1/2 pound smoked sausage, cut in pieces
1 (21-ounce) can apple pie filling	1/2 cup packed brown sugar
1/2 cup barbecue sauce	1/2 cup chopped onion

Preheat the oven to 350 degrees. Combine the ingredients in a large bowl; mix well. Pour into a greased 9x13-inch baking dish. Bake, covered, for 1 1/2 hours. Yield: 6 to 8 servings.

Marian K. Perusek, Xi Lambda Sigma
East Lake, Ohio

SPINACH QUICHE

This is an easy, delicious, inexpensive recipe especially good for those who need extra iron in their diet.

2 (16-ounce) cans spinach, drained	1 envelope onion soup mix
2 large or 3 small eggs, beaten	1 (28-ounce) package French-fried real onions, crumbled
1/2 cup sour cream	
1/2 cup cottage cheese	

Preheat the oven to 350 degrees. Spread the spinach in a greased 8x12-inch baking dish. Combine the eggs, sour cream, cottage cheese and onion soup mix; mix well. Pour the sour cream mixture evenly over the spinach. Cover with French-fried onions. Bake for about 45 minutes or until wooden pick comes out clean. Let stand for 15 minutes before serving. Yield: 6 to 8 servings.

Margaret Nell Flanagan, Laureate Mu
Coffeyville, Kansas

SPINACH SOUFFLE

3 eggs, beaten	Salt and pepper to taste
1 (10-ounce) package frozen spinach, thawed, drained	1 cup small-curd cottage cheese
1/4 cup (1/2 stick) butter, softened	1 cup cubed American cheese
1/4 cup flour	1 cup cubed brick cheese

Preheat the oven to 350 degrees. Combine the eggs, spinach, butter, flour, salt and pepper in a large bowl; stir to blend. Stir in the cottage cheese, American cheese and brick cheese. Spoon the mixture into a greased 2-quart baking dish. Bake for 50 to 60 minutes or until set. Yield: 6 servings.

Louise Cunniff, Preceptor Epsilon Epsilon
St. Charles, Missouri

❖ SWEET POTATO CRISP

8 ounces cream cheese, softened	2/3 cup chopped cranberries
1 (40-ounce) can cut syrup-pack sweet potatoes, drained	1/2 cup flour
	1/2 cup quick-cooking rolled oats
1/4 cup packed brown sugar	1/2 cup brown sugar
1/4 teaspoon cinnamon	1/3 cup margarine
1 cup chopped peeled apple	1/4 cup chopped pecans

Preheat the oven to 350 degrees. Combine the cream cheese, sweet potatoes, 1/4 cup brown sugar and cinnamon in a large bowl; beat until smooth. Spoon into a greased 10x16-inch baking pan. Sprinkle with the chopped apple. Sprinkle with the cranberries. Combine the flour, rolled oats and 1/2 cup brown sugar in a medium bowl; stir well. Cut in the margarine until mixture resembles coarse crumbs. Stir in the pecans. Sprinkle flour mixture over the cranberries. Bake for 35 to 40 minutes or until hot and bubbly. Yield: 8 servings.

Helen Cheseldine, Xi Iota Omega
Florissant, Missouri

FESTIVE VEGETABLES

Great for a potluck dinner, this vegetable casserole can be frozen in the baking dish before baking.

2 carrots	1 tablespoon sugar
1 rib celery	1/2 teaspoon basil
1/2 turnip, peeled	1/2 teaspoon savory
1 cup chicken broth	Salt and pepper to taste
1/4 cup (1/2 stick) butter	1 cup brussels sprouts, trimmed
2 tablespoons fresh lemon juice	8 small onions, peeled

Preheat the oven to 350 degrees. Cut the carrots, celery and turnip into 2-inch strips. Combine the chicken broth, butter, lemon juice, sugar, basil, savory and salt and pepper in a large kettle. Bring to a boil. Stir in the carrots, celery, turnip, brussels sprouts and onions. Reduce heat and simmer uncovered for 3 minutes. Pour into a greased 2-quart baking dish. Bake uncovered for 1 hour. Yield: 12 servings.

Catherine Hardy, Alpha Epsilon
Kelowna, British Columbia, Canada

ZUCCHINI CARROT CASSEROLE

1 pound ground beef	1 (10-ounce) can cream of chicken soup
2 medium zucchini, shredded	1 cup sour cream
1 cup shredded carrots	1/2 cup water
1 (6-ounce) package stove-top stuffing mix	1/2 cup milk

Preheat the oven to 350 degrees. Brown the ground beef in a skillet, stirring until crumbly; drain. Layer the ground beef, zucchini, carrots and stuffing mix in a 9x13-inch baking dish. Combine the cream of chicken soup, sour cream, water and milk in a medium bowl; mix well. Pour soup mixture over stuffing layer. Bake uncovered for 1 hour. Yield: 6 servings.

Angela Reder, Lambda
Fruitdale, South Dakota

MICROWAVE ZUCCHINI STRATA

6 medium zucchini	1 (6-ounce) package stove-top stuffing mix
1 medium onion, chopped	
1 (10-ounce) can cream of chicken soup	1 tablespoon butter or margarine, melted
1/2 cup sour cream	

Cut zucchini into 1/2-inch cubes. Combine the zucchini and onion in a large microwave-safe dish. Microwave, loosely covered, on High for 7 to 8 minutes or until tender. Combine the cream of chicken soup and sour cream in a small bowl; mix well. Stir the soup mixture into the zucchini mixture. Toss together the stuffing mix and butter in a medium bowl. Layer the zucchini mixture and stuffing mix 1/2 at a time in a 2-quart baking dish, forming 4 layers. Microwave uncovered on High for 12 minutes. Let stand for 3 or 4 minutes before serving. Yield: 6 to 8 servings.

Toni Dell-Imaginé, Laureate Gamma
Edmonds, Washington

Candy Cable, Beta Sigma, Nicholasville, Kentucky, bakes 4 potatoes for Veggie-Stuffed Potatoes, scoops out and mashes the pulp to mix with 1/4 cup each chopped green and red bell peppers and onion. After mixing in 1/2 cup yogurt and 1/3 cup shredded Cheddar cheese, she spoons the mixture into the potato shells, bakes at 350 degrees for 5 minutes, tops with additional cheese and bakes for 5 to 10 minutes longer. Serve with additional yogurt or sour cream.

APPLES AND COINS OF GOLD

This comfort food is reminiscent of the Oregon farm where I grew up. We always had apples at our meals, often served with pork or ham.

6 medium tart apples, peeled, sliced	1/3 cup sugar
6 medium carrots, thinly sliced	1/2 teaspoon nutmeg
1/2 cup orange juice	1/2 teaspoon cinnamon
1/3 cup flour	1/4 teaspoon salt
	2 tablespoons cold butter or margarine

Preheat the oven to 350 degrees. Combine the apples and carrots in a greased shallow 2-quart baking dish. Drizzle with the orange juice. Bake, covered, for 45 minutes. Combine the flour, sugar, nutmeg, cinnamon and salt in a small bowl. Cut in the butter until crumbly. Sprinkle over the apple mixture. Bake uncovered for 15 minutes longer or until carrots are tender. Yield: 6 to 8 servings.

Norma Gilkey, Laureate Pi
Glendopa, California

❖ BAKED CRANBERRY RELISH

This recipe may be halved or doubled, depending on your needs.

1 pound fresh cranberries, washed, dried	1 (8-ounce) jar orange marmalade
1 3/4 cups sugar	Grated orange zest (optional)
2 tablespoons water	1/2 cup brandy (optional)
3 to 4 tablespoons lemon juice	Chopped pecans (optional)

Preheat the oven to 325 degrees. Spread the cranberries in a 9x13-inch baking dish. Sprinkle the sugar and water evenly over the cranberries. Cover tightly with foil. Bake for 30 to 45 minutes or until cranberries begin to pop, shaking pan once or twice during baking. Remove from oven. Stir in the lemon juice, orange marmalade, orange zest, brandy and pecans. Chill, covered, for at least 3 hours before serving. Yield: 3 1/2 cups.

Shirley J. Bird, Xi Alpha Nu
Eureka Springs, Arkansas

Joyce Hoepker, Creston, Iowa, makes Summer Pepper Surprise by finely chopping 2 green bell peppers and 1 large Vidalia onion and mixing in 1 1/2 teaspoons olive oil and a pinch of salt. She serves it with grilled meats, especially hamburgers and baked beans.

SLOW-COOKER DRESSING

1 (8x8-inch) pan cooked corn bread	2 eggs, beaten
5 slices white or whole wheat bread	1 (10-ounce) can cream of celery soup
4 cups chicken broth	2 (10-ounce) cans cream of chicken soup
1 cup chopped celery	1 teaspoon pepper
1 onion, chopped	3 teaspoons sage

Crumble the corn bread and white bread into a 4-quart slow cooker. Pour the chicken broth over the bread. Cook the celery and onion in a small amount of water in a saucepan over medium heat for 5 minutes or until tender. Stir celery mixture into bread mixture. Combine the eggs, cream of celery soup, cream of chicken soup, pepper and sage in a medium bowl; mix well. Stir the soup mixture into the bread mixture. Dot with 4 or 5 pats of butter. Cook on High for 2 to 3 hours, stirring every 20 minutes for last hour of cooking time. Yield: 12 to 15 servings.

Ruth H. Poe, Preceptor Laureate Rho
Harrison, Arkansas

CORN BREAD DRESSING

To prepare a day ahead of time, chill, covered, before the final baking step. Remove from the refrigerator and let stand for 30 minutes. Bake at 350 degrees for 55 minutes.

2 cups cornmeal	1/2 cup chopped green onions
1 tablespoon sugar	
1 tablespoon baking powder	3 eggs, beaten
1 teaspoon salt	2 (14-ounce) cans chicken broth
2 eggs, beaten	1 (10-ounce) can cream of chicken soup, undiluted
1 (12-ounce) can evaporated milk	
1/4 cup vegetable oil	3/4 cup sliced almonds
3 tablespoons butter or margarine	1 teaspoon poultry seasoning
2 cups chopped fresh mushrooms	1/2 teaspoon sage
1 cup chopped celery	1/4 teaspoon pepper
	Dash of parsley flakes

Preheat the oven to 350 degrees. Combine the cornmeal, sugar, baking powder and salt in a large bowl. Stir in the eggs, evaporated milk and vegetable oil; mix well. Heat a well greased 10-inch cast-iron skillet in the oven for 5 minutes. Remove from oven. Spoon the cornmeal mixture into the hot skillet. Bake, uncovered, for 35 to 40 minutes or until lightly browned. Cool. Crumble the corn bread into a large bowl. Melt the butter in a skillet over medium heat and sauté the mushrooms, celery and green onions for 3 to 4 minutes or until tender. Stir the mushroom mixture, eggs, chicken broth, cream of chicken soup, almonds, poultry seasoning, sage, pepper and parsley flakes into the corn bread; mix well. Spoon into a greased 9x13-inch baking dish. Bake, uncovered, for 45 minutes. Garnish with a fluted mushroom and fresh parsley at serving time. Yield: 12 servings.

Leslie O'Neal, Xi Alpha Zeta
Bentonville, Arkansas

POLISH PIEROGI

My mother always made a traditional Polish dinner for every holiday, and these pierogi were the best part of a delicious meal.

1 pound sauerkraut, or 1 medium head cabbage, finely chopped	Pinch of salt
	Pinch of pepper
	2 eggs, beaten
4 to 6 ounces dried Polish mushrooms	1/4 cup water
	2 cups sifted flour
1/2 small onion, grated	2 tablespoons butter, melted (optional)

Soak the sauerkraut in water to cover for 1 hour; drain well. Combine the sauerkraut, mushrooms, onion, salt and pepper in a large bowl; set aside. Combine the eggs and water in a medium bowl. Beat in flour gradually with a wooden spoon, adding flour until dough becomes too stiff to beat. Knead the dough by hand for 5 minutes or until smooth and elastic. Roll dough 1/4 inch thick on a floured surface. Cut into 3-inch rounds. Place 2 teaspoons sauerkraut mixture over each round. Brush edges with water. Fold over dough, enclosing filling. Press edges together to seal. Crimp with a fork. Drop into boiling water. Boil for 10 minutes or until pierogi float to the top. Remove from water with a slotted spoon. Brush melted butter over pierogi if desired. Yield: 6 to 8 servings.

Stephnie B. Palasinski, Laureate Alpha Nu
Melbourne Beach, Florida

HORSERADISH RELISH

Serve with baked ham or roast beef.

1 (3-ounce) package lemon gelatin	3/4 cup horseradish, drained
1 cup hot water	1 cup whipping cream, whipped
1 tablespoon vinegar	
3/4 teaspoon salt	

Dissolve the gelatin mix in the hot water in a small bowl. Stir in the vinegar and salt. Chill, covered, for 45 minutes or until slightly thickened. Fold in the horseradish and whipped cream. Pour into a 4-cup salad mold. Chill, covered, for 2 to 3 hours or until set. Yield: 10 servings.

Barb Stein, Xi Delta Rho
LeRoy, New York

MACARONI AND CHEESE

1/4 cup butter	2 cups 1/2-inch cubes Cheddar cheese
3 tablespoons flour	1 cup fresh bread crumbs
2 cups milk	2 tablespoons butter, melted
8 ounces cream cheese, softened	2 tablespoons chopped fresh parsley
1/2 teaspoon salt	
1/2 teaspoon pepper	
2 teaspoons country-style Dijon mustard	
1 (7-ounce) package elbow macaroni, cooked	

Preheat the oven to 400 degrees. Melt 1/4 cup butter in a 3-quart saucepan. Whisk in the flour. Cook over medium heat for 1 minute or until smooth and bubbly, stirring constantly. Stir in the milk, cream cheese, salt, pepper and mustard. Cook for 3 to 4 minutes or until thickened, stirring constantly. Stir in the macaroni and Cheddar cheese. Pour into a greased 2-quart baking dish. Combine the bread crumbs, 2 tablespoons butter and parsley in a small bowl. Sprinkle over the macaroni and cheese. Bake for 15 to 20 minutes or until heated through. Yield: 6 to 8 servings.

Berlita Anderson, Laureate Kappa
Beatrice, Nebraska

TOSSED PARMESAN PASTA

2 to 4 tablespoons olive oil	Enough cooked, drained pasta to serve 4
1/2 to 1 cup coarsely chopped onion	1/2 cup grated Parmesan cheese
1 or 2 garlic cloves, pressed	Seasoned salt to taste
1 to 2 cups chopped fresh parsley	

Heat the olive oil in a skillet over medium heat and sauté the onion for 5 to 7 minutes or until lightly browned. Add the garlic. Cook briefly, stirring. Add the parsley. Cook for 1 or 2 minutes or until wilted, stirring constantly. Toss with the pasta, Parmesan cheese and seasoned salt. Serve hot. Yield: 4 servings.

Joanne Kozarek, At Large
Wyoming, Michigan

FRESH PEACH CHUTNEY

3 cups chopped peeled
  peaches, about
  5 medium
1/2 cup golden raisins
1/2 tablespoon freshly
  grated gingerroot

1/4 cup chopped onion
1/2 cup packed brown
  sugar
1/3 cup cider vinegar
1/4 teaspoon salt

Combine the peaches, raisins, gingerroot, onion, brown sugar, vinegar and salt in a 3-quart microwave-safe dish. Microwave, covered, on High for 18 to 20 minutes or until thickened, stirring 3 times during cooking. Ladle into 3 hot sterilized 8-ounce jars, leaving 1/2 inch headspace; seal with 2-piece lids. Process in a boiling water bath for 10 minutes. Yield: 2 2/3 cups.

Carolyn M. Cline, Laureate Omicron
Jamestown, New York

BUCKET PICKLES

4 cups sugar
2 cups white vinegar
2 tablespoons pickling
  salt
1 teaspoon turmeric
1 teaspoon celery seeds
1 teaspoon mustard
  seeds

1 large red bell pepper,
  sliced
1 large green bell pepper,
  sliced
1 large Spanish onion,
  sliced
5 or more cucumbers,
  sliced

Combine the sugar, vinegar, pickling salt, turmeric, celery seeds and mustard seeds in a 4-quart ice cream bucket; stir well. Add the red pepper, green pepper, Spanish onion and enough of the cucumbers to fill bucket to the level that the vegetables are just covered by liquid. Let stand for 2 hours. Stir. Add more cucumber slices if mixture has settled. Cover. Store in the refrigerator for up to 6 months.
Yield: 2 1/2 to 3 quarts.

Edna Ferrel, Laureate Tau
Penticton, British Columbia, Canada

MOM'S MUSTARD PICKLES

12 large cucumbers
1 large head cauliflower
12 large onions
2 green bell peppers
2 red bell peppers
1/2 cup coarse salt
5 cups cold water
8 cups mild vinegar
  (4 cups vinegar plus
  4 cups water)

6 cups sugar
1 tablespoon mustard
  seeds
1 tablespoon celery
  seeds
3/4 cup flour
6 tablespoons dry
  mustard
1 tablespoon turmeric

Chop the cucumbers, cauliflower, onions, green peppers and red peppers. Place in a large crock. Sprinkle the coarse salt over the vegetables. Add the 5 cups water. Let stand for 1 to 10 hours. Stir well; drain. Combine the mild vinegar, sugar, mustard seeds and celery seeds in a large stockpot over medium heat. Bring just to a boil. Combine the flour, mustard and turmeric in a small bowl. Stir in enough of the hot vinegar mixture to make a smooth paste. Add the flour mixture to the hot vinegar mixture. Cook for 5 minutes or until thick and smooth, stirring constantly. Stir in the well drained vegetables. Cook for 20 minutes, stirring occasionally. Pack into hot sterilized jars. Add the boiling liquid, leaving 1/2 inch headspace; seal with 2-piece lids. Process in a boiling water bath for 10 minutes. Yield: 8 quarts.

Debora Blazieko
Melville, Saskatchewan, Canada

BAKED PINEAPPLE

2 (20-ounce) cans
  pineapple chunks
1 cup (2 sticks) butter,
  melted
1 1/2 cups sugar

1/4 cup milk
3 eggs, beaten
10 slices fresh bread,
  torn into pieces

Preheat the oven to 325 degrees. Combine the undrained pineapple, butter, sugar, milk, eggs and bread in a 2-quart baking dish and mix well. Bake, covered, for about 1 hour, removing cover for the last 10 to 15 minutes of baking time to allow browning. Yield: 8 to 10 servings.

Lettie Loveleen Turner, Preceptor Zeta Tau
Orange Park, Florida

SPANISH RICE

2 tablespoons vegetable
  oil
1 1/2 cups rice
1 pound lean ground
  beef, browned,
  drained
1/2 green bell pepper,
  chopped

1 small onion, chopped
1/4 cup packed brown
  sugar
1 (10-ounce) can tomato
  soup
1 (10-ounce) soup can
  water

Heat the oil in a saucepan over medium heat and sauté the rice for 3 to 5 minutes. Stir in the beef, green pepper, onion, brown sugar, tomato soup and water. Bring to a simmer. Reduce heat and cook, tightly covered, for 15 to 20 minutes or until rice is tender, adding water as needed. Yield: 4 to 6 servings.

Donna Smith, Preceptor Epsilon Theta
St. Petersburg, Florida

Breads

FLUFFY TEA BISCUITS

Some prefer to bake these biscuits until they begin to brown; others prefer to remove them from the oven before there is any hint of browning.

3 cups flour
1¹/2 teaspoons baking soda
1 teaspoon baking powder
3 teaspoons cream of tartar
1 teaspoon salt
¹/2 cup (1 stick) butter, chilled
¹/2 cup shortening
1¹/2 cups milk

Preheat the oven to 450 degrees. Combine the flour, baking soda, baking powder, cream of tartar and salt in a large bowl. Cut in the butter and shortening until crumbly. Stir in the milk gradually. Dust the work surface with flour. Knead the dough on the work surface. Roll the dough ¹/2 inch thick. Cut into 3-inch circles with a cookie cutter. Bake on an ungreased baking sheet for 10 to 12 minutes or until done to taste. Yield: 6 to 8 servings.

Sally Cochrane, Xi Epsilon
Riverview, New Brunswick, Canada

CARROT MUSHROOM CHEESE ROLLS

Instead of forming 12 small circles, you may prefer to pat the dough into a large circle on the baking sheet. Cut into wedges to serve.

2¹/2 cups flour
1 tablespoon baking powder
¹/2 teaspoon salt
¹/2 cup (1 stick) chilled butter, sliced
2 cups coarsely shredded sharp Cheddar cheese
1 medium onion, minced
¹/2 cup finely chopped mushrooms
¹/2 cup finely chopped carrot
1 tablespoon freshly chopped parsley
³/4 cup milk
1 egg, lightly beaten

Preheat the oven to 450 degrees. Combine the flour, baking powder and salt in a medium bowl. Cut in the butter until crumbly. Stir in 1¹/2 cups of the Cheddar cheese, onion, mushrooms, carrot and parsley; mix well. Combine the milk and egg in a small bowl; mix well. Stir the egg mixture into the flour mixture just until moistened. Drop by spoonfuls onto a lightly greased baking sheet, forming 12 circles that barely touch each other. Sprinkle with the remaining ¹/2 cup Cheddar cheese. Bake for 15 minutes or until golden brown. Cool for 5 minutes. Yield: 24 rolls.

Shirley MacLeod, Preceptor Gamma Rho
Kemptville, Ontario, Canada

SKILLET WHITE CORN BREAD

This corn bread is moister and denser than today's standard yellow corn bread. My grandmother used to make it on her wood-burning stove. She would soften fresh churned butter in a warm place and use a glass of cold fresh cow's milk from the well-house cooler. I bake this corn bread when I want to step back in time to days that went at a gentler, slower pace.

2 cups boiling water
1½ cups white cornmeal
1 cup milk
1¼ teaspoons salt
3 teaspoons baking
    powder

2 tablespoons butter,
    softened
3 eggs, well beaten

Preheat the oven to 400 degrees. Stir the water into the cornmeal in a mixer bowl. Cool for at least 15 minutes. Beat in the milk, salt, baking powder, butter and eggs on medium speed. Pour into a greased 10-inch iron skillet. Bake for 30 to 35 minutes or until tests done. Yield: 8 servings.

Mary Helen Goldberg, Psi Beta
Plattsburg, Missouri

LUCY'S SPOON BREAD

The key to avoiding lumps in the batter is to make sure you pour the boiling water very slowly over the cornmeal while stirring. The 8x8-inch baking dish makes the thicker bread that I prefer, but you may use a buttered 9x13-inch baking dish if you want a flat bread. The women in my chapter always request this spoon bread for our annual chili supper. The recipe can be doubled.

2 cups boiling water
1 cup cornmeal
2 tablespoons butter or
    margarine, softened
1 (12-ounce) can
    evaporated milk

1 teaspoon salt
2 teaspoons baking
    powder
3 eggs, well beaten

Preheat the oven to 375 degrees. Pour the boiling water slowly over the cornmeal in a bowl, stirring constantly so there are no lumps. Add the butter, stirring until smooth. Cool slightly. Combine the evaporated milk, salt, baking powder and eggs in a medium bowl; mix well. Pour the egg mixture into the cornmeal mixture, stirring while pouring. Pour into an 8x8-inch buttered baking dish. Bake for 40 to 45 minutes. Yield: 9 servings.

Donna Howell, Xi Alpha Beta
Aiken, South Carolina

ALMOST BLINTZES

You can freeze the uncovered "blintzes" before baking for 15 minutes and remove to a sealable plastic bag for longer storage. Do not thaw before baking.

8 ounces cream cheese,
    softened
¼ cup sugar
1 egg yolk
1 tablespoon cinnamon
¾ cup sugar

1 to 1½ loaves large
    sandwich bread,
    crusts trimmed
½ to 1 cup (1 to 2 sticks)
    margarine, melted

Beat the cream cheese, ¼ cup sugar and egg yolk in a bowl until light and fluffy. Combine the cinnamon and ¾ cup sugar in a small bowl. Roll each slice of sandwich bread flat with a rolling pin. Spread cream cheese mixture over bread slices. Roll up each slice from a corner; cream cheese mixture should hold the bread in rolled form. Dip each roll in the margarine. Roll in cinnamon mixture. Arrange on a baking sheet. Preheat the oven to 350 degrees. Bake for 20 to 25 minutes or until just beginning to brown. Yield: 6 to 10 servings.

Kim McClain, Epsilon Xi
Conway, Arkansas

QUICK AND EASY CINNAMON BUNS

These cinnamon buns are great for Christmas mornings.

1 (6-ounce) package
    vanilla pudding and
    pie filling mix
Nuts and raisins to
    taste
2 (1-pound) loaves
    frozen bread dough,
    thawed, cut into
    pieces

½ cup (1 stick) butter,
    melted
1 cup packed brown
    sugar
1 to 2 teaspoons
    cinnamon
2 to 4 tablespoons milk

Preheat the oven to 350 degrees. Cook the vanilla pudding using package directions. Sprinkle nuts and raisins over the bottom of a greased 9x13-inch baking pan. Arrange the bread dough pieces over the nuts and raisins. Combine the vanilla pudding, butter, brown sugar, cinnamon and 2 tablespoons of the milk in a medium bowl and mix well; add additional milk if needed to make the desired consistency. Pour the pudding mixture over the bread dough. Bake for 25 minutes. Yield: 6 to 8 servings.

Sharon L. Robinson, Xi Epsilon Mu
Acworth, Georgia

CHERRY BRICKLE COFFEE CAKE

1 (2-layer) package
    white cake mix
    (non-pudding)
2 (2½-ounce) packages
    almond brickle pieces
    (about 2⅔ cups)
1 (21-ounce) can cherry
    pie filling
½ cup flour
½ cup packed brown
    sugar
½ teaspoon cinnamon
1 cup (½ stick) butter or
    margarine, sliced
½ cup slivered almonds
1 cup sifted
    confectioners' sugar
4 to 5 teaspoons water

Preheat the oven to 350 degrees. Prepare the cake mix using package directions, adding ⅔ cup of the almond brickle pieces to the batter. Pour into a greased and floured 9x13-inch cake pan. Layer the pie filling over the batter. Combine the flour, brown sugar and cinnamon in a medium bowl. Cut in the butter until crumbly. Stir in the almonds and the remaining almond brickle pieces. Sprinkle the brown sugar mixture over the pie filling. Bake for 1 hour. Combine the confectioners' sugar and enough water to make an icing of desired consistency. Remove cake from oven and drizzle icing over the top. Serve warm or cool. Yield: 15 servings.

Dee Borger, Laureate Psi
Centerville, Ohio

ONE-STEP TROPICAL COFFEE CAKE

1½ cups flour
1 cup sugar
2 teaspoons baking
    powder
½ teaspoon salt
1 (8-ounce) container
    pineapple yogurt, or
    1 cup dairy sour
    cream
½ cup vegetable oil
2 eggs
1 cup shredded coconut
    or chopped nuts
1 teaspoon cinnamon
⅓ cup sugar

Preheat the oven to 350 degrees. Combine the flour, 1 cup sugar, baking powder, salt, yogurt, vegetable oil and eggs in a large bowl; stir just until moistened. Pour into a greased 9x9-inch or 7x11-inch cake pan. Combine the coconut, cinnamon and ⅓ cup sugar in a small bowl. Sprinkle over batter. Bake for 35 to 45 minutes or until wooden pick inserted in center comes out clean. May substitute apricot, orange or lemon yogurt for the pineapple yogurt and use a mixture of coconut and chopped nuts for the 1 cup coconut. Yield: 12 servings.

Sandi Keim, Alpha Mu Master
Wooster, Ohio

RASPBERRY STREUSEL COFFEE CAKE

This coffee cake is especially good when served with ice cream.

2 cups flour
¾ cup sugar
½ cup milk
¼ cup butter, softened
1 egg
½ teaspoon salt
2 teaspoons baking
    powder
½ teaspoon nutmeg
1 cup fresh or frozen
    raspberries
Streusel Topping

Preheat the oven to 375 degrees. Combine the flour, sugar, milk, butter, egg, salt, baking powder and nutmeg in a mixer bowl. Beat on low speed for 1 to 2 minutes. Fold the raspberries gently into the batter. Spread in a greased and floured 9x9-inch cake pan. Sprinkle with Streusel Topping. Bake for 30 to 35 minutes. Yield: 10 to 12 servings.

STREUSEL TOPPING

½ cup sugar
⅓ cup flour
½ teaspoon cinnamon
½ teaspoon nutmeg
¼ cup butter

Combine the sugar, flour, cinnamon and nutmeg in a small bowl. Cut in the butter until crumbly.

Marilyn Stewart, Xi Rho
Miramichi, New Brunswick, Canada

BLUEBERRY FRENCH TOAST

12 slices white bread,
    cut into 1-inch cubes
16 ounces cream cheese,
    cut into 1-inch cubes
1 cup fresh or frozen
    blueberries
12 eggs, beaten
2 cups milk
⅓ cup honey or maple
    syrup

Layer half the bread cubes in a greased 9x13-inch baking pan. Layer the cream cheese cubes over the bread. Layer the blueberries and remaining bread cubes over the cream cheese. Combine the eggs, milk and honey in a medium bowl; beat well. Pour the egg mixture evenly over the top of the bread layer. Chill, covered, for 8 to 10 hours. Remove from refrigerator 30 minutes before baking time. Preheat the oven to 350 degrees. Bake, covered, for 30 minutes. Bake, uncovered, for 25 to 30 minutes longer or until lightly browned. Serve with sour cream, whipped cream and/or extra syrup. Yield: 12 servings.

Jo Prusha, Preceptor Gamma
Omaha, Nebraska

❖ CREME BRULEE FRENCH TOAST

This exquisite recipe is from a French country inn in Spring Lake, New Jersey.

1/2 cup (1 stick) unsalted
  butter
1 cup packed brown
  sugar
1/4 cup corn syrup
1 (8- to 9-inch) round
  loaf country-style
  bread

5 large eggs
1 1/2 cups half-and-half
1 teaspoon vanilla
  extract
1 teaspoon Grand
  Marnier
1/4 teaspoon salt

Melt the butter with the brown sugar and corn syrup in a small heavy saucepan over medium heat, stirring until smooth. Pour butter mixture into a 9x13-inch baking dish. Cut six 1-inch-thick slices from the center of bread, reserving ends for another use, and trim crusts. Arrange the bread slices in one layer in the baking dish, squeezing them slightly to fit. Combine the eggs, half-and-half, vanilla, Grand Marnier and salt in a medium bowl; whisk well until blended. Pour evenly over the bread slices. Chill, covered, for 8 to 24 hours. Preheat the oven to 350 degrees. Bring bread mixture to room temperature. Bake, uncovered, in center of oven for 35 to 40 minutes or until puffed and edges are pale golden. Serve immediately. Yield: 6 servings.

Alice R. McClure, Xi Sigma
Vancouver, Washington

OVERNIGHT CARAMEL FRENCH TOAST

2 tablespoons light corn
  syrup
1/2 cup (1 stick) butter
1 cup packed brown
  sugar
12 (1-inch) slices white
  or whole wheat bread

6 eggs
1 1/2 cups milk
1 teaspoon vanilla
  extract
1/4 teaspoon salt

Combine the corn syrup, butter and brown sugar in a small saucepan over medium heat. Simmer for 10 minutes or until syrupy, stirring occasionally. Pour into a greased 9x13-inch baking pan. Arrange 6 slices of the bread over the syrup. Combine the eggs, milk, vanilla and salt in a medium bowl; mix well. Pour half the egg mixture over bread layer in baking pan. Layer the remaining slices of bread over the egg mixture. Pour the remaining egg mixture evenly over the top. Chill, covered, for 8 to 10 hours. Preheat the oven to 350 degrees before baking time. Bake, uncovered,

for 45 minutes or until lightly browned. Serve with maple syrup and bacon, ham or sausage. Yield: 6 servings.

Karen Ann Meng, Xi Alpha Mu
Terre Haute, Indiana

OVERNIGHT FRUITY FRENCH TOAST

1 (1-pound) loaf French
  bread
5 eggs, well beaten
3/4 cup milk
1/4 teaspoon baking
  powder
1 tablespoon vanilla
  extract
1 (20-ounce) package
  frozen whole
  strawberries, thawed

4 ripe bananas, sliced
1 cup sugar
1 tablespoon apple pie
  spice
1 tablespoon cinnamon-
  sugar mixture

Cut the bread into 8 thick slices. Arrange in a medium bowl. Combine the eggs, milk, baking powder and vanilla in a bowl; mix well. Pour the egg mixture over the bread. Chill, covered, for 8 to 10 hours. Mix the strawberries, bananas, sugar and apple pie spice in a bowl. Pour into a greased 9x13-inch baking pan. Preheat the oven to 450 degrees. Cover the strawberry mixture evenly with the soaked bread. Sprinkle with the cinnamon-sugar mixture. Bake for 20 to 25 minutes or until lightly browned. Yield: 6 to 8 servings.

Ellen A. O'Bryan, Preceptor Gamma
Hannibal, Missouri

❖ PINEAPPLE UPSIDE DOWN FRENCH TOAST

This splendid marriage of French toast and pineapple needs no maple syrup.

8 (3/4-inch-thick) slices
  egg bread
6 eggs
1 1/2 cups milk
1/4 cup sugar
1 teaspoon vanilla
  extract

1/4 teaspoon cinnamon
2 tablespoons butter
1 cup packed brown
  sugar
8 round slices canned
  pineapple, drained

Arrange the bread slices in a single layer in a 9x13-inch shallow baking dish. Combine the eggs, milk, sugar, vanilla and cinnamon in a bowl; mix well. Pour the egg mixture over the bread. Turn bread slices once. Let stand for about 10 minutes or until liquid is absorbed. Bread can be chilled, covered, for up to 12 hours. Preheat the oven to 375 degrees. Heat the butter in another 9x13-inch baking dish in the oven for 5 to 8 minutes or until melted. Turn dish to spread melted butter evenly over the bottom. Sprinkle the brown sugar evenly over butter. Arrange the pineapple slices over the brown sugar layer. Layer the bread slices over the pineapple. Bake for 30 to 40 minutes or until bread is puffed and golden. Cool for 5 minutes. Cut between bread slices to separate. Invert bread slice with pineapple over each plate. Yield: 8 servings.

Myrtle Davies, Kappa Master
Guelph, Ontario, Canada

OJALDAS

2 cups flour	3/4 cup hot water
1 teaspoon baking	1/2 cup milk
powder	2 tablespoons canola oil
1 teaspoon salt	Canola oil for frying

Combine the flour, baking powder and salt in a medium bowl. Combine the water, milk and oil in a small bowl; mix well. Add the milk mixture to the flour mixture, stirring gently just until moistened. Heat 1/4 inch of oil in a heavy skillet over medium heat. Remove a large spoonful of dough from the bowl. Use your hands to pull and smooth out the spoonful, allowing holes to appear in the dough. Drop into the hot oil and brown on each side. Yield: 6 servings.

Treva Bedwell, Preceptor Lambda Psi
Corpus Christi, Texas

MAPLE BACON OVEN PANCAKE

1 1/2 cups buttermilk	1/4 cup maple syrup
baking mix	1 1/2 cups shredded
1 tablespoon sugar	Cheddar cheese
3/4 cup milk	8 ounces bacon, crisp-
2 eggs, beaten	fried, crumbled

Preheat the oven to 425 degrees. Combine the baking mix, sugar, milk, eggs, maple syrup and 1/2 cup of the Cheddar cheese in a bowl; mix well. Pour into a greased 9x13-inch baking dish. Bake, covered, for 10 to 15 minutes or until wooden pick inserted near center comes out clean. Sprinkle with the bacon and remaining Cheddar cheese. Bake, uncovered, for 3 to 5 minutes longer or until cheese melts. Serve with extra syrup if desired. Yield: 12 servings.

Cindy Seitz, Beta Lambda
Beavercreek, Ohio

MOM'S PANCAKES

1 cup flour	1/2 teaspoon salt
1 tablespoon sugar	1 egg, beaten
1 teaspoon baking	1 cup buttermilk
powder	1 cup sour cream
1 teaspoon baking soda	

Combine the flour, sugar, baking powder, baking soda and salt in a large bowl. Combine the egg, buttermilk and sour cream in a medium bowl. Add the egg mixture to the flour mixture, beating well to blend. Let stand for at least 10 minutes. Pour 1/4 cup at a time onto hot lightly greased griddle. Bake until bubbles appear on surface and underside is golden brown. Turn pancake over. Bake until other side is golden brown. Yield: 4 to 6 servings.

Leslie Peacock, Xi Upsilon Rho
Oxnard, California

BIG DUTCH BABIES (PANNUKUKKA)

If you want to use a 3-quart baking pan and make a larger amount, use 1/3 cup butter, 4 eggs, and 1 cup each of milk and flour. For a 4-quart baking pan, use 1/2 cup butter, 5 eggs, and 1 1/4 each of milk and flour. For a 5-quart baking pan, use 1/2 cup butter, 6 eggs, and 1 1/2 cups each of milk and flour.

1/4 cup (1/2 stick) butter	3/4 cup milk
3 eggs	3/4 cup flour

Preheat the oven to 425 degrees. Place the butter in a 2-quart baking pan in the oven until melted. Process the eggs in a blender at high speed for 1 minute. Pour the milk into the blender in a thin stream and sprinkle in the flour, processing constantly until smooth. Blend for 30 seconds longer. Remove baking pan from oven. Pour the egg mixture over the melted butter. Return to oven. Bake 20 to 25 minutes or until puffy and well browned. Dust with powdered sugar, drizzle with syrup or garnish with fruit. Yield: 4 servings.

Janeen Pullins, Xi Delta Eta
Austin, Colorado

Carol De Biase, Xi Mu Eta, Houston, Texas, makes Thin-Crust Pizza Dough by dissolving 1 envelope yeast in 1 cup warm water and adding 2 1/2 cups unbleached flour and 1 teaspoon salt. She kneads it for 10 minutes, adding up to 1/2 cup flour, lets it rise for 45 to 60 minutes, punches it down and lets it rest and then shapes, adds toppings and bakes at 350 to 375 degrees for 30 minutes.

SWEDISH BROWN BREAD

My grandmother was German but this was a favorite recipe.

2 eggs	1 teaspoon cinnamon
1 cup sugar	1 teaspoon ground
1/2 cup packed brown	cloves
sugar	2 1/4 cups flour
1 cup milk	3 tablespoons melted
1 teaspoon baking soda	margarine

Preheat the oven to 350 degrees. Combine the eggs, sugar, brown sugar and milk in a mixer bowl; mix well. Sift together the baking soda, cinnamon, cloves and flour. Add the flour mixture and margarine to the egg mixture. Mix at medium speed for 1 to 2 minutes or until well blended. Turn into a greased and floured loaf pan. Bake for 50 minutes or until loaf tests done. Yield: 12 slices.

Lois Van De Sompele, Laureate Gamma Mu
Apple Valley, California

THE BEST CHOCOLATE BREAD

Do not overbake this bread; cover loosely with foil about halfway through baking time if necessary. I divide the recipe and bake smaller loaf pans of bread to use as Christmas gifts.

8 tablespoons unsalted	1 cup sour cream
butter, softened	1 teaspoon baking
1 1/4 cups sugar	powder
1 teaspoon vanilla	1/2 teaspoon baking soda
extract	1/4 teaspoon salt
2 large eggs	1 3/4 cups flour
1 cup sweetened baking	Confectioners' sugar
cocoa	

Preheat the oven to 350 degrees. Beat the butter, sugar and vanilla extract in a large mixer bowl for 3 to 5 minutes or until pale and fluffy. Scrape down the sides of the bowl. Beat in the eggs, 1 at a time, scraping bowl after each addition. Stir in the baking cocoa, sour cream, baking powder, baking soda and salt. Mix at low speed until well blended. Scrape the bowl. Add the flour, mixing at low speed only until blended. Spread the batter in a greased 5x9x3-inch loaf pan. Bake for 1 hour or until a wooden pick comes out clean. Cool. Dust top with confectioners' sugar before serving. Serve with your favorite whipped topping. Yield: 12 to 15 slices.

Sheilah Harber, Alpha Epsilon Gamma
Blue Springs, Missouri

CHOCOLATE CHIP BANANA NUT BREAD

All ingredients should be mixed, but not overmixed. This is wonderful when served at breakfast with cream cheese.

1/2 cup shortening	3 bananas, mashed
1 cup sugar	2 cups flour
2 eggs, beaten	1 teaspoon baking soda
1/2 teaspoon vanilla	1/2 cup chopped pecans
extract	1/2 cup chocolate chips

Preheat the oven to 350 degrees. Cream the shortening and sugar in a large bowl until light and fluffy. Stir in the eggs, vanilla extract and bananas. Stir in the flour and baking soda. Fold in the pecans and chocolate chips. Pour into a greased and floured loaf pan. Bake for 1 to 1 1/2 hours or until lightly browned and just beginning to look dry on top. Yield: 12 slices.

Patricia Perez, Alpha Rho
Mountain Home, Idaho

CITRUS NUT BREAD

This bread is great as a breakfast snack or in a lunchbox.

4 1/2 cups flour	1 teaspoon grated lemon
1 3/4 cups sugar	zest
4 teaspoons baking	2 eggs
powder	1 cup milk
1 teaspoon baking soda	1 cup orange juice
1 1/2 teaspoons salt	1/4 cup melted margarine
1 1/2 cups chopped	or butter
walnuts	
2 tablespoons grated	
orange zest	

Preheat the oven to 350 degrees. Combine the flour, sugar, baking powder, baking soda and salt in a large bowl; mix well. Stir in the walnuts, orange zest and lemon zest. Combine the eggs, milk, orange juice and margarine in a small bowl; beat until smooth. Add the egg mixture to the flour mixture, stirring just until moistened. Pour into 2 greased loaf pans. Bake for 50 to 60 minutes or until wooden pick comes out clean. Cool for 10 minutes in pans before removing to wire racks. Serve warm or cool. Yield: 2 loaves.

Terry Munro, Theta Pi
Spokane, Washington

EGGNOG BREAD

1/4 cup butter or margarine, melted	1 cup dairy or canned eggnog
3/4 cup sugar	1/2 cup chopped pecans or walnuts
2 eggs, beaten	
2 1/4 cups flour	1/2 cup raisins
2 teaspoons baking powder	1/2 cup chopped red and green candied cherries
1 teaspoon salt	

Preheat the oven to 350 degrees. Combine the butter, sugar and eggs in a large bowl; mix well. Combine the flour, baking powder and salt in a small bowl. Add the flour mixture alternately with the eggnog, mixing lightly after each addition just until moistened. Fold in the pecans, raisins and cherries. Spoon into a greased 4 1/2x8 1/2-inch loaf pan. Yield: 1 loaf.

Margaret Palmtag, Upsilon Master
West Grove, Pennsylvania

HAWAIIAN BREAD

2 3/4 cups flour	1 (8-ounce) can crushed pineapple
1 teaspoon baking soda	
1 1/2 cups sugar	1/2 cup flaked or shredded coconut
1 teaspoon salt	
1 cup pecans or walnuts, chopped	2 medium bananas, mashed
1 cup vegetable oil	2 eggs, beaten
1 teaspoon vanilla extract	

Preheat the oven to 350 degrees. Combine the flour, baking soda, sugar and salt in a bowl; mix well. Add the pecans, vegetable oil, vanilla extract, undrained pineapple, coconut, bananas and eggs, stirring just until blended. Place in 2 well-greased 5x9-inch loaf pans. Bake for 1 hour. Yield: 2 loaves.

Pauline M. Witte, Preceptor Theta
Pierre, South Dakota

IRISH SODA BREAD

3 cups flour	1 teaspoon salt
1/3 cup sugar	1 egg, lightly beaten
1 tablespoon baking powder	2 cups buttermilk
1 teaspoon baking soda	1/4 cup (1/2 stick) butter, melted

Preheat the oven to 325 degrees. Combine the flour, sugar, baking powder, baking soda and salt in a large bowl; stir to blend well. Blend the egg and buttermilk in a small bowl. Add buttermilk mixture all at once to flour mixture; stir until moistened. Stir in the butter; mix well. Pour into a greased 5x9x3-inch loaf pan.

Bake for 65 to 75 minutes or until a wooden pick comes out clean. Do not underbake. Remove from pan. Cool on a wire rack. Store in an airtight wrap for at least 8 hours before serving. Yield: 1 loaf.

Sheila Merrill, Xi Eta Pi
Princeton, Missouri

LEMON POPPY SEED BREAD

1 (2-layer) package lemon pudding-type cake mix	4 eggs
	1 cup water
	1/2 cup vegetable oil
1 (3-ounce) package lemon instant pudding	2 tablespoons poppy seeds

Preheat the oven to 350 degrees. Combine the cake mix, pudding mix, eggs, water, vegetable oil and poppy seeds in a large mixer bowl. Beat at medium speed for 4 minutes. Pour into 2 greased and floured loaf pans or a bundt pan. Bake loaves for 40 to 50 minutes (bundt for 45 to 55 minutes) or until bread tests done. Remove from pans. Cool on a wire rack. Yield: 16 or more servings.

Ann B. Lucas, Laureate Lambda
Polson, Montana

MINCEMEAT NUT BREAD

1 1/2 cups flour	1 egg
2 teaspoons baking powder	1/2 cup milk or mocha mix
3/4 teaspoon cinnamon	1 1/2 cups prepared mincemeat
1/4 teaspoon cloves	
1/2 cup sugar	1 teaspoon baking soda
2 tablespoons shortening	2/3 cup chopped walnuts

Preheat the oven to 350 degrees. Sift the flour, baking powder, cinnamon and cloves into a large bowl. Combine the sugar, shortening, egg and milk in a medium bowl; beat until light and fluffy. Stir the sugar mixture into the flour mixture; mix well. Combine the mincemeat and baking soda. Fold mincemeat mixture and walnuts gently into the batter. Spray a 5x9-inch loaf pan with nonstick cooking spray and flour lightly. Pour the batter into the loaf pan. Bake for 55 minutes or until wooden pick comes out clean. Cool in the pan for 10 minutes. Remove from pan; cool completely on a wire rack. Serve with apple butter, ice cream, whipped topping or brandy sauce. Yield: 12 servings.

Dottie Kellogg Bastyr, Laureate Eta Tau
Morgan Hill, California

OATMEAL HONEY BREAD

This great alternative to corn bread is good with soups and stews, even chili.

1 cup flour	1/4 cup honey
1 cup quick-cooking oats	1 cup milk
1 tablespoon baking powder	1 egg
1/2 teaspoon salt	1/4 cup melted butter or margarine

Preheat the oven to 400 degrees. Combine the flour, oats, baking powder, salt, honey, milk, egg and butter in a large bowl; mix well. Spread in a greased 8- or 9-inch square baking dish. Bake for 15 to 20 minutes or until lightly browned. Yield: 6 servings.

Karen Coppin, Beta Nu
Joseph, Oregon

PEACH PECAN BREAD

1 1/2 cups chopped peeled peaches	3/4 cup all-purpose flour
2 eggs, beaten	3/4 cup whole wheat flour
1/3 cup buttermilk	1 1/2 teaspoons baking powder
1/2 cup natural bran	1/2 teaspoon baking soda
1 teaspoon vanilla extract	1/2 teaspoon salt
1/2 cup packed brown sugar	1/4 teaspoon ginger
1/3 cup butter	1/4 teaspoon nutmeg
	1/2 cup ground pecans

Preheat the oven to 350 degrees. Combine the peaches, eggs, buttermilk, bran and vanilla in a large bowl. Let stand for 15 minutes. Cream the brown sugar and butter in a bowl until light and fluffy. Add to the peach mixture. Combine the all-purpose and whole wheat flours, baking powder, baking soda, salt, ginger and nutmeg in a medium bowl. Beat into the peach mixture with a few light, rapid strokes, just until moistened. Stir in the pecans. Spoon batter into a well-greased 5x9-inch loaf pan. Bake for 45 to 50 minutes or until cake tester comes out clean. Cool completely on a wire rack before cutting. Yield: 12 servings.

Vera Esson, Mu Zeta
Tillsonburg, Ontario, Canada

Mildred Sharp, Kappa Master, McClave, Colorado, makes a delicious Orange Syrup for pancakes by blending 1/2 cup sugar, 1/4 cup thawed orange juice concentrate, 1/4 cup butter and 1/4 cup light corn syrup in a saucepan and bringing it to a boil. Serve warm.

RHUBARB LEMON BALM TEA BREAD

1 1/2 cups packed brown sugar	1 1/2 cups chopped fresh rhubarb
2/3 cup vegetable oil	1/2 cup sugar
1 cup buttermilk	1/3 cup finely chopped lemon balm
1 egg	1 teaspoon grated lemon zest
1 teaspoon vanilla extract	1 tablespoon butter, at room temperature
1 teaspoon baking soda	
1 teaspoon salt	
2 1/2 cups flour	

Preheat the oven to 350 degrees. Combine the brown sugar and vegetable oil in a large bowl; mix well. Combine the buttermilk, egg and vanilla in a small bowl; beat well. Add the buttermilk mixture to the brown sugar mixture; blend well. Combine the baking soda, salt and flour. Stir the flour mixture gradually into the brown sugar mixture. Fold in the rhubarb. Pour batter into a 5x9-inch loaf pan lined with waxed paper. Combine the sugar, lemon balm, lemon zest and butter in a small bowl. Sprinkle lemon balm mixture over the batter. Bake for 50 minutes to 1 hour or until a wooden pick inserted in the center comes out clean. Let cool in pan for 10 minutes. Remove from pan and finish cooling on a wire rack. Remove the waxed paper when loaf is cool. Yield: 1 loaf.

Tami Walker, Alpha Rho
Harana, Illinois

APPLESAUCE PUFFS

This recipe makes 8 regular muffins or 24 tiny gems. The fragrance of these wonderful muffins is likely to bring a guest to your door.

2 cups baking mix	1 egg, lightly beaten
1/2 cup sugar	2 tablespoons vegetable oil
1 1/4 teaspoons cinnamon	
1/2 cup applesauce	2 tablespoons melted butter or margarine
1/4 cup milk	

Preheat the oven to 400 degrees. Combine the baking mix, 1/4 cup of the sugar and 1 teaspoon of the cinnamon in a large bowl. Stir in the applesauce, milk, egg and vegetable oil. Beat vigorously for 30 seconds. Fill greased muffin cups 2/3 full. Bake for 12 minutes or until golden. Remove from muffin cups. Stir together the remaining 1/4 cup sugar, 1/4 teaspoon cinnamon and the melted butter. Roll muffins in butter mixture. Yield: 8 muffins.

Mary A. Silva, Laureate Alpha Phi
Brecksville, Ohio

BRAN MARASCHINO CHERRY MUFFINS

1 cup flour	1 egg
1½ teaspoons baking powder	½ cup applesauce
½ teaspoon baking soda	1 tablespoon vanilla extract
1 tablespoon cinnamon	15 maraschino cherries, chopped
2 cups 100% bran cereal	
1¼ cups 2% low-fat milk	1 cup raisins
⅓ cup packed brown sugar	¾ cup chopped walnuts

Preheat the oven to 400 degrees. Combine the flour, baking powder, baking soda and cinnamon in a large bowl. Combine the cereal, milk and brown sugar in a medium bowl; let stand for 5 minutes. Stir the egg, applesauce, vanilla extract, cherries, raisins and walnuts into the cereal mixture. Add to the flour mixture, stirring just until moistened. Spray muffin cups with nonstick cooking spray. Fill the prepared muffin cups ⅔ full. Bake for 20 minutes or until golden brown. Yield: 12 muffins.

Lillian Laing, Preceptor Epsilon Delta
Garden Grove, California

ANGEL CORN BREAD MUFFINS

1½ cups cornmeal	½ teaspoon baking soda
1 cup flour	1 teaspoon salt
1 envelope dry yeast	2 eggs, beaten
2 tablespoons sugar	2 cups buttermilk
1½ teaspoons baking powder	½ cup canola oil

Preheat the oven to 450 degrees. Combine the cornmeal, flour, yeast, sugar, baking powder, baking soda and salt in a large bowl. Combine the eggs, buttermilk and canola oil in a medium bowl; mix well. Add the egg mixture to the cornmeal mixture, stirring just until moistened. Bake in greased muffin cups for 12 to 15 minutes or until golden brown. Yield: 3 dozen.

Shonda Judy, Gamma Chi
Cynthiana, Kentucky

ORANGE GRANOLA MUFFINS

1½ cups flour	½ cup orange juice
1½ cups granola	½ cup margarine, melted
½ cup sugar	
1 teaspoon baking soda	1 teaspoon grated orange zest
½ teaspoon salt	
2 eggs	

Preheat the oven to 375 degrees. Combine the flour, granola, sugar, baking soda and salt in a medium bowl. Beat the eggs, orange juice and margarine in a small bowl. Add the egg mixture and the orange zest into the flour mixture, stirring just until moistened. Fill 12 paper-lined muffin cups ⅔ full. Bake for 15 to 20 minutes or until golden and wooden pick comes out clean. Yield: 12 muffins.

Julia Gatsos, Preceptor Sigma
New Albany, Indiana

STREUSEL MUFFINS

2¼ cups flour	¼ cup packed brown sugar
1½ cups packed brown sugar	
	¼ cup chopped walnuts or pecans
1 teaspoon baking soda	
1 egg	3 tablespoons rolled oats
1 cup yogurt	
½ cup vegetable oil	½ teaspoon cinnamon
2 cups diced apples	1 tablespoon margarine, melted
¾ cup cranberries (optional)	

Preheat the oven to 375 degrees. Combine the flour, 1½ cups brown sugar and baking soda in a large bowl. Combine the egg, yogurt and vegetable oil in a small bowl. Add the egg mixture to the flour mixture, stirring just until moistened. Stir in the apples and cranberries. Fill muffin cups ⅔ full. Mix ¼ cup brown sugar, nuts, rolled oats, cinnamon and margarine in a bowl. Sprinkle over the top. Bake for 25 minutes or until browned. Yield: 12 muffins.

Nancy Leduc, Kappa Zeta
Tweed, Ontario, Canada

CASSEROLE BREAD

¼ cup sugar	2 envelopes dry yeast
1 teaspoon salt	½ cup warm water
¼ cup (½ stick) margarine	1 egg
	4½ cups flour
1 cup milk, scalded	

Combine the sugar, salt, margarine and hot milk in a mixer bowl. Cool to lukewarm. Dissolve the yeast in the water. Stir the yeast mixture, egg and 3 cups of the flour into the milk mixture; beat at medium speed for 3 to 4 minutes or until smooth. Stir in the remaining 1½ cups flour. Pour into a greased round baking dish or bundt pan. Let rise in a warm place for about 1 hour or until doubled in bulk. Preheat the oven to 350 degrees. Bake for 40 minutes or until bread tests done. Yield: 1 round loaf.

Alice White, Preceptor Gamma Kappa
Chesapeake, Virginia

CHEDDAR OATMEAL BREAD

1 envelope active dry yeast	1/2 cup hot water
1/2 cup warm water	2 1/2 cups shredded sharp Cheddar cheese
1 cup old-fashioned rolled oats	2 tablespoons sugar
1/2 cup milk, scalded	2 teaspoons salt
	3 cups flour

Dissolve the yeast in the warm water. Combine the oats, hot milk and hot water in a large bowl. Cool to lukewarm. Stir in the yeast mixture, Cheddar cheese, sugar, salt and 2 1/2 cups of the flour; mix well. Knead for 3 to 5 minutes on a floured work surface, working in the remaining 1/2 cup flour. Place in a lightly greased bowl, turning to coat the surface. Let rise, covered, in a warm place for about 1 hour or until doubled in bulk. Punch down. Shape into a loaf in a well-greased 5x9-inch loaf pan. Preheat the oven to 350 degrees. Let dough rise, covered, for 30 minutes. Bake for 45 to 50 minutes or until deep golden. Remove from pan immediately. Yield: 1 loaf.

Patricia R. Soard, Theta Psi
Cookeville, Tennessee

❖ FOCACCIA

2 teaspoons active dry yeast	2 teaspoons salt
1 1/2 cups warm water	1 medium onion, diced, caramelized
4 cups flour	8 to 10 leaves fresh basil, finely chopped
8 roasted garlic cloves, crushed	1 cup feta cheese
4 tablespoons extra-virgin olive oil	1 1/2 teaspoons kosher salt

Preheat the oven to 425 degrees. Sprinkle 1 teaspoon of the yeast over 1/2 cup of the warm water in a large bowl. Let stand for about 10 minutes. Stir in 3/4 cup of the flour; mix well. Let rise, covered, in a warm place for about 45 minutes or until doubled in bulk. Sprinkle the remaining 1 teaspoon yeast over the remaining 1 cup warm water in a large mixer bowl; let stand for about 10 minutes. Stir in 4 of the garlic cloves, 3 tablespoons of the olive oil, the remaining 3 1/4 cups flour and 2 teaspoons salt. Beat with the electric mixer's dough hook for 3 to 4 minutes. Finish kneading the dough by hand on a floured surface, adding more flour as needed. Dough should be smooth and slightly sticky. Place in an oiled bowl, turning once to coat, and let rise, covered, in a warm place for about 1 1/4 hours or until doubled in bulk. Roll dough into an 11x17-inch rectangle or a 15-inch circle. Spread the remaining 4 garlic cloves over the dough. Layer the onion, basil, feta cheese, the

remaining 1 tablespoon olive oil and kosher salt over the garlic layer. Bake for 30 to 40 minutes or until crusty and browned. Serve warm. Yield: 15 to 20 appetizer servings, 8 entrée servings.

Mildred Buzby, Laureate Eta
Wasilla, Alaska

BREAD MACHINE TWELVE-GRAIN BREAD

Please use the type of yeast specified in your bread machine instructions.

2 1/2 cups bread flour	2 teaspoons salt
1 1/4 cups whole wheat flour	2 tablespoons sugar
3/4 cup twelve-grain cereal	2 tablespoons butter
	1 2/3 cups milk
	2 teaspoons yeast

Combine the bread flour, whole wheat flour, cereal, salt, sugar, butter, milk and yeast in the container of a bread machine in order recommended by bread machine instructions. Set the machine on the Whole Wheat cycle. Yield: 1 loaf.

Alice Steadman, Xi Master
Sudbury, Ontario, Canada

WHOLE WHEAT BREAD

2 envelopes active dry yeast	1/4 cup canola oil
1 teaspoon sugar	2 teaspoons salt
1 1/2 cups warm water	3 cups whole wheat flour
3/4 cup warm skim milk	3 to 4 cups all-purpose flour
1/3 cup honey	

Combine the yeast, sugar and 1/2 cup of the warm water in a small bowl. Let stand for 10 minutes. Combine the remaining 1 cup warm water, skim milk, honey, canola oil and salt in a large mixer bowl; mix well. Add the yeast mixture and whole wheat flour; beat well at medium speed for 1 minute. Stir in enough of the all-purpose flour (about 2 cups) with a wooden spoon to make a soft dough. Knead on a floured surface for 6 to 7 minutes or until smooth and elastic, adding remaining 1 cup flour as needed. Let rise, covered, in a warm place for about 45 minutes or until doubled in bulk. Preheat the oven to 375 degrees. Divide the dough into 2 portions. Shape each portion into a loaf in a 5x9x3-inch loaf pan. Let rise, covered, for about 20 minutes. Bake for 35 to 40 minutes or until crust is deep golden. Yield: 2 loaves.

Joan E. Petainen, Laureate Delta Eta
Sault Ste. Marie, Ontario, Canada

CARAMEL ROLLS

1 cup water	1/3 cup sugar
1 egg	2 teaspoons cinnamon
3 1/4 cups flour	1 cup packed brown
1/4 cup sugar	sugar
1 teaspoon salt	2 tablespoons corn
1 envelope active dry	syrup
yeast	
1 cup plus 2 tablespoons	
soft margarine	

Place the water, egg, flour, 1/4 cup sugar, salt, yeast and 2 tablespoons of the margarine in the container of a bread machine in order recommended by bread machine instructions. Prepare the dough using the Dough cycle. Roll dough into a 10x15-inch rectangle on a floured surface. Spread 1/3 cup of the margarine over the dough. Sprinkle with 1/3 cup sugar and cinnamon. Combine the remaining 2/3 cup margarine, brown sugar and corn syrup in a small saucepan. Heat until margarine melts; stir well. Spread the brown sugar mixture over the bottom of a 9x13-inch baking pan. Roll up the dough rectangle tightly, enclosing sugar and cinnamon. Slice into 12 rolls. Arrange rolls cut side down in the prepared baking pan. Let rise, covered, in a warm place for 45 minutes to 1 hour or until doubled in bulk. Preheat the oven to 375 degrees. Bake for 20 to 25 minutes or until golden brown. Yield: 12 rolls.

Judy Oberhelman, Iota Omicron
Renwick, Iowa

GRANDDAD'S CINNAMON ROLLS

Use a hard-wheat bread flour for these rolls; do not use regular all-purpose flour. This recipe was a blue-ribbon winner at the Guadalupe County Fair. Granddad is 94 years old and still baking.

1 egg, beaten	1 teaspoon lemon juice
1 teaspoon salt	1 cup plus 1 tablespoon
3 tablespoons sugar	water
1 1/2 teaspoons active dry	Cinnamon Roll Filling
yeast	Chopped pecans or
3 3/4 cups bread flour	walnuts (optional)
3 tablespoons vegetable	Pecan or walnut halves
oil	

Combine the egg, salt, sugar and yeast in a small bowl. Combine the flour, vegetable oil, lemon juice and water in a large bowl. Stir in the egg mixture; mix to form a soft dough. Let rise, covered, in a warm place for at least 1 hour or until doubled in bulk. Punch down. Divide into 4 portions. Roll each portion into a 1/8-inch-thick (6x8-inch) rectangle on a floured surface, stretching the dough by hand if necessary. Spread a thin layer of Cinnamon Roll Filling over each rectangle. Sprinkle with the chopped pecans. Roll up the rectangle slowly, making sure layers of filling and chopped nuts remain even. Grease an 8x12-inch baking pan. Cover bottom of pan with a thin (1/4 inch or less) layer of Cinnamon Roll Filling. Arrange pecan halves over the filling layer. Cut each cylinder of dough into short rolls about 1 1/2 inches long. Arrange cut side down in the baking pan over the filling layer, leaving about 1/2 inch between each roll. Let rise, covered, with a dish towel, in a warm place for about 1 hour or until rolls almost touch. Preheat the oven to 350 degrees. Bake for 20 minutes. Remove pan from oven and turn upside down immediately over a sheet of waxed paper, allowing the extra syrup and nut halves to flow onto the rolls. Can be served immediately. Yield: 12 to 15 rolls.

CINNAMON ROLL FILLING

2 cups packed brown	3 tablespoons dark corn
sugar	syrup
1/2 cup (1 stick) butter	1 tablespoon cinnamon

Combine the brown sugar, butter and corn syrup in a microwave-safe bowl. Microwave on Medium until butter melts, making sure mixture does not boil, or heat in a small saucepan over the stove. Stir mixture until creamy. Stir in the cinnamon; mix well.

Marjorie McNealy, Beta Gamma Master
El Paso, Texas

DILLY ROLLS

1 cup cottage cheese	1 1/2 tablespoons (scant)
1 tablespoon butter or	dillweed
margarine	1/4 teaspoon baking soda
1/4 cup warm water	2 1/2 cups flour
1 egg	2 tablespoons sugar
1 tablespoon dried	2 1/4 teaspoons dry active
minced onion	yeast
1 1/2 teaspoons salt	

Place the first 9 ingredients in the container of a bread machine in the order listed. Sprinkle the sugar and yeast over the flour. Select Dough setting to prepare dough. Form dough into 12 rolls and place on a baking sheet. Let rise, covered, in a warm place for about 45 minutes or until doubled in bulk. Preheat the oven to 350 degrees. Bake for 20 to 25 minutes or until golden brown. Yield: 12 rolls.

Cindy Snavely, Preceptor Nu
Salina, Kansas

EASY EXCELLENT ROLLS

1 envelope active dry yeast	1/2 cup sugar
2 cups warm milk	1 egg
3/4 cup (1 1/2 sticks) butter, melted	4 cups self-rising flour

Preheat the oven to 400 degrees. Dissolve the yeast in the warm milk in a small bowl. Combine the butter, sugar, egg and flour in a large bowl. Stir in the yeast mixture. Pour into greased muffin cups. Bake for 15 to 20 minutes or until golden.
Yield: 1 1/2 to 2 dozen rolls.

Jane Ann Ashley, Xi Epsilon Epsilon
Evansville, Indiana

ERMA'S ROLLS

Once you taste these rolls and see how easy they are to prepare, you may never want to serve another type of dinner roll. You can prepare the dough ahead of time and chill, covered, until baking time. Remove from the refrigerator and let rise, lightly covered, in a warm place for 45 minutes to an hour. Follow baking instructions. Be sure rolls are very brown on top. They may look as if they are about to burn, but they need the extra baking time.

1/3 cup powdered milk	1/2 cup sugar
1 envelope active dry yeast	1 teaspoon salt
1 cup lukewarm water	1/4 cup vegetable oil
1 egg	3 cups flour

Combine the powdered milk, yeast and water in a blender container; process until smooth. Let stand for 5 minutes. Process at medium speed for 20 seconds. Add the egg, sugar, salt and vegetable oil to the yeast mixture; process for 10 seconds. Place the flour in a large bowl. Pour the yeast mixture over the flour; mix well. Let rise, covered, in a warm place for 2 hours or until doubled in bulk. Punch down. Roll out dough about 1/2 inch thick with a floured rolling pin on a floured surface, using plenty of flour to avoid stickiness. Cut into rounds with a floured cutter. Dip rolls in melted butter and arrange close together in buttered baking pans. Let rise, covered, for 25 minutes or until double in bulk. Preheat the oven to 350 degrees. Bake for 20 minutes or until very brown on top. Yield: 2 dozen rolls.

Rosy W. Bromell, Eta Omicron
Ruston, Louisiana

SOUTHERN SWEET POTATO ROLLS

1 tablespoon active dry yeast	2/3 cup butter, softened
2/3 cup warm water	2/3 cup sugar
1 cup mashed cooked sweet potatoes	2 eggs, lightly beaten
	6 cups flour
	Cinnamon to taste

Dissolve the yeast in the water. Combine the next 4 ingredients in a large bowl. Stir in the yeast mixture. Add the flour and cinnamon gradually, stirring until well mixed. Let rise, covered, for about 2 hours or until doubled in bulk. Punch down. Shape into small dinner rolls. Arrange on a greased baking sheet. Let rise, loosely covered, until almost doubled in bulk. Preheat the oven to 375 degrees. Bake for 10 to 12 minutes or until golden brown.
Yield: 2 to 3 dozen rolls.

Sara Lucas, Zeta Phi
Virginia Beach, Virginia

YEASTY BREAKFAST ROLLS

3/4 cup milk	2 envelopes active dry yeast
1/2 cup water	
1/4 cup butter or margarine	1 egg
1/4 cup sugar	1 teaspoon salt
3 1/4 cups flour	Breakfast Roll Topping

Combine the milk, water, butter, and sugar in a saucepan over low heat. Heat for 5 to 10 minutes or until butter is melted and mixture is lukewarm, stirring occasionally. Pour into a large mixer bowl with 1 1/2 cups of the flour, yeast, egg and salt; beat at high speed for 3 minutes. Stir in the remaining 1 3/4 cups flour by hand. Let rise, covered, in a warm place for 30 minutes or until doubled in bulk. Pour the Breakfast Roll Topping into a 9x13-inch baking dish. Preheat the oven to 375 degrees. Stir dough. Drop dough by tablespoons over the topping layer. Bake for 15 minutes or until golden. Remove from oven and invert over a serving plate. Yield: 8 servings.

BREAKFAST ROLL TOPPING

3/4 cup (1 1/2 sticks) butter or margarine	1 tablespoon corn syrup
1 cup packed brown sugar	1 tablespoon water
1 teaspoon cinnamon	3/4 cup chopped pecans or walnuts (optional)

Combine the ingredients in a saucepan over low heat. Heat for 5 to 10 minutes or until butter is melted and mixture is lukewarm, stirring occasionally.

Cathy Jennings, Zeta Nu
Queen City, Missouri

Delightful Desserts

Any meal becomes an extraordinary event with a picture-perfect finalé. And you're simply set to steal the show with our *Delightful Desserts* waiting in the wings. Expresso Chocolate Cheesecake will win rave reviews, while White Chocolate Cranberry Cookie Bars is a certain curtain lifter. From the daintiest delicacy to the most provocative *patisserie*, you'll be sure to captivate your audience with these savory recipes. So let the last act put you in the limelight, whether you're playing to a packed house or your own precious peanut gallery.

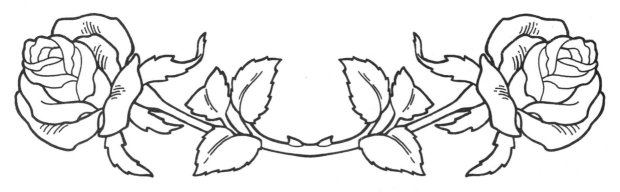

AMISH CAKE

2 cups flour
2 cups sugar
2 teaspoons baking soda
1/4 teaspoon salt
2 eggs, beaten
1 (15-ounce) can crushed
    pineapple
1 teaspoon vanilla
    extract
1 1/2 to 2 cups pecans or
    walnuts, finely
    chopped
Amish Cake Frosting

Preheat the oven to 350 degrees. Combine the first 4 ingredients in a large bowl; stir. Combine the eggs, undrained pineapple and vanilla in a small bowl; mix well. Add the pineapple mixture to the flour mixture, stirring just until moistened. Fold in 3/4 of the chopped pecans. Pour into a greased 9x13-inch cake pan. Bake for 45 minutes or until cake tests done. Cool. Frost with Amish Cake Frosting. Sprinkle with remaining chopped nuts. Yield: 15 servings.

AMISH CAKE FROSTING

1/4 cup (1/2 stick) butter,
    softened
4 ounces cream cheese,
    softened
1 teaspoon vanilla
    extract
2 cups (or more)
    confectioners' sugar

Combine the butter, cream cheese, vanilla extract and enough confectioners' sugar to make of spreading consistency. Beat at high speed until smooth, adding confectioners' sugar as necessary to achieve proper consistency.

Betty I. Doil, Laureate Gamma
Las Cruces, New Mexico

APPLE CAKE

2 cups sugar
1/2 cup vegetable oil
4 eggs
1 teaspoon vanilla
    extract
2 cups flour
1 teaspoon baking soda
2 teaspoons nutmeg
2 teaspoons cinnamon
4 cups chopped peeled
    Granny Smith apples
1 cup broken pecans or
    walnuts

Preheat the oven to 350 degrees. Cream the sugar, oil and eggs in a bowl until light and fluffy. Beat in the vanilla extract. Combine the flour, baking soda, nutmeg and cinnamon in a bowl. Add the flour mixture to the egg mixture, stirring until well mixed and smooth. Batter will be thick. Stir in the apples and pecans. Pour into a greased 9x13-inch cake pan. Bake for 45 minutes to 1 hour or until wooden pick inserted in center comes out clean. Yield: 36 servings.

Gloria P. Lewis, Preceptor Laureate Rho
Valley Springs, Arkansas

APPLE CAKE WITH BUTTER SAUCE

1 1/2 cups sugar
1 cup (2 sticks) butter,
    softened
1 egg
2 cups chopped peeled
    apples
1 cup flour
1 teaspoon baking soda
1 teaspoon cinnamon
1/4 teaspoon salt
1/2 cup chopped pecans
    or walnuts
1/2 cup packed brown
    sugar
1/2 cup heavy cream

Preheat the oven to 350 degrees. Cream 1 cup of the sugar and 1/2 cup of the butter in a bowl until light and fluffy. Add the egg, apples, flour, baking soda, cinnamon, salt and pecans 1 ingredient at a time, mixing well after each addition. Pour into a greased 9x9-inch cake pan. Bake for 35 to 40 minutes or until cake tests done. Cool. Combine the remaining 1/2 cup sugar, 1/2 cup butter, brown sugar and cream in a saucepan. Bring to a boil over medium heat. Boil for 1 minute. Pour the hot mixture over the cooled cake. Garnish with whipped cream. Yield: 16 servings.

Nancy Anderson, Preceptor Zeta
Moorhead, Minnesota

CINNAMON APPLE CAKE

If you substitute 1/2 cup unsweetened applesauce for 1/2 cup of the shortening, the cake will still be moist and delicious . . . but lower in fat.

2 cups sugar
1 cup shortening
2 eggs
2 teaspoons vanilla
    extract
1/4 teaspoon black
    walnut extract
3 cups flour
2 teaspoons cinnamon
2 teaspoons baking soda
1 teaspoon salt
1 cup brewed coffee
2 cups finely chopped
    peeled apples
2/3 cup packed brown
    sugar
1 cup chopped walnuts

Preheat the oven to 325 degrees. Cream the sugar and shortening in a mixer bowl until light and fluffy. Add the eggs, vanilla and black walnut extract; beat until smooth. Sift the flour, cinnamon, baking soda and salt together. Add the flour mixture to the creamed mixture alternately with the coffee, mixing well after each addition. Stir in the apples. Pour into a greased 9x13-inch cake pan. Combine the brown sugar and walnuts. Sprinkle walnut mixture over the batter. Bake for 40 to 45 minutes or until cake tests done. Serve plain or with ice cream or whipped topping. Yield: 18 servings.

Ella Sears, Xi Alpha Mu
Bozeman, Montana

SURPRISE APPLE CAKE

2 cups flour	1 cup vegetable oil
2 teaspoons baking powder	16 ounces sauerkraut, rinsed, squeezed dry
2 teaspoons cinnamon	1 large Granny Smith
1 teaspoon baking soda	apple, cored, peeled,
1 teaspoon salt	coarsely grated,
1/2 teaspoon nutmeg	squeezed dry
1 cup sugar	1 cup coarsely chopped
1/2 cup packed brown sugar	walnuts or pecans
4 large eggs	Cream Cheese Frosting

Preheat the oven to 350 degrees. Line 2 greased 8-inch round cake pans with greased and floured waxed paper. Combine the flour, baking powder, cinnamon, baking soda, salt and nutmeg in a medium bowl; mix well. Combine the sugar and brown sugar in a large bowl, stirring to break up any lumps. Whisk in the eggs. Add the oil, whisking until well blended. Stir in the sauerkraut, apple and walnuts. Add the flour mixture, stirring just until moistened. Spoon into the prepared cake pans. Bake for about 35 minutes or until cake begins to pull away from side of pan and wooden pick comes out clean. Cool in pans for 10 minutes. Invert onto wire racks to cool completely. Frost with Cream Cheese Frosting. Yield: 12 servings.

CREAM CHEESE FROSTING

16 ounces cream cheese, softened	2 tablespoons grated orange zest
1 cup confectioners' sugar	1 teaspoon cinnamon
3 1/2 tablespoons heavy cream	2 teaspoons vanilla extract

Beat the cream cheese in a large bowl. Add the confectioners' sugar, gradually beating until light and fluffy. Beat in the cream, orange zest, cinnamon and vanilla extract.

Glenda Whitcomb, Xi Beta Pi
Birmingham, Alabama

SAUCY APPLE SWIRL CAKE

1/4 cup sugar	1 2/3 cups applesauce
2 teaspoons cinnamon	3 eggs
1 (2-layer) package yellow cake mix	

Preheat the oven to 350 degrees. Mix the sugar and cinnamon together. Grease a 10-inch bundt or tube pan. Dust with about 1 tablespoon of the cinnamon mixture. Combine the cake mix, applesauce and eggs in a mixer bowl. Beat using package directions. Pour all but 1 1/2 cups of batter into the prepared pan. Sprinkle with the remaining cinnamon mixture. Pour reserved batter over the cinnamon mixture. Bake for 35 to 45 minutes or until cake tests done. Cool in pan for 15 minutes. Invert onto a serving platter. Yield: 8 to 10 servings.

Doris Morley, Sigma Lambda
Camino, California

WEST VIRGINIA BLACK WALNUT APPLE CAKE

4 cups chopped peeled apples	1/2 teaspoon nutmeg
2 cups sugar	2 teaspoons vanilla extract
3 eggs, lightly beaten	1 teaspoon cinnamon
2 cups sifted flour	3/4 cup vegetable oil
1 teaspoon salt	1 cup chopped black
2 teaspoons baking soda	walnuts

Preheat the oven to 350 degrees. Combine the apples and sugar in a small bowl. Let stand while preparing other ingredients. Combine the eggs, flour, salt, baking soda, nutmeg, vanilla, cinnamon and oil in a large bowl; mix well. Stir in the apple mixture and walnuts; mix well. Pour into a greased and floured tube pan. Bake for 1 hour. Yield: 16 servings.

Dorothy Metz, Laureate Eta Gamma Sigma
Oroville, California

MOTHER'S APPLESAUCE CAKE

2 cups cold sweetened applesauce	1/2 teaspoon nutmeg
1/2 cup shortening	1/2 teaspoon cloves
1 cup sugar	1 cup raisins or currants
3 cups sifted flour	1 cup chopped dates or
1/4 teaspoon salt	figs
1 teaspoon baking soda	1 cup chopped pecans or
1 teaspoon cinnamon	walnuts

Preheat the oven to 350 degrees. Cream the applesauce, shortening and sugar in a mixer bowl until light and fluffy. Combine the flour, salt, baking soda and spices. Combine the flour mixture and applesauce mixture; mix to form a stiff batter. Mix raisins and dates with a small amount of additional flour. Fold with walnuts into batter. Pour into a greased and floured bundt pan. Bake for 1 hour or until cake tests done. Serve plain or drizzle with confectioners' sugar mixed with lemon juice. Yield: 16 servings.

Eleonora Donahue, Alpha Zeta Master
Kansas City, Missouri

BUTTER PECAN BUNDT CAKE

This moist cake can be served with whipped topping or ice cream, but it is rich by itself.

1 (2-layer) package butter pecan cake mix	4 eggs
1 package homestyle coconut pecan frosting mix	1 cup water
	1 cup vegetable oil
	1 cup shredded coconut
	1 cup chopped pecans

Spray a bundt pan generously with nonstick cooking spray; dust with sugar. Preheat the oven to 350 degrees. Beat the cake mix, frosting mix, eggs, water and oil in a large mixer bowl at medium speed for 1¹/₂ minutes. Add the coconut and pecans; mix well. Pour into the prepared bundt pan. Bake for 65 minutes or until cake tests done. Yield: 14 to 16 servings.

Mary Dobbins, Epsilon Master
Broken Arrow, Oklahoma

BURNT SUGAR CAKE

1 (2-layer) package butter brickle cake mix	1 tablespoon plus 1 teaspoon burnt sugar flavoring
1 (4-ounce) package butterscotch instant pudding mix	¹/₄ cup brown sugar
4 eggs	2 tablespoons margarine
³/₄ cup vegetable oil	2 tablespoons milk
³/₄ cup water	1 cup confectioners' sugar

Preheat the oven to 350 degrees. Combine the cake mix, pudding mix, eggs, oil, water and the 1 tablespoon burnt sugar flavoring in a large mixer bowl; beat at medium speed for 5 minutes. Pour into a greased and floured bundt pan. Bake for 50 minutes or until cake tests done. Remove from pan. Combine the brown sugar, margarine and milk in a small saucepan over medium heat. Heat, stirring occasionally, until margarine melts. Stir in the 1 teaspoon burnt sugar flavoring and the confectioners' sugar. Pour and spread over the hot cake to make a thin glaze. Yield: 16 servings.

Laura J. Nevins, Alpha Phi
Paris, Missouri

Gwen Spalding, Xi Zeta, Nashville, Tennessee, makes Hot Fudge Cake by preparing and baking a fudge cake mix in a 9x13-inch cake pan, poking holes in it with a wooden pick and drizzling a can of sweetened condensed milk over the top. Let stand for 1 hour. Drizzle with about 1¹/₂ cups chocolate syrup. Chill, covered, for 4 hours and top with whipped topping and pecans.

LOW-FAT CARROT CAKE

This comfort food is loved by kids after school on a cold day.

2 cups flour	1 cup plain low-fat yogurt
1¹/₂ cups sugar	¹/₄ cup egg substitute
2 teaspoons baking soda	¹/₄ cup vegetable oil
1 teaspoon baking powder	3 cups shredded carrots
2 teaspoons cinnamon	³/₄ cup raisins
1 cup crushed pineapple, drained	Yogurt Topping

Preheat the oven to 325 degrees. Spray a 9x13-inch cake pan with nonstick cooking spray. Combine the flour, sugar, baking soda, baking powder and cinnamon in a large bowl. Stir in the pineapple, yogurt, egg substitute and oil; mix well. Stir in the carrots and raisins. Pour into prepared baking pan. Bake for 40 to 45 minutes or until wooden pick comes out clean. Cool on a wire rack. Spread the Yogurt Topping over the cooled cake. Yield: 18 servings.

YOGURT TOPPING

1¹/₂ cups low-fat plain yogurt	1 teaspoon vanilla extract
3 tablespoons brown sugar	

Line a sieve with cheesecloth. Place the sieve over a bowl. Drain the yogurt in the sieve for 2 hours in the refrigerator. Discard liquid. Combine the drained yogurt, brown sugar and vanilla extract in a small bowl; mix well. Chill, covered, until ready to use.

Beverly Brown, Laureate Alpha Xi
North Vancouver, British Columbia, Canada

CHERRY CAKE

¹/₂ cup (1 stick) butter, softened	¹/₂ teaspoon baking soda
1¹/₂ cups sugar	¹/₂ teaspoon allspice
3 eggs	¹/₂ teaspoon ground cloves
3 cups flour	¹/₄ teaspoon salt
2 teaspoons baking powder	1 cup milk
1 teaspoon cinnamon	1 (16-ounce) can red sour cherries, drained

Preheat the oven to 350 degrees. Cream the butter and sugar in a mixer bowl until light and fluffy. Beat in the eggs 1 at a time. Combine the flour, baking powder, cinnamon, baking soda, allspice, cloves and salt in a small bowl. Add the mixture of dry ingredients alternately with the milk, mixing well after each addition. Stir in the cherries. Spoon into a greased

9x13-inch cake pan, smoothing the top. Bake for 40 minutes or until cake springs back when touched lightly. Cool completely. Frost with a butter frosting. Yield: 15 servings.

Betty Jo King, Xi Alpha Alpha Beta
Frisco, Texas

CHOCOLATE CHERRY SOUR CREAM CAKE

1¹/2 cups flour
¹/3 cup baking cocoa
2 teaspoons butter
   substitute
1 cup sugar
1 cup water
¹/4 cup light corn syrup
1 teaspoon vanilla
   extract

¹/2 cup fat-free sour
   cream
¹/2 teaspoon vinegar
¹/2 teaspoon baking soda
³/4 cup fat-free sour
   cream
¹/3 cup sugar
1 (21-ounce) can cherry
   pie filling

Combine flour, baking cocoa and butter substitute in a large bowl; mix well. Beat 1 cup sugar, water, corn syrup, vanilla, ¹/2 cup sour cream, vinegar and baking soda in a large mixer bowl until smooth. Add the dry ingredients gradually, beating at medium speed. Pour into a 9x13-inch cake pan sprayed with nonstick baking spray. Mix the remaining ³/4 cup sour cream and ¹/3 cup sugar in a small bowl. Drop the pie filling by spoonfuls over the cake batter. Drop spoonfuls of the sour cream mixture over the pie filling. Bake in a preheated 350-degree oven for 45 to 50 minutes or until cake tests done. Yield: 12 servings.

Marcia Smith, Iota Master
Kearney, Nebraska

CINNAMON STREUSEL CAKE WITH CONFECTIONERS' SUGAR ICING

1¹/2 cups graham cracker
   crumbs
¹/2 cup chopped pecans
³/4 cup packed brown
   sugar
1¹/2 teaspoons cinnamon
1 (2-layer) package
   yellow cake mix
1 cup water

¹/4 cup vegetable oil
3 eggs
²/3 cup melted butter
1 cup confectioners'
   sugar
1 teaspoon vanilla
   extract
Water

Combine graham cracker crumbs, pecans, brown sugar and cinnamon in a bowl. Combine cake mix, 1 cup water, oil and eggs in a large mixer bowl; beat at medium speed for 2 minutes or until well mixed. Layer the batter and graham cracker mixture, ¹/2 at a time, in a greased 9x13-inch cake pan, ending with the graham cracker mixture. Pour melted butter

evenly over the top. Swirl a knife through the cake a few times to pull the butter through the cake. Bake in a preheated 350-degree oven for 35 minutes. Cool slightly. Mix confectioners' sugar, vanilla and enough water to make of drizzling consistency in a small bowl. Drizzle over the cake. Yield: 12 to 14 servings.

Lori Kirkpatrick, Alpha Delta Nu
Kimberling City, Missouri

SPICY CHIFFON CAKE WITH CREAMY NUT ICING

2 cups flour
1¹/2 cups sugar
1 tablespoon baking
   powder
1 teaspoon salt
1 teaspoon cinnamon
¹/2 teaspoon nutmeg
¹/2 teaspoon allspice
¹/2 teaspoon cloves
¹/2 cup vegetable oil
7 egg yolks
³/4 cup cold water
¹/2 teaspoon cream of
   tartar

7 egg whites
¹/2 cup shortening,
   melted
2¹/2 tablespoons flour
¹/4 teaspoon salt
¹/2 cup milk
¹/2 cup packed brown
   sugar
2 cups sifted
   confectioners' sugar
¹/2 cup chopped pecans
1 tablespoon vanilla
   extract

Sift 2 cups flour, sugar, baking powder, 1 teaspoon salt, cinnamon, nutmeg, allspice and cloves into a large bowl. Add the oil, egg yolks and water; beat until smooth. Beat the cream of tartar and egg whites in a large bowl until very stiff peaks form; peaks should be much stiffer than for meringue. Fold the flour mixture gently into the egg whites. Pour into a greased 10-inch tube pan. Bake in a preheated 325-degree oven for 55 minutes. Increase oven temperature to 350 degrees and bake for 10 to 15 minutes longer or until cake tests done. Mix the shortening, 2¹/2 tablespoons flour, ¹/4 teaspoon salt and milk in a saucepan. Boil for 1 minute, stirring constantly. Stir in the brown sugar. Remove the saucepan to a pan of cold water. Beat in the confectioners' sugar until of spreading consistency. Stir in the pecans and vanilla. Spread over the cooled cake. Yield: 16 servings.

Pat Trantham, Alpha Delta Rho
Chillicothe, Missouri

Ann Locke, Laureate Eta Pi, West Columbia, Texas, says the secret of her Mother's Devil's Food Cake was using coffee as the liquid and baking in square pans to get four corners—the best part of the cake.

GUILTLESS CHOCOLATE CAKE

Be sure not to stir the boiling water into the batter.

1 cup unbleached flour
2 teaspoons baking
   powder
1 teaspoon salt
2/3 cup sugar
6 tablespoons baking
   cocoa

1/2 cup skim milk, soy
   milk or rice milk
1 teaspoon vanilla
   extract
1 cup packed brown
   sugar
1 1/2 cups boiling water

Preheat the oven to 350 degrees. Combine the flour, baking powder, salt, sugar and 2 tablespoons of the baking cocoa in a large bowl; mix well. Stir in the milk and vanilla extract; mix just until smooth. Pour into a 1-quart baking dish coated with nonstick baking spray. Combine the brown sugar with the remaining 4 tablespoons cocoa in a medium bowl. Sprinkle the brown sugar mixture over the batter. Pour the boiling water evenly over all; do not stir. Bake for 40 minutes. Serve warm, sauce side up. Yield: 8 servings.

Delight Colby, Preceptor Sigma
Holden, Maine

EASY CHOCOLATE CAKE

2 cups flour
2 cups sugar
1 cup (2 sticks)
   margarine
1 cup water
3 tablespoons baking
   cocoa
2 eggs
1 teaspoon vanilla
   extract
1 teaspoon baking soda
1/2 cup buttermilk

1/2 teaspoon cinnamon
1/2 cup (1 stick)
   margarine
3 tablespoons baking
   cocoa
6 tablespoons milk
1 pound confectioners'
   sugar
1 teaspoon vanilla
   extract
1 cup chopped pecans or
   walnuts

Preheat the oven to 400 degrees. Combine the flour and sugar in a large bowl. Combine 1 cup of the margarine, water and 3 tablespoons of the baking cocoa in a saucepan over medium-high heat. Bring to a boil. Pour over the flour mixture. Add the eggs, 1 teaspoon vanilla, baking soda, buttermilk and cinnamon; mix well. Pour into a greased 9x13-inch cake pan. Bake for 20 minutes. Combine 1/2 cup margarine, milk and 3 tablespoons cocoa in a saucepan. Bring to a boil over medium-high heat. Remove from heat. Stir in the confectioners' sugar and remaining vanilla. Stir in the pecans. Pour hot frosting over hot chocolate cake. Yield: 25 to 30 servings.

Joanne Donaldson, Xi Kappa Chi
Largo, Florida

ROY'S CHOCOLATE CAKE

2 cups sugar
3 eggs
1 cup shortening
3/4 cup buttermilk
2 1/2 cups flour

2/3 cup hot water
3 tablespoons baking
   cocoa
1 teaspoon baking soda
Chocolate Icing

Preheat the oven to 350 degrees. Combine the sugar, eggs, shortening, buttermilk and flour in a large bowl; beat well to mix. Combine the hot water, cocoa and baking soda in a separate bowl. Add the cocoa mixture to the sugar mixture; beat well. Pour into 3 greased and floured 9-inch round cake pans. Bake for 20 minutes. Frost cake while still warm. Yield: 12 to 14 servings.

CHOCOLATE ICING

1 pound confectioners'
   sugar
1 cup (2 sticks)
   margarine, softened
4 tablespoons baking
   cocoa

1 tablespoon vanilla
   extract
2 tablespoons (or more)
   water
1 cup chopped pecans

Cream the confectioners' sugar and margarine in a bowl until light and fluffy. Add the cocoa, vanilla and enough water to make of spreading consistency. Stir in the pecans.

Delores J. Stone, Preceptor Mu Phi
Plano, Texas

MILKY WAY CAKE

4 (2-ounce) Milky Way
   candy bars
1 cup (2 sticks)
   margarine, softened
2 cups sugar

4 eggs
1/2 teaspoon baking soda
1 1/2 cups buttermilk
2 1/2 cups sifted flour
1 cup chopped pecans

Preheat the oven to 325 degrees. Melt the candy bars and half the margarine in a small saucepan over low heat. Remove from heat. Cream the sugar and the remaining 1/2 cup margarine in a bowl until light and fluffy. Add the eggs 1 at a time, beating well after each addition. Stir the baking soda into the buttermilk. Add the flour and the buttermilk mixture alternately to the creamed mixture, mixing well after each addition. Stir in the melted candy bar mixture. Stir in the pecans. Pour into a greased 10-inch tube pan. Bake for 70 minutes or until cake tests done. Frost with your favorite chocolate icing. Yield: 16 servings.

Lee Bowey, Iota Master
Sterling, Colorado

DEATH BY CHOCOLATE

21 ounces bittersweet
chocolate, chopped
3/4 cup unsalted butter,
chopped
6 large eggs, separated
12 tablespoons sugar

2 teaspoons vanilla
extract
1/2 cup heavy cream
1/2 cup corn syrup
1 ounce white chocolate

Cut a circle of parchment paper to fit the bottom of a 9-inch springform pan. Grease the parchment paper. Line the sides of the pan with foil. Preheat the oven to 350 degrees. Melt 12 ounces of the bittersweet chocolate with the butter in a saucepan over medium-low heat. Cool to lukewarm. Combine the egg yolks, 6 tablespoons of the sugar and vanilla in a mixer bowl; beat at medium speed for 3 minutes. Fold into the melted chocolate mixture. Beat the egg whites and the remaining 6 tablespoons sugar in a mixer bowl until soft peaks form. Fold into the chocolate mixture; do not overmix. Pour into the prepared pan. Bake for 50 minutes. Invert onto a serving platter to cool. Heat the remaining 9 ounces bittersweet chocolate, cream and corn syrup in a saucepan over medium heat until chocolate melts, stirring occasionally. Pour about 1/4 cup of the mixture over the cooled cake; place in the freezer for 3 minutes. Pour the remaining cream mixture over the cake. Decorate with dribbles of melted white chocolate. Yield: 16 or more servings.

Susan Booker, Theta Zeta
Cranbrook, British Columbia, Canada

CHOCOLATE SPICE CUPCAKES

1 cup cake flour
3 tablespoons baking
cocoa
2 teaspoons baking
powder
1 teaspoon cinnamon
1/4 teaspoon nutmeg
1/2 teaspoon salt

Dash of ground cloves
1/3 cup butter, softened
2/3 cup sugar
1 egg
1/3 cup water
1 teaspoon vanilla
extract

Preheat the oven to 375 degrees. Combine the flour, cocoa, baking powder, cinnamon, nutmeg, salt and cloves in a small bowl; stir to blend. Cream the butter and sugar in a bowl until light and fluffy. Beat in the egg, water and vanilla. Add the flour mixture, stirring just until moistened. Fill greased muffin cups 2/3 full. Bake for 20 minutes or until cupcakes test done. Remove from oven. Sprinkle with confectioners' sugar. Yield: 12 servings.

Judith Barker, Xi Master
Cocoa, Florida

EASY HOT FUDGE PUDDING CAKE

1 cup flour
2 teaspoons baking
powder
1/4 teaspoon salt
3/4 cup sugar
2 tablespoons baking
cocoa
1/2 cup plus
2 tablespoons milk

2 tablespoons vegetable
oil
1 cup chopped nuts
(optional)
1 cup packed brown
sugar
4 tablespoons baking
cocoa
1 1/4 cups hot water

Preheat the oven to 350 degrees. Combine the flour, baking powder, salt, sugar and 2 tablespoons of the cocoa in a bowl; mix well. Add the milk and oil; mix well. Spread in a greased 8x8-inch cake pan. Mix the brown sugar with 4 tablespoons cocoa. Sprinkle over the batter. Pour the hot water evenly over the top; do not stir. Bake for 30 to 40 minutes or until cake begins to pull away from sides of pan. Be careful not to overbake. Invert onto a serving plate. Serve warm with vanilla or peppermint ice cream or with whipped cream. Yield: 6 servings.

Cheryl Dotson, Xi Mu
Nathrop, Colorado

COFFEE SCOTCH FUNNY CAKE AND SAUCE

1/2 cup (1 stick) butter or
margarine
1 cup packed brown
sugar
1/4 cup light corn syrup
1/2 cup minus
1 tablespoon strong
brewed coffee
1/4 cup shortening
1 1/4 cups cake flour,
sifted

1 teaspoon baking
powder
1/2 teaspoon salt
3/4 cup sugar
1 egg
1/2 cup milk
1 teaspoon vanilla
extract
1 unbaked (9-inch) pie
shell

Combine the the first 3 ingredients in a saucepan. Bring to a boil over low heat, stirring frequently. Stir in the coffee. Boil gently for 2 minutes. Remove from heat. Cool. Place the shortening in a mixer bowl. Sift the flour, baking powder, salt and sugar over the shortening. Add the egg, milk and vanilla. Beat at low speed until moistened. Beat at medium speed for 2 minutes. Pour into the pie shell. Pour the brown sugar sauce gently over the top. Bake for 50 to 55 minutes or until set. Sauce will form a layer between cake and pie shell. Yield: 8 servings.

Shirley LaDue, Laureate Beta Rho
Normal, Illinois

CRANBERRY SAUCE CAKE

3 cups sifted flour
1 cup sugar
2 teaspoons baking soda
1 teaspoon salt
1 cup chopped walnuts
1 (16-ounce) can whole
 cranberry sauce
1 cup mayonnaise
1/2 cup orange juice

Preheat the oven to 350 degrees. Grease a 9-inch tube pan and line the bottom with a circle of waxed paper. Sift the flour, sugar, baking soda and salt into a large bowl. Add the walnuts, cranberry sauce and mayonnaise; mix well. Stir in the orange juice. Pour into the prepared pan. Bake for 1¼ hours. Frost with a buttercream frosting. Yield: 16 servings.

Dottie Bokanovich, Laureate Mu
Cayce, South Carolina

SUPER SIMPLE LEMON CRUNCH CAKE

1½ cups sugar
1/3 cup water
1/4 cup light corn
 syrup
1 teaspoon baking
 powder
Dash of oil of lemon
10-inch sponge or angel
 food cake
Dash of lemon extract
2 cups heavy cream,
 whipped

Combine the sugar, water and corn syrup in a heavy saucepan. Cook over medium heat to 300 degrees on a candy thermometer, stirring occasionally. Remove from heat. Quickly stir in the baking powder and oil of lemon. Pour the mixture onto a 12-inch square of buttered foil. Cool. Break into coarse crumbs. Slice the sponge cake into 3 layers. Blend the lemon extract into the whipped cream. Spread 3/4 of the whipped cream between layers. Frost top and sides with the remaining whipped cream. Pat crushed candy generously over top and sides. Yield: 10 servings.

Flora L. Simay, Alpha Sigma Master
Palm Desert, California

❖ SWEET LEMON CAKE

1 (2-layer) package
 lemon or yellow cake
 mix
1 (4-ounce) package
 lemon instant
 pudding mix
4 eggs
1/3 cup vegetable oil
1 cup water
1 (14-ounce) can
 sweetened condensed
 milk
1/2 cup lemon juice
5 drops yellow food
 coloring
Seven Minute Icing

Preheat the oven to 350 degrees. Combine the cake mix, pudding mix, eggs, oil and water in a large bowl; mix well. Pour into a well greased bundt pan. Bake for 45 to 50 minutes or until cake tests done. Cool in the pan for 10 minutes. Remove from pan and cool for 1 hour on a wire rack. Cut the cake in half horizontally. Scoop out cake from bottom half, leaving a 1-inch shell. Reserve the scooped-out cake for another use. Combine the condensed milk, lemon juice and yellow food coloring in a small bowl; whisk to mix well. Pour into the shell. Cover the filled bottom half of the cake with the top half. Frost with Seven Minute Icing. Yield: 12 to 15 servings.

SEVEN MINUTE ICING

3 egg whites
2¼ cups sugar
1/8 teaspoon salt
1/2 cup water
1 teaspoon light corn
 syrup
1/2 teaspoon cream of
 tartar
1½ teaspoons lemon or
 vanilla extract

Whisk the egg whites, sugar, salt, water, corn syrup and cream of tartar in the top of a double boiler. Cook over boiling water, beating constantly with a hand-held electric mixer for 7 minutes or until satiny and fluffy. Cool slightly. Beat in the lemon extract.

Maureen Bearb, Xi Delta Pi
Breaux Bridge, Louisiana

MANGO CAKE

2½ cups mashed ripe
 mangoes
2 cups flour
2 cups sugar
2 teaspoons baking soda
2 eggs
1 teaspoon vanilla
 extract
1 cup chopped walnuts
8 ounces cream cheese,
 softened
1/2 cup margarine,
 softened
2 teaspoons vanilla
 extract
3/4 cup confectioners'
 sugar

Preheat the oven to 350 degrees. Combine the mangos, flour, sugar, baking soda, eggs and 1 teaspoon vanilla in a mixer bowl; beat until smooth. Stir in the walnuts. Spoon into a greased 9x13-inch cake pan. Bake for 35 to 40 minutes or until cake tests done. Cool on a wire rack. Beat the cream cheese, margarine and 2 teaspoons vanilla in a mixer bowl until light. Add the confectioners' sugar; beat until smooth. Spread over the cooled cake.
Yield: 15 servings.

Linda Lewis, Alpha Alpha Chi
Fort Myers, Florida

BANANA SOUR CREAM POUND CAKE

2 cups sifted flour
3 cups sugar
1/4 teaspoon baking soda
1 cup (2 sticks) butter,
    chopped
1 tablespoon shortening
6 eggs
1 cup sour cream
1 cup mashed ripe
    bananas
1/4 teaspoon vanilla
    extract
1/4 teaspoon lemon
    extract
1/4 teaspoon almond
    extract

Preheat the oven to 325 degrees. Combine the flour, sugar and baking soda in a large mixer bowl. Cut in the butter until crumbly. Beat in the shortening, eggs and sour cream. Beat at medium speed for 5 minutes. Stir in the bananas, vanilla, lemon and almond extracts. Beat for 2 minutes longer. Pour the batter into a greased and floured 10-inch tube pan or 2 greased and floured 5x9-inch loaf pans, filling pans no more than 3/4 full. Bake for 90 minutes or until a sharp knife inserted deep in cake comes out clean. Let cool in pan for 5 minutes. Invert onto serving plate Yield: 16 to 20 servings.

Polly Cray, Chi Zeta
Dunnellon, Florida

BLUE RIBBON POUND CAKE

4 cups sifted flour
1 teaspoon baking
    powder
1/2 teaspoon salt
    (optional)
Large pinch of ground
    nutmeg
2 cups unsalted butter,
    at room temperature
3 cups sugar
6 large eggs, at room
    temperature
1 cup milk, at room
    temperature
2 teaspoons lemon,
    vanilla or almond
    extract
Confectioners' sugar
    (optional)

Preheat the oven to 300 degrees. Sift the flour, baking powder, salt and nutmeg together. Cream the butter in a mixer bowl. Add the sugar gradually, beating at high speed until light and fluffy. Add the eggs 1 at a time, beating just enough to mix after each addition. Combine the milk and lemon extract. Add the flour mixture to the creamed mixture alternately with the milk, beginning and ending with dry ingredients, making 4 or 5 additions and mixing at low speed. Pour into a well buttered and floured bundt pan. Bake for 1 hour 20 minutes. Cool the cake in the pan for about 10 minutes. Invert onto a serving plate. Serve with sugared strawberries. Yield: 20 servings.

Belinda Holland, Xi Zeta Lambda
Fort Stockton, Texas

COCONUT POUND CAKE

1 cup shortening
3 cups sugar
5 eggs
2 cups flour
1 1/2 teaspoons baking
    powder
1 teaspoon salt
1 cup buttermilk
1 1/2 teaspoons coconut
    flavoring
1 1/2 cups shredded
    coconut
1/2 cup water

Cream the shortening with 2 cups of the sugar in a mixer bowl until light and fluffy. Add the eggs; beat until smooth. Combine the flour, baking powder and salt. Combine the buttermilk and 1 teaspoon of the coconut flavoring; blend well. Add the flour mixture to the creamed mixture alternately with the buttermilk mixture, mixing after each addition. Stir in the coconut. Pour into 2 greased and sugared loaf pans. Bake for 55 minutes to 1 hour or until cake tests done. Remove from pans. Cool on wire racks. Combine the remaining cup of sugar with the water in a saucepan over medium-high heat. Bring to a boil. Remove from heat. Stir in the remaining 1/2 teaspoon coconut flavoring. Pour over the cooled cakes. Wrap in foil. Let stand for several hours. Yield: 10 servings.

Karen L. Foster, Preceptor Alpha Omega
Coffeyville, Kansas

COLD OVEN POUND CAKE

1 cup (2 sticks) butter or
    margarine, softened
1/2 cup shortening
3 cups sugar
1/4 teaspoon salt
5 large eggs
3 cups flour
1 (6-ounce) can
    evaporated milk
4 tablespoons water
2 tablespoons vanilla
    butternut flavoring

Cream the butter, shortening, sugar and salt in a mixer bowl until light and fluffy. Add the eggs 1 at a time, beating well after each addition. Add the flour alternately with the milk, mixing after each addition and ending with flour. Fold in the vanilla butternut flavoring. Pour into a greased 10-inch tube pan. Place in a cold oven. Heat oven to 325 degrees. Bake for 1 hour 45 minutes; do not open oven door while baking. Yield: 16 servings.

Mary Beth Crowgey, Laureate Alpha Omicron
Roanoke, Virginia

Catherine Foote, Beta, Halifax, Nova Scotia, Canada, microwaves a mixture of 1/2 cup each sugar and brown sugar, 2 tablespoons flour, 1 tablespoon butter and 3/4 cup hot water for 3 minutes, stirring every minute to make Caramel Sauce.

PUMPKIN PECAN PRALINE CAKE

This handsome cake has been a popular seller at our garden club bazaar and church auction. It is also a favorite at sorority meetings. Serve with a cup of good, hot coffee.

1 (2-layer) package yellow cake mix	**¹⁄₂ teaspoon allspice**
1 cup canned pumpkin	**4 eggs**
¹⁄₂ cup vegetable oil	**¹⁄₂ cup packed dark brown sugar**
³⁄₄ cup packed light brown sugar	**¹⁄₄ cup heavy cream or evaporated milk**
¹⁄₄ cup water	**4 tablespoons butter**
1 teaspoon cinnamon	**¹⁄₂ cup chopped pecans**
¹⁄₄ teaspoon nutmeg	

Preheat the oven to 350 degrees. Combine the cake mix, pumpkin, oil, light brown sugar, water, cinnamon, nutmeg and allspice in a mixer bowl. Beat at medium speed for 1 minute. Add the eggs 1 at a time, beating well after each addition. Pour into a greased bundt pan. Bake for 1 hour. Cool in the pan on a wire rack for 10 minutes. Invert onto a serving plate. Combine the dark brown sugar, cream, butter and pecans in a small saucepan over medium-low heat. Heat until sugar is dissolved, stirring occasionally. Spoon over the warm bundt cake.
Yield: 14 to 16 servings.

Joy LeMasters, Alpha Eta Master
Beaumont, Texas

QUEEN ELIZABETH CAKE

1 cup chopped dates	**1 cup (or less) sugar**
1 teaspoon baking soda	**1 egg, beaten**
1 cup boiling water	**1 teaspoon vanilla extract**
1¹⁄₂ cups sifted flour	**¹⁄₂ cup chopped walnuts**
1 teaspoon baking powder	**Caramel Icing**
¹⁄₂ teaspoon salt	
¹⁄₂ cup (1 stick) butter, softened	

Preheat the oven to 350 degrees. Combine the dates and baking soda in a small bowl. Pour the boiling water over the dates and baking soda. Cool for at least 15 minutes. Sift the flour, baking powder and salt together. Cream the butter and sugar in a mixer bowl until light and fluffy. Add the egg and vanilla; mix well. Add the sifted dry ingredients to the creamed mixture alternately with the date mixture, mixing well after each addition. Stir in the walnuts. Pour into a greased 7x11- or 9x9-inch baking pan. Bake for 35 minutes or until cake tests done. Frost cooled cake with Caramel Icing. Yield: 15 servings.

CARAMEL ICING

7¹⁄₂ tablespoons brown sugar	**4 tablespoons butter**
7¹⁄₂ tablespoons heavy cream	

Combine the brown sugar, cream and butter in a heavy saucepan. Bring to a boil over medium heat. Boil gently for 12 minutes, stirring occasionally.

Judy Siegers, Xi Alpha Epsilon
Whitecourt, Alberta, Canada

CINNAMON RAISIN CAKE

2 cups boiling water	**¹⁄₄ teaspoon baking soda**
1 cup raisins	**¹⁄₂ cup (1 stick) margarine, softened**
1²⁄₃ cups flour	**1 cup packed brown sugar**
¹⁄₄ teaspoon salt	
1 teaspoon cinnamon	
¹⁄₄ teaspoon allspice	**1 teaspoon vanilla extract**
2¹⁄₂ teaspoons baking powder	**2 eggs**

Preheat the oven to 350 degrees. Combine the water and raisins in a saucepan. Simmer, covered, for 15 to 20 minutes or until only 1 cup of water appears to remain. Reserve ¹⁄₄ cup liquid for icing if desired. Combine the flour, salt, cinnamon, allspice, baking powder and baking soda in a bowl; mix well. Cream the margarine, brown sugar, vanilla and eggs in a bowl until light and fluffy. Add the flour mixture alternately with the remaining raisin liquid, mixing well after each addition. Fold in the raisins. Pour into a greased and floured 8¹⁄₂-inch cake pan. Bake for 30 to 35 minutes or until cake tests done.
Yield: 12 servings.

Sandy Gale, Xi Alpha
Pierrefonds, Quebec, Canada

RHUBARB SKILLET CAKE

My dear grandmother, who lived to be 101, baked this cake with fresh rhubarb from her garden every spring.

³⁄₄ cup sugar	**1 cup packed brown sugar**
¹⁄₂ teaspoon salt	
1¹⁄₂ cups flour	**¹⁄₂ cup milk**
2 teaspoons baking powder	**1 egg, beaten**
3 tablespoons butter	**2 cups chopped fresh rhubarb**

Preheat the oven to 350 degrees. Combine the sugar, salt, flour and baking powder. Melt the butter with the brown sugar in a 10-inch cast-iron skillet over medium heat. Stir in the milk and egg. Remove from heat. Stir in the rhubarb. Layer the flour mixture evenly over the rhubarb mixture. Bake for 30 minutes. Cool in the pan for 1 or 2 minutes. Invert onto a serving plate. Serve with ice cream or other topping. Yield: 8 to 10 servings.

Doris L. Kane, Xi Omega
Washington, Indiana

OLD-FASHIONED RHUBARB CAKE

1 cup buttermilk
1 teaspoon vanilla
  extract
2 cups flour
1 teaspoon baking soda
1 teaspoon salt
1/2 cup (1 stick) butter or
  margarine, softened
1 cup sugar

1 egg
2 cups chopped rhubarb
1/4 cups sugar
1/2 teaspoon cinnamon
1 1/2 cups milk
1/3 cup sugar
1 teaspoon vanilla
  extract

Preheat the oven to 350 degrees. Combine the buttermilk and vanilla in a small bowl. Combine the flour, baking soda and salt in a bowl. Cream the butter and 1 cup sugar in a mixer bowl. Beat in the egg. Add the dry ingredients alternately with the buttermilk mixture, mixing well after each addition. Stir in the rhubarb. Spread in a greased 9x13-inch cake pan. Combine 1/4 cup sugar and cinnamon. Sprinkle over the batter. Bake for 35 minutes or until cake tests done. Cut into 12 squares. Blend the milk, 1/3 cup sugar and vanilla in a bowl. Spoon over cake at serving time. Yield: 12 servings.

Cheryol Miller, Xi Lambda Gamma
Mansfield, Ohio

SEVEN-UP CAKE

1 (2-layer) package
  strawberry cake mix
1 (4-ounce) package any
  flavor instant
  pudding mix
4 eggs
1 cup vegetable oil

7 ounces of Seven-Up
1 (20-ounce) can crushed
  pineapple, drained
1 cup sugar
4 teaspoons cornstarch
1/4 cup (1/2 stick) butter
1 cup shredded coconut

Preheat the oven to 350 degrees. Prepare the cake batter according to the package directions using the cake mix, pudding mix, eggs, oil and Seven-Up. Pour into 3 greased 9-inch round cake pans. Bake for 30 minutes or until cake tests done. Cool using package directions. Combine the pineapple, sugar and cornstarch in a saucepan. Cook over medium-low heat for 3 minutes or until thickened, stirring constantly. Stir

in the butter and coconut. Remove from heat. Spread frosting between layers and over top and side of cake. Yield: 12 servings.

Naomi Brannon, Preceptor Psi
Texas City, Texas

BAKED-IN STRAWBERRY SHORTCAKE

1 cup flour
2 teaspoons baking
  powder
1/2 cup sugar
1 egg
1/2 cup milk
2 tablespoons melted
  margarine

1 1/2 cups sliced
  strawberries
1/2 cup flour
1/2 cup sugar
1/4 cup (1/2 stick)
  margarine, sliced

Preheat the oven to 375 degrees. Sift 1 cup flour and baking powder into a mixer bowl. Add 1/2 cup sugar, egg, milk and melted margarine; beat at low speed until moistened. Beat at medium speed for 2 minutes. Pour into a greased 8-inch square cake pan. Layer the strawberries over the batter. Combine 1/2 cup flour and 1/2 cup sugar in a small bowl. Cut in margarine until crumbly. Sprinkle over the strawberries. Bake for 35 to 40 minutes or until cake tests done. Yield: 9 servings.

Nancy Costello, Xi Omega
Asheville, North Carolina

WINE CAKE

1 (2-layer) package
  yellow cake mix
1 (4-ounce) package
  vanilla instant
  pudding mix

4 eggs
3/4 cup vegetable oil
3/4 cup pale dry sherry
1 tablespoon nutmeg
Confectioners' sugar

Preheat the oven to 350 degrees. Combine the cake mix, pudding mix, eggs, oil, sherry and nutmeg in a bowl; mix until moistened. Pour into a greased and lightly floured bundt pan. Bake for 45 to 50 minutes or until cake tests done. Cool in pan for 10 minutes. Invert onto a serving plate. Dust with confectioners' sugar. Yield: 12 servings.

Patty Chamberlain, Laureate Eta Alpha
Benicia, California

Lavina Blake, Mu Tau, Wichita, Kansas, mixes a 10-ounce package of thawed sweetened strawberries with 1 cup confectioners' sugar and 1 cup butter to make Yummy Strawberry Syrup for pancakes, waffles and other warm goodies.

CHOCOLATE PEANUT BUTTER FROSTING

This frosting is wonderful for devil's food cake.

3 cups confectioners'
  sugar
1/2 cup baking cocoa
1/2 teaspoon vanilla
  extract

1/2 cup peanut butter
1 tablespoon margarine,
  softened
1 cup (about) cold
  brewed coffee

Combine the confectioners' sugar, cocoa and vanilla in a mixer bowl. Beat in the peanut butter and margarine. Beat in enough cold coffee gradually to make of spreading consistency. Yield: 1 1/2 cups.

Shannon Ramsey, Eta Eta
Cocoa, Florida

ALMOND GOOEY BARS

10 tablespoons butter,
  melted
1 (2-layer) package
  butter recipe yellow
  cake mix
1 egg, lightly beaten
1 pound confectioners'
  sugar

8 ounces cream cheese,
  softened
2 eggs
1 teaspoon almond
  extract
Sliced almonds

Preheat the oven to 350 degrees. Combine the butter, cake mix and 1 egg in a large bowl; mix well. Press into a greased and floured 9x13-inch baking pan. Cream the confectioners' sugar and cream cheese in a bowl until light and fluffy. Stir in 2 eggs and almond flavoring. Pour the cream cheese mixture over the cake mix layer. Sprinkle with almonds. Bake for 30 to 40 minutes or until lightly browned. Cool and cut into squares. Yield: 2 dozen.

Maureen Silko, Alpha Phi Nu
Carrollton, Texas

ALMOND ROCA COOKIES

1 cup (2 sticks) butter,
  softened
1/2 cup sugar
1/2 cup packed brown
  sugar
1 teaspoon vanilla
  extract

1 egg yolk, beaten
1 cup flour
1/2 teaspoon salt
2 cups chocolate chips
1/4 cup chopped almonds

Preheat the oven to 325 degrees. Combine the butter, sugar, brown sugar, vanilla, egg yolk, flour and salt in a bowl; mix well. Spread evenly in an ungreased 10x15-inch baking pan. Bake for 20 to 25 minutes or until lightly browned. Sprinkle the chocolate chips evenly over the top. Bake for 5 minutes or until

chocolate is melted. Remove from oven. Spread the chocolate evenly. Sprinkle with the chopped almonds. Cut into squares while still slightly warm. Yield: 6 dozen.

Debra Lind, Preceptor Laureate Zeta
Silverdale, Washington

ANGEL FOOD COOKIES

1 1/2 cups (3 sticks)
  margarine
4 cups flour
5 egg yolks
3 tablespoons vinegar
1/2 cup water
1 package angel food
  cake mix

3/4 cup water
1 pound walnuts, finely
  ground
1 cup sugar
2 (10-ounce) jars
  maraschino cherries,
  drained, chopped

Cut the margarine into the flour until crumbly. Combine the egg yolks, vinegar and 1/2 cup water in a small bowl. Add to the flour mixture; mix well. Divide dough into 6 equal portions. Chill, wrapped in plastic wrap, for 3 hours. Preheat the oven to 350 degrees. Prepare the angel food cake mix using the package directions, reducing water to 3/4 cup. Set aside. Roll each dough ball into a 10x12-inch rectangle on a well-floured sheet of foil. Combine the walnuts and sugar in a bowl. Sprinkle down the center of the rolled dough. Add a layer of cherries over the walnut mixture. Spoon the angel food cake batter over the cherries in a 1 1/2 inch thick layer. Fold 1 side of the dough rectangle over to enclose filling and pinch ends to seal. Place on a lightly greased baking sheet. Bake for 30 minutes. Remove from oven. Sprinkle with confectioners' sugar while still hot. Cool completely. Cut into 1/2-inch slices. Repeat with remaining ingredients. Yield: 6 rolls.

Michaelene Campana, Laureate Epsilon Eta
Monessen, Pennsylvania

APPLESAUCE COOKIES

1/2 cup shortening
1 cup sugar
1 egg
1 teaspoon baking soda
1 cup applesauce
2 cups flour

1/2 teaspoon salt
1 teaspoon cinnamon
1/2 teaspoon nutmeg
1/2 teaspoon ground
  cloves
1 cup rolled oats

Preheat the oven to 350 degrees. Cream the shortening and sugar in a large bowl until light and fluffy. Add the egg and blend well. Mix the baking soda and applesauce in a small bowl. Combine the flour, salt, cinnamon, nutmeg and cloves. Add the flour mixture to the creamed mixture alternately with the applesauce mixture, mixing after each addition. Stir in the oats. Drop by tablespoonfuls onto a greased cookie sheet. Bake for 15 to 20 minutes or until golden brown. Yield: 3 dozen.

Jennifer L. Johnson, Nu Psi
Lexington, Missouri

APRICOT WRAP COOKIES

1³/₄ cups flour
¹/₂ teaspoon baking
  powder
¹/₄ teaspoon salt
3 tablespoons unsalted
  butter, softened
3 tablespoons
  margarine, softened
¹/₂ cup sugar
1 egg
¹/₂ teaspoon vanilla
  extract
2 teaspoons grated
  orange zest
¹/₂ cup chopped dried
  apricots
¹/₃ cup orange juice
2 tablespoons light
  brown sugar

Combine the flour, baking powder and salt. Cream the butter, margarine and sugar in a large bowl until light and fluffy. Add the egg, vanilla and orange zest; mix well. Stir in the flour mixture. Shape into a disk. Chill, wrapped in plastic wrap, for several hours. Preheat the oven to 350 degrees. Combine the apricots, orange juice and brown sugar in a small saucepan. Simmer, covered, over medium heat for 10 minutes or until apricots are soft. Purée the apricot mixture in a food processor until smooth, adding additional orange juice if necessary. Divide the dough into thirds. Roll each third into a 6-inch square on a lightly floured surface. Cut each square into nine 2-inch squares. Spread a scant teaspoonful apricot filling from one corner of each small square diagonally across to its opposite corner. Fold over to form a triangle, enclosing filling; press to seal. Place on a greased cookie sheet. Bake for 10 to 12 minutes or until lightly browned. Sprinkle with confectioners' sugar. Yield: 2 dozen.

Blanche N. Goldsmith, Eta Master
Las Cruces, New Mexico

Cordelia M. Holst, Preceptor Rho, Miles City, Montana, makes Strawberry Wonder Cake by dissolving a small package of strawberry gelatin in 1 cup boiling water, adding 1 large package of frozen strawberries and chilling until partially set. Prepare a small package of vanilla instant pudding mix with 1 cup milk and blend in a pint of softened ice cream. Layer a torn angel food cake, pudding mixture and gelatin mixture in a 9x13-inch cake pan. Chill until firm and top with whipped cream.

ARKANSAS TRAVELERS

All the children in the neighborhood used to come to our house when my mother made these cookies. She would serve them warm with cold milk.

1 cup (2 sticks) butter,
  softened, or
  shortening
1 teaspoon vanilla
  extract
1 cup packed brown
  sugar
1 cup sugar
2 eggs
1 cup peanut butter
3 cups sifted flour
2 teaspoons baking
  powder
1 cup chopped dates or
  peanuts (optional)

Preheat the oven to 300 degrees. Cream the butter and vanilla in a mixer bowl. Add the brown sugar and sugar gradually, creaming until light and fluffy. Add the eggs 1 at a time, beating well after each addition. Stir in the peanut butter; mix well. Sift the flour and baking powder into the creamed mixture; mix well. Stir in the dates. Roll the dough into small balls. Arrange on a greased cookie sheet. Flatten the balls with the tines of a fork that has been dipped in water. Bake for 10 to 15 minutes or just until brown. Yield: 5 dozen.

Sandy Larson, Laureate Alpha Epsilon
Fayetteville, Arkansas

BANANA BONANZA COOKIES

2 cups flour
1 cup butterscotch chips
¹/₄ cup (¹/₂ stick)
  margarine or butter,
  softened
¹/₄ cup applesauce
¹/₂ cup packed brown
  sugar
1 egg
³/₄ cup chopped banana
1 teaspoon baking soda
1 cup rolled oats
1 cup chopped nuts
1 cup shredded coconut
1 cup white chocolate
  chips

Preheat the oven to 350 degrees. Process the flour and butterscotch chips in a food processor or blender until the butterscotch chips are as fine as the flour. Cream the butter, applesauce, brown sugar and egg in a mixer bowl until light and fluffy. Beat in the banana and baking soda. Add the butterscoth and flour mixture; mix well. Stir in the rolled oats, nuts, coconut and white chocolate chips. Drop dough by heaping teaspoonfuls onto greased cookie sheets. Bake for 12 to 14 minutes or until golden brown. Cool on the cookie sheets for 1 minute. Remove from cookie sheets to wire racks to cool completely. Yield: 4 dozen.

Lillian Cook, Laureate Alpha Zeta
Matheny, West Virginia

BANANA SPICE COOKIES

1/2 cup (1 stick)
margarine, softened
1 cup packed brown
sugar
2 eggs
1 1/2 cups mashed
bananas
2 cups flour
1/4 teaspoon baking soda
1/4 teaspoon salt
1/4 teaspoon cinnamon

2 teaspoons baking
powder
Dash of ground cloves
1 cup chopped pecans
1/2 banana, mashed
1 tablespoon margarine,
softened
1/2 teaspoon vanilla
extract
1 pound confectioners'
sugar, sifted

Cream 1/2 cup margarine and brown sugar in a large bowl until light and fluffy. Add the eggs and 1 cup bananas; mix well. Sift the flour, baking soda, salt, cinnamon, baking powder and cloves together. Add to the margarine mixture; mix well. Chill dough, covered, for at least 3 hours. Preheat the oven to 350 degrees. Drop by teaspoonfuls onto ungreased cookie sheets. Bake for 10 to 12 minutes or until lightly browned. Make the frosting while cookies are baking. Combine 1/2 banana, 1 tablespoon margarine, vanilla and confectioners' sugar in a small bowl; mix until smooth. Frost the cookies while still warm. Yield: 3 dozen.

Lavonda Wentworth, Laureate Omega
Enid, Oklahoma

CHOCOLATE CHIP BANANA COOKIES

2 1/4 cups flour
1 cup sugar
2 teaspoons baking
powder
1/4 teaspoon baking soda
3/4 teaspoon salt
2/3 cup shortening

2 eggs
1 cup mashed bananas
2 teaspoons vanilla
extract
1 cup chocolate chips
3 tablespoons sugar
3/4 teaspoon cinnamon

Preheat the oven to 350 degrees. Sift the flour, 1 cup of the sugar, baking powder, baking soda and salt into a large bowl. Cut in the shortening until crumbly. Add the eggs, banana and vanilla; mix well. Stir in the chocolate chips. Drop by heaping teaspoonfuls onto an ungreased cookie sheet. Mix the remaining 3 tablespoons sugar with the cinnamon. Sprinkle half the cinnamon mixture over cookie dough. Bake for 10 minutes. Sprinkle the remaining cinnamon mixture over cookies while still warm. Remove from cookie sheet. Cool. Yield: 5 dozen.

Joyce Bell, Xi Epsilon Upsilon
Isabel, Kansas

CAPPUCCINO BISCOTTI

2 cups flour
1 cup sugar
1/3 cup chopped walnuts
1/4 cup unsweetened
baking cocoa
1/2 teaspoon baking
powder
1/2 teaspoon baking soda
1/2 teaspoon salt

1/2 teaspoon ground
cinnamon
2 teaspoons instant
coffee granules
2 teaspoons hot water
1 teaspoon vanilla
extract
2 eggs
1 egg white

Preheat the oven to 325 degrees. Combine the flour, sugar, walnuts, cocoa, baking powder, baking soda, salt and cinnamon in a large bowl. Dissolve the coffee granules in water in a small bowl. Add the vanilla, eggs and egg white; mix well. Add the coffee mixture to the flour mixture; mix well. Knead dough lightly 7 or 8 times on a lightly floured surface. Shape into a 16 inch long roll. Place the roll on a greased cookie sheet. Flatten to 1-inch thickness. Bake for 30 minutes. Remove roll from cookie sheet to a wire rack. Cool for 10 minutes. Cut roll diagonally into 1/2-inch-wide slices. Arrange the slices cut side down on the cookie sheet. Bake for 10 minutes. Turn the slices over. Bake for 10 minutes longer. Cool completely on a wire rack. Yield: 1 1/2 to 2 dozen.

Carol J. Aubrey, Xi Alpha Eta
Vero Beach, Florida

RED AND WHITE BISCOTTI

1/4 cup (1/2 stick)
margarine, softened
3/4 cup sugar
1 tablespoon freshly
grated orange zest
1/2 teaspoon vanilla
extract
2 eggs

1 egg white
2 cups flour
1 1/2 teaspoons baking
powder
1/4 teaspoon salt
2 (1-ounce) squares white
chocolate, chopped
1/2 cup dried cranberries

Cream the margarine, sugar, orange zest and vanilla in a large mixer bowl until light and fluffy. Beat in the eggs and egg white. Beat in the flour, baking powder and salt. Stir in the chocolate and cranberries. Chill dough for 1 hour. Preheat the oven to 325 degrees. Shape the dough into 2 logs, each 12 inches long and 3 inches wide. Arrange 2 or 3 inches apart on a greased cookie sheet. Bake for 30 minutes or until golden brown. Cool for 10 minutes. Cut logs diagonally into 1-inch slices. Arrange slices cut side down on the cookie sheet. Bake for 15 minutes longer. Cool completely. Store in an airtight container. Yield: 2 dozen.

Brenda Hansen, Xi Alpha Nu
Baker, Montana

WALNUT BISCOTTI

1/2 cup sugar
2 tablespoons
    margarine, softened
1 large egg
1 1/2 teaspoons vanilla
    extract
1 1/4 cups flour
1 teaspoon baking
    powder

1/4 teaspoon ground
    nutmeg
Dash of salt
1/2 cup chopped walnuts
1/4 cup Old English fruit
    and peel mix
    (optional)

Preheat the oven to 350 degrees. Cream the sugar and margarine in a large bowl until light and fluffy. Beat in the egg and vanilla. Combine the flour, baking powder, nutmeg and salt. Add the flour mixture to the sugar mixture gradually, mixing well. Mix in walnuts and fruit mix. Knead dough lightly 7 times on a lightly floured surface. Shape into a 12-inch roll. Place roll on a greased cookie sheet. Flatten to 1-inch thickness. Bake for 30 minutes. Cool on a wire rack for 10 minutes. Cut roll diagonally into sixteen 1/2-inch slices. Arrange slices cut side down on the cookie sheet. Bake for 5 minutes. Turn slices over. Bake for 5 minutes longer. Yield: 16 servings.

Jean Portner, Preceptor Zeta Kappa
Rock Falls, Illinois

BISHOP'S CAKE

Bishop's Cake is a bar-type cookie. It was traditionally served when the bishop came to visit the Methodist church in Elmira, New York. I usually triple the recipe and bake in a 9x13-inch pan.

1 egg, beaten
1/3 cup sugar
1/3 cup sifted flour
1 1/8 teaspoons salt
1/4 teaspoon baking
    powder

1/3 cup chocolate chips
2/3 cup chopped nuts
1/3 cup chopped dates
1/3 cup chopped candied
    cherries

Preheat the oven to 375 degrees. Add the sugar gradually to the egg in a large mixer bowl, beating until light and fluffy. Sift the flour, salt and baking powder together. Add the chocolate chips, nuts and fruit to the flour mixture; mix well. Fold the chocolate chip mixture into the egg mixture. Pour into a greased shallow 7x7-inch baking pan. Bake for 20 minutes or until lightly browned. Cool and cut into bars.
Yield: 1 dozen.

Valeria K. Martin, Xi Delta Beta
State College, Pennsylvania

CHOCOLATE FROSTED BROWNIES

1/2 cup (1 stick)
    margarine, softened
1 cup sugar
4 eggs
1 teaspoon vanilla
    extract
1 cup plus 1 tablespoon
    flour

1 (16-ounce) can
    chocolate syrup
1/2 cup chopped nuts
6 tablespoons margarine
6 tablespoons milk
1 1/2 cups sugar
1/2 cup chocolate chips

Preheat the oven to 350 degrees. Beat 1/2 cup margarine, sugar and eggs in a large bowl until light and fluffy. Add the vanilla, flour, chocolate syrup and nuts; mix well. Spread in a 10x15-inch baking pan. Bake for 30 minutes. Combine 6 tablespoons margarine, milk and sugar in a saucepan. Bring to a rolling boil over medium heat and boil for 30 seconds. Remove from heat. Add the chocolate chips; beat until smooth. Frost warm brownies.
Yield: 2 dozen.

Celia A. Reed, Xi Nu Kappa
Kearney, Missouri

GERMAN CREAM CHEESE BROWNIES

2 (8-ounce) packages
    German's sweet
    chocolate
10 tablespoons butter
8 ounces cream cheese,
    softened
1/2 cup sugar
2 eggs
2 tablespoons flour
1 teaspoon vanilla
    extract

4 eggs
1 1/2 cups sugar
1 teaspoon baking
    powder
1/2 teaspoon salt
2 teaspoons vanilla
    extract
1 teaspoon almond
    extract
1 cup flour
1 cup pecans, chopped

Preheat the oven to 350 degrees. Melt the chocolate and 6 tablespoons of the butter in a saucepan over low heat, stirring constantly. Set aside. Beat the remaining 4 tablespoons butter with the cream cheese until soft. Add 1/2 cup of the sugar gradually, beating until light and fluffy. Blend in 2 eggs, 2 tablespoons flour and 1 teaspoon vanilla. Set aside. Beat 4 eggs in a bowl until light and fluffy. Beat in 1 1/2 cups sugar gradually. Add the baking powder, salt, 2 teaspoons vanilla, almond extract, 1 cup flour, pecans and chocolate mixture. Spread half the chocolate mixture in a greased 9x13-inch baking pan. Spread with cream cheese mixture. Spoon on the remaining chocolate mixture. Swirl with a spatula to create a marbled effect. Bake for 35 to 40 minutes. Cool and cut into bars. Yield: 3 dozen.

Ruth Corley, Laureate Zeta Eta
College Station, Texas

TEXAS BROWNIES

1 (16-ounce) package
   light brown sugar
4 eggs
2 cups buttermilk
   baking mix

2 teaspoons vanilla
   extract
1½ cups nuts
Easy Penuche Frosting

Preheat the oven to 350 degrees. Combine the sugar, eggs, baking mix, vanilla and nuts in a large bowl; mix well. Spread in a greased and floured 9x13-inch pan. Bake for 25 to 30 minutes or until brownies pull from side of pan. Cool. Frost with Easy Penuche Frosting. Yield: 3 dozen.

EASY PENUCHE FROSTING

½ cup (1 stick) butter
1 cup packed brown
   sugar

¼ cup milk
1¾ to 2 cups
   confectioners' sugar

Melt the butter in a medium saucepan over low heat. Stir in the brown sugar. Bring to a boil. Boil for 2 minutes, stirring constantly. Stir in the milk. Bring to a boil, stirring constantly. Cool to lukewarm. Add the confectioners' sugar gradually. Beat until of spreading consistency.

Susan Gafnea, Xi Alpha Xi
Hueytown, Alabama

CHOCOLATE CRUNCH BROWNIES

1 cup (2 sticks) butter or
   margarine, softened
2 cups sugar
4 eggs
6 tablespoons baking
   cocoa
1 cup flour
2 teaspoons vanilla
   extract

½ teaspoon salt
1 (7-ounce) jar
   marshmallow creme
1 cup creamy peanut
   butter
2 cups semisweet
   chocolate chips
3 cups crisp rice cereal

Preheat the oven to 350 degrees. Cream the butter and sugar in a mixer bowl until light and fluffy. Add the eggs 1 at a time, beating well after each addition. Stir in the cocoa, flour, vanilla and salt. Spread in a greased 9x13-inch baking pan. Bake for 25 minutes or until brownies test done. Cool. Spread the marshmallow creme over the cooled brownies. Melt the peanut butter and chocolate chips in a small saucepan over low heat, stirring constantly. Remove from heat. Add the cereal, stirring until coated. Spread over marshmallow creme layer. Chill for at least 1 hour before cutting. Keep refrigerated. Yield: 3 dozen.

Anna M. Hoge, Xi Zeta Epsilon
Kalamazoo, Michigan

BLONDE BROWNIES

1 cup flour
½ teaspoon baking
   powder
⅛ teaspoon baking soda
½ teaspoon salt
½ cup pecans, chopped
⅓ cup vegetable oil
1 tablespoon hot water

1 cup packed brown
   sugar
1 egg
1 teaspoon vanilla
   extract
1 cup semisweet
   chocolate chips

Preheat the oven to 350 degrees. Mix the flour, baking powder, baking soda and salt in a small bowl. Stir in the pecans. Beat the eggs, vanilla and oil in a large bowl. Beat in the hot water. Add the flour mixture, brown sugar, egg, vanilla and chocolate chips; mix well. Spread in a greased 8x8-inch baking pan. Bake for 20 to 25 minutes. Yield: 2 dozen.

Carla J. White, Xi Gamma Nu
Alva, Oklahoma

FUDGY BROWNIES

1 cup (2 sticks) unsalted
   butter
4 (1-ounce) squares
   unsweetened
   chocolate
5 large eggs

2 cups sugar
1 teaspoon vanilla
   extract
1½ cups flour
1 teaspoon salt
3 cups chopped walnuts

Preheat the oven to 325 degrees. Melt the butter and chocolate in a saucepan over low heat. Cool. Beat the eggs in a mixer bowl at high speed until foamy. Add the sugar, beating until pale yellow and slightly thickened. Beat in the cooled chocolate mixture and vanilla. Add the flour, salt and walnuts, stirring just until flour is incorporated. Spread in a greased 9x13-inch baking pan. Bake for 30 to 35 minutes. Do not overbake. Dust with confectioners' sugar. Yield: 3 dozen.

Karen Regennitter, Xi Delta Chi
Ritzville, Washington

CHOCOLATE COFFEE BROWNIES

2 cups flour
2 cups sugar
½ cup (1 stick)
   margarine
½ cup shortening
1 cup strong brewed
   coffee
¼ cup baking cocoa
½ cup buttermilk
2 eggs
1 teaspoon baking soda

1 teaspoon vanilla
   extract
½ cup (1 stick)
   margarine
2 teaspoons baking
   cocoa
¼ cup milk
3½ cups unsifted
   confectioners' sugar
1 teaspoon vanilla
   extract

Preheat the oven to 400 degrees. Combine the flour and sugar in a large mixer bowl. Combine 1/2 cup margarine, shortening, coffee and 1/4 cup cocoa in a heavy saucepan. Bring to a boil over medium heat. Pour boiling mixture over the flour mixture; mix well. Beat in the buttermilk, eggs, baking soda and 1 teaspoon vanilla. Mix well at high speed. Spread in a greased 11x13-inch baking pan. Bake for 20 minutes or until firm in the center. Combine 1/2 cup margarine, 2 teaspoons cocoa and milk in a small saucepan. Bring to a boil over medium heat, stirring constantly. Add the confectioners' sugar and 1 teaspoon vanilla; beat until smooth. Pour the warm frosting over the brownies as soon as they come out of the oven. Yield: 4 dozen.

Lucy Sabo, Preceptor Gamma Eta
Caledonia, Ontario, Canada

PEANUT BUTTER BROWNIES

1/2 cup (1 stick) butter or margarine, softened	*1 cup flour*
1/2 cup sugar	*1 cup rolled oats*
1/2 cup packed brown sugar	*1 cup chocolate chips*
1 egg	*1/2 cup confectioners' sugar*
1/3 cup peanut butter	*2 to 3 tablespoons peanut butter*
1/2 teaspoon each salt and baking soda	*2 to 3 tablespoons evaporated milk*
1/2 teaspoon vanilla extract	

Preheat the oven to 325 degrees. Cream the butter, sugar and brown sugar in a large bowl until light and fluffy. Beat in the egg, 1/3 cup peanut butter, salt, baking soda and vanilla. Stir in the flour and rolled oats. Spread in a 9x13-inch greased baking pan. Bake for 15 to 20 minutes. Sprinkle the chocolate chips over the top while brownies are still warm. Let chips melt, then spread evenly. Combine the confectioners' sugar, 2 to 3 tablespoons peanut butter and evaporated milk. Drizzle over brownies. Cut into bars. Yield: 1 1/2 dozen.

Christi Bently, Epsilon Xi
Marshall, Missouri

BROWN SUGAR BARS

2 cups flour	*3 eggs*
1 1/2 teaspoons baking powder	*1 1/2 teaspoons vanilla extract*
1/2 teaspoon salt	*3/4 cup melted margarine*
3 cups packed brown sugar	*1 1/2 cups chopped nuts*

Preheat the oven to 350 degrees. Combine the flour, baking powder, salt, brown sugar, eggs and vanilla in a large bowl. Add the melted butter; mix well. Add nuts. Spread in a greased and floured 9x13-inch baking pan. Bake for 30 minutes. Cool before cutting. Yield: 2 dozen.

Judith Wells, Beta Sigma Phi
Lindsay, Oklahoma

PORTUGUESE BUTTERHORNS

2 cups flour	*1 cup sugar*
1 cup (2 sticks) butter or margarine	*1 teaspoon cinnamon*
1 egg yolk	*1/4 cup packed brown sugar*
3/4 cup buttermilk	*3/4 cup chopped nuts*

Combine the flour, butter and egg yolk in a large bowl; mix well with hands. Add the buttermilk; mix well. Dough will be very soft. Form three balls of dough; wrap in waxed paper. Chill overnight. Preheat the oven to 325 degrees. Combine the sugar, cinnamon, brown sugar and nuts. Roll each ball of dough into a circle. Sprinkle with the nut mixture. Cut each circle into 8 equal wedges. Roll the pieces from the small end to enclose filling. Shape into horns on a greased cookie sheet. Bake for 20 to 25 minutes. Yield: 2 dozen.

Lorna Barrowcliff, Laureate Zeta Epsilon
Redwood Valley, California

CHOCOLATE CHIP BUTTERSCOTCH BARS

2 cups flour	*2 teaspoons vanilla extract*
1/2 teaspoon baking soda	*1 cup chopped pecans*
1 cup packed dark brown sugar	*1 1/2 cups semisweet chocolate chips*
3/4 cup butter, softened	
1 large egg	

Preheat the oven to 300 degrees. Combine the flour and baking soda in a medium bowl. Cream the brown sugar and butter in a large mixer bowl. Add the egg and vanilla; beat until light and fluffy. Add the flour mixture, pecans and chocolate chips. Mix at low speed just until combined. Do not overmix. Spread in a greased 8x8-inch baking pan. Level the top with a spatula. Bake for 35 to 45 minutes or until a wooden pick comes out clean but center is still soft. Cool. Cut into 1x2-inch bars. Yield: 1 to 1 1/2 dozen.

Gina Birkmaier, Beta Nu
Enterprise, Oregon

CHOCOLATE MINT COOKIES

2½ cups flour
1½ teaspoons baking
powder
¾ teaspoon salt
1 cup sugar
¾ cup vegetable oil
2 eggs
1 teaspoon vanilla
extract

8 drops red or green food
coloring (optional)
1 (10-ounce) package
semisweet mint
chocolate chips
¼ cup sugar

Preheat the oven to 350 degrees. Combine the flour, baking powder and salt in a small bowl. Blend 1 cup sugar and oil in a large bowl. Beat in the eggs, vanilla and food coloring. Add the flour mixture gradually, stirring until smooth. Stir in the chocolate chips. Shape by teaspoonfuls into small balls. Roll in the remaining ¼ cup sugar; arrange on a greased cookie sheet. Bake for 8 to 10 minutes or until crisp around the edges. Yield: 2½ dozen.

Jill Sellers, Beta Beta Chi
Cedar Hill, Texas

GRAHAM CRACKER COOKIES

20 marshmallows,
chopped
6 tablespoons butter,
melted
1 teaspoon vanilla
extract
3½ cups graham cracker
crumbs

1 cup chopped nuts
2 (1-ounce) squares
unsweetened
chocolate
1 cup milk
2 cups sugar
¼ teaspoon salt

Combine the marshmallows, butter, vanilla, graham cracker crumbs and nuts in a bowl; mix well. Combine the chocolate, milk, sugar and salt in a heavy saucepan. Bring to a boil over medium heat. Cook to soft-ball stage like fudge, but not too hard, stirring constantly. Remove from heat. Stir in the marshmallow mixture gradually. Spoon into a greased 8x11-inch baking pan. Spread to ½-inch thickness. Cut into squares when set. Yield: 4 dozen.

Patti Kruse, Xi Tau Chi
San Diego, California

Patricia Epp, Preceptor Gamma Tau, Sorrento, British Columbia, Canada, shares this recipe from a friend in Borneo. Melt 3 Mars bars with 6½ tablespoons butter, mix with 3 cups rice Krispies and press into a greased 8x12-inch dish. Melt 7 ounces milk chocolate with 3 tablespoons butter. Pour over the cereal layer. Chill and cut into squares for Chocolate-Topped Crunch.

CHOCOLATE CHERRY COOKIES

1 (10-ounce) jar
maraschino cherries
1½ cups flour
½ cup baking cocoa
¼ teaspoon baking
powder
¼ teaspoon baking soda
¼ teaspoon salt
½ cup (1 stick) butter,
softened

1 cup sugar
1 egg
1½ teaspoons vanilla
extract
1 cup chocolate chips
½ cup sweetened
condensed milk
4 to 5 teaspoons
maraschino cherry
juice

Preheat the oven to 350 degrees. Drain the cherries, reserving juice. Stir the flour, cocoa, baking powder, baking soda and salt together. Cream the butter and sugar in a large mixer bowl. Add the egg and vanilla; beat until light and fluffy. Mix in the flour mixture gradually until well blended. Shape the dough into 1-inch balls. Arrange on ungreased cookie sheets. Make an indentation in the center of each ball; place a cherry in each indentation. Combine the chocolate chips and condensed milk in a small saucepan. Melt over low heat. Stir in the cherry juice, adding more if mixture is too thick. Spoon 1 teaspoon of the melted chocolate mixture over each ball, covering the cherry. Bake for 10 minutes; do not overbake. Cool on a wire rack. Freezes nicely. Yield: 3 dozen.

Kay Goodroad, Gamma Nu
Bristow, Oklahoma

WHITE CHOCOLATE CRANBERRY COOKIE BARS

2 cups flour
1 teaspoon baking
powder
1 teaspoon salt
4 eggs
1¾ cups sugar
1 teaspoon vanilla
extract

1 (12-ounce) package
white chocolate chips
½ cup (1 stick)
margarine
1 cup dried cranberries

Preheat the oven to 350 degrees. Combine the flour, baking powder and salt in a medium bowl. Beat the eggs, sugar and vanilla in a small bowl with a wire whisk. Melt 1 cup of the chocolate chips with the margarine in a large saucepan over low heat, stirring occasionally. Remove from heat. Let cool slightly. Stir the egg mixture slowly into the chocolate mixture. Stir in the flour mixture gradually. Stir in the remaining white chocolate chips and cranberries. Spread in a greased 9x13-inch baking pan. Bake for 40 minutes or until center springs back up when lightly touched. Cool on a wire rack. Cut into bars. Yield: 1½ dozen.

Barbara Anderson, Laureate Eta
Parmington, Connecticut

✤ CRANBERRY ORANGE CHEESECAKE BARS

1 (15-ounce) package sugar cookie mix	6 ounces cream cheese, softened
1 tablespoon water	¼ cup sugar
1 (12-ounce) package cranberry orange sauce, drained	1 egg
	1 teaspoon vanilla extract

Preheat the oven to 350 degrees. Combine the cookie mix (including shortening pouch) and water; mix until crumbly. Set aside 1 cup of the crumb mixture for the topping. Press the remaining crumb mixture evenly into a lightly greased 9-inch square baking pan. Bake for 12 to 15 minutes or until lightly browned. Cool slightly. Spread the cranberry orange sauce evenly over the crust. Combine the cream cheese, sugar, egg and vanilla in a small mixer bowl; beat until creamy. Pour evenly over the cranberry layer. Sprinkle with the reserved crumb mixture. Return to the oven. Bake for 30 minutes longer. Cool completely. Cut into bars and chill. Serve cold. Yield: 16 bars.

Brenda Crumley, Preceptor Delta Upsilon
Dayton, Ohio

✤ WHITE CHOCOLATE BISCOTTI

Prepare these at least 10 days in advance for a special occasion.

½ cup (1 stick) butter, softened	1½ teaspoons baking powder
¾ cup sugar	¼ teaspoon baking soda
2 eggs	¼ teaspoon salt
1 teaspoon vanilla extract	⅔ cup chopped nuts
2 tablespoons amaretto	⅔ cup white chocolate chips
2 cups plus 2 tablespoons flour	

Preheat the oven to 325 degrees. Cream the butter and sugar in a mixer bowl until light and fluffy. Beat in the eggs, vanilla and amaretto. Combine the flour, baking powder, baking soda and salt in a small bowl; mix well. Add the flour mixture to the butter mixture; mix well. Fold in the nuts and chocolate chips. Divide dough in half. Form 2 logs about 1½ inches wide, 14 inches long and ½ inch thick. Place at least 2 inches apart on a greased and floured cookie sheet.

Bake in the middle of the oven for 25 minutes. Remove from oven. Cool on a wire rack for 5 minutes. Cut the logs into ½-inch-thick slices. Arrange the slices cut side down on the cookie sheet. Bake for 8 minutes longer. Cool. Store in an airtight container. Yield: 3 dozen.

Conni Grod, Omega Sigma
San Jose, California

CREAM CHEESE COOKIES

Every time I take these cookies to a gathering, people just go on talking about how good they are. Now I take the recipe with me to hand out!

1 cup (2 sticks) margarine, softened	1 teaspoon vanilla extract
8 ounces cream cheese, softened	1 cup chopped pecans
2 cups sugar	2 cups flour

Preheat the oven to 350 degrees. Cream the margarine and cream cheese in a mixer bowl. Add the sugar, vanilla and chopped pecans; mix well. Add the flour gradually, mixing well. Drop by teaspoonfuls onto a greased cookie sheet. Bake for 12 to 15 minutes or until light brown. Yield: 3 dozen.

Jill Spencer, Beta Nu
Crossville, Illinois

EASTER EGG COOKIES

These cookies eventually replaced real hard-boiled eggs as "our family Easter eggs."

1 cup (2 sticks) butter, softened	3 cups flour
½ cup packed brown sugar	1 cup quick-cooking oats, uncooked
1 teaspoon almond extract	1 recipe frosting
1 egg	Food colorings
½ teaspoon salt	Cookie toppings (optional)

Preheat the oven to 325 degrees. Cream the butter and brown sugar in a large bowl until light and fluffy. Add the flavoring and egg. Add a mixture of the salt and flour gradually to the butter mixture. Stir in the oats. Shape dough into about 3 dozen egg shapes. Place on an ungreased cookie sheet. Bake for 20 to 25 minutes. Cool. Decorate with your favorite frosting tinted in pastel colors and add cookie toppings. Store in an airtight container. Yield: 3 dozen.

Marti Timmel, Preceptor Alpha Theta
Oakton, Virginia

GUMDROP COOKIE BARS

2 tablespoons water
4 eggs
2 cups packed brown
   sugar
1¹/₂ cups flour
¹/₄ teaspoon salt

¹/₄ teaspoon baking soda
1 teaspoon cinnamon
³/₄ cup coarsely chopped
   pecans
1 cup chopped fruit-
   flavor gumdrops

Preheat the oven to 375 degrees. Combine the water and eggs in a bowl; beat until light and fluffy. Stir in the brown sugar. Add the flour, salt, baking soda and cinnamon; mix well. Stir in the pecans and gumdrops. Spread in a greased 9x13-inch baking dish. Bake for 30 to 35 minutes or until a wooden pick comes out clean. Cool. Cut into small squares. Roll in confectioners' sugar. Yield: 1¹/₂ dozen.

Irene M. Davis, Preceptor Delta Lambda
Taylorville, Illinois

PAPA'S ICEBOX COOKIES

My German grandfather loved these cookies. He would keep the dough in the refrigerator and bake a few each morning. The house smelled wonderful! They are great dunked in coffee.

1 cup (2 sticks) butter or
   margarine
¹/₂ cup sugar
¹/₂ cup packed brown
   sugar
2 eggs
2³/₄ cups sifted flour

¹/₂ teaspoon baking soda
1 teaspoon salt
2 teaspoons cinnamon
1 teaspoon vanilla
   extract
¹/₂ cup chopped nuts

Combine the butter, sugar, brown sugar and eggs in a mixer bowl; mix at low speed. Stir in the flour, baking soda, salt, cinnamon, vanilla and nuts; mix with hands. Form into a smooth roll. Wrap in waxed paper and chill for 2 hours. Preheat the oven to 400 degrees. Cut roll into slices ¹/₁₆ to ¹/₈ inch thick. Place on an ungreased cookie sheet. Bake for 6 to 8 minutes or until light brown. Yield: 6 dozen.

Amy Jones, Xi Chi Pi
Albany, Texas

LEMON BUTTER COOKIES

5 cups sifted cake flour
2 cups sugar
1 cup (2 sticks) unsalted
   butter
1 cup shortening

6 egg yolks
1 cup sour cream
Juice and grated zest of
   1 lemon
6 egg whites

Preheat the oven to 350 degrees. Combine the flour and sugar in a bowl. Cut in the butter and shortening with a pastry blender until crumbly. Stir in the egg

yolks, sour cream, lemon juice and lemon zest. Knead gently to blend the ingredients. Roll the dough ¹/₂ inch thick on a lightly floured surface. Cut with a round cutter. Arrange on a nonstick cookie sheet. Brush with egg whites and sprinkle with additional sugar. Bake for 10 to 12 minutes or until light brown. Yield: 3 dozen.

Anne Schroeder, Preceptor Alpha Zeta
Appleton, Wisconsin

OLD-FASHIONED FILLED COOKIES

1 cup shortening
2 cups sugar
2 teaspoons baking
   powder
1 teaspoon baking soda
1 teaspoon salt

3¹/₂ to 4 cups flour
3 eggs, beaten
2 teaspoons vanilla
   extract
5 tablespoons milk
Marmalade Filling

Cream the shortening and sugar in a mixer bowl until light and fluffy. Sift the baking powder, baking soda, salt and flour together. Add the eggs and sifted mixture alternately to the creamed mixture, mixing well after each addition and adding milk as needed. Chill, covered. Preheat the oven to 350 degrees. Roll out dough on a floured surface. Cut into circles. Arrange half the circles on a lightly greased cookie sheet. Spoon about 1 teaspoon Marmalade Filling over each. Cover with remaining dough circles and crimp edges to seal. Bake for 10 to 12 minutes. Cookies should not be brown. Yield: 3 dozen.

MARMALADE FILLING

2 tablespoons (heaping)
   cornstarch
3 or 4 tablespoons water
3 quarts chopped
   rhubarb
4 cups sugar, or to taste

2 oranges, chopped
1 (16-ounce) package
   brown or golden
   raisins
1 (20-ounce) can crushed
   pineapple

Blend the cornstarch and water in a small bowl and set aside. Combine the rhubarb, sugar, oranges, raisins and pineapple in a saucepan. Cook over low heat for 5 to 10 minutes or until thickened, stirring constantly. Add the cornstarch mixture. Cook for about 10 minutes longer, stirring constantly. May add chopped nuts if desired. Cool overnight or seal in pint jars. This filling will keep for 3 to 4 weeks in the refrigerator or may be frozen.

Sharon R. Gump,
Fairmont Convention Hospitality Committee
Barrackville, West Virginia

MINCEMEAT-FILLED CRUMB BARS

3½ cups flour
1 cup finely chopped
   walnuts
1½ cups (3 sticks)
   margarine or butter,
   softened

1¼ cups sifted
   confectioners' sugar
2 cups All-Fruit
   Mincemeat
1 tablespoon flour

Preheat the oven to 375 degrees. Combine 3½ cups flour and walnuts in a medium bowl. Cream the margarine in a large mixer bowl at medium speed. Add the confectioners' sugar; beat until light and fluffy. Add the flour mixture. Beat at low speed. Press ⅔ of the dough in an ungreased 9x13-inch baking pan. Spread the Mincemeat over the top. Mix 1 tablespoon flour with the remaining dough until slightly crumbly. Sprinkle over the mincemeat layer. Bake for 25 minutes or until golden. Cool completely. Cut into bars. Yield: 4 dozen.

ALL-FRUIT MINCEMEAT

4 cups chopped unpeeled
   apples
2 cups raisins, chopped
1 cup chopped dried
   apricots
1 (6-ounce) can frozen
   apple juice
   concentrate, thawed

¾ cup water
¼ cup honey
1 teaspoon allspice
½ teaspoon salt
2 teaspoons brandy

Combine the apples, raisins, apricots, apple juice concentrate, water, honey, allspice and salt in a 4½-quart Dutch oven over medium-high heat. Bring to a boil. Reduce heat and simmer, covered, for 50 minutes, stirring occasionally. Uncover and simmer for 10 to 15 minutes longer or until liquid has nearly evaporated, stirring occasionally. Stir in the brandy. May use in other mincemeat recipes. Yield: 4 cups.

Karen Windhausen, Laureate Eta
Edmonds, Washington

Dorothy Crockatt, Laureate Beta Nu, Etobicoke, Ontario, Canada, makes Pinkies or Greenies by blending ½ cup butter with ½ cup sugar, ¼ cup baking cocoa, ⅛ teaspoon salt and 2 eggs in a double boiler. Cook over boiling water until thickened, stirring constantly. Stir in 1 teaspoon vanilla and 25 crushed arrowroot cookies. Pour into a buttered 8x8-inch glass dish and chill. Frost with pink or green confectioners' sugar icing. Chill; cut into squares.

DUNKIN' PLATTERS

For kids' snacks add M&Ms, Smarties, dried cranberries, or other favorites.

2 cups (4 sticks)
   margarine, melted
2 cups packed brown
   sugar
2 cups sugar
4 eggs
2 teaspoons vanilla
   extract
2 cups rolled oats

2 cups cornflakes
4 cups flour
2 teaspoons baking soda
2 teaspoons baking
   powder
1½ cups raisins
1 cup shredded coconut
2½ cups chocolate chips

Preheat the oven to 350 degrees. Mix the margarine, brown sugar, sugar, eggs and vanilla in a large bowl. Combine the oats, cornflakes, flour, baking soda and baking powder in a separate bowl. Add the oat mixture gradually to the margarine mixture. Fold in the remaining ingredients. Drop by spoonfuls onto greased cookie sheets. Bake for 8 to 12 minutes or until brown. Yield: 6 to 8 dozen.

Yvonne Brueckert, Preceptor Alpha Omicron
Abbotsford, British Columbia, Canada

JELLY BARS

1½ cups flour
1 cup sugar
Dash of salt
¾ cup (1½ sticks)
   margarine
2 cups quick-cooking
   oats

1½ cups favorite jelly or
   jam
1½ cups chopped nuts
   (optional)

Preheat the oven to 350 degrees. Combine the flour, sugar and salt in a large bowl. Cut in the margarine until crumbly. Reserve 1½ cups of the mixture. Press the remaining mixture into a lightly greased 9x13-inch baking pan. Spread the jelly evenly over the mixture. Sprinkle the reserved mixture over the jelly layer. Pat down lightly. Top with the nuts. Bake for 25 minutes. Yield: 8 to 10.

Flora Lou Alexander, Xi Xi Rho
Arlington, Texas

Mary Hill, Alpha Rho, Mountain Home, Idaho, prepares Yum Yum Dessert by mixing 60 crushed butter crackers with ¾ cup melted butter and ¼ cup sugar and pressing half into a 9x13-inch pan. Pour on a mixture of a can of sweetened condensed milk, a 6-ounce can of lemonade or limeade concentrate and a large container of whipped topping. Top with the remaining crumb mixture. Chill or freeze until firm.

COCOA SHORTBREAD COOKIES

2 cups flour	1¹/₃ cups sifted
¹/₃ cup baking cocoa	confectioners' sugar
¹/₂ teaspoon (or less) salt	1¹/₂ teaspoons vanilla
1¹/₄ cups (2¹/₂ sticks)	extract
butter, softened	

Preheat the oven to 350 degrees. Combine the flour, baking cocoa and salt in a small bowl; mix well. Cream the butter in a large mixer bowl until light and fluffy. Beat in the confectioners' sugar gradually. Add the vanilla. Stir in the flour mixture gradually; mix well. If the dough is too soft to roll and cut, chill for about 15 minutes. Roll dough ¹/₃ at a time to ¹/₈-inch thickness on a lightly floured board. Cut out shapes with a floured cutter. Place on ungreased cookie sheets. Bake for 8 to 10 minutes. Yield: 3 to 4 dozen.

Sheila A. LeBlanc, Gamma Master
Bedford, Nova Scotia, Canada

SASKATCHEWAN'S OWN OATMEAL SHORTBREAD

Serve with fresh or canned fruit.

1¹/₄ cups (2¹/₂ sticks)	3 cups rolled oats
butter, softened	2¹/₂ cups flour
¹/₂ cup packed brown	2 teaspoons baking
sugar	powder
¹/₃ cup sugar	1 teaspoon salt
1 teaspoon vanilla	
extract	

Preheat the oven to 325 degrees. Cream the butter, brown sugar, sugar and vanilla in a large bowl until light and fluffy. Stir in the rolled oats. Sift the flour, baking powder and salt together. Add to the butter mixture, mixing to make a stiff dough. Roll dough into 5x12-inch rectangles. Cut into 2-inch squares. Place on greased cookie sheets. Bake for 20 to 30 minutes or until golden brown. Yield: 4 dozen.

Phyllis MacKay, Epsilon Master
Prince Albert, Saskatchewan, Canada

SPECULAAS

1 cup (2 sticks) butter,	1¹/₄ tablespoons
softened	cinnamon
1 cup packed brown	³/₄ teaspoon crushed
sugar	anise seeds
2 cups flour	¹/₂ teaspoon ground
¹/₂ teaspoon salt	cloves
1¹/₄ teaspoons nutmeg	2¹/₂ teaspoons finely
³/₄ teaspoon pepper	grated orange zest
1 tablespoon baking	2 tablespoons milk
powder	

Preheat the oven to 450 degrees. Cream the butter and brown sugar in a mixer bowl until light and fluffy. Sift the flour, salt, nutmeg, pepper, baking powder, cinnamon, anise seeds, cloves and orange zest into the butter mixture; mix well. Add the milk gradually, mixing at medium speed. Roll out the dough ¹/₂ inch thick on a lightly floured board. Cut with desired shape cookie cutters. Arrange on a greased cookie sheet. Bake at 450 degrees for 7 minutes. Reduce oven temperature to 325 degrees. Bake for 20 minutes longer or until light brown. Cool on the cookie sheet for 1 minute. Remove from the cookie sheet to a wire rack to cool completely. Yield: 2 dozen.

Corina Schanoski, Theta
Moose Jaw, Saskatchewan, Canada

SWEET PASTRY POCKETS

I entered this recipe in the Nevada state cookie bake-off when I was 16 years old—and won. It was a very exciting experience.

³/₄ cup packed brown	¹/₂ cup chopped walnuts
sugar	³/₄ cup (1¹/₂ sticks)
3 ounces cream cheese,	butter, softened
softened	2 cups flour
¹/₈ teaspoon salt	¹/₂ teaspoon salt
1 teaspoon vanilla	2 tablespoons
extract	confectioners' sugar
¹/₂ cup shredded coconut	1 egg yolk
¹/₂ cup chocolate chips	¹/₄ cup water

Preheat the oven to 400 degrees. Cream the brown sugar and cream cheese in a medium bowl until smooth. Add ¹/₈ teaspoon salt and vanilla; mix well. Stir in the coconut, chocolate chips and walnuts. Chill, covered, while preparing dough. Combine the butter, flour, ¹/₂ teaspoon salt, confectioners' sugar and egg yolk in a large mixer bowl; mix well. Add the water, mixing to form a stiff dough. Divide the dough into 2 equal portions. Roll each portion to ¹/₈-inch thickness on a lightly floured board. Cut with a 2- to-3-inch round floured cutter. Place ¹/₂ teaspoon cream cheese filling in the center of each circle. Fold over and press edges to seal. Arrange on ungreased cookie sheets. Make a ¹/₂-inch cut in the top of each cookie to allow steam to escape. Bake for 8 to 10 minutes or until golden brown. Cool on the cookie sheet for 1 minute. Remove from the cookie sheet to a wire rack to cool completely. Garnish with a sprinkle of additional confectioners' sugar. Yield: 3 dozen.

Lesa Speyer, Xi Pi
Riverton, Wyoming

WHISKEY LIZZIES

1½ pounds candied fruit	*2 eggs, well beaten*
2 ounces whiskey	*1½ cups flour*
⅓ cup butter or	*½ teaspoon salt*
margarine	*1½ teaspoons baking*
½ cup sugar or packed	*soda*
brown sugar	*1½ tablespoons milk*

Preheat the oven to 325 degrees. Soak the fruit in the whiskey in a small dish. Cream the butter and sugar in a mixer bowl until light and fluffy. Beat in the eggs. Combine the flour, salt and baking soda. Add the flour mixture to the butter mixture; mix well. Stir in the milk and whiskey mixture. Drop by spoonfuls onto greased cookie sheets. Bake for 15 minutes or until edges are lightly browned. Yield: 3 dozen.

Joya Hill, Preceptor Tau
Weiser, Idaho

APPLE BUTTER CRUMBLE PIE

1 cup solid-pack	*¼ teaspoon nutmeg*
pumpkin	*¼ teaspoon salt*
1 cup apple butter	*3 eggs, lightly beaten*
¼ cup packed dark	*1 cup evaporated milk*
brown sugar	*1 unbaked (9-inch) pie*
½ teaspoon cinnamon	*shell*
¼ teaspoon ginger	

Preheat the oven to 375 degrees. Combine the pumpkin, apple butter, brown sugar, cinnamon, ginger, nutmeg and salt in a large bowl. Stir in the eggs and evaporated milk. Mix well. Pour into the pie shell. Bake for 50 to 60 minutes. Sprinkle Crumble Topping over the pie and bake for 15 minutes longer.
Yield: 8 servings.

CRUMBLE TOPPING

½ cup flour	*⅓ cup chopped pecans*
5 tablespoons sugar	*3 tablespoons butter*

Combine the flour, sugar and pecans in a small bowl. Cut in the butter until crumbly.

Cayla Armatti, Xi Nu Rho
Ocala, Florida

APPLE CREAM PIE

⅔ cup sugar	*1 egg, lightly beaten*
2 tablespoons flour	*2 cups finely chopped*
Pinch of salt	*apples*
1 cup sour cream	*1 unbaked (9-inch) pie*
1 teaspoon vanilla	*shell*
extract	*Cinnamon Topping*

Preheat the oven to 425 degrees. Combine the sugar, flour and salt in a mixer bowl. Stir in the sour cream, vanilla and egg. Beat until smooth. Stir in the apples. Pour into the pie shell. Sprinkle Cinnamon Topping over the pie. Bake for 25 to 30 minutes or until set. Yield: 6 to 8 servings.

CINNAMON TOPPING

⅓ cup flour	*1 teaspoon cinnamon*
⅓ cup sugar	*½ stick butter, sliced*

Combine the flour, sugar and cinnamon in a small bowl. Cut in the butter until crumbly.

Barbara Imber, Laureate Gamma Epsilon
Toledo, Ohio

CARAMEL APPLE PIE

6 ounces cream cheese,	*1 (9-inch) graham*
softened	*cracker pie shell*
1 egg	*1 (12-ounce) package*
1½ teaspoons vanilla	*frozen escalloped*
extract	*apples, thawed*
3 tablespoons sugar	*⅓ cup caramel topping*
1 tablespoon flour	*½ teaspoon cinnamon*

Preheat the oven to 375 degrees. Combine the cream cheese, egg, vanilla, sugar and flour in a bowl; beat until smooth. Pour the mixture into the pie shell. Combine the escalloped apples, caramel topping and cinnamon in a medium bowl; mix well. Spoon over the cream cheese mixture, keeping 2 distinct layers. Bake for 40 to 45 minutes or until apples bubble up around the edge. Serve at room temperature. Yield: 6 to 8 servings.

Lynda Klasel, Xi Omega Nu
Rosenberg, Texas

HEAVENLY BANANA CREAM PIE

1 (14-ounce) can	*1 cup cold water*
sweetened condensed	*16 ounces whipped*
milk	*topping*
1 (4-ounce) package	*6 large bananas, sliced*
vanilla instant	*1 baked (11-inch) pie*
pudding mix	*shell*

Combine the first 3 ingredients in a large bowl. Whisk until smooth and thickened. Fold in ¾ of the whipped topping. Fold in the bananas. Pour into the pie shell. Cover with remaining whipped topping. Chill, covered, for at least 4 hours. Yield: 12 servings.

Helen Boorman, Preceptor Beta
Los Alamos, New Mexico

CARAMEL PIE

½ cup sugar
3 egg yolks
½ cup sugar
½ cup flour
2 cups milk
1 tablespoon butter or
    margarine
1 baked (10-inch) pie
    shell

3 egg whites
⅓ cup sugar
½ teaspoon cream of
    tartar
Pinch of salt
1 teaspoon vanilla
    extract

Preheat the oven to 425 degrees. Caramelize ½ cup sugar in a heavy saucepan over low heat. Combine the egg yolks, ½ cup sugar, flour and milk in a blender container; blend until smooth. Whisk the milk mixture into the melted sugar over medium-low heat. Cook until thickened, stirring constantly. Stir in the butter. Pour into the pie shell. Bake for 15 minutes or until set. Beat the egg whites at high speed until stiff peaks form. Add remaining ⅓ cup sugar, cream of tartar, salt and vanilla gradually, beating constantly. Spread over the baked layer, sealing to edge. Bake for 2 or 3 minutes longer or until browned. Yield: 6 to 8 servings.

Judy Williams
Glen Rose, Texas

SOUTHERN CHESS PIE

1½ cups sugar
1 tablespoon (heaping)
    flour
3 eggs
½ cup (1 stick) butter,
    softened

1 teaspoon vanilla
    extract
1 teaspoon vinegar
¼ cup milk
1 unbaked (10-inch) pie
    shell

Preheat the oven to 350 degrees. Blend the sugar, flour, eggs, butter, vanilla, vinegar and milk in a bowl. Pour into the pie shell. Bake for 40 to 45 minutes or until firm in the center. Yield: 8 servings.

Leatrice T. Cole, Master
Huntsville, Alabama

SWEET CHOCOLATE ANGEL PIE

2 egg whites
⅛ teaspoon salt
⅛ teaspoon cream of
    tartar
½ cup sugar
½ cup finely chopped
    nuts
½ teaspoon vanilla
    extract

4 ounces German's
    chocolate
3 tablespoons water
1 teaspoon vanilla
    extract
1 cup whipping cream,
    whipped

Preheat the oven to 300 degrees. Combine the egg whites, salt and cream of tartar in a mixer bowl; beat at high speed until foamy. Add the sugar, 2 tablespoons at a time, beating well after each addition. Mixture should stand in very stiff peaks. Fold in the nuts and ½ teaspoon vanilla. Spread over bottom and side of a lightly greased 8-inch pie pan, building up side ½ inch above the rim. Bake for 50 to 55 minutes or until set. Cool to room temperature. Combine German's chocolate and 3 tablespoons water in a heavy saucepan. Cook over low heat until melted, stirring frequently. Remove from heat. Cool until thickened. Stir in the remaining 1 teaspoon vanilla. Fold the chocolate mixture into the whipped cream. Spoon into the meringue shell. Chill, covered, for at least 2 hours before serving. Yield: 6 to 8 servings.

LuAnn Petty, Lambda Tau
Meriden, Kansas

NO-BAKE CHOCOLATE CARAMEL PIE

½ cup pecans, toasted
1 chocolate crumb pie
    shell
1 (14-ounce) can
    sweetened condensed
    milk
6 tablespoons butter or
    margarine
¼ cup sugar
1½ cups semisweet
    chocolate chips

⅔ cup whipping cream
3 tablespoons butter or
    margarine
1½ cups semisweet
    chocolate chips
1 cup heavy whipping
    cream
⅓ cup evaporated milk,
    chilled

Sprinkle the pecans in the pie shell. Combine the condensed milk, butter and sugar in a heavy saucepan. Cook over medium-low heat until butter melts, stirring frequently. Bring to a slow boil. Boil for 6 minutes or until thickened, stirring constantly. Pour over the pecans. Chill, covered, for 1 hour or until firm. Combine 1½ cups chocolate chips, ⅔ cup whipping cream and butter in a heavy saucepan. Cook over medium-low heat for 5 minutes or until melted, stirring constantly. Pour over the caramel layer. Chill, covered, until set. Melt 1½ cups chocolate chips in a heavy saucepan. Cool slightly. Whip 1 cup whipping cream in a large chilled mixer bowl. Reserve ½ cup whipped cream. Beat the cooled chocolate into the remaining whipped cream until well blended. Beat the cold evaporated milk until thick enough for beaters to leave a trail. Beat into the chocolate mixture. Spread over the chocolate layer. Chill until set. Serve with reserved whipped cream. Yield: 12 servings.

Renell Bell, Kappa Upsilon
Colby, Kansas

MYSTERY PIE

1 (3-ounce) package
   vanilla pudding and
   pie filling mix
2 cups milk
1 baked (9-inch) pie
   shell
1 (16-ounce) can pecan-
   coconut frosting

1/4 cup milk
2 tablespoons margarine
8 ounces whipped
   topping
Chopped pecans

Cook the pudding mix with 2 cups milk, using package directions. Cool. Pour into the pie shell. Combine the frosting, 1/4 cup milk and margarine in a saucepan. Cook over medium-low heat until margarine melts, stirring frequently. Cool slightly. Pour over the pudding layer. Cool completely. Top with whipped topping. Sprinkle with pecans. Chill until ready to serve. Yield: 8 servings.

Ines Wilson, Laureate Xi
Riverton, Wyoming

COCONUT OATMEAL PIE

3 eggs, well beaten
1 cup packed brown
   sugar
2/3 cup sugar
2 tablespoons
   margarine, melted
1 teaspoon vanilla
   extract

2/3 cup quick-cooking
   oats
2/3 cup flaked coconut
1 unbaked (9-inch) pie
   shell
Whipped topping

Preheat the oven to 350 degrees. Combine the eggs, brown sugar, sugar, margarine, vanilla, oats and coconut in a medium bowl; mix well. Pour into the pie shell. Bake for 35 minutes or until set. Cool. Serve with whipped topping. Yield: 8 servings.

Ruby G. Hartje, Xi Gamma Nu
Anna, Illinois

COCONUT PEACH PIE

3/4 cup flaked coconut
1/4 cup flour
1/3 cup packed brown
   sugar
3 tablespoons butter,
   softened
1 unbaked (9-inch) pie
   shell

4 cups sliced peaches
1 tablespoon lemon
   juice
2/3 cup sugar
1/3 cup packed brown
   sugar
1/4 cup quick-cooking
   tapioca

Preheat the oven to 425 degrees. Combine the coconut, flour, 1/3 cup brown sugar and butter in a bowl; mix well. Spread 1/3 of the coconut mixture in the pie shell. Combine the peaches, lemon juice, sugar, 1/3 cup brown sugar and tapioca in a bowl. Pour over the coconut mixture in the pie shell. Cover with the remaining coconut mixture. Bake for 40 minutes or until set. Yield: 6 to 8 servings.

Joyce Greenough, Sigma Master
29 Palms, California

PECAN PUMPKIN PIE

2 eggs, lightly beaten
1 cup canned pumpkin
1 cup 2% evaporated
   milk
2/3 cup packed brown
   sugar
1 tablespoon flour
1/2 teaspoon cinnamon
1/4 teaspoon cloves
Pinch of nutmeg

1/2 teaspoon ginger
Pinch of salt
1/3 cup ground pecans
1/3 cup packed brown
   sugar
2 tablespoons butter,
   softened
1 unbaked (9-inch) pie
   shell

Preheat the oven to 400 degrees. Combine the eggs, pumpkin, evaporated milk, 2/3 cup brown sugar, flour, cinnamon, cloves, nutmeg, ginger and salt in a large bowl; mix well. Combine the pecans, 1/3 cup brown sugar and butter in a small bowl; mix well. Press the pecan mixture evenly into the pie shell. Pour the pumpkin mixture over the pecan mixture. Bake for 50 minutes or until set. Garnish with pecan halves. Serve with whipped cream. Yield: 8 servings.

Linda Anderson, Preceptor Alpha Phi
Greely, Ontario, Canada

PINEAPPLE SOUR CREAM PIE

1 baked (9-inch) pie
   shell
3/4 cup sugar
1/4 cup flour
1/2 teaspoon salt
2 1/2 cups crushed
   pineapple with juice

1 cup sour cream
1 tablespoon lemon
   juice
3 egg yolks, beaten
3 egg whites
1 teaspoon cold water
6 tablespoons sugar

Preheat the oven to 350 degrees. Combine 3/4 cup sugar, flour and salt in a heavy saucepan. Stir in the pineapple, sour cream, lemon juice and egg yolks. Cook over medium-low heat until mixture boils and thickens, stirring constantly. Pour into the pie shell. Beat the egg whites with water to form soft peaks. Add 6 tablespoons sugar 1 tablespoon at a time, beating until stiff peaks form. Spread over the pie, sealing to the edge. Bake for 15 minutes or until golden brown. Yield: 6 servings.

Mae Belle Herczeg, Lambda Master
Vancouver, British Columbia, Canada

PINEAPPLE CHEESE PIE

1 (12-ounce) carton
    cottage cheese,
    drained
1/2 cup sugar
2 tablespoons flour
2 eggs
1 cup evaporated milk
2 tablespoons lemon
    juice

1/4 teaspoon salt
1/2 teaspoon vanilla
    extract
1 unbaked (10-inch) pie
    shell
1/3 cup sugar
1 (9-ounce) can crushed
    pineapple
1 tablespoon cornstarch

Preheat the oven to 450 degrees. Beat the cottage cheese in a mixer bowl at high speed until smooth and creamy. Beat in 1/2 cup sugar and flour gradually until well mixed. Add the eggs 1 at a time, beating well after each addition. Stir in the evaporated milk, lemon juice, salt and vanilla; blend well. Pour into the pie shell. Bake for 10 minutes. Reduce heat to 350 degrees. Bake for 20 minutes longer. Cool. Combine 1/3 cup sugar, pineapple and cornstarch in a saucepan. Cook over medium heat until thick, stirring constantly. Spread over the pie. Yield: 6 servings.

Rosa M. Eaches, Preceptor Alpha
Colorado Springs, Colorado

BUTTER CRACKER PIE

3 egg whites
1 cup sugar
1/2 teaspoon baking
    powder
1 teaspoon vanilla
    extract
1/2 cup chopped pecans

14 butter crackers,
    crumbled
1 (3-ounce) package
    French vanilla
    instant pudding mix
8 ounces whipped
    topping

Preheat the oven to 350 degrees. Beat the egg whites in a mixer bowl at high speed until stiff peaks form. Beat the sugar, baking powder and vanilla gradually into the egg whites. Stir in the pecans and crackers. Pour into a greased 9-inch pie pan. Bake for 30 minutes. Cool until center of pie sinks. Prepare the pudding using package directions. Fold in the whipped topping. Pour into the meringue shell. Chill, covered, until serving time. Yield: 6 servings.

Shirley Quick, Mu Gamma
Tell City, Indiana

Dorothy Knecht, Preceptor Alpha Xi, Natchitoches, Louisiana, layers half a can of fruit pie filling in a graham cracker shell and adds a blend of 8 ounces cream cheese, 1 cup milk, lemon instant pudding mix and half an 8 ounce tub of whipped topping. Layer remaining topping and pie filling to make Fluffy Lemon Fruit Pie.

GRANDMA BESSIE'S SQUASH PIE

2 cups cooked squash
1 (14-ounce) can
    sweetened condensed
    milk
2 egg yolks
1 teaspoon pumpkin pie
    spice

1 teaspoon cinnamon
1/2 teaspoon nutmeg
1/3 cup packed brown
    sugar
2 egg whites
1 unbaked (9-inch) pie
    shell

Preheat the oven to 425 degrees. Combine the squash, condensed milk, egg yolks, pumpkin pie spice, cinnamon, nutmeg and brown sugar in a large bowl; mix well. Beat the egg whites until stiff peaks form. Fold into the squash mixture. Pour into the pie shell. Bake for 15 minutes. Reduce heat to 350 degrees. Bake for 35 to 40 minutes longer or until knife inserted in center of pie comes out clean. Serve with whipped topping or vanilla ice cream.
Yield: 6 to 8 servings.

Cathi R. Holt, Xi Zeta Mu
Lebanon, Kansas

OLD TIME VINEGAR PIE

2 tablespoons
    margarine, softened
3/4 cup sugar
3 egg yolks
1/4 cup flour
1/4 cup apple cider
    vinegar

3/4 cup water
1 tablespoon vanilla
    extract
3 egg whites
Dash of salt
1 unbaked (9-inch) pie
    shell

Preheat the oven to 425 degrees. Cream the margarine and sugar in a bowl until light and fluffy. Add the egg yolks; blend well. Add the flour; blend well. Combine the vinegar, water and vanilla. Stir the vinegar mixture into the egg yolk mixture, blending well. Beat the egg whites with a dash of salt until stiff peaks form. Fold egg whites gently into the flour mixture. Pour into the pie shell. Bake for 12 to 15 minutes. Reduce heat to 350 degrees. Bake for 30 to 35 minutes longer or until set. Cool completely before cutting. Sprinkle confectioners' sugar over the top if desired. Yield: 6 to 8 servings.

Nadine Hitt, Laureate Omicron
Rogers, Arkansas

SPICED LOUISIANA YAM PIE

3/4 cup packed brown
    sugar
2 teaspoons cinnamon
1/4 teaspoon ginger
1/4 teaspoon nutmeg
1/4 teaspoon ground
    cloves

3/4 teaspoon salt
1 1/2 cups mashed cooked
    sweet potatoes
3 eggs, beaten
1 (12-ounce) can
    evaporated milk

Preheat the oven to 350 degrees. Combine the brown sugar, cinnamon, ginger, nutmeg, cloves and salt in a large bowl; blend well. Add the sweet potatoes, eggs and evaporated milk; mix until smooth and well blended. Pour into a greased 9-inch pie pan. Bake for 55 minutes or until a knife inserted in the center comes out clean. Yield: 6 servings.

Oma Mackey, Xi Beta Sigma
Sulphur, Oklahoma

ZUCCHINI PIE

4 cups sliced, peeled zucchini	**1½ teaspoons cream of tartar**
2 tablespoons lemon juice	**3 tablespoons flour**
Dash of salt	**Dash of nutmeg**
1¼ cups sugar	**1 recipe (2-crust) pie pastry**
1½ teaspoons cinnamon	**Butter**

Preheat the oven to 400 degrees. Cook the zucchini in a small amount of water over medium heat until tender; drain. Combine the zucchini, lemon juice and salt in a bowl. Combine the sugar, cinnamon, cream of tartar, flour and nutmeg in a small bowl. Stir into the zucchini mixture; mixture will be runny. Pour into a pastry-lined pie plate. Dot with butter. Top with the remaining pastry, sealing edge and cutting vents. Bake for 40 minutes or until golden brown. Yield: 6 to 8 servings.

Donna Yauger, Beta Nu
Connellsville, Pennsylvania

CREAMY CHEESE AND FRUIT TARTS

2 (15-count) packages frozen prebaked phyllo tart shells	**½ cup lemon juice**
	1 teaspoon vanilla extract
1 (14-ounce) can sweetened condensed milk	**Sliced strawberries**
	Blueberries
	Sliced bananas
8 ounces cream cheese, softened	

Thaw the tart shells at room temperature for 10 minutes. Combine the condensed milk and cream cheese in a mixer bowl; beat until smooth and creamy. Beat in the lemon juice and vanilla. Spoon the cream cheese filling into the tart shells; smooth the filling with a knife. Arrange the strawberry slices, blueberries and banana slices brushed lightly with a small amount of additional lemon juice in a decorative pattern on the filling. Chill, covered, until ready to serve. Yield: 30 or more servings.

Margaret J. West, Preceptor Beta Chi
Ocala, Florida

HAWAIIAN MACADAMIA TARTS

3 ounces cream cheese, softened	**1 egg**
	Pinch of salt
½ cup (1 stick) butter, softened	**1 teaspoon vanilla extract**
1 cup flour	**¾ cup ground macadamia nuts**
¾ cup packed brown sugar	**24 whole macadamia nuts**
1 tablespoon butter, softened	

Preheat the oven to 325 degrees. Combine the cream cheese, ½ cup butter and flour in a medium bowl; mix well. Roll into 24 small balls. Press over bottoms and sides of miniature muffin cups or tart pans. Combine the brown sugar, the 1 tablespoon butter, egg, salt, vanilla and ground macadamia nuts in a bowl; mix well. Fill the tart shells ¾ full. Press a whole macadamia nut into each tart. Bake for 25 minutes or until crusts are lightly browned. Yield: 12 servings.

Patricia Weitz, Laureate Beta
Kailua, Hawaii

PEACHES AND CREAM TART

9 soft coconut macaroon cookies, crumbled	**¼ teaspoon almond extract**
1 cup ground pecans	**½ cup whipping cream, whipped**
3 tablespoons margarine, softened	**3 peaches, peeled, thinly sliced**
8 ounces cream cheese, softened	**2 tablespoons lemon juice**
2 teaspoons orange juice	
⅓ cup sugar	**½ cup fresh raspberries**
1 teaspoon vanilla extract	**¼ cup apricot preserves**
	2 teaspoons honey

Preheat the oven to 350 degrees. Combine the macaroons, pecans and margarine in a medium bowl; mix well. Press crumbs over the bottom and side of a 9-inch pie plate. Bake for 15 minutes. Beat the cream cheese in a mixer bowl until fluffy. Add the orange juice, sugar, vanilla and almond extract; beat until smooth. Fold the whipped cream into the mixture gently. Spread into the cooled cookie crust. Chill for 2 to 4 hours. Toss the peaches in the lemon juice just before serving. Arrange the peaches and raspberries over the pie filling. Combine the apricot preserves and honey in a small saucepan. Cook over medium-low heat until runny, stirring constantly. Spoon over the top. Yield: 8 servings.

Carol Welden, Alpha Xi
Cupar, Saskatchewan, Canada

GRILLED APPLE MELT

This is a great recipe for using up leftover pound cake.

Butter, softened
2 slices pound cake
2 slices American or
  Cheddar cheese
1/2 cup canned apple pie
  filling

Spread butter on 1 side of each slice of pound cake. Place 1 slice of cake buttered side down in a skillet. Layer 1 slice of the cheese, the apple pie filling and the remaining slice of cheese. Cover with the remaining slice of pound cake, buttered side up. Cook over low heat until golden brown on both sides and cheese is melted, turning carefully. Yield: 1 serving.

Myrtle Pion, Laureate Gamma Kappa
Lakeland, Florida

APPLE LASAGNA

2 cups shredded Cheddar
  cheese
1 cup ricotta cheese
1 egg, lightly beaten
1/4 cup sugar
1 teaspoon almond
  extract
2 (21-ounce) cans apple
  pie filling
8 lasagna noodles,
  cooked, rinsed,
  drained
6 tablespoons flour
6 tablespoons brown
  sugar
1/4 cup quick-cooking
  oats
1/2 teaspoon ground
  cinnamon
Dash of ground nutmeg
3 tablespoons margarine
1 cup sour cream
1/3 cup packed brown
  sugar

Preheat the oven to 350 degrees. Combine the Cheddar cheese, ricotta cheese, egg, sugar and almond extract in a medium bowl; mix well. Spread 1 can of apple pie filling in a greased 9x13-inch baking dish. Layer half the noodles, cheese mixture, the remaining noodles and the remaining pie filling in the dish. Combine the flour, 6 tablespoons brown sugar, oats, cinnamon and nutmeg in a small bowl; cut in the margarine until crumbly. Sprinkle over the apple pie filling. Bake for 45 minutes. Cool for 15 minutes. Combine the sour cream and 1/3 cup brown sugar in a small bowl while dessert is baking; blend well. Chill, covered, until ready to serve. Cut the lasagna into squares. Top with dollops of sour cream mixture. Yield: 12 to 15 servings.

JoAnn J. Kresky, Laureate Alpha Chi
Lansing, Michigan

S'MORE BANANA DESSERT

3/4 cup graham cracker
  crumbs
1/2 cup buttermilk
  baking mix
2 tablespoons sugar
1/4 cup (1/2 stick)
  margarine or butter,
  melted
2 to 3 medium bananas,
  sliced
3 tablespoons lemon
  juice
1 1/3 cups milk
1 (4-ounce) package
  vanilla instant
  pudding mix
3/4 cup miniature
  marshmallows
16 chocolate stars

Combine the cracker crumbs, baking mix and sugar in a small bowl. Stir in the margarine until moistened. Press in an 8x8x2-inch microwave-safe dish. Microwave on High for 1 1/2 to 3 minutes or until mixture bubbles up slightly and then begins to flatten, rotating dish 1/2 turn every minute. Cool for 10 minutes on a wire rack. Dip the bananas into lemon juice. Arrange over the crumb crust. Combine the milk and pudding mix in a bowl; beat until smooth. Stir in the marshmallows. Spread the pudding mixture over the banana slices. Arrange the chocolate stars evenly over pudding mixture. Chill, covered, for at least 1 hour. Yield: 16 servings.

Meleese Cook, Laureate Alpha Mu
Enterprise, Oregon

BUTTER ROLL

2 cups evaporated milk
1/2 cup (1 stick) butter
2 cups sugar
1 teaspoon vanilla
  extract
2 cups flour
2 teaspoons baking
  powder
1 teaspoon salt
2/3 cup shortening
1/2 cup milk
1/2 cup (1 stick) butter

Combine the evaporated milk, 1/2 cup butter, sugar and vanilla in a heavy saucepan. Bring to a boil over medium heat, stirring frequently. Remove from heat. Sift the flour, baking powder and salt into a large bowl. Cut in the shortening until crumbly. Add milk 1 tablespoon at a time, mixing with a fork until mixture forms a ball. Preheat the oven to 350 degrees. Roll the dough into a rectangle. Chop the remaining 1/2 cup butter and arrange over the rectangle. Sprinkle generously with additional sugar. Roll as for jelly roll, enclosing butter and sugar. Place in a greased 9x11-inch baking dish. Pour the evaporated milk mixture over the roll. Sprinkle with additional sugar. Bake for 30 minutes. Yield: 10 to 12 servings.

Irma Paul, Preceptor Zeta Gamma
Rusk, Texas

CARAMEL APPLE CHEESECAKE

1 (21-ounce) can apple pie filling	1/4 teaspoon vanilla extract
1 (10-inch) graham cracker pie shell	2 eggs
16 ounces cream cheese, softened	1/4 cup caramel topping
	12 pecan halves
1/2 cup sugar	2 tablespoons chopped pecans

Preheat the oven to 350 degrees. Set aside 3/4 cup of the apple pie filling. Spoon the remaining pie filling over the pie shell. Cream the cream cheese, sugar and vanilla in a mixer bowl until light and fluffy. Add the eggs 1 at a time, beating well after each addition. Pour over the pie filling. Bake for 35 minutes or until center is set. Cool. Combine the reserved 3/4 cup pie filling and caramel topping in a small saucepan. Cook over medium heat for 1 minute, stirring constantly. Arrange the apple slices from the caramel mixture evenly around the edge of the cooled cheesecake. Spoon the caramel sauce over the cheesecake; spread evenly. Press the pecan halves on the surface to decorate. Sprinkle with chopped pecans. Chill, covered, until serving time. Yield: 8 to 12 servings.

Lela Patteson, Xi Alpha Tau
Ardmore, Oklahoma

ESPRESSO CHOCOLATE CHEESECAKE

1 cup chocolate cookie crumbs	1 teaspoon vanilla extract
1/2 cup unsalted butter, melted	2 tablespoons baking cocoa
1 cup sugar	2 1/2 cups sour cream, room temperature
4 large eggs	
24 ounces cream cheese, softened	1/2 cup brewed espresso, chilled
1 (16-ounce) package semisweet chocolate	1 cup shaved white chocolate

Blend the cookie crumbs and half the melted butter in a small bowl. Press crumb mixture over the bottom of a 10-inch springform pan. Chill, covered, for 1 hour. Preheat the oven to 425 degrees. Beat the sugar and eggs in a large mixer bowl until light and fluffy. Beat in the cream cheese gradually. Melt the chocolate in the top of a double boiler over boiling water. Remove from heat and cool slightly. Beat the chocolate into the cream cheese mixture. Beat the mixture at low speed while adding the remaining melted butter, vanilla, baking cocoa, sour cream and espresso. Pour the chocolate mixture over the chilled crumb crust. Place the springform pan on a baking sheet.

Bake for 1 hour; center will be soft. Cool on a wire rack. Cover with foil. Chill overnight. Loosen from side of pan and remove pan side. Garnish with the shaved white chocolate. Yield: 16 to 24 servings.

Lesley Cryderman, Mu Epsilon
Jefferson City, Missouri

CHOCOLATE PUMPKIN CHEESECAKE

To minimize cracking, place a shallow pan half full of water on the lower rack during baking time.

1 1/2 cups (about 19 cookies) crushed creme-filled chocolate sandwich cookies	3 tablespoons flour
	2 teaspoons cinnamon
	1 teaspoon ginger
	1/2 teaspoon ground cloves
2 tablespoons margarine or butter, softened	1 cup canned pumpkin
	4 eggs
24 ounces cream cheese, softened	1 1/2 cups miniature semisweet chocolate chips
1 cup sugar	

Preheat the oven to 325 degrees. Combine the crushed cookies and margarine in a medium bowl; mix well. Press over the bottom and up the side of an ungreased 9-inch springform pan. Chill, covered, until ready to use. Combine the cream cheese, sugar, flour, cinnamon, ginger and cloves in a large mixer bowl; beat until smooth. Beat in the pumpkin and eggs. Stir in the chocolate chips. Pour into the chilled crumb crust. Bake for 1 hour or until edges are set; center will be soft. Turn off the oven. Let cheesecake stand in oven with door ajar at least 4 inches for 30 minutes or until center is set. Remove from oven. Cool to room temperature on a wire rack. Loosen from side of pan and remove pan side. Chill overnight. Yield: 16 to 20 servings.

Kathy Hilton, Preceptor Mu
Mitchell, South Dakota

Syble Ann Shoults, Xi Alpha Xi, Bessemer, Alabama, prepares Butterfinger Banana Pudding as an emergency dessert for unexpected company. Prepare 2 large packages vanilla instant pudding according to the package directions and fold in 12 ounces whipped topping. Crush 4 Butterfinger candy bars and reserve 1/2 cup for topping. Fold the remaining candy and 6 sliced bananas into the pudding. Alternate layers of pudding and vanilla wafers in a large glass bowl. Top with reserved candy and chill.

CHOCOLATE TRUFFLE CHEESECAKE

1½ cups chocolate wafer crumbs	1 cup sugar
2 tablespoons sugar	⅓ cup baking cocoa
¼ cup (½ stick) butter, melted	3 eggs
	1 teaspoon vanilla extract
¼ cup semisweet chocolate chips	1½ cups semisweet chocolate chips
¼ cup whipping cream, whipped	¼ cup whipping cream
24 ounces cream cheese, softened	1 teaspoon vanilla extract

Preheat the oven to 350 degrees. Mix the crumbs and 2 tablespoons sugar in a small bowl. Stir in the butter. Press over the bottom and 1½ inches up the side of a greased 10-inch springform pan. Bake for 10 minutes. Cool on a wire rack. Reduce heat to 325 degrees. Melt ¼ cup chocolate chips in a saucepan over low heat; stir until smooth. Remove from heat. Blend in ¼ cup cream. Beat the cream cheese and 1 cup sugar in a large mixer bowl until smooth. Add the cocoa and eggs, beating at low speed just until combined. Add the chocolate mixture and 1 teaspoon vanilla, stirring just until smooth. Pour over the cooled crust. Bake for 45 minutes or until center is almost set. Melt 1½ cups chocolate chips in a saucepan over low heat, stirring until smooth. Remove from heat. Stir in ¼ cup cream and 1 teaspoon vanilla. Spread evenly over the cheesecake. Chill overnight. Loosen from side of pan; remove side. Garnish with whipped cream and miniature chocolate kisses just before serving. Yield: 12 servings.

Barbara Hinson, Preceptor Laureate Rho
Harrison, Arkansas

FROZEN PEACH CHEESECAKE

⅓ cup butter, melted	2 tablespoons lemon juice
1¼ cups graham cracker crumbs	1 to 2 teaspoons almond extract
¼ cup sugar	3 cups puréed peach halves
16 ounces cream cheese, softened	8 ounces whipped topping
1 (14-ounce) can sweetened condensed milk	

Mix the butter, graham cracker crumbs and sugar in a small bowl. Press over the bottom of a 10-inch springform pan. Beat the cream cheese in a large mixer bowl until fluffy. Add the condensed milk; beat until smooth. Stir in the lemon juice, almond extract and peach purée. Fold in the whipped topping. Pour into the prepared springform pan. Freeze, covered, until firm. Remove to the refrigerator 15 minutes before serving. Garnish with peach quarters. Yield: 10 to 12 servings.

Sandra Rompf, Laureate
Goderich, Ontario, Canada

PEANUT BUTTER CHEESECAKE

1¼ cups graham cracker crumbs	1⅔ cups peanut butter chips, melted
⅓ cup sugar	4 eggs
¼ cup baking cocoa	2 teaspoons vanilla extract
⅓ cup butter, melted	1 cup miniature semisweet chocolate chips
24 ounces cream cheese, softened	
1 (14-ounce) can sweetened condensed milk	

Preheat the oven to 300 degrees. Mix the crumbs, sugar, cocoa and butter. Press over the bottom of a 9-inch springform pan. Beat the cream cheese in a large mixer bowl until fluffy. Beat in the condensed milk gradually. Beat in the peanut butter chips until smooth. Add the eggs and vanilla; beat well. Stir in chocolate chips. Pour over the crumb mixture. Bake for 55 to 65 minutes or until center is set. Cool. Chill, covered, until ready to serve. Yield: 12 servings.

Marjorie Duckworth, Pi Eta
Seguin, Texas

LIME CHEESECAKE

1 cup sweetened shredded coconut	¾ cup sugar
2 tablespoons flour	¾ cup water
2 tablespoons melted butter	16 ounces cream cheese, softened
1 envelope unflavored gelatin	¼ cup fresh lime juice
¼ cup cold water	Grated zest of 1 lime
3 egg yolks, beaten	1 cup whipping cream, whipped
	3 egg whites

Preheat the oven to 350 degrees. Combine the coconut, flour and butter in a small bowl. Press into an 8- or 9-inch springform pan. Bake for 8 to 12 minutes or just until brown around the edges. Soften the gelatin in ¼ cup of the cold water. Beat the egg yolks in a saucepan. Add the sugar to the egg yolks gradually, beating at medium speed. Stir in ¾ cup water slowly; mixture will foam too much if beaten. Cook over medium heat for 5 to 7 minutes, stirring constantly. Add the gelatin, stirring until dissolved.

Remove from heat. Add to the cream cheese gradually, beating well. Stir in the lime juice and zest. Fold in the whipped cream. Beat the egg whites until stiff but not dry. Fold into the cream cheese mixture. Pour over the baked crust. Chill for 3 hours or until firm. Garnish with lime twists. Yield: 8 to 9 servings.

Peggy Borgerson, Kappa Master
Nanaimo, British Columbia, Canada

PUMPKIN CHEESECAKE

½ cup finely crushed graham cracker crumbs	*16 ounces cream cheese, softened*
¼ cup finely crushed gingersnaps	*1 cup sugar*
	4 eggs
2 tablespoons finely chopped pecans	*1 (15-ounce) can pumpkin*
1 tablespoon flour	*¼ cup milk*
1 tablespoon confectioners' sugar	*½ teaspoon cinnamon*
	¼ teaspoon ginger
2 tablespoons butter or margarine, melted	*¼ teaspoon nutmeg*

Preheat the oven to 350 degrees. Combine the graham cracker crumbs, crushed gingersnaps, pecans, flour, confectioners' sugar and butter in a bowl; mix well. Press evenly over the bottom of a 9-inch springform pan. Beat the cream cheese and sugar at medium speed in a large mixer bowl until fluffy. Add 3 eggs all at once; beat at low speed just until combined. Remove 1 cup of the cream cheese mixture to a medium mixer bowl. Add the remaining egg, pumpkin, milk, cinnamon, ginger and nutmeg to the 1 cup cream cheese mixture; beat at low speed just until combined. Pour pumpkin mixture into the prepared pan. Top with the cream cheese mixture, swirling through the layers gently with a knife to marbleize. Place springform pan in a shallow baking pan. Bake for 40 to 45 minutes or until center appears set when shaken. Cool for 15 minutes on a wire rack. Loosen from side of pan. Cool for 30 minutes longer. Remove side of pan. Cool completely. Chill, covered, for at least 4 hours. Yield: 12 to 16 servings.

Kristin M. George, Eta Eta
Port St. John, Florida

Frances Wood, Xi Delta Rho, LeRoy, New York, makes Pistachio Hash by mixing a package of pistachio instant pudding mix with a 20-ounce can of crushed pineapple, 8 ounces whipped topping and 1 cup each miniature marshmallows and nuts.

CHOCOLATE LINZER TORTE

¾ cup (1½ sticks) butter, softened	*1 teaspoon cloves*
1 cup sifted confectioners' sugar	*1½ cups flour*
	1 cup chopped almonds
3 tablespoons mayonnaise	*1 cup semisweet chocolate chips*
1 teaspoon cinnamon	*1 cup raspberry preserves*

Preheat the oven to 300 degrees. Cream the butter and confectioners' sugar in a large bowl until light and fluffy. Mix in the mayonnaise, cinnamon and cloves. Add the flour gradually, beating constantly. Stir in the almonds and chocolate chips. Form dough into 2 balls. Chill, wrapped in plastic wrap, for 30 minutes. Flatten 1 ball of dough into the bottom of a 9-inch pie pan. Spread with the raspberry preserves. Roll the remaining ball of dough a little larger than pan between 2 sheets of waxed paper. Place over preserves and crimp edges to seal. Bake for 45 minutes. Cool completely. Serve with ice cream.
Yield: 16 servings.

Victoria Urbanik, Xi Alpha Sigma
Stansbury Park, Utah

A DELICATE DESSERT

1 (6-ounce) package orange gelatin	*2 tablespoons flour*
	½ cup sugar
1 (3-ounce) package lemon gelatin	*2 eggs, beaten*
	1 cup pineapple juice
1 (20-ounce) can crushed pineapple, drained	*1 cup whipping cream, whipped*
2 bananas, mashed	*½ cup shredded mild Cheddar cheese*
⅔ cup miniature marshmallows	

Prepare orange gelatin using package directions. Pour into an 8x13-inch glass dish. Chill until firm. Prepare lemon gelatin using package directions; cool but do not chill. Pour the lemon gelatin over the set orange gelatin. Chill, covered, until firm. Combine the pineapple and bananas in a bowl; mix well. Spread the pineapple mixture evenly over the lemon gelatin. Cover with the marshmallows. Combine the flour and sugar in a medium saucepan. Combine the eggs and pineapple juice. Stir into the flour mixture. Bring to a boil over medium-high heat, stirring constantly. Remove from heat. Cool. Fold the whipped cream into the cooled egg mixture. Spread over the lemon gelatin layer. Sprinkle with Cheddar cheese. Yield: 10 servings.

Wilena Walton, Laureate Iota
Maysville, Kentucky

FOOD FOR THE GODS

Use a light hand when folding the walnut mixture, bread crumbs and baking soda into the beaten egg whites. Be sure not to overmix or the egg whites will fall.

4 egg whites	**4 tablespoons bread**
3/4 cup sugar	**crumbs**
4 ounces dates, finely	**1/2 teaspoon baking**
chopped	**powder**
4 ounces walnuts,	
chopped	

Preheat the oven to 350 degrees. Beat the egg whites and sugar until the consistency of a meringue. Combine the dates and walnuts. Fold the walnut mixture into the egg whites. Fold in the bread crumbs and baking powder. Pour into a 13-inch springform pan. Bake for 1 to 1 1/2 hours or until firm and dry. Remove from oven. Cool. Serve with whipped cream or whipped topping. Yield: 8 servings.

Bronwyn Stich, Xi Lambda Epsilon
Fort Pierce, Florida

APRICOT SPUMONI

2 1/2 cups crushed vanilla	**Vanilla ice cream,**
wafers	**softened**
1/2 cup melted butter	**Apricot preserves**
1 tablespoon almond	**1/2 cup slivered almonds,**
extract	**toasted**

Combine the vanilla wafers, butter and almond extract in a bowl; mix well. Cover the bottom of a 5x9-inch loaf pan with half the crumb mixture. Layer ice cream, apricot preserves and almonds over the crumb layer. Finish with another layer of ice cream. Top with the remaining crumb mixture. Cover and freeze. Will keep indefinitely. Yield: 12 servings.

Connie Leetsch, Laureate Delta Eta
Abilene, Texas

CINNAMON ICE CREAM

1 1/2 cups sugar	**1 quart half-and-half**
3 tablespoons flour	**1 tablespoon vanilla**
1/2 teaspoon salt	**extract**
3 eggs	**1 tablespoon cinnamon**
1 quart milk	
1 (14-ounce) can	
sweetened condensed	
milk	

Whisk the sugar, flour and salt together in a large saucepan. Whisk in the eggs. Add the milk. Cook over medium-low heat for 10 minutes or until thick-ened, stirring constantly. Remove from heat. Add the condensed milk, half-and-half, vanilla and cinnamon; blend well. Chill, covered, for several hours. Pour into the ice cream freezer. Add additional milk to reach the fill line. Follow manufacturer's instructions for freezing. Yield: 1 gallon.

Jane Wherritt, Xi Alpha Kappa
Guymon, Oklahoma

CLUB FREEZER DESSERT

1 1/2 cups crushed club	**4 tablespoons lemon**
crackers	**juice**
1/4 cup sugar	**1 cup sugar**
1/2 cup (1 stick)	**6 tablespoons**
margarine, softened	**margarine, melted**
1 quart vanilla ice	**2 eggs, beaten**
cream, softened	
1 quart lemon sherbet,	
softened	

Combine the crushed crackers, 1/4 cup sugar and the softened 1/2 cup margarine in a bowl; mix well. Pat the mixture evenly into a 9x13-inch pan. Combine the ice cream and sherbet in a large bowl; mix well. Spoon evenly over the crumb layer. Freeze until firm. Combine the lemon juice, 1 cup sugar, melted margarine and eggs in a small saucepan. Cook over medium-low heat for 2 minutes or until thickened, stirring constantly. Let stand for 10 to 15 minutes to cool and slightly thicken. Swirl over the frozen dessert. Return to the freezer. Yield: 15 to 18 servings.

Marlys Montz, Preceptor Alpha Epsilon
Marshalltown, Iowa

KAHLUA KRUNCH

6 to 12 ice cream	**Butter brickle pieces**
sandwiches	**Pecan pieces**
3/4 cup Kahlúa	**Maraschino cherries,**
16 ounces whipped	**quartered**
topping	

Line a 9x13-inch baking dish with the ice cream sandwiches, cutting the sandwiches as necessary to fit snuggly in the dish. Drizzle the Kahlúa evenly over the sandwiches. Cover with the whipped topping. Sprinkle with the butter brickle and pecan pieces. Arrange the maraschino cherries decoratively over the top. Freeze, covered, until ready to serve. Cut into squares. Keep leftovers frozen. Yield: 12 servings.

Judy Trevarrow, Preceptor Gamma Mu
Troy, Michigan

PEACH BUTTERMILK ICE CREAM

1 envelope unflavored gelatin	2 teaspoons vanilla extract
2/3 cup sugar	1/4 teaspoon salt
1 1/2 cups buttermilk	1 1/2 cup mashed peeled peaches
1 egg, beaten	
3 cups heavy cream	3 tablespoons sugar

Combine the gelatin, 2/3 cup sugar and buttermilk in a heavy 2-quart saucepan. Cook over low heat until gelatin is dissolved, stirring occasionally. Stir a small amount of the hot mixture into the egg. Stir the egg into the hot mixture. Cook for 1 minute, stirring constantly. Remove from heat. Stir in the cream, vanilla and salt. Combine the peaches and 3 tablespoons sugar. Stir peaches into the cooked mixture. Chill. Pour into ice cream freezer and freeze using manufacturer's instructions. Let ripen for 3 hours. Yield: 2 quarts.

Judith Dougherty, Delta Kappa
Jacksonville, Arkansas

LEMON BISQUE

2 1/2 cups vanilla wafer or graham cracker crumbs	1/4 cup sugar
	Juice and grated zest of 1 lemon
1 (3-ounce) package lemon gelatin	1 (12-ounce) can evaporated milk, chilled
1 1/2 cups boiling water	

Press crumbs into the bottom of a deep 9x12-inch dish. Prepare gelatin using package instructions, adding sugar, lemon juice and zest. Cool gelatin until partially set. Beat until frothy. Add chilled evaporated milk; mix well. Pour over the crumb layer. Chill, covered, until set. Yield: 8 to 10 servings.

Mary Jo Kennel, Preceptor Alpha Psi
Midlothian, Virginia

COOL AND CREAMY MINT TORTE

15 chocolate creme-filled sandwich cookies, crushed	16 ounces cream cheese, softened
3 tablespoons butter or margarine, softened	1/2 cup confectioners' sugar
2/3 cups mint chocolate chips, or 2/3 cup chopped creme de menthe thins	1/4 cup milk
	8 ounces whipped topping

Combine the crushed cookies and the butter in a small bowl; mix well. Press into the bottom of an 8-inch springform pan. Chill until firm. Microwave the chocolate chips on High in a microwave-safe bowl for 1 to 1 1/2 minutes or until melted, stirring every 30 seconds. Cool slightly. Cream the cream cheese in a large mixer bowl. Add confectioners' sugar and mix well. Add the milk and chocolate gradually, mixing until smooth. Reserve 1/2 cup of the whipped topping. Fold the remaining whipped topping into the cream cheese mixture. Spread evenly over the crumb layer. Chill, covered, for 1 to 2 hours. Remove side of pan. Garnish with reserved whipped topping. Yield: 12 servings.

Beverley Neff, Laureate Tau
South Charleston, West Virginia

PEACH COBBLER

3 cups sliced ripe peaches	1/8 teaspoon salt
	1/2 cup milk
1/2 cup sugar	1 cup boiling water or peach juice
1 cup flour	
2 teaspoons baking powder	3/4 cup sugar
	1/2 cup (1 stick) butter

Preheat the oven to 375 degrees. Spread the peaches in a 9x11-inch baking pan. Combine 1/2 cup sugar, flour, baking powder, salt and milk in a bowl; mix well. Pour the mixture over the peaches. Pour the boiling water over the top. Sprinkle with 3/4 cup sugar and dot with butter. Bake for 50 minutes to 1 hour or until golden. Yield: 12 servings.

Barbara Lindsey, Psi Omicron Lambda
Blythe, California

PINEAPPLE TORTE

1 cup (2 sticks) butter or margarine, softened	1 cup sugar
	2 tablespoons (heaping) cornstarch
2 tablespoons sugar	4 egg whites, stiffly beaten
1 1/4 cups flour	
3 1/2 cups crushed pineapple	

Preheat the oven to 350 degrees. Cream the butter and 2 tablespoons sugar in a bowl until light and fluffy. Add the flour; mix well. Spread evenly in an ungreased 10x10-inch baking pan. Bake for 25 minutes or until light brown. Combine the pineapple, 1 cup sugar and cornstarch in a saucepan. Cook over low heat, until thickened, stirring frequently. Cook for 3 minutes longer. Cool. Fold the stiffly beaten egg whites into the cooled pineapple mixture. Pour over the baked crust. Bake for 15 to 20 minutes or until firm but not brown. Serve chilled. Yield: 10 servings.

Marjorie Davison, Laureate Delta Sigma
Ocala, Florida

POPPY SEED DESSERT

1/2 cup flour
1/2 cup graham cracker
  or vanilla wafer
  crumbs
1/2 cup (1 stick) butter or
  margarine, melted
1/2 cup chopped pecans
  or almonds
1 cup sugar
3 tablespoons
  cornstarch
1 envelope unflavored
  gelatin

3/4 cup poppy seeds,
  ground
2 cups milk
4 egg yolks, beaten
4 egg whites, beaten
1/4 teaspoon cream of
  tartar
1/4 cup sugar
Vanilla extract to taste
1 1/4 cups whipping
  cream, whipped

Preheat the oven to 375 degrees. Mix the flour, crumbs, butter and pecans in a medium bowl. Press into an 8x8-inch baking pan. Bake for 5 to 10 minutes or until edges begin to brown. Combine 1 cup sugar, cornstarch, gelatin and poppy seeds. Bring to a boil over medium-high heat, stirring constantly. Cook for 1 minute or until thick and bubbly. Stir a small amount of hot mixture into egg yolks; stir eggs into hot mixture. Cook for 1 minute longer, stirring constantly. Cool, covered, until partially set. Beat the egg whites and cream of tartar to soft peaks. Add the 1/4 cup sugar, beating until stiff peaks form. Add the vanilla to the poppy seed mixture. Fold in the egg whites gently. Spread over the cooled crust. Cover with whipped cream. Garnish with chopped nuts. Yield: 10 to 12 servings.

Linda Ortynsky, Xi Zeta
Yorkton, Saskatchewan, Canada

PINA COLADA WEDGES

8 ounces cream cheese,
  softened
1/3 cup sugar
2 tablespoons rum, or
  1/2 teaspoon rum
  extract

8 ounces whipped
  topping
1 (8-ounce) can crushed
  pineapple
2 2/3 cups flaked coconut

Beat the cream cheese with sugar and rum until smooth. Fold in 2 cups of the whipped topping, undrained pineapple and 2 cups of the coconut. Spread evenly in an 8-inch round cake pan lined with plastic wrap. Invert the pan onto a serving plate. Remove the pan and plastic wrap. Spread with the remaining whipped topping. Sprinkle with the remaining coconut. Freeze for about 2 hours or until firm. Cut into wedges to serve. Garnish with pineapple and cherries. Yield: 6 to 8 servings.

Kathy Bowers, Theta Rho
Cuero, Texas

AUSTRALIAN CHRISTMAS CREAM

3 eggs, separated
2 teaspoons sugar
2 teaspoons unflavored
  gelatin
1/2 cup cold water
Juice of 1 lemon
1/2 cup 2% milk
1 (16-ounce) can passion
  fruit, drained,
  mashed

4 medium mint leaves
1 (4-ounce) jar red
  glacéed cherries
1 (4-ounce) jar green
  glacéed cherries
1/2 cup chopped nuts
1 cup whipping cream,
  whipped

Beat the egg yolks with the sugar in a large mixer bowl. Soften the gelatin in water in a saucepan. Heat until dissolved. Cool. Add to the egg yolk mixture with the lemon juice, milk and passion fruit. Chill until almost set. Whisk well. Beat the egg whites in a bowl until stiff peaks form. Fold into the egg yolk mixture. Pour into a decorative 2-quart bowl. Chill. Garnish with mint leaves, glacéed cherries and nuts. Serve with whipped cream. Yield: 4 servings.

Maxine Houser, Preceptor Eta Omicron
West Sacramento, California

VANILLA BANANA PUDDING

This is a perfect cool summer dessert that is especially popular at potlucks. The ingredients are easy to keep on hand, and in a pinch, you can leave out the bananas. It is delicious.

2 (4-ounce) packages
  vanilla instant
  pudding mix
1 (14-ounce) can
  sweetened condensed
  milk

12 ounces whipped
  topping
2 cups milk
1 or 2 bananas, sliced
Vanilla wafers

Combine the pudding mix, condensed milk, whipped topping and milk in a large bowl; mix well. Line a 9x13-inch dish with the vanilla wafers. Layer the bananas and pudding mixture in the dish. Sprinkle about 1/2 cup of crushed wafers on top. Chill, covered, for at least 1 hour. Yield: 12 to 15 servings.

Joy A. Hoyder, Rho Beta
Goodland, Kansas

Mary Gail Lewis, Xi Zeta Mu, Borger, Texas, makes a Healthy Banana Split that is not just a dessert but a balanced meal. She places a banana split lengthwise on a plate, spreads it with 2 tablespoons of peanut butter and adds a cup of cottage cheese, 1/2 cup of crushed pineapple and a maraschino cherry.

MOMMIE BESSIE'S BANANA PUDDING

4 egg yolks, well beaten
2 cups milk
1/3 cup flour
3/4 cup sugar
1/2 teaspoon vanilla
extract

1 (12-ounce) box vanilla
wafers
6 bananas, sliced
4 egg whites
1 tablespoon
confectioners' sugar

Combine the egg yolks and milk in a medium saucepan. Stir in the flour and sugar with a wire whisk. Whisk in the vanilla. Cook over medium heat for about 5 minutes or until pudding thickens, stirring constantly. Remove from heat. Layer the vanilla wafers, bananas and pudding half at a time in a 2-quart baking dish or 9x11-inch baking pan. Beat the egg whites and confectioners' sugar in a mixer bowl at high speed until stiff peaks form. Spread over the pudding, sealing to the edge. Broil until meringue is lightly browned. Yield: 8 servings.

Connie Stallard, Theta Theta
Clintwood, Virginia

BANANA BREAD PUDDING

4 cups cubed stale
French bread
1/4 cup (1/2 stick)
margarine, melted
3 eggs, beaten
2 cups milk
1/2 cup sugar

2 teaspoons vanilla
extract
1/2 teaspoon cinnamon
1/2 teaspoon nutmeg
1/2 teaspoon salt
1 cup sliced bananas
Vanilla Sauce

Preheat the oven to 375 degrees. Place the bread cubes in a 2-quart baking dish. Pour the margarine over the bread and toss to coat. Beat the eggs with the milk, sugar, vanilla, cinnamon, nutmeg and salt. Stir in the bananas. Pour over the bread cubes. Stir until well coated. Bake, uncovered, for 40 minutes or until a knife inserted near the center comes out clean. Serve with warm Vanilla Sauce. Yield: 6 servings.

VANILLA SAUCE

3 tablespoons melted
butter
2 tablespoons sugar
1 tablespoon cornstarch

3/4 cup milk
1/4 cup light corn syrup
1 teaspoon vanilla
extract

Blend butter, sugar and cornstarch in a saucepan. Blend in milk and corn syrup. Cook until thickened, stirring constantly. Blend in vanilla.

Joyce Homan, Laureate Delta Eta
Abilene, Texas

BREAD AND BUTTER PUDDING

1 cup plus 2 tablespoons
milk
1 cup plus 2 tablespoons
heavy cream
6 tablespoons butter
Salt to taste
3 fresh vanilla beans

5 eggs
1/2 cup sugar
1 loaf white bread
2 tablespoons raisins,
plumped
2 tablespoons cinnamon
sugar

Preheat the oven to 350 degrees. Combine the milk, cream, butter, salt and vanilla beans in a saucepan. Bring just to a boil over medium heat. Beat the eggs and sugar in a large bowl. Stir in the hot milk mixture. Strain. Slice the bread into thin slices and trim off the crusts. Discard the crusts or reserve for another purpose. Layer half the bread slices, raisins, and remaining bread slices in a buttered 9x11-inch baking dish. Pour the milk mixture over the bread. Place the dish in a roasting pan filled 1/3 with water. Bake for 40 to 50 minutes or until golden brown. Sprinkle with cinnamon sugar. Serve with a vanilla sauce. Yield: 16 servings.

Kathryn Charley, Chi Zeta
Dunellon, Florida

DOUBLE CHOCOLATE BREAD PUDDING

Sourdough bread
1/2 cup (1 stick) butter,
melted
1 cup semisweet
chocolate chips
1/2 cup chopped apricots
or dates
4 eggs, beaten
1/2 cup sugar
2 cups evaporated milk

1 teaspoon vanilla
extract
1 teaspoon brandy
extract
1 teaspoon cinnamon
1/2 cup slivered almonds
1/4 cup butter
1/4 cup sugar
1 cup white chocolate
chips

Preheat the oven to 375 degrees. Cube enough of the bread to fill a 9x13-inch baking pan. Place the bread in a large bowl; toss with 1/2 cup butter. Add chocolate chips and apricots and toss until well mixed. Turn into the buttered baking pan. Combine eggs, 1/2 cup sugar, evaporated milk, vanilla, brandy extract and cinnamon in a bowl and mix well. Pour over the bread mixture. Let stand for 15 minutes. Bake for 40 minutes. Brown the almonds in 1/4 cup butter with 1/4 cup sugar in a skillet. Cool. Sprinkle the almond mixture and white chocolate chips over the pudding just after removing from oven. Yield: 8 to 12 servings.

Jimmie Lee Foster, Preceptor Delta Nu
Amarillo, Texas

NEW ORLEANS BREAD PUDDING WITH WHISKEY SAUCE

1 (10-ounce) loaf stale
  French bread, cut into
  1-inch cubes
2 cups milk
2 cups heavy cream
½ cup (1 stick) butter,
  melted
3 eggs, beaten
2 tablespoons vanilla
  extract
1½ cups raisins
1½ cups chopped pecans
1 teaspoon cinnamon
½ teaspoon nutmeg
Whiskey Sauce

Preheat the oven to 350 degrees. Combine the bread, milk, cream, butter, eggs, vanilla, raisins, pecans, cinnamon and nutmeg in a large bowl; mix well. The mixture should be moist, but not soupy. Pour into a greased 9x13-inch baking pan. Bake on the center rack of the oven for 1 hour and 15 minutes or until top is golden brown. Serve warm with Whiskey Sauce. Shredded coconut and a variety of fruits may be used in place of or in addition to raisins and pecans. Yield: 20 servings.

WHISKEY SAUCE

½ cup (1 stick) butter
1½ cups confectioners'
  sugar
2 egg yolks
½ cup bourbon, or
  to taste

Combine the butter and confectioners' sugar in a heavy saucepan over medium heat. Heat until all butter is melted and absorbed, stirring constantly. Remove from heat. Beat in the egg yolks. Stir in the bourbon gradually. The sauce will thicken as it cools. Serve warm over bread pudding. May substitute any fruit juice or liqueur for the bourbon.

Lauren Iannaci, Xi Beta Theta
Lakeville, Minnesota

NEW MEXICO BREAD PUDDING

A simple sugar lemon sauce is great with this pudding.

½ loaf French bread
1 cup milk
½ cup (1 stick butter),
  melted
½ cup raisins
¼ cup chopped pine nuts
1 (12-ounce) can
  evaporated milk
1 (8-ounce) can juice-
  pack crushed
  pineapple
¼ cup sugar
¼ cup packed brown
  sugar
3 eggs, beaten
1 tablespoon lemon
  juice
1½ teaspoons vanilla
  extract

Preheat the oven to 350 degrees. Tear the bread into small pieces. Soak the bread in the milk. Drain the bread and squeeze with fingers; discard the drained milk. Combine the bread, butter, raisins, pine nuts, evaporated milk, undrained pineapple, sugar, brown sugar, eggs, lemon juice and vanilla in a large bowl; mix well. Pour into a buttered 8x12-inch baking pan. Bake for 1 hour. Yield: 10 servings.

Hugh Ann Payne, Preceptor Alpha Omicron
Farmington, New Mexico

WHITE CHOCOLATE BREAD PUDDING

This bread pudding can be served with a sauce made by melting 12 ounces white chocolate chips in the top of a double boiler and stirring in ⅓ cup heavy cream.

1 quart heavy cream
14 ounces white
  chocolate chips
1½ cups milk
½ cup sugar
3 eggs
15 egg yolks
2 loaves French bread,
  cut into 2-inch pieces

Preheat the oven to 300 degrees. Heat the cream in a large saucepan over medium-low heat until warm; do not boil. Remove from heat. Add the chocolate chips to the hot cream, stirring until melted and smooth. Beat the milk, sugar, eggs and egg yolks in a double boiler over barely simmering water. Heat until warm. Blend the egg mixture into the cream mixture. Layer the bread and half the egg mixture in a greased 11x13-inch baking pan. Let stand for 30 minutes. Pour on the remaining egg mixture. Bake, covered with foil, for 1 hour. Bake, uncovered, for 15 minutes longer or until golden brown.
Yield: 15 to 20 servings.

Gwen Newburn, Preceptor Beta Gamma
Jacksonville, Texas

BROWN SUGAR PUDDING

2 tablespoons butter
1½ cups packed brown
  sugar
1¾ cups boiling water
½ cup sugar
1 cup flour
1 teaspoon vanilla
  extract
½ cup cold water
2 teaspoons baking
  powder

Preheat the oven to 350 degrees. Combine the butter, 1 cup of the brown sugar and water in a saucepan over medium-high heat. Bring to a boil. Boil for 5 minutes, stirring frequently. Combine the remaining ½ cup brown sugar, sugar, flour, vanilla, cold water and baking powder in a bowl; mix well. Pour the boiling brown sugar syrup into the center of a greased 9x13-inch baking pan. While syrup is still

bubbling, pour the flour mixture all around the edges. Bake for 20 to 25 minutes.
Yield: 9 to 12 servings.

Sara B. Hunsucker, Laureate Delta Mu
Wichita Falls, Texas

FLAN

This was a favorite dessert for my family when I was growing up in Lima, Peru.

4 eggs, room temperature	1 (14-ounce) can sweetened condensed milk
1 teaspoon vanilla extract	10 teaspoons sugar
1 (12-ounce) can evaporated milk	5 drops of water

Preheat the oven to 350 degrees. Combine the eggs, vanilla, evaporated milk and condensed milk in a blender container; process until smooth. Combine the sugar and water in a heavy saucepan. Cook over medium heat until it begins to turn a light golden color, stirring constantly. Remove from heat. Pour the caramelized sugar into a 9-inch pie plate. Pour the milk mixture over the caramelized sugar. Place the pie plate in a cake pan filled with 1 cup water. Bake for 45 minutes to 1 hour or until set. Chill, covered, until serving time. Serve by sliding and flipping portions onto a plate so the caramelized sugar faces up.
Yield: 8 servings.

Gloria Burton, Laureate Psi
Altus, Oklahoma

PEACHY RICE DESSERT

2 cups cooked rice	1 (15-ounce) can sliced peaches, drained
1 1/2 cups milk	1/3 cup packed brown sugar
1/4 cup sugar	
Pinch of salt	1/2 teaspoon cinnamon
2 eggs, lightly beaten	1/4 cup sour cream (optional)
1/2 teaspoon vanilla extract	

Combine the rice, milk, sugar and salt in a heavy saucepan. Bring to a boil over medium heat. Reduce heat. Simmer, uncovered, for 10 minutes, stirring occasionally. Stir a small amount of the rice mixture into the eggs. Add the egg mixture to the rice mixture in the pan. Cook for 2 to 3 minutes or to 160 degrees on a candy thermometer, stirring constantly. Remove from heat. Stir in the vanilla. Pour into a greased shallow 1-quart baking dish. Cover with peaches. Mix the brown sugar and cinnamon. Sprinkle 1 tablespoon of the cinnamon mixture over the peaches. Broil 6 inches from heat for 3 to 5 minutes or until browned. Let stand for 5 to 10 minutes. Spoon into serving bowls. Sprinkle with the remaining cinnamon mixture. Top with sour cream. Yield: 4 servings.

Tamara Pichon, Chi Beta
Mt. Carmel, Illinois

PUMPKIN ORANGE LAYERED DESSERT

1 1/2 cups flour	1/2 teaspoon nutmeg
1 1/2 cups chopped pecans	1 1/4 cups canned pumpkin
3/4 cup (1 1/2 sticks) butter or margarine, softened	1 teaspoon grated orange zest
1 envelope unflavored gelatin	1/4 cup orange juice
1/2 cup milk	8 ounces cream cheese, softened
3 eggs, separated, at room temperature	1 cup sifted confectioners' sugar
1 cup sugar	2 cups sugar
1/2 teaspoon ginger	3 cups whipped topping
1/2 teaspoon cinnamon	

Preheat the oven to 350 degrees. Mix the flour, pecans and butter in a bowl. Press into a shallow 9x13-inch baking dish. Bake for 30 to 35 minutes or until edges begin to brown. Cool completely. Beat the egg yolks and milk together. Soften the gelatin in milk. Combine the egg yolk mixture, 1/2 cup sugar, ginger, cinnamon and nutmeg in a large saucepan over medium heat. Bring to a boil, stirring constantly. Remove from heat. Stir in the pumpkin, orange zest and orange juice. Chill, covered, for 30 minutes or until partially set. Beat the egg whites with 1/2 cup sugar until stiff peaks form. Fold the egg white mixture into the partially set pumpkin mixture. Cream the cream cheese and confectioners' sugar in a bowl until light and fluffy. Fold in 1 cup of the whipped topping. Spread over the cooled crust. Spread the pumpkin mixture over the cream cheese layer. Spread the remaining 2 cups whipped topping over the pumpkin layer. Chill, covered, for 2 hours or longer. Garnish with shredded orange zest.
Yield: 15 servings.

Betty Rutledge, Laureate Rho
Stillwater, Oklahoma

Peggy Lynne Rickey, Psi Upsilon, Trimble, Missouri, soaks a loaf of stale bread in 1 quart milk and mixes in 3 eggs, 2 cups sugar, 1/2 cup raisins, 2 tablespoons vanilla, 1 teaspoon each cinnamon and nutmeg and a can of apple, peach or cherry pie filling. She bakes her Fruity Bread Pudding in 2 well-buttered loaf pans at 375 degrees for 45 to 60 minutes or until very firm and serves warm.

ITALIAN RASPBERRY TORTE

1¼ cups flour
½ teaspoon baking soda
½ teaspoon baking
  powder
¼ teaspoon salt
⅔ cup sugar
¾ cup sour cream
½ cup (1 stick) butter,
  melted

2 eggs
½ teaspoon vanilla
  extract
½ teaspoon almond
  extract
8 ounces cream cheese,
  softened
¼ cup sugar
2 cups fresh raspberries

Preheat the oven to 350 degrees. Combine the flour, baking soda, baking powder and salt. Beat ⅔ cup sugar, ½ cup of the sour cream and butter in a large mixer bowl until light and fluffy. Add the eggs, vanilla and ¼ teaspoon of the almond extract; mix well. Beat in the flour mixture. Pour into a greased 9-inch springform pan. Bake for 15 minutes. Beat the cream cheese and ¼ cup sugar in a mixer bowl until smooth. Beat in the remaining ¼ cup sour cream and the remaining ¼ teaspoon almond extract. Spoon the cream cheese mixture over the partially baked cake layer, spreading carefully to the edges. Bake for 20 to 25 minutes or until top is set and edges are brown. Remove to a wire rack. Mound the raspberries over the torte. Cool for 10 minutes. Loosen from the side of the pan. Cool for 30 minutes. Remove the side of the pan. Chill, covered, until serving time. Garnish with sprigs of mint. Yield: 12 to 16 servings.

Jan Meredith, Preceptor Alpha Zeta
Woodbridge, Virginia

CHOCOLATE RASPBERRY TRIFLE

1 (2-layer) package
  chocolate fudge cake
  mix
1 (4-ounce) package
  vanilla instant
  pudding mix

¼ to ½ cup raspberry
  liqueur
½ cup raspberry jam
16 ounces whipped
  topping

Prepare and bake the cake using package directions. Cool. Prepare the pudding mix using package directions. Crumble half the cake into a large glass bowl. Pour half the raspberry liqueur over the crumbled cake. Thin the jam with a little water or raspberry liqueur; drizzle or spread over the crumbled cake. Add layers of half the pudding and half the whipped topping. Repeat the layers with the remaining ingredients. Drizzle a little jam in a circle over the top. Chill, covered, for 24 hours before serving.
Yield: 15 to 20 servings.

Jackie N. Latta, Theta Chi
Chesapeake, Virginia

RASPBERRY ANGEL DESSERT

1 envelope unflavored
  gelatin
½ cup cold milk
3 eggs, separated
1½ cups milk
¾ cup sugar
1 teaspoon vanilla
  extract

1 cup whipping cream,
  stiffly whipped
1 angel food cake
2 (10-ounce) packages
  frozen raspberries,
  thawed
1 tablespoon cornstarch

Soften the gelatin in the ½ cup milk; set aside. Beat the egg yolks in the top of a double boiler. Add 1½ cups milk and sugar. Cook over boiling water until mixture coats the spoon, stirring constantly. Remove from heat. Add the vanilla and gelatin mixture and stir until gelatin dissolves completely. Cool completely. Beat the egg whites in a mixer bowl until soft peaks form. Fold the whipped cream and beaten egg whites into the cooled egg yolk mixture. Crumble the angel food cake into a 9x13-inch baking dish. Pour the egg mixture evenly over the cake. Refrigerate, covered. Combine the raspberries and cornstarch in a small saucepan. Cook over medium heat for 1 minute or until thickened, stirring constantly. Cool. Pour evenly over the top. Chill, covered, for 2 or 3 hours before serving. Yield: 15 to 20 servings.

Marla Von Moos, Preceptor Xi Phi
Patterson, California

SWEET POTATO COBBLER

I won second place at the Sweet Potato Festival with this recipe.

¼ cup (½ stick) butter,
  softened
2 cups mashed cooked
  sweet potatoes
½ cup milk
2 eggs
1 cup sugar
Pinch of salt
½ cup shredded coconut

1 teaspoon vanilla
  extract
1 (8-ounce) can crushed
  pineapple, drained
½ cup sugar
½ cup (1 stick) butter,
  melted, cooled
¼ cup self-rising flour
1 egg

Preheat the oven to 350 degrees. Combine the softened butter, sweet potatoes, milk, eggs, 1 cup sugar, salt, coconut and vanilla in a large bowl; mix well. Pour evenly into a 2-quart baking dish. Combine the pineapple, ½ cup sugar, melted butter, flour and egg in a bowl; mix well. Spread evenly over the sweet potato mixture. Bake, uncovered, for 30 to 45 minutes or until golden. Yield: 8 servings.

Bobbie Moody, Eta
Florence, South Carolina

Men's Specialties

With today's busy lifestyles, it's not
surprising that the men in your sorority
sisters' lives actually know how to cook.
What's surprising is that these men
know how to cook so well. From simple
snacks to party pleaser (?), our *Men's
Specialties* chapter is devoted exclusively
to recipes submitted by husbands,
fathers, sons, and the other men "behind"
Beta Sigma Phi sisters. Perhaps "beside"
is more politically correct, since there's
no apparent gender gap in your kitchens.
Warmest congratulations to
these many chefs!

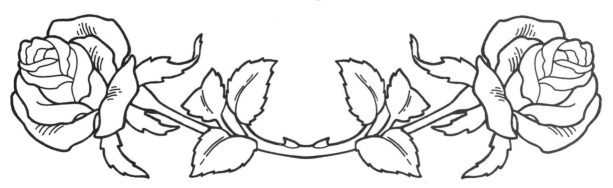

BLACK-EYED PEA DIP

2 (15-ounce) cans black-
  eyed peas, drained
1 (10-ounce) can
  tomatoes with green
  chiles
1 green bell pepper,
  chopped
1 onion, chopped
1 tomato, chopped

1 (3-ounce) can black
  olives, chopped
  (optional)
Chopped jalapeño
  peppers to taste
  (optional)
1/4 cup zesty Italian
  salad dressing
  (or more)

Combine the black-eyed peas and tomatoes with green chiles in a bowl. Add the green pepper, onion, tomato, olives and jalapeño peppers. Stir in Italian dressing. Serve with corn chips. Yield: 4 cups.

Jon (Karlese) Butler, Eta Sigma
Watonga, Oklahoma

RANDY'S SUPER SIMPLE PARTY DIP

16 ounces cream cheese,
  softened
2 (6-ounce) cans crab
  meat, oysters or
  popcorn shrimp

1 (16-ounce) jar hot or
  mild salsa

Combine the cream cheese and crab meat in a bowl; mix well. Spread evenly in a 10x10-inch serving dish. Cover with a layer of salsa. Chill, covered, for 10 to 15 minutes or until cream cheese is slightly firm. Serve with nacho chips. Yield: 10 to 12 servings.

Randy Sherrill, son-in-law of Juanita Koehler, Xi Alpha Tau
Dandridge, Tennessee

MUSHROOM DELIGHTS

12 large white
  mushrooms, rinsed,
  drained
1/2 cup red wine
3 ribs celery, finely
  chopped
1/2 medium onion, finely
  chopped

1 medium red bell
  pepper, finely
  chopped
1 pound fresh lump crab
  meat
1/4 cup Italian bread
  crumbs

Discard the mushroom stems or save for another use. Cook the mushroom caps with the wine in a nonstick skillet over medium heat for 5 to 10 minutes or until caps fill with liquid. Remove mushroom caps from skillet and arrange rounded side down in a 9x13-inch baking dish sprayed with nonstick cooking spray. Preheat the oven to 350 degrees. Add the celery, onion, red pepper and crab meat to the mushroom liquid in the skillet and sauté over low heat for 5

minutes. Combine the crab mixture and the bread crumbs in a bowl; mix well. Overfill each mushroom cap with crab mixture. Bake for 15 minutes. Yield: 6 servings.

Edwin (Ann) Jones, Alpha Zeta Theta
Houston, Texas

SAUSAGE STARS

The wonton shells can be made days ahead and stored in a sealable plastic bag. The filling can be made a day ahead. Or stuff the shells and freeze.

1 (12-ounce) package
  wonton wraps
1/4 cup vegetable oil
1 pound hot sausage
1 cup ranch dressing
1 cup shredded
  Monterey Jack cheese

1 cup shredded Cheddar
  cheese
1 (4-ounce) can sliced
  black olives

Preheat the oven to 350 degrees. Brush wonton wraps with oil. Press each wrap into a mini muffin cup, folding out edges to form a star. Bake for 8 to 10 minutes or until golden. Brown the sausage in a skillet, stirring until crumbly; drain. Combine the sausage, ranch dressing, Monterey Jack cheese, Cheddar cheese and olives in a medium bowl; mix well. Fill the wonton shells with sausage mixture. Bake for 10 minutes. Yield: 24 to 32 servings.

Greg (Mary) Goforth, Sigma Eta
Wildwood, Missouri

GIL'S MEXICAN OYSTERS

12 flat oyster shells
  collected at the beach
4 or 5 garlic cloves,
  minced
1/2 onion, chopped
4 tablespoons butter
1/2 cup wine

1/2 cup salsa
12 oysters or scallops,
  each cut into 3 pieces
Shredded mozzarella
  cheese
Grated Parmesan cheese

Scrub the oyster shells until clean and smooth inside. Preheat the oven to 485 degrees. Mix the garlic and onion in a bowl. Rub each shell with 1 tablespoon of the garlic mixture and arrange shells on a baking sheet. Place 1 tablespoon of the butter, 1 tablespoon of the wine and 3 oyster pieces in each shell. Drizzle salsa over shell fillings. Sprinkle with mozzarella cheese and Parmesan cheese. Bake for 5 to 10 minutes or until Parmesan cheese begins to darken. Yield: 6 servings.

Gil (Harriet) Hudgin, Laureate Nu
Comox, British Columbia, Canada

WILD BILL'S CHILI BEAN SOUP

1 pound ground beef
1/4 cup vegetable oil
2 cups chopped onions
1 cup dried parsley
2 tablespoons minced
  garlic
6 (10-ounce) cans beef
  broth
1 (6-ounce) can tomato
  paste

4 (15-ounce) cans kidney
  beans, rinsed, drained
1 (16-ounce) jar
  spaghetti sauce
1 teaspoon chili powder
1/4 cup hot sauce or to
  taste
Dash of cinnamon
Salt to taste

Brown the ground beef with the oil and onions in a skillet, stirring until beef is crumbly; drain. Combine the beef mixture, parsley, garlic, beef broth, tomato paste, beans, spaghetti sauce, chili powder, hot sauce, cinnamon and salt in a 4-quart kettle. Simmer for 45 minutes to 1 hour. Yield: 15 to 20 servings.

William (Heidi) Przybylowicz
Stevensville, Montana

CRAB BISQUE SOUP

1/3 cup chicken broth
4 ounces mushrooms,
  chopped
1 large onion, chopped
2 garlic cloves, chopped
3 large ribs celery and
  leaves, chopped
  separately
3 large carrots, chopped
8 ounces crab meat
1/2 cup skim milk

2 (10-ounce) cans 98%
  fat-free mushroom
  soup
4 teaspoons Old Bay
  seasoning
2 teaspoons each lemon
  pepper, garlic powder,
  white pepper and
  celery salt
Dash of celery seeds

Combine the chicken broth, mushrooms, onion, garlic, celery ribs and carrots in a 3-quart saucepan over medium heat. Bring to a simmer. Cook for 8 to 9 minutes, stirring occasionally, until tender-crisp. Stir in the remaining ingredients. Bring to a simmer. Cook for 5 minutes, stirring occasionally. Adjust seasonings. Yield: 6 servings.

Tom (Karen) Walsh, Nu Mu
Centralia, Illinois

Wes Mears, son of Karen Moss, Alpha Kappa Nu, Fort Worth, Texas, makes a Taste Delight breakfast-lunch combo by dipping a peanut butter and jelly sandwich into an egg beaten with 2 tablespoons water and 1/2 teaspoon cinnamon and browning on both sides in 1 tablespoon butter. Serve with confectioners' sugar, syrup and crisp bacon. Bananas are good, too.

HALIBUT CHOWDER

Serve with a large loaf of round bread that you can pull apart and dip in the chowder.

1 pound bacon
2 large onions, chopped
2 cups diced celery
1 1/2 cups diced carrots
3 cups diced peeled
  potatoes
4 cups water
1 teaspoon thyme

3 teaspoons salt
1/2 teaspoon pepper
1 cup evaporated milk
1 to 2 pounds halibut,
  cut into 1-inch cubes
1 cup instant potato mix
2 cups heavy cream

Cook the bacon over medium-high heat until crisp; drain and crumble. Remove bacon from skillet. Sauté the onions, celery, carrots and potatoes in the bacon drippings over medium-low heat for 5 to 10 minutes or until tender-crisp; drain. Combine the onion mixture, water, thyme, salt and pepper in a large kettle over medium heat. Simmer for 10 to 15 minutes or until tender. Stir in the evaporated milk. Bring to a boil. Stir in the halibut. Reduce heat and simmer for 20 minutes. Add the instant potatoes and cook for 5 minutes or until thickened, stirring occasionally. Stir in the cream and heat through. Do not boil. Stir in the bacon. Yield: 8 to 10 servings.

Phil Lightner, friend of Stephanie Hadden, Xi Theta
Anchorage, Alaska

SLOW-COOKER MINESTRONE

1 medium onion,
  chopped
2 garlic cloves, chopped
1 small green bell
  pepper, sliced
1 medium zucchini, cut
  into 1/2-inch slices
2 (14-ounce) cans low-
  sodium beef broth
2 (15-ounce) cans kidney
  beans, drained
2 medium carrots, thinly
  sliced

2 ribs celery, cut into 1/2-
  inch pieces
2 (14-ounce) cans
  Italian-style stewed
  tomatoes
1/4 teaspoon coarsely
  ground pepper
Oregano, basil, thyme
  and leaf-form
  rosemary to taste
1 1/2 cups cooked rice

Combine the onion, garlic, green pepper, zucchini, beef broth, beans, carrots, celery, tomatoes, pepper, oregano, basil, thyme and rosemary in a slow cooker. Cook on Low for 8 to 10 hours. Stir in the rice at serving time. Adjust seasonings. Yield: 6 to 8 servings.

Vergil (Joan) Eness, Preceptor Alpha Upsilon
Mason City, Iowa

SPICY POTATO SOUP

The ground beef can be browned in a covered 2-quart glass baking dish in the microwave if desired.

1 pound ground beef
4 cups 1/2-inch cubed
  peeled potatoes
1 small onion, chopped
3 (8-ounce) cans tomato
  sauce

4 cups water
2 teaspoons salt
1 1/2 teaspoons pepper
1/2 to 1 teaspoon hot
  pepper sauce

Brown the ground beef in a large kettle, stirring until crumbly; drain. Stir in the potatoes, onion, tomato sauce, water, salt, pepper and hot pepper sauce. Bring to a boil. Reduce heat and simmer for 1 hour or until potatoes are tender and soup has thickened. Yield: 6 to 8 servings.

Rusty (Sherry) Craig, Beta Eta
Webster City, Iowa

BROWN DERBY BURGERS WITH DIABLO SAUCE

Our children always ask their dad to prepare this dinner when they come home to visit.

2 pounds ground beef
1 egg
2 cups chicken broth
1/2 teaspoon mustard
1 teaspoon salt

1 teaspoon pepper
2 tablespoons
  Worcestershire sauce
Diablo Sauce

Combine the ground beef, egg, chicken broth, mustard, salt, pepper and Worcestershire sauce in a large bowl; mix well. Form 8 thick patties, using about 1 cup of beef mixture for each patty. Brown patties in vegetable oil in a heavy skillet over medium heat; drain. Preheat the oven to 350 degrees. Arrange patties in an 11x13-inch baking dish. Cover with Diablo Sauce. Bake for 30 minutes or until hot and bubbly. Serve with onion rings sprinkled over the top. Yield: 8 servings.

DIABLO SAUCE

1 (10-ounce) can beef
  gravy
2 tablespoons
  Worcestershire sauce

2 tablespoons butter or
  margarine
2 teaspoons A-1 sauce
5 1/2 cups catsup

Combine the beef gravy, Worcestershire sauce, butter, A-1 Sauce and catsup in a saucepan over medium heat. Bring to a boil. Cook for 2 minutes, stirring occasionally. Recipe may be doubled if you want plenty of gravy.

Jack (Frances Chase) Parks, Laureate Beta Sigma
St. Charles, Missouri

THE COOKS' VEGGIE SALAD DELIGHT

1/2 pound broccoli florets
1/2 pound cauliflowerets
1/2 cup chopped red
  onion
1/2 cup sliced fresh
  mushrooms

1/2 cup crumbled bacon
  bits
1/2 cup roasted sunflower
  seeds
1/2 cup raisins
Orange Salad Dressing

Cut broccoli and cauliflowerets into bite-size pieces. Combine the broccoli and cauliflowerets with the red onion, mushrooms, bacon bits, sunflower seeds and raisins in a large salad bowl. Toss. Drizzle the Orange Salad Dressing over the salad; toss thoroughly. Chill, tightly covered, for 3 to 10 hours before serving. Yield: 10 to 15 servings.

ORANGE SALAD DRESSING

3/4 cup mayonnaise
3 tablespoons orange
  juice

3 tablespoons vinegar
1/3 cup sugar

Combine the mayonnaise, orange juice, vinegar and sugar in a bowl; blend well.

John A. (Susan) Cook, Xi Delta Chi
Sturgis, Michigan

TAILGATE SALAD

2 cups small macaroni
1/2 cup Catalina salad
  dressing
1/2 cup mayonnaise-type
  salad dressing
1 cup water
1 (20-ounce) package
  frozen mixed
  vegetables
2 cups chopped cooked
  ham

1 cup chopped celery
1 cup sliced or diced
  cucumber
2 tablespoons chopped
  onion
1 teaspoon salt or to
  taste
1/2 teaspoon pepper
1 cup shredded Cheddar
  or Swiss cheese

Cook macaroni until tender using package directions. Rinse, drain and cool. Combine macaroni with the Catalina salad dressing and mayonnaise-type salad dressing in a large bowl. Let stand while preparing rest of salad. Bring the water to a boil in a medium saucepan. Add the frozen mixed vegetables. Return to a boil. Cook for 1 minute; drain. Cool. Stir into the macaroni mixture. Stir in the ham, celery, cucumber, onion, salt and pepper. Place in a large serving bowl and sprinkle with shredded Cheddar cheese. Yield: 6 to 8 servings.

Tom (Elaine) Badger, Preceptor Beta Psi
Manhattan, Kansas

SAUERKRAUT SALAD

This savory salad keeps well for several weeks in the refrigerator.

1 (16-ounce) jar
   sauerkraut, drained
2 cups shredded carrots
2 cups chopped celery
1 green bell pepper,
   chopped

1 red onion, chopped
1/2 cup red wine vinegar
1/2 cup vegetable oil
1 1/2 cups sugar

Combine the sauerkraut, carrots, celery, green pepper, red onion, vinegar, vegetable oil and sugar in a large bowl; mix well. Chill, covered, for 8 to 10 hours. Yield: 12 to 15 servings.

John (Sara) Westfahl, Laureate Zeta Alpha
Eureka, California

PAUL'S TORTELLINI SALAD

1 (9-ounce) package
   cheese tortellini
2 cups shredded red
   cabbage
6 cups torn fresh
   spinach
2 cups cherry tomatoes,
   halved

1/2 cup sliced green
   onions
1 (8-ounce) bottle ranch
   salad dressing
8 bacon slices, crisp-
   fried, crumbled

Cook tortellini using package directions; rinse and drain. Layer the cabbage, spinach, tortellini, cherry tomatoes and green onions in a large glass serving bowl. Pour the dressing evenly over all. Sprinkle with the crumbled bacon. Chill, covered, for at least 1 hour. Yield: 6 to 8 servings.

Paul (Sue) Beams, Alpha Upsilon
Dalzell, South Carolina

CHINESE CHICKEN SALAD

1 head lettuce, chopped
2 bunches green onions,
   chopped
2 bunches celery,
   chopped
2 teaspoons chopped
   almonds
2 teaspoons toasted
   sesame seeds

2 ounces wonton wraps,
   cut into strips, deep-
   fried
2 to 3 bundles rice sticks
3 to 4 chicken breasts,
   cooked, chopped
Chinese Dressing

Layer the lettuce, green onions, celery, almonds, sesame seeds, fried wontons, rice sticks and chicken in a large salad bowl. Add the Chinese Dressing. Toss and serve. Yield: 4 servings.

CHINESE DRESSING

1/4 cup sugar
2 teaspoons salt
1 teaspoon MSG
1 teaspoon pepper
1/2 cup vegetable oil

2 tablespoons sesame
   oil
6 tablespoons rice
   vinegar

Combine the sugar, salt, MSG, pepper, vegetable oil, sesame oil and rice vinegar in a bowl. Blend well.

Edward (Nancy) Walker, Xi Theta Phi
Geneseo, Illinois

DAD'S POT ROAST

The sauce becomes a thick, rich, sweet-and-sour barbecue-type sauce as the roast cooks. Don't tell anyone the secret ingredient in the sauce until they rave about it . . . and they will!

2 1/2- to 3-pound pot
   roast
1 (12-ounce) can of Coke
   or Pepsi

2 3/4 to 3 cups catsup
1 onion, chopped
1 or 2 garlic cloves,
   minced

Preheat the oven to 350 degrees. Place the roast in a large Dutch oven or roasting pan. Combine the Coke, catsup, onion and garlic in a bowl; mix well. Pour the Coke mixture over the roast. Bake, covered, for 2 1/2 to 3 hours or until done to taste. Slice and serve with the sauce. Yield: 6 servings.

Jim (Dena) Stewart, Xi Beta Mu
Terrace, British Columbia, Canada

JIM'S MEAT LOAF

8 ounces extra-lean
   ground beef
3 garlic cloves, chopped
8 ounces bacon, crisp-
   fried, crumbled
1 large white onion,
   chopped
2 pounds lean ground
   beef

3 ribs celery, chopped
1 (10-ounce) can tomato
   juice
1 1/2 cups cracker crumbs
2 eggs
Salt and pepper to taste
Catsup

Preheat the oven to 350 degrees. Brown the 8 ounces extra-lean ground beef with the garlic, bacon and half the onion in a skillet, stirring until the ground beef is crumbly. Combine with the 2 pounds ground beef, the remaining onion, celery, tomato juice, cracker crumbs, eggs, salt and pepper in a large bowl; mix well. Shape into a loaf in a 10x10-inch baking dish. Cover with catsup. Bake for 1 1/2 hours or until cooked through. Yield: 8 servings.

Jim (Ruth) Zinn, Laureate Zeta Beta
Canyon, Texas

CURTIS' MY-WIFE-IS-WORKING-LATE MIX-ALL

On some days I work until 6:00, and I often come home to a home-cooked meal. Thank you, sweetie!

1 pound ground beef
1 small onion, chopped
1 small green bell
  pepper, chopped
1 teaspoon garlic salt
1 teaspoon pepper
1 (15-ounce) can whole
  kernel corn, drained

1 (15-ounce) can kidney
  beans, drained
1 (15-ounce) can diced
  tomatoes, drained
Salt to taste
1 package boil-in-bag
  rice

Brown the ground beef with the onion and green pepper in a 4-quart kettle, stirring until beef is crumbly; drain. Stir in the garlic salt, pepper, corn, beans and tomatoes. Add salt to taste. Prepare rice in the microwave oven, following package directions. Serve the beef mixture over rice.
Yield: 4 to 6 servings.

Curtis (Jennifer) Short, Beta Zeta Lambda
Victoria, Texas

ENCHILADA CASSEROLE

2 pounds ground beef
1 medium onion,
  chopped
Salt and pepper to taste
1 (8-ounce) can tomato
  sauce
1 (8-ounce) jar picante
  sauce
1 envelope enchilada
  sauce mix
1 (10-ounce) can cream
  of chicken soup

1 (10-ounce) can cream
  of mushroom soup
1 (4-ounce) can chopped
  green chiles
2 cups shredded Colby
  cheese
8 slices American cheese
1 package corn tortillas,
  quartered

Brown the ground beef with the onion, salt and pepper in a skillet, stirring until beef is crumbly; drain. Preheat the oven to 350 degrees. Combine the tomato sauce, picante sauce, enchilada mix, cream of chicken soup, cream of mushroom soup and green chiles in a bowl; mix well. Line the bottom of a 9x13-inch baking dish with half the tortillas. Layer the beef mixture, soup mixture and Colby cheese 1/2 at a time over the tortillas. Repeat the layers, starting with tortillas and ending with Colby cheese. Bake for 30 minutes. Arrange American cheese slices over the top. Bake for 15 minutes longer or until cheese is melted. Yield: 6 to 8 servings.

Bill (Pamela) Palmer, Xi Delta
Ponca City, Oklahoma

PAUL'S TORTILLA PIE

I received this recipe from a U.S. Army cook at Fort Ord, California. It was originally made in quantities that served 200 people. Serve with a salad and hot rolls.

1 1/2 pounds ground beef
1 teaspoon minced
  garlic
1 large onion, finely
  chopped
1 (14-ounce) can
  Mexican-style stewed
  tomatoes
1 (15-ounce) can chili
  hot beans

1 (16-ounce) package
  frozen corn
1 Old El Paso Burrito
  Dinner
3 cups (12 ounces)
  shredded Cheddar
  cheese
1 (6-ounce) can large
  black olives, cut in
  halves

Preheat the oven to 350 degrees. Brown the ground beef in a skillet, stirring until crumbly; drain. Add the garlic and onion, cooking over medium-low heat for 5 to 10 minutes or until onions are soft and translucent. Remove from heat. Crush the stewed tomatoes with a potato masher in a bowl. Add the tomatoes, beans, corn and seasoning packet from Burrito Dinner to the beef mixture; stir well. Return to heat. Bring to a boil. Reduce heat and simmer, uncovered, for 15 minutes. Spread 1/3 of the beef mixture in two 2-quart baking dishes and cover each layer with a tortilla from the Burrito Dinner. Repeat layers until all beef mixture and tortillas are used. Sprinkle with Cheddar cheese and olives. Bake for 30 minutes.
Yield: 12 servings.

Paul (Katherine) Rines, Delta Iota
Palm Bay, Florida

RICHARD'S HAMBURGERS

2 pounds ground beef
2 slices fresh bread,
  finely chopped
2 eggs
1/4 cup Heinz 57 steak
  sauce
2 tablespoons catsup
1 1/2 teaspoons dry
  mustard
1 teaspoon dried mint

2 teaspoons salt
1/2 teaspoon pepper or
  hot sauce
1 teaspoon dillweed
1 1/2 teaspoons paprika
1/8 teaspoon garlic
  powder, or 1 clove
  fresh garlic, finely
  chopped

Prepare the grill or preheat the broiler. Combine the ground beef, bread, eggs, Heinz 57, catsup, mustard, mint, salt, pepper, dillweed, paprika and garlic powder in a large bowl; mix well. Shape into patties. Grill or broil until done to taste. Yield: 12 servings.

Richard (Mary) Niefer, Xi Delta
St. John's, Newfoundland, Canada

PAUL'S STUFFED GREEN PEPPERS

I challenged my brother on the number of onions he uses in this recipe. He wagered me twenty dollars that his stuffed peppers would be superior to my 3-onion recipe. He won!

10 medium onions, chopped	1 tablespoon salt
Butter	1/4 teaspoon pepper
1 pound ground beef	1/4 teaspoon paprika
1 pound ground pork	4 (10-ounce) cans
2 large eggs, beaten	tomato soup
2/3 cup uncooked long grain rice	8 to 10 green bell peppers, seeded

Sauté the onions in butter in a skillet over medium heat for 5 to 10 minutes. Combine the onions, beef, pork, eggs, rice, salt, pepper, paprika and about 3 tablespoons of the tomato soup in a large bowl; mix well. Spread the remaining contents of 1 can of the tomato soup over the bottom of a Dutch oven. Arrange the green pepper shells over the tomato soup layer and fill shells with the beef mixture. Pour the remaining 3 cans tomato soup over the green peppers, first stirring in a little water if necessary to make enough to cover peppers completely. Bring to a boil. Reduce heat and simmer, covered, for 1 to 1 1/2 hours, or until rice is cooked. Cook, uncovered, for a few minutes if a thicker sauce is desired.
Yield: 6 to 8 servings.

Paul Czetto, brother of Mary C. Henchon, Laureate Beta
Trenton, New Jersey

COWBOY POTATOES

10 to 12 large potatoes, peeled, sliced	Salt and pepper to taste
1 large yellow onion, sliced	1 dozen flour tortillas (optional)
2 or 3 garlic cloves, thinly sliced	2 cups shredded Cheddar cheese (optional)
Vegetable oil	1 (16-ounce) jar salsa (optional)
1 (12-ounce) can corned beef	

Cook the potatoes with the onion and garlic in a small amount of oil in a cast-iron skillet over medium-low heat for about 20 minutes or until tender, stirring occasionally. Stir in the corned beef, salt and pepper. Heat through. Place in a warmed flour tortilla with shredded cheese and salsa and roll like a burrito. Yield: 4 to 6 servings.

Russell (Terry) Wolfe, Xi Lambda
Gilroy, California

GEORGE'S CHILI RECIPE

2 tablespoons vegetable oil	1 (12-ounce) can beer
1 medium onion, chopped	1 cup barbecue sauce
1 medium green bell pepper, chopped	2 tablespoons chili powder
2 garlic cloves, minced	1 1/2 teaspoons cumin
1 pound lean stew beef	1 teaspoon oregano
1 pound lean ground beef	1/2 teaspoon cayenne pepper
1/2 pound bulk hot Italian sausage	1 cup water
1 cup chopped celery	3 beef bouillon cubes
1 (15-ounce) can tomato paste	1 (15-ounce) can pinto beans, drained
1 (16-ounce) can whole tomatoes	1 (15-ounce) can kidney beans, drained

Heat the oil in a heavy skillet and sauté the onion, green pepper and garlic for 3 to 4 minutes. Add the stew beef, ground beef and sausage. Brown, stirring until crumbly. Stir in the celery, tomato paste, tomatoes, beer, barbecue sauce, chili powder, cumin, oregano, cayenne pepper, water and bouillon cubes. Bring to a boil. Reduce heat and simmer, uncovered, for 1 to 1 1/2 hours. Stir in the pinto beans and kidney beans. Simmer, covered, for 30 to 45 minutes longer. Yield: 12 or more servings.

George M. Cusick III, son of Dorothy L. Cusick
Preceptor Phi
Galveston, Texas

KICKED-UP CHILI

2 pounds ground beef	2 tablespoons garlic powder
1 large onion, chopped	3 tablespoons sugar
6 garlic cloves, chopped	3 (10-ounce) cans tomato soup
15 button mushrooms, chopped	6 tablespoons catsup
2/3 cup chili powder	2 (15-ounce) cans kidney beans
2 teaspoons salt	
2 teaspoons freshly ground pepper	

Brown the ground beef in a skillet, stirring until crumbly; drain. Add the onion, garlic, mushrooms, chili powder, salt, pepper, garlic powder and sugar. Cook, stirring frequently, until onions and mushrooms are soft. Stir in the tomato soup, catsup and beans. Simmer until heated through.
Yield: 15 to 20 servings.

Mike (Fran) Drozdowski, Nu
Surrey, British Columbia, Canada

CROWN ROAST OF PORK WITH CRANBERRY APPLE DRESSING

Place extra cranberry dressing in a baking dish and bake, covered, alongside the roast.

1 (14- to 16-ounce) package stuffing mix
2 envelopes onion soup mix
1¹/₂ cups chopped pecans or walnuts
2 tablespoons minced onion
1¹/₂ cups fresh cranberries, coarsely chopped
1 cup hot water
2 medium apples, chopped
3 ribs celery, chopped
1 teaspoon salt
1 teaspoon pepper
3¹/₂ cups apple cider
15- to 18-rib crown roast of pork

Preheat the oven to 325 degrees. Combine the stuffing mix, 1 of the envelopes of onion soup mix, pecans, onion, cranberries, water, apples, celery, salt, pepper and apple cider in a bowl; mix well. Line a roasting pan with aluminum foil. Rub the pork roast with the remaining envelope of onion soup mix, sprinkling any leftover mix into the roasting pan. Place roast in pan and fill center with cranberry mixture. Bake for 1 hour before roast is removed from the oven. Cover roast with foil and bake for 20 to 22 minutes per pound. Yield: 6 to 8 servings.

James (Peg) McVitty, Beta Mu
Forest, Ohio

PORK TENDERLOIN WITH MUSTARD AND THYME

¹/₂ cup whole grain mustard
4 large garlic cloves, crushed
2 tablespoons dried thyme
¹/₄ teaspoon pepper
2 tablespoons balsamic vinegar
¹/₄ cup dry red wine
2 tablespoons olive oil
2 pounds pork tenderloin

Combine the mustard, garlic, thyme, pepper, vinegar, wine and olive oil in a large bowl. Add the pork, turning to coat well. Marinate, covered, in the refrigerator for 1 to 10 hours, turning occasionally. Prepare the grill or preheat the broiler. Remove pork from marinade. Grill or broil for 13 to 14 minutes or until meat thermometer registers 160 degrees, turning 3 times and brushing with marinade. Watch carefully to make sure pork does not become dry.
Yield: 8 servings.

Joseph (Eleanor) Toth, Phi Master
Grosse Ile, Michigan

SHERRIED PORK CHOPS AND PEARS

If you want more sauce, use ³/₄ cup sherry and ³/₄ teaspoon each of the cornstarch and water.

8 center-cut (³/₄-inch-thick) pork chops, trimmed
Salt to taste
4 firm ripe Anjou pears, halved lengthwise, cored
2 tablespoons fresh lemon juice
¹/₄ cup packed brown sugar
¹/₂ teaspoon cinnamon
¹/₄ cup dry sherry
1 tablespoon butter or margarine
¹/₂ teaspoon cornstarch
¹/₂ teaspoon water

Preheat the oven to 350 degrees. Heat a small piece of pork fat in a large heavy skillet, stirring until skillet is lightly coated. Remove fat. Arrange the pork chops in the skillet without crowding. Brown well on all sides over medium heat. Sprinkle lightly with salt. Arrange the chops along one side of a large, shallow baking dish. Arrange pear halves cut side up beside the pork chops. Sprinkle the lemon juice over the pork and fruit. Combine the brown sugar and cinnamon in a small bowl; sprinkle over the pork and fruit. Pour the sherry over all. Place a small dot of butter in the center of each pear hollow. Bake, covered, for 20 minutes. Remove cover and bake for 20 minutes longer. Spoon out pan juices and place in a small saucepan. Stir a mixture of cornstarch and water into the pan juices. Bring to a boil, stirring constantly. Pour the sauce over the pork and fruit. Yield: 8 servings.

A nephew of Glee Tappan, Preceptor Beta Alpha
Vancouver, Washington

BARBECUE HAM LOAF

2¹/₂ pounds ground ham
2¹/₂ pounds ground pork
1 pound ground beef
3 eggs
2 cups crushed graham crackers
2 cups milk
2 tablespoons vinegar
1 tablespoon dry mustard
1 cup packed brown sugar
¹/₄ cup catsup
1 teaspoon orange juice

Preheat the oven to 325 degrees. Combine the ham, pork, ground beef, eggs, graham crackers and milk in a large bowl; mix well. Shape into a loaf and place in a large baking pan. Bake for 1¹/₂ hours. Combine the vinegar, mustard, brown sugar, catsup and orange juice in a small bowl; mix well. Pour over the ham loaf for the last 30 minutes of baking time.
Yield: 15 servings.

Scott D. Worth, son of Marilyn E. Worth
Preceptor Alpha Tau
Dalton, Nebraska

SATISFYING SPICY VENISON TIPS

Serve this award-winning recipe with a baked potato or rice and add a favorite vegetable.

¹/₂ cup finely chopped onion	1¹/₂ teaspoons chili powder
¹/₂ cup white wine	¹/₂ teaspoon salt
3 tablespoons vegetable oil	¹/₂ teaspoon black pepper
3 tablespoons soy sauce	1 teaspoon lemon juice
2 tablespoons brown sugar	¹/₄ teaspoon crushed red pepper flakes
3 teaspoons ground coriander	2 pounds venison or sirloin tips, cubed

Combine the onion, wine, vegetable oil, soy sauce, brown sugar, coriander, chili powder, salt, black pepper, lemon juice and red pepper flakes in a 1-quart saucepan over medium-high heat. Bring to a boil. Boil for 4 minutes, stirring occasionally. Remove from heat. Cool to room temperature. Add the venison tips to the wine mixture, stirring to coat well. Marinate, covered, for 1 hour at room temperature. Preheat a 10- to 12-inch skillet over high heat and sear the venison, stirring constantly, for 10 to 15 minutes or until done to taste. Yield: 8 servings.

Raymond (Carolyn) Saldi, Laureate Epsilon Chi
Voorhees, New Jersey

PORTOBELLO MUSHROOM AND SAUSAGE PIZZA

8 (4-inch) portobello mushrooms, stemmed, dark gills removed	Dried crushed red pepper
	1 cup marinara sauce
Olive oil	1 cup (4 ounces) shredded mozzarella cheese
3 sweet Italian sausages	

Preheat the oven to 350 degrees. Brush mushrooms with olive oil. Arrange mushrooms rounded side down on a baking sheet. Bake for 8 minutes or until almost tender. Brown the sausages in a skillet over medium-high heat until cooked through, breaking sausages into small pieces with spoon. Remove from skillet with a slotted spoon. Divide sausages into 8 portions. Spread each portion over a mushroom. Sprinkle red pepper, 2 tablespoons marinara sauce and 2 tablespoons mozzarella cheese over each mushroom. Bake for 10 minutes or until cheese begins to brown. Yield: 8 servings.

Bob (Marlene) Morwick, Laureate Beta
Boulder City, Nevada

TOM'S OIL-FREE BARBECUED CHICKEN

Serve with corn-on-the-cob grilled in the husks, a tossed salad, fresh sliced tomatoes and bruschetta.

4 boneless skinless chicken breast halves	2 teaspoons brown sugar
¹/₄ cup catsup	1 large garlic clove, minced
3 tablespoons cider vinegar	¹/₈ teaspoon thyme
1 tablespoon horseradish	¹/₄ teaspoon pepper

Rinse chicken and pat dry. Preheat broiler or gas grill. Combine the catsup, vinegar, horseradish, brown sugar, garlic and thyme in a small saucepan over medium-high heat; mix well. Bring to a boil. Cook for 5 minutes or until thickened, stirring constantly. Remove from heat. Stir in pepper. Brush over chicken breasts. Arrange chicken sauce side down under broiler or on grill, 3 inches from heat. Cook, turning and basting with remaining sauce, for 5 to 7 minutes or until no longer pink in center. Yield: 4 servings.

Tom (Charlotte) Hurley, Laureate Alpha Lambda
Parkersburg, West Virginia

BUTTERFLY LAKE CHICKEN

The specialty of the house for guests to our home on Butterfly Lake.

¹/₄ cup minced scallions or green onions	2 teaspoons sesame oil, or 2 teaspoons sunflower oil plus 1 teaspoon sesame seeds
2 tablespoons soy sauce	
1 tablespoon honey	
1 tablespoon minced garlic	
1 tablespoon minced fresh gingerroot, or ¹/₂ teaspoon ground ginger	2 medium carrots, sliced julienne-style
¹/₄ teaspoon freshly ground pepper	4 boneless skinless chicken breast halves

Combine the scallions, soy sauce, honey, garlic, gingerroot and pepper in a small bowl; mix well. Heat the sesame oil in a medium skillet over medium heat and sauté the carrots for 2 to 3 minutes. Stir in the scallion mixture. Add the chicken, turning once to coat both sides. Cook, covered, over low heat for about 50 minutes or until tender and cooked through. Serve with sauce over cooked rice. Yield: 4 servings.

Alan (Marianne) Williamson, Preceptor Gamma Phi
Sioux Lookout, Ontario, Canada

CREAMY CHICKEN CORDON BLEU

4 boneless skinless
    chicken breasts
Deli-thin honey ham,
    cut into 1/2-inch strips
Sliced aged Swiss
    cheese, cut into
    1/2-inch strips

1/4 cup (about) flour
    mixed with paprika
    to taste
1 tablespoon butter
1 1/2 cups dry white wine
3 cups heavy cream

Rinse chicken and pat dry. Pound to a uniform thickness. Place 5 strips ham and 5 strips Swiss cheese over each chicken breast; roll up chicken and secure with a wooden pick. Dredge chicken rolls in flour mixture. Melt butter in a heavy skillet and brown the chicken on all sides. Add the wine. Simmer, covered, for 30 minutes. Remove chicken to a serving dish and keep warm. Add the cream to the skillet; simmer gently until mixture is reduced by half. Pour the cream mixture over the chicken and serve.
Yield: 4 servings.

Jim (Angie) Mutz, Iota Chi
O'Fallon, Missouri

FENTON FAJITAS

This recipe is Derek's version of a favorite dish from the Mexican restaurant where he worked during high school.

1 1/2 pounds boneless
    skinless chicken
    breasts, sliced, or
    1 1/2 pounds London
    broil steak, thinly
    sliced
1 onion, thinly
    sliced

1 (10- to 12-ounce)
    package shredded
    Cheddar cheese
10 (12-inch) flour
    tortillas
Butter or margarine,
    softened
1/2 head lettuce, sliced

Rinse chicken and pat dry. Preheat the oven to 350 degrees. Heat a small amount of vegetable oil in a large wok or skillet and stir-fry the chicken for a few minutes or until no longer pink. Remove chicken to a bowl. Stir-fry the onion, using more oil if necessary, for a few minutes or until tender-crisp. Place 1 or 2 spoonfuls of chicken, onion and Cheddar cheese over each tortilla. Fold over edges. Spread butter over both sides of folded tortilla. Fry each tortilla folded side first in wok or skillet. Arrange the fried tortillas in a 9x13-inch baking dish or on a large baking sheet. Bake for about 5 minutes. Top with lettuce. Serve with salsa, sour cream, and/or guacamole.
Yield: 4 servings.

Derek Fenton, son of Lorraine Fenton, Xi Omicron
Uxbridge, Massachusetts

❖ PAPA ROYD'S JUMPIN' JAMBALAYA

2 pounds chicken parts
1/2 teaspoon cayenne
    pepper
2 tablespoons vegetable
    oil
8 ounces spicy smoked
    sausage, cut into
    1/4-inch slices
1 medium onion, chopped
1 medium green bell
    pepper, seeded,
    chopped
1 rib celery, sliced
2 garlic cloves, minced

1 teaspoon dried thyme
1 cup long grain rice
1 (16-ounce) can juice-
    pack whole tomatoes
1/2 cup fish stock or
    bottled clam juice
1 cup water
1 bay leaf
4 green onions
3/4 teaspoon hot pepper
    sauce
8 ounces peeled jumbo
    shrimp

Rinse chicken and pat dry. Sprinkle all sides of the chicken with cayenne pepper. Heat the vegetable oil in a large heavy saucepan over medium-high heat, add the chicken and cook for 4 minutes on each side. Add the sausage and cook for 3 minutes or until brown, stirring occasionally. Remove the chicken and sausage to a plate with a slotted spoon. Add the onion, green pepper, celery and garlic to the skillet and cook for 4 minutes or until vegetables begin to soften, stirring frequently. Add the thyme and rice. Cook for 1 minute or until rice is coated with oil, stirring constantly. Stir in the tomatoes, breaking them up with a fork. Stir in the fish stock, 1/2 cup of the water, bay leaf, green onions and hot sauce. Return chicken and sausage to the skillet. Bring to a simmer over medium-high heat. Turn heat to low and cook, covered, for 15 minutes. Scatter the shrimp over the top, pressing slightly into the rice. Cook, covered, for 15 minutes longer or until chicken and shrimp are cooked through. If rice absorbs all of liquid, add up to 1/2 cup more water. Discard bay leaf.
Yield: 4 servings.

Nic, son-in-law of Rosemary Mumford, Xi Theta Psi
Anaheim Hills, California

MICHAEL'S CILANTRO CHICKEN

1 whole chicken, cut up,
    skinned or 6 to 8
    skinless thighs
1 tablespoon olive oil
1 large onion, sliced
1 teaspoon minced
    garlic
1/4 to 1/2 cup red wine
1 (14-ounce) can
    tomatoes with green
    chiles

1 (10-ounce) can low-fat
    chicken broth
1 teaspoon cumin
1 teaspoon dried
    cilantro, or
    2 teaspoons fresh
    cilantro or parsley
Salt and pepper to taste

Rinse chicken and pat dry. Heat the olive oil in a large skillet and brown the chicken. Remove from skillet. Sauté the onion in the skillet until translucent. Add the garlic and sauté for 1 minute. Add the wine, scraping bottom of skillet to deglaze. Add the chicken, tomatoes with green chiles, chicken broth, cumin and cilantro. Simmer over medium heat for 20 to 30 minutes. Serve over steamed rice.
Yield: 4 to 6 servings.

Michael (Kathleen) Copeland, Iota Chi
St. Charles, Missouri

ROSEMARY CHICKEN

4 chicken breast halves	*2 garlic cloves, minced*
1/2 red bell pepper, cut into 1-inch pieces	*2 1/2 tablespoons vegetable oil*
1/2 yellow bell pepper, cut into 1-inch pieces	*1 1/2 teaspoons crushed rosemary*
1/4 green bell pepper, cut into 1-inch pieces	*Salt and pepper to taste*
3/4 pound small red potatoes, halved	*1 tablespoon fresh lemon juice*
3 shallots, blanched, peeled, halved	*1/2 cup chicken broth*

Rinse chicken and pat dry. Preheat the oven to 450 degrees. Combine the red pepper, yellow pepper, green pepper, potatoes, shallots, garlic, 2 tablespoons of the oil, rosemary, salt and pepper in a bowl. Layer bell pepper mixture in a 9x13-inch baking dish. Combine the remaining 1/2 tablespoon oil with lemon juice. Rub over the chicken. Arrange chicken skin side up over the vegetables. Drizzle the chicken broth over chicken. Bake, uncovered, for 20 minutes or until chicken sizzles. Reduce oven heat to 375 degrees. Bake for 10 to 20 minutes longer or until chicken and vegetables test done. Yield: 4 servings.

John (Margaret) Whitworth, Laureate Omicron
Terre Haute, Indiana

CHICKEN IN SHERRY

6 boneless skinless chicken breasts	*2 small onions, diced*
1/2 cup flour	*1 1/2 cups cooking sherry*
1 teaspoon salt	*1/3 cup water*
1/2 teaspoon paprika	*6 servings hot cooked rice*
1/4 teaspoon pepper	*1 cup mayonnaise*
1/2 cup vegetable oil	*Parsley flakes to taste*

Rinse chicken and pat dry. Combine the flour, salt, paprika and pepper in a sealable plastic bag. Add the chicken, seal the bag and shake to coat. Heat the vegetable oil in a large skillet and brown the chicken on both sides, cooking for 10 to 15 minutes. Do not drain. Add the onions, sherry and water. Simmer, covered, for 1 hour. Arrange hot rice on a large platter. Arrange chicken over the rice, leaving sherry mixture in the skillet. Keep chicken warm in a warm oven. Whisk the mayonnaise and parsley flakes into the sherry mixture. Heat through. Pour over the chicken and serve. Yield: 6 servings.

Bob (Kathy) Galinak, Xi Epsilon Beta
Abilene, Texas

BEER BATTER FISH

1/2 cup vegetable oil, or enough to fill saucepan 1 1/2 inches	*1 cup plus 3 to 4 tablespoons baking mix*
1 pound fish fillets or cooked large shrimp	*1/2 teaspoon salt*
	1 egg
	1/2 cup beer

Heat the vegetable oil to 350 degrees in a deep-fat fryer or heavy saucepan. Coat the fish lightly with 3 to 4 tablespoons baking mix. Combine the remaining baking mix, salt, egg and beer in a small bowl; beat until smooth. Dip fish into the batter, letting excess batter drip back into bowl. Deep-fry for 2 minutes on each side or until golden brown. Drain.
Yield: 4 servings.

Andy (Glendola) King, Xi Gamma Omicron
Pryor, Oklahoma

CLAM FETTUCCINI

6 tablespoons (3/4 stick) butter	*1 (3-ounce) can sliced mushrooms*
1/2 medium onion, chopped	*2 cups half-and-half*
3 tablespoons flour	*Salt and pepper to taste*
2 (7-ounce) cans chopped clams	*Pinch of thyme*
	Cooked noodles

Melt the butter in a small skillet over medium heat and sauté the onion and flour for 3 to 5 minutes or until brown. Drain the clams, reserving juice. Combine the clam juice, mushrooms, half-and-half, salt, pepper and thyme in a 2-quart saucepan over medium heat. Bring to a gentle boil; do not scorch. Stir in the clams and onion mixture. Simmer for 5 minutes or until thickened, stirring frequently. Serve over noodles. Yield: 4 servings.

Gregg (Kathi) Bruni, Preceptor Gamma
Boise, Idaho

OLD-FASHIONED SCALLOPED OYSTERS

If you want to double or triple this recipe, use a larger shallow baking dish. Never use more than 2 layers of oysters, or casserole will not cook through.

1 pint shucked oysters	1/2 cup (1 stick) butter,
1/2 cup dried bread	melted
crumbs	Salt and pepper to taste
1 cup cracker crumbs	1 tablespoon milk

Preheat the oven to 450 degrees. Drain the oysters, reserving 1 tablespoon liquor. Combine the bread crumbs, cracker crumbs and butter in a small bowl. Spray a shallow 8x8-inch baking dish with nonstick cooking spray. Spread 1/3 of the crumb mixture over the bottom of the baking dish. Layer half the oysters over the crumb layer. Sprinkle with salt and pepper. Blend the milk and reserved oyster liquid. Drizzle half the milk mixture over the oysters in baking dish. Add layers of half the remaining crumb mixture and remaining oysters. Sprinkle with salt and pepper. Drizzle the remaining milk mixture over the oysters. Cover with the remaining crumb mixture. Bake for 30 minutes. Yield: 4 to 5 servings.

Harry K. (Michelle) Oxrider III, Preceptor Zeta Mu
Cincinnati, Ohio

OYSTER STEW VERA CRUZ

1/2 pint (or more)	2 tablespoons flour
shucked oysters or	2 tablespoons chili
clams	powder
3 tablespoons margarine	1/2 teaspoon dry mustard
or butter	1/2 teaspoon oregano
1 medium onion,	1/2 teaspoon thyme
chopped	2 cups milk
2 tablespoons chopped	1/4 cup dry sherry
green bell pepper	Pinch of salt

Drain oysters, reserving liquor. Melt the margarine in a 3-quart saucepan over medium heat and sauté the onion and green pepper for about 5 minutes or until soft. Stir in the flour, chili powder, mustard, oregano and thyme. Cook for 5 minutes longer or until bubbly. Whisk in the milk and 1 cup of the reserved oyster liquor. Heat until bubbly, stirring constantly. Add the oysters. Cook for 5 to 10 minutes or until the oysters curl at the edges. Yield: 4 servings.

Harry (June Marie) Binar, Preceptor Psi
LaMarque, Texas

BARBECUED SALMON

2 pounds salmon fillets	1/4 cup cream cheese
1 tablespoon fresh	with onions and
lemon juice	chives
2 tablespoons butter,	1/4 cup mayonnaise
softened	

Prepare the grill for cooking. Rinse the salmon and pat dry. Rub the lemon over the salmon. Combine the butter, cream cheese and mayonnaise in a small bowl; beat until light and fluffy. Spread heavy-duty foil over the hot grill. Arrange the salmon skin side down on the foil. Spread half the cream cheese mixture over the salmon. Grill for 8 to 10 minutes. Turn carefully onto clean spots on the foil, allowing skin to separate and remain on foil. Cover salmon with remaining cream cheese mixture. Grill for 10 minutes longer, or until fish flakes easily with a fork. Remove to a warm platter. Serve immediately.
Yield: 4 servings.

Ray (Judy) Stewart, Preceptor Alpha Theta
Richland, Washington

SALMON CROQUETTES

2 (10-ounce) cans	1/2 cup egg substitute
salmon, drained,	1/2 cup milk
deboned	1 tablespoon chopped
1 1/2 cups yellow	parsley
cornmeal	Olive oil for frying

Flake the salmon with a fork in a medium bowl. Add the cornmeal, continuing to mix with the fork. Add the egg substitute; mix well. Add the parsley; mix well. Adjust proportions of ingredients if necessary to achieve a good packing consistency. Form the salmon mixture into 15 patties. Heat the olive oil in a large skillet over medium heat. Fry the salmon patties on both sides for 10 to 15 minutes or until golden brown. Yield: 15 patties.

Keith (Rhea Borysiak-) Fix, Alpha Chi
Little Rock, Arkansas

POACHED SALMON A LA DISHWASHER

You won't believe how good this is. It comes out perfect every time.

1 (3-pound) whole	1 small onion, sliced
salmon, head and tail	1 small lemon, sliced
removed	1/2 cup white wine
Salt and pepper to taste	
2 tablespoons cold	
butter, cut into pieces	

Rinse the salmon and pat dry. Sprinkle liberally inside and out with salt and pepper. Place on a piece of aluminum foil large enough to wrap fish completely. Arrange the butter, onion and lemon in cavity of fish. Sprinkle with wine. Fold the foil around the salmon, making a watertight package. Wrap several more layers of foil around the package. Place the fish on the top rack of the dishwasher. Do not add detergent. Set the dishwasher for its full cycle, including drying cycle. When cycle is complete, open the foil package. Discard the onion and lemon. Lift out the salmon's backbone, scrape off discolored spots and remove the fins. Serve warm or cold, garnished with parsley, lemon wedges or your favorite seafood sauce. Yield: 6 servings.

Harold (Dolores) Dunker, Kappa Master
Fremont, Nebraska

PASTA WITH SHRIMP AND JALAPENO ORANGE SAUCE

This dish can be prepared 4 hours ahead of serving time, in which case you would cover and refrigerate the shrimp and sauce in separate containers before reheating.

6 tablespoons (³/4 stick) unsalted butter	¹/2 cup dry white wine
24 large shrimp, peeled, deveined	1¹/2 cups orange juice
2 tablespoons minced shallots	³/4 cup heavy cream
	Salt and pepper to taste
1 small jalapeño pepper, seeded, thinly sliced	12 ounces angel hair pasta
	Minced fresh parsley

Melt the butter in a large heavy skillet over medium-high heat and sauté the shrimp just until pink. Remove the shrimp to a plate and sauté the shallots and jalapeño pepper for 1 minute. Stir in the wine. Bring to a boil. Stir in the orange juice and cream. Boil gently for about 10 minutes or until reduced to a thin sauce, stirring occasionally. Add salt and pepper to taste. (If you are preparing the dish ahead of serving time, cover and refrigerate the shrimp and sauce in separate containers for up to 4 hours.) Cook the pasta in a large pot of boiling water for 3 to 4 minutes or just until tender but still firm to the bite, stirring occasionally to prevent sticking; drain. Bring the sauce to a simmer in a large kettle. Stir the shrimp into the simmering sauce. Add the warm pasta, tossing well to coat. Divide the pasta among 4 plates. Sprinkle with parsley and serve. Yield: 4 servings.

Robert (Sherran) Ereth, Zeta Rho
Redlands, California

SEAFOOD ALFREDO PASTA

2 tablespoons olive oil	Dash of garlic powder
1 pound cooked shrimp	Dash of pepper
1 pound cooked crab meat	16 ounces spaghetti or linguine, cooked, drained
1 (10-ounce) can white clam sauce	
1 (26- to 32-ounce) jar alfredo sauce	

Heat the olive oil in a large skillet. Sauté the shrimp and crab meat for 1 minute. Stir in the white clam sauce and alfredo sauce. Season with garlic powder and pepper. Cook for 5 minutes or until heated through. Serve over hot pasta. Yield: 4 servings.

Nolan Geiss, son of Adrienne Geiss, Preceptor Beta Lambda
Rochester, New York

SPAGHETTI A LA CARBONARA

8 ounces bacon, crisp-fried	Salt and pepper to taste
3 eggs, beaten	3 tablespoons butter
¹/2 cup heavy cream	16 ounces spaghetti, cooked, drained
1 cup grated Parmesan cheese	2 teaspoons olive oil

Cut the bacon into ¹/2-inch pieces. Combine the eggs, cream, Parmesan cheese, salt and pepper in a medium bowl; blend well. Melt the butter in a large skillet and stir in the spaghetti, heating until warm. Add the egg mixture and cook, stirring frequently, for 10 to 15 minutes or until eggs are cooked and absorbed. Yield: 4 servings.

Craig Lenhard (Kimi) Robinson, Alpha Rho
Mountain Home, Idaho

BARBECUED BEANS

1 pound bacon slices, cut into thirds	¹/4 cup Worcestershire sauce
1 large onion, chopped	1 (12-ounce) bottle catsup
5 (16-ounce) cans pork and beans	¹/4 cup prepared mustard
2¹/4 cups packed brown sugar	2 teaspoons liquid smoke

Preheat the oven to 325 degrees. Crisp-fry the bacon in a 4- to 6-quart Dutch oven over medium heat. Add the onion. Sauté until tender. Stir in the remaining ingredients. Bake, uncovered, for 3 hours or until reduced to desired consistency. Yield: 20 servings.

Mike (Jo) Dowling, Zeta Eta
Derby, Kansas

LARRY'S BLACK-EYED PEAS

16 ounces dried black-
eyed peas
2 pounds smoked ham,
cubed, or 2 ham
hocks

2 ribs celery, chopped
1 yellow onion, chopped
1 teaspoon crushed red
pepper flakes
Salt and pepper to taste

Soak peas in water to cover for 4 hours; drain. Place the ham with water to cover in a large kettle. Bring to a boil. Reduce heat and simmer, covered, for 2 hours. Stir in the peas and remaining ingredients. Cook for 45 minutes or until tender. Yield: 6 servings.

Larry (Sheri) Abernathy, Preceptor Beta Beta
Portland, Oregon

HONEYED BRUSSELS SPROUTS

6 tablespoons (3/4 stick)
butter, melted
6 tablespoons honey
1 garlic clove, crushed

2 pints brussels sprouts,
cooked, drained
Salt and pepper to taste
1/4 teaspoon nutmeg

Combine the butter, honey and garlic in a medium saucepan over medium-low heat. Stir in the brussels sprouts. Add salt and pepper. Sprinkle with nutmeg. Yield: 8 servings.

Steve Bailey, friend of Bill Ross
Kansas City, Missouri

FRIED CORN

6 slices turkey bacon
1 onion, chopped
1/3 cup chopped green
bell pepper
1/4 cup water

2 cups fresh corn kernels
1 teaspoon salt
1 teaspoon freshly
ground pepper

Fry the turkey bacon in a nonstick skillet; drain, leaving 2 tablespoons bacon drippings in the skillet. Crumble the bacon and set aside. Sauté the onion and green pepper in the bacon drippings until soft. Add the water, corn, salt and pepper. Simmer, covered, for 5 minutes. Uncover and boil gently to reduce liquid. Stir in the bacon. Yield: 4 servings.

Byerl (Karen) Sawyer, Xi Epsilon Kappa
Douglasville, Georgia

Louis (Emily) Larsen, Preceptor Beta Epsilon, Bay Village, Ohio, makes Famous Macaroni Supreme by cooking 8 ounces of macaroni and mixing in 1 can of cream of mushroom soup, 2 cups canned tomatoes, 1 cup shredded Cheddar cheese and half a can of French-fried onions. Spoon into a casserole, top with the remaining onions and bake at 350 degrees for 30 minutes.

BRUNCH TIMBALES

1 pound sausage
1 (10- to 12-inch)
zucchini
2 (15-ounce) cans cream-
style corn
2/3 cup water
6 large eggs
11/4 tablespoons flour

1 teaspoon sugar
1/2 teaspoon salt
1/2 teaspoon freshly
ground pepper
2 cups shredded sharp
Cheddar cheese
1 (2-ounce) jar diced
pimentos

Preheat the oven to 350 degrees. Cook the sausage in a skillet until brown and crumbly and drain well. Cut the ends from the zucchini. Slice 12 long, very thin strips from the zucchini with a vegetable peeler. Chop the remaining zucchini coarsely and place in a blender container with the corn, water, eggs, flour, sugar, salt and pepper. Process at medium speed for about 1 minute or until the zucchini is finely chopped. Pour the corn mixture into a large bowl. Stir in the sausage and Cheddar cheese. Spray two 6-cup muffin pans with nonstick cooking spray. Loop each zucchini strip into a circle and place to form a band around the curved side of each muffin cup. Ladle the sausage mixture into the cups, filling to the top of the zucchini strips. Place muffin pans in two 9x13-inch baking pans. Add very hot water carefully to the pans, about 1 inch deep. Bake for about 35 minutes or until wooden pick comes out clean. Top with diced pimentos. Serve hot. Yield: 12 servings.

Jerry (Jean) Kyle, Preceptor Delta
Montgomery, Alabama

YUMMY POTATO PANCAKES

6 to 8 potatoes, peeled
1 medium onion, grated
3 tablespoons flour
1 tablespoon baking
soda
1 tablespoon seasoned
salt

1 teaspoon pepper
2 eggs
Margarine and
vegetable oil for
frying

Grate the potatoes into a large bowl and squeeze dry with paper towels. Add the onion, flour, baking soda, salt, pepper and eggs; mix well. Heat the desired amount of a mixture of margarine and oil in a skillet over medium heat. Drop large spoonfuls of the potato mixture into the hot margarine mixture. Fry until brown. Yield: 4 servings.

David (Donna) Kott
Novi, Michigan

BUCCANEER BARLEY

Serve instead of rice as a side dish for fish or any other entrée.

5 tablespoons butter	1¹/₂ cups barley
1 medium onion, chopped	3 (10-ounce) cans chicken broth
1 (10-ounce) can mushrooms (stems and pieces), drained	

Preheat the oven to 350 degrees. Melt the butter in a skillet and sauté the onion and mushrooms until lightly browned. Add the barley and brown slightly. Pour into a greased 3- to 4-quart baking dish. Stir in the chicken broth. Bake, covered, for 1 hour or until liquid is absorbed. Garnish with fresh parsley if desired. Yield: 6 servings.

Dan (Juanita) Bean, Theta Master
Sparks, Nevada

NEW ORLEANS GRITS

If you are not ready to bake right after the mixing stage, cover the baking dish with foil and let it stand in a warm oven until ready to bake.

1¹/₂ cups grits	3 eggs, beaten
6 cups water	¹/₂ cup half-and-half
¹/₂ cup (1 stick) butter, sliced	¹/₂ cup chopped onion, lightly browned
1 pound Velveeta cheese, cubed	2 tablespoons chopped pimentos
4 cups shredded sharp Cheddar cheese	3 teaspoons seasoned salt

Preheat the oven to 350 degrees. Cook grits in boiling water in a large pot for 12 minutes. Stir in the butter, Velveeta cheese, Cheddar cheese, eggs, half-and-half, onion, pimentos and seasoned salt; mix well. Pour into a buttered large baking dish. Bake, uncovered, for 1 hour. Yield: 10 servings.

Larry Fair, brother of Dianne Fair, Laureate Alpha Delta
Cleveland, Tennessee

SPANISH RICE

3 tablespoons vegetable oil	2 cups water
1 cup rice	¹/₄ cup catsup
1 medium onion, sliced	1 teaspoon salt
¹/₄ cup chopped green bell pepper or jalapeño peppers	¹/₈ teaspoon pepper
1 (16-ounce) can tomatoes	¹/₈ to ¹/₄ teaspoon chili powder (optional)

Heat the vegetable oil in a skillet and sauté the rice, onion and green pepper for 5 to 10 minutes or until onion is tender. Stir in the tomatoes, water, catsup, salt, pepper and chili powder. Simmer, covered, over low heat for about 30 minutes or until rice is tender and has absorbed all liquid. Yield: 5 servings.

Henry "Hank" (Orlene) Biggert, Alpha Tau Master
Mission Viejo, California

WILD RICE CASSEROLE

We always serve this at wild game feeds. Even if you don't like the game, you can fill up on the rice.

²/₃ cup wild rice	1 cup chopped celery
3 cups water	1 (10-ounce) can beef consommé
¹/₃ cup white rice	1 (10-ounce) can French onion soup
¹/₄ cup (¹/₂ stick) butter, sliced	
8 ounces fresh mushrooms, sliced	

Preheat the oven to 350 degrees. Rinse the wild rice until water runs clear. Bring 3 cups of water to a boil in a saucepan. Boil the wild rice and white rice for 10 minutes; drain. Combine the rice, butter, mushrooms, celery, consommé and onion soup in a large bowl; mix well. Pour mixture into a greased 3-quart baking dish. Bake, uncovered, for 45 minutes. Cover and bake for 45 minutes longer. Yield: 6 to 8 servings.

Gary (Pamela) Bartness, Xi Epsilon Xi
New Hampton, Iowa

HOT CORN BREAD

My husband makes this for potlucks and there is never any left. I tell him not to fix it for home because I can't stay away from it.

3 cups buttermilk cornmeal mix	1 large onion, chopped
3 tablespoons sugar	3 eggs
1 teaspoon salt	2 green hot peppers, chopped
1¹/₂ cups shredded Cheddar cheese	1¹/₂ cups milk
³/₄ cup vegetable oil	1 (14-ounce) can cream-style corn

Preheat the oven to 400 degrees. Combine the cornmeal mix, sugar, salt, Cheddar cheese, vegetable oil, onion, eggs, hot peppers, milk and corn in a large bowl 1 at a time, stirring after each addition. Pour into a greased 9x13-inch baking pan. Bake for 30 to 40 minutes or until wooden pick comes out clean. Let cool for 5 minutes before cutting. Yield: 12 servings.

Dave (Sandra) Edmondson, Xi Beta Alpha
Jeffersonville, Indiana

TOM'S MEXICALI CORN BREAD

This is wonderful served with posole.

3 large eggs, beaten	1 cup melted shortening
1 (14-ounce) can cream-style corn	2 cups yellow cornmeal
5 teaspoons baking powder	1½ teaspoons salt
	2 (7-ounce) cans whole chile peppers
2 cups small-curd cottage cheese	1½ cups shredded Cheddar cheese

Preheat the oven to 350 degrees. Combine the eggs, corn, baking powder, cottage cheese, shortening, cornmeal and salt in a large bowl; mix until smooth. Pour half the batter into a greased 9x13-inch baking pan. Rinse the chile peppers and pat dry. Layer the chile peppers, half the Cheddar cheese and the remaining batter over the first half. Cover with the remaining cheese. Bake for 1 hour or until edges begin to brown. Cool before cutting.
Yield: 12 servings.

Thomas (Cheryl) Kramer, Preceptor Lambda Mu
Ridgecrest, California

DAD'S HEALTHY WHOLE WHEAT BREAD

My father, at 91 years of age, still makes this bread by hand, in larger quantities. I remember waking up late at night as a child to the delicious aroma of baking bread. Our family was known to consume an entire hot loaf before going back to bed. If making in a bread machine, which is my version, be sure to use the kind of yeast that is meant to be used in a bread machine.

1¼ cups all-purpose flour	1 teaspoon dry yeast
¾ cup whole wheat flour	4 teaspoons vegetable oil
½ teaspoon salt	1 cup minus 2 tablespoons water
4 teaspoons brown sugar	

Place the all-purpose flour, whole wheat flour, salt, brown sugar, yeast, vegetable oil and water in a bread machine in order directed by manufacturer. Set the machine for the light setting (2 hours and 8 minutes) or the equivalent for your machine. Remove the loaf after baking to cool on a wire rack. Yield: 1 loaf.

Arthur Roy, father of Sheila Woodard
Lewiston, Maine

JOHN'S WHOLE WHEAT BREAD

Serve with honey butter.

5 to 5½ cups whole wheat flour	2 teaspoons salt
2 envelopes dry yeast	2 cups milk
2 tablespoons sugar	½ cup (1 stick) butter
	1 egg white

Combine 2 cups of the flour, yeast, sugar and salt in a mixer bowl. Heat the milk and butter to 120 to 130 degrees in a small saucepan over medium heat. Add the milk mixture to the flour mixture and beat at medium speed for 2 minutes. Add by hand enough of the remaining flour to form a dough. Knead the dough on a floured surface for 10 minutes, gradually adding more flour as necessary. Place in a greased bowl, turning to coat. Let rise, covered, in a warm place for 1 hour and 15 minutes or until doubled in bulk. Punch down. Divide into 2 portions. Form into loaves on a greased baking sheet. Let rise, covered with a tea towel, for 45 minutes longer or until doubled in bulk. Preheat the oven to 375 degrees. Brush loaves with the egg white. Slash loaf tops. Bake for 35 minutes or until bread tests done. Yield: 12 servings.

John (Liz) Hein, Pi Theta
Wichita, Kansas

THE ULTIMATE FRENCH TOAST

Serve this great weekend treat with crisp bacon and tall glasses of ice cold milk.

4 (1½-inch-thick) slices French bread	4 eggs, lightly beaten
3 ounces miniature chocolate chips	½ cup milk
	Grated zest of 1 orange
½ cup strawberry preserves	½ cup sugar
	1 teaspoon vanilla extract
4 tablespoons cream cheese, softened	½ teaspoon cinnamon
	2 tablespoons butter

Cut almost through each bread slice to form a pocket. Stuff ¼ of the chocolate chips, ¼ of the strawberry preserves and 1 tablespoon cream cheese into each pocket. Combine the eggs, milk, orange zest, sugar, vanilla and cinnamon in a shallow dish; blend well. Add the filled bread slices and soak for 5 minutes, turning once. Melt the butter on a griddle. Bake French toast, turning once, until crisp and golden on both sides. Serve on warmed plates with warmed strawberry syrup. Yield: 4 servings.

Brady Rohlfs, son of Nina Rohlfs, Preceptor Tau
Unadilla, Nebraska

BEER BATTER PANCAKES

This recipe makes 6 large or 12 small fluffy, tasty pancakes.

2 eggs, separated	1 (12-ounce) can beer
1¹/₃ cups flour	¹/₂ cup vegetable oil
¹/₂ teaspoon salt	
1 tablespoon baking powder	

Preheat the griddle. Beat the egg yolks in a medium bowl. Add the flour, salt, baking powder, beer and vegetable oil; beat until smooth. Beat the egg whites in a separate bowl until stiff peaks form. Fold the egg whites into the beer batter. Drop by spoonfuls onto the greased griddle. Bake until brown on both sides, turning once. Yield: 6 servings.

David Mills, son of Bonnie F. Mills, Xi Zeta Epsilon
Schoolcraft, Michigan

BUCKWHEAT PANCAKES

1¹/₂ cups buckwheat flour	2 large eggs
2¹/₂ teaspoons baking powder	1¹/₄ cups rice milk or milk
¹/₂ teaspoon salt	1 teaspoon vanilla extract
1 tablespoon sugar	¹/₃ cup canola oil

Combine the buckwheat flour, baking powder, salt, sugar, eggs, rice milk, vanilla and canola oil in a large bowl; beat until smooth. Pour 1 large spoonful at a time onto hot, lightly greased griddle. Bake until puffed and bubbles appear on surface. Turn pancake over and complete baking. Serve hot with maple syrup. Yield: 6 servings.

Wayne Scott, son of Susanna Scott, Preceptor Tau
Comox, British Columbia, Canada

❖ PUFFED PANCAKE WITH STRAWBERRY SAUCE

6 eggs	1 (16-ounce) package
1 cup milk	frozen strawberries in
1 cup flour	syrup, thawed
¹/₄ cup orange juice	2 tablespoons orange
¹/₂ cup sugar	juice
¹/₄ teaspoon salt	Confectioners' sugar
¹/₂ cup (1 stick) margarine	Sour cream

Preheat the oven to 425 degrees. Combine the eggs, milk, flour, ¹/₄ cup orange juice, sugar and salt in a blender container; process until smooth. Melt the margarine in a 9x13-inch baking dish in the oven, removing from oven after margarine sizzles but before it browns. Pour the batter into the baking dish over the butter. Bake in the middle of the oven for 20 minutes or until puffed and brown. Heat the strawberries and 2 tablespoons orange juice in a small saucepan over low heat while pancake is baking. Remove pancake from oven and sprinkle with confectioners' sugar. Serve with warm strawberry sauce and sour cream. Yield: 4 servings.

Tony (Linda) Davito, Preceptor Theta Xi
Pleasanton, California

PERFECT POPOVERS

3 eggs	1 cup milk
1 cup flour	2 tablespoons vegetable oil
1 teaspoon salt	

Combine the eggs, flour, salt and half the milk in a blender container; process for several seconds. Add the vegetable oil and the remaining milk. Process for 2 minutes, without scraping sides. Pour the batter into greased popover cups. Place in a cool oven. Turn on oven to 450 degrees. Bake for 20 minutes. Reduce temperature to 350 degrees. Bake for 20 minutes longer. Yield: 6 servings.

Renard (Candace) Bergstrom, Xi Tau
Devil's Lake, North Dakota

BLUE CORN WAFFLES

1 cup flour	2 egg yolks, slightly beaten
1 tablespoon baking powder	1³/₄ cups milk
¹/₂ teaspoon salt	¹/₂ cup vegetable oil
³/₄ cup blue cornmeal	2 egg whites

Combine the flour, baking powder, salt and cornmeal in a large bowl. Add the egg yolks, milk and vegetable oil; mix well. Beat the egg whites in a separate bowl until stiff peaks form. Fold egg whites into flour mixture. Do not overmix. Bake in waffle iron using manufacturer's instructions. Yield: 6 servings.

Rick Martinez (Pamela Smith), Xi Alpha
Albuquerque, New Mexico

Jack (Margaret) Schilling, Preceptor Xi Tau, Paradise, California, makes a fabulous Brandied Cranberry Sauce by sprinkling 4 cups cranberries in a baking dish with 2 cups sugar and baking at 350 degrees for 30 minutes, stirring occasionally. While still bubbling, stir in ¹/₄ cup sugar and ¹/₄ cup brandy.

TWENTY-MINUTE FUDGE CAKE

1/2 cup (1 stick) margarine, sliced	2 cups sugar
4 tablespoons baking cocoa	2 eggs
1/4 cup shortening	1/2 cup buttermilk
1 cup water	1 teaspoon baking soda
2 cups flour	1 teaspoon vanilla extract
	Fudge Frosting

Preheat the oven to 400 degrees. Combine the margarine, baking cocoa, shortening and water in a large saucepan. Bring to a boil, stirring occasionally. Remove from heat. Add the flour and sugar; mix well. Add the eggs, buttermilk, baking soda and vanilla 1 ingredient at a time, beating well after each addition. Pour the batter into a greased and floured 9x13-inch cake pan. Bake for 20 minutes or until the cake tests done. Prepare Fudge Frosting during the last 5 minutes of baking time. Spread the hot frosting over the hot cake. Yield: 12 servings.

FUDGE FROSTING

1/2 cup (1 stick) margarine, sliced	1 teaspoon vanilla extract
4 tablespoons baking cocoa	1 cup chopped pecans or walnuts
1/3 cup milk	
1 (1 pound) package confectioners' sugar	

Combine the margarine, baking cocoa and milk in a saucepan. Bring to a boil, stirring constantly. Remove from heat. Stir in the confectioners' sugar and vanilla; beat until smooth. Stir in the pecans.

Jim (Betty) Chiasson, Preceptor Kappa Psi
Port Neches, Texas

PLUM SPICE CAKE

2 cups self-rising flour	1 cup chopped pecans
2 cups sugar	1 teaspoon (rounded) cinnamon
1 cup vegetable oil	1/2 teaspoon ground cloves
3 eggs	
2 (4-ounce) jars baby food plums	

Preheat the oven to 350 degrees. Combine the flour, sugar, vegetable oil, eggs, plums, pecans, cinnamon and cloves in a large bowl; mix well. Spray a nonstick bundt pan heavily with nonstick cooking spray. Pour the batter into the pan. Bake for 1 hour. Cool for 10 minutes before removing from pan.
Yield: 12 servings.

Ben Linder, cousin of Marilyn Cloud, Preceptor Alpha Xi
Cleveland, Tennessee

HAWAIIAN PIES

1 1/4 cups sugar	1 cup coarsely chopped walnuts or pecans
1/4 cup flour	1/2 cup shredded coconut (optional)
1 (20-ounce) can crushed pineapple	2 baked (9-inch) deep-dish pie shells
1 (3-ounce) package orange gelatin	1 (16-ounce) container frozen whipped topping
1 (16-ounce) can sour cherries	
5 bananas, sliced	

Combine the sugar and flour in a medium saucepan. Stir in the undrained pineapple. Bring just to a boil over medium-high heat, stirring constantly. Remove from heat. Add the gelatin, stirring until dissolved. Stir in the undrained cherries. Cool to room temperature. Stir in the bananas, walnuts and coconut. Spoon into the pie shells. Chill for several hours before serving. Serve with whipped topping.
Yield: 12 servings.

Jerry (Anita) Wilson, Omega Master
Mansfield, Ohio

❖ SHANE'S CIRCUS PIZZA

1 (18-ounce) package refrigerator sugar cookie dough	1/2 teaspoon vanilla extract
8 ounces cream cheese, softened	2 medium baking apples, peeled, cored, sliced
1/2 cup packed brown sugar	Lemon juice
1/4 cup creamy peanut butter	1 tablespoon cinnamon
	1/3 cup caramel ice cream topping
	1/2 cup peanuts, chopped

Preheat the oven to 350 degrees. Soften the cookie dough by bringing to room temperature. Shape into a ball. Place on a 16-inch pizza pan. Roll out with a lightly floured rolling pin to a 14-inch circle about 1/4 inch thick. Bake for 15 to 18 minutes or until light golden brown. Remove the cookie crust to a wire rack. Cool completely. Combine the cream cheese, brown sugar, peanut butter and vanilla in a medium bowl; mix well. Spread evenly over the cooled crust. Dip the apple slices in lemon juice to prevent darkening. Arrange apples over cream cheese mixture. Sprinkle with cinnamon. Microwave the caramel topping on High for 30 seconds; stir. Microwave for 15 seconds longer or until warm. Drizzle over the apples. Sprinkle with chopped peanuts. Serve with vanilla ice cream. Yield: 16 servings.

Shane Bee Bush, grandson of Sara Bee-Gay, Xi Theta Pi
Chillicothe, Ohio

HAZELNUT POPPY SEED CAKE

2¹/₂ cups sugar
1¹/₂ cups butter, softened
5 eggs
1 teaspoon vanilla
    extract
3 cups flour
1 teaspoon baking
    powder
³/₄ cup milk

¹/₄ cup hazelnut liqueur
1¹/₂ cups coarsely
    chopped roasted
    Oregon hazelnuts
¹/₄ cup poppy seeds
¹/₂ cup dried cranberries,
    blueberries, cherries
    or chopped apricots
    (optional)

Beat the sugar, butter, eggs and vanilla in a large bowl at low speed just until blended. Beat at high speed for 5 minutes or until light and fluffy. Mix the flour and baking powder together. Blend the milk with the liqueur. Add the flour mixture and milk mixture alternately to the creamed mixture, beating well after each addition. Stir in the hazelnuts, poppy seeds and dried fruit. Pour into a greased and floured 10-inch bundt pan. Bake at 350 degrees for 1 hour and 25 minutes or until the cake tests done. Cool in the pan on a wire rack for 20 minutes. Invert onto the wire rack to cool completely. Garnish with a dusting of confectioners' sugar. Yield: 12 to 16 servings.

HAZELNUT COFFEE CAKE

2¹/₄ cups flour
³/₄ cup sugar
2 teaspoons baking
    powder
¹/₂ teaspoon baking soda
¹/₄ teaspoon salt
¹/₂ cup finely chopped
    roasted hazelnuts

³/₄ cup chilled butter
³/₄ cup sour cream
1 egg, lightly beaten
Cream Cheese Filling
1 cup prepared cherry
    pie filling
¹/₂ cup coarsely chopped
    roasted hazelnuts

Preheat the oven to 350 degrees. Position oven rack in the lower one-third of the oven. Combine the first 5 ingredients in a food processor. Pulse several times. Add the finely chopped hazelnuts and butter cut into ¹/₂-inch cubes. Process for 20 seconds or until crumbly. Reserve 1 cup of the mixture. Add the sour cream and egg to the remaining mixture and process just until moistened. Spread evenly over the bottom and 2 inches up the side of a greased 9-inch spring-form pan. Spoon in the Cream Cheese Filling. Spoon on the cherry pie filling. Sprinkle with the reserved crumb mixture and the coarsely chopped hazelnuts. Bake for 60 minutes or until the center is set. Let stand at room temperature for 15 minutes. Loosen the coffee cake from the side of the pan and remove the ring. Let stand until cooled to room temperature before removing the bottom of the pan.
Yield: 10 to 12 servings.

CREAM CHEESE FILLING

8 ounces cream cheese,
    softened
¹/₃ cup sugar
2 eggs

1 tablespoon fresh
    lemon juice
1 teaspoon grated lemon
    zest

Combine the cream cheese, sugar, eggs, lemon juice and zest in a bowl and mix until smooth and creamy.

APRICOT HAZELNUT MUFFINS

1¹/₂ cups flour
1 teaspoon baking soda
¹/₂ cup hazelnut meal
²/₃ cup buttermilk
¹/₄ cup orange juice
2 teaspoons grated
    orange zest
³/₄ cup sugar
6 tablespoons butter,
    softened

1 egg
¹/₂ cup coarsely chopped
    roasted hazelnuts
¹/₂ cup coarsely chopped
    dried apricots
³/₄ cup confectioners'
    sugar
1¹/₂ tablespoons milk
¹/₄ cup finely chopped
    roasted hazelnuts

Sift the flour and baking soda together, mix in the hazelnut meal and set aside. Combine the buttermilk, orange juice and half the zest and set aside. Cream the sugar and butter in a large bowl until light and fluffy. Add the egg and beat until smooth. Add the flour mixture and buttermilk mixture alternately, beating well after each addition. Stir in the coarsely chopped hazelnuts and apricots. Spoon into 12 greased muffin cups. Bake at 375 degrees for 18 to 20 minutes or until the muffins are golden brown and spring back when lightly touched. Cool in the pan on a wire rack for 5 minutes. Remove to a wire rack to cool completely. Blend the confectioners' sugar, milk and remaining zest in a small bowl. Drizzle over the cooled muffins. Sprinkle with the finely chopped hazelnuts. Yield: 12 muffins.

HOW TO ROAST HAZELNUTS

Spread shelled hazelnuts in a shallow baking pan. Roast at 275 degrees for 20 to 30 minutes or until the skins crack and the nutmeats turn light golden in color. Pour the hot hazelnuts into the center of a heavy terrycloth kitchen towel. Pull the corners of the towel together and twist tightly. Let stand for about 5 minutes to allow the nuts to steam. Rub the nuts vigorously in the towel to remove as much of the skin as possible. Remove the nuts and discard the skins. Do not be concerned if some of the skins cling tenaciously to the nuts, this is their nature and the light-dark colors give the hazelnuts their distinctive look. One pound of hazelnuts will yield about 3 cups.

Photograph for these recipes is on the Cover.

Metric Equivalents

Although the United States has opted to postpone converting to metric measurements, most other countries, including England and Canada, use the metric system. The following chart provides convenient approximate equivalents for allowing use of regular kitchen measures when cooking from foreign recipes.

Volume

These metric measures are approximate benchmarks for purposes
of home food preparation.
1 milliliter = 1 cubic centimeter = 1 gram

Liquid	Dry
1 teaspoon = 5 milliliters	1 quart = 1 liter
1 tablespoon = 15 milliliters	1 ounce = 30 grams
1 fluid ounce = 30 milliliters	1 pound = 450 grams
1 cup = 250 milliliters	2.2 pounds = 1 kilogram
1 pint = 500 milliliters	

Weight	Length
1 ounce = 28 grams	1 inch = $2\frac{1}{2}$ centimeters
1 pound = 450 grams	$\frac{1}{16}$ inch = 1 millimeter

Formulas Using Conversion Factors

When approximate conversions are not accurate enough, use these
formulas to convert measures from one system to another.

Measurements	Formulas
ounces to grams:	# ounces x 28.3 = # grams
grams to ounces:	# grams x 0.035 = # ounces
pounds to grams:	# pounds x 453.6 = # grams
pounds to kilograms	# pounds x 0.45 = # kilograms
ounces to milliliters:	# ounces x 30 = # milliliters
cups to liters:	# cups x 0.24 = # liters
inches to centimeters	# inches x 2.54 = # centimeters
centimeters to inches:	# centimeters x 0.39 = # inches

Approximate Weight to Volume

Some ingredients which we commonly measure by volume are measured by weight in foreign recipes. Here are a few examples for easy reference.

flour, all-purpose, unsifted	1 pound = 450 grams = 3 1/2 cups
flour, all-purpose, sifted	1 pound = 450 grams = 4 cups
sugar, granulated	1 pound = 450 grams = 2 cups
sugar, brown, packed	1 pound = 450 grams = 2 1/4 cups
sugar, confectioners'	1 pound = 450 grams = 4 cups
sugar, confectioners', sifted	1 pound = 450 grams = 4 1/2 cups
butter	1 pound = 450 grams = 2 cups

Temperature

Remember that foreign recipes frequently express temperatures in Centigrade rather than Fahrenheit.

Temperatures	Fahrenheit	Centigrade
room temperature	68°	20°
water boils	212°	100°
baking temperature	350°	177°
baking temperature	375°	190.5°
baking temperature	400°	204.4°
baking temperature	425°	218.3°
baking temperature	450°	232°

Use the following formulas when temperature conversions are necessary.

Centigrade degrees x $9/5$ + 32 = Fahrenheit degrees
Fahrenheit degrees - 32 x $5/9$ = Centigrade degrees

American Measurement Equivalents

1 tablespoon = 3 teaspoons	12 tablespoons = 3/4 cup
2 tablespoons = 1 ounce	16 tablespoons = 1 cup
4 tablespoons = 1/4 cup	1 cup = 8 ounces
5 tablespoons + 1 teaspoon = 1/3 cup	2 cups = 1 pint
8 tablespoons = 1/2 cup	4 cups = 1 quart
	4 quarts = 1 gallon

Merit Winners

QUICK CREATIONS
First Place
Braganza, Mary, page 37
Second Place
Young, Michelle, page 6
Third Place
Wood, Donna, page 40
Honorable Mention
Bailey, Marjorie A., page 37
Ball, Anne-Marie, page 42
Bush, Freda I., page 35
Carter, Pam, page 8
Dennis, Pauline, page 23
Glorioso, Judy, page 31
Goetz, Pennie, page 11
Griffey, Pat, page 8
Hawkings, Sabra, page 32
Higgins, Stephanie, page 16
Hoskins, Frances, page 52
Huse, Linda, page 62
Irish, Dawn C., page 49
Johnson, Kimberly, page 28
Kemerling, Carmel-Beth,
    page 48
Lively, Lucylee, page 47
McCurdy, Penny, page 37
Melton, Barbara, page 20
Mowrey, Judy, page 22
Munn, Rose Ann, page 36
Neumann, Ruth, page 60
Nichols, Ginny, page 29
O'Halloran, Madeline, page 34
Pender, Grace, page 55
Peterson, Heather, page 43
Phillips, Karen, page 24
Reader, Lisa C., page 7
Reid, Judy, page 13
Reiners, Anne, page 33
Schroeder, Cheryl, page 56
Shockey, Delona, page 46
Snavely, Karen, page 19
Snyder, Marjorie, page 47
Steward, Sue, page 37
Stinson, Julia, page 34
Sublette-Peyton, Melody,
    page 18
Suchan, Berny, page 26
Tanner, Doris, page 40

Taylor, Patricia, page 29
Teasdale, Vera, page 44
Vance, Patricia Kyle, page 44
Varnum, Shirley, page 11
Wall, LuAnn, page 15
Waller, Delma J., page 13
Webb, Kellie, page 31
Welsch, Keri, page 45
Williams, Leslie, page 32

BRISK BEGINNINGS
First Place
Jones, Jean, page 64
Second Place
Murrill, Judith, page 65
Third Place
Hamilton, Janet, page 71
Honorable Mention
Cook, Kathy, page 71
Flynn, Patience, page 72
Janes, Cathy, page 70
Mercer, Susan, page 74
Miller, Daphene D., page 72
Parrish, Karon, page 73
Parsons, Dorothy, page 69
Poindexter, Susie, page 64
Weaver, Walda, page 68

SIMPLE SOUPS & SALADS
First Place
Lahey, Patricia Kelley, page 91
Second Place
Summers, Alice, page 77
Third Place
Day, Shirley, page 88
Honorable Mention
Brown, Sue, page 90
Bubonovich, Beth, page 91
Burns, Mildred, page 95
Carter, Nancy, page 85
Derichsweiler, Sandy, page 86
Duntz, Iva Jean, page 76
Evans, MaryAnn, page 95
Finucan, Marilyn, page 90
Harper, Patricia A., page 80
Kelarek, Margie, page 91
LaFerrara, L. Robin, page 96
Mallinson, Diane, page 78

McPherson, Lora Jane, page 78
Nicely, Patricia, page 83
Olds, Michel, page 89
Rodgers, Barbara, page 94
Smit-Briggs, "Al", page 80
Sweeney, Toni, page 82
Tauzin, Brenda, page 85
Valdez-Fitzgibbons, Valerie R.,
    page 94
Van Winkle, Sharon, page 81
Wishart, Lonnie Gloria, page 86

ENTERTAINING ENTREES
First Place
Nygren, Connie, page 104
Second Place
Champa, Naomi E., page 102
Third Place
Allen, Idella, page 111
Honorable Mention
Bernier, Elayne, page 98
Bonvillian, Lilitha, page 110
Bowers, Tina, page 113
Bray, Marie M., page 105
Corral, Heather, page 112
Davis, R. Jeen, page 101
Dixon, Barbara, page 109
Dorman, Marjorie, page 112
Ebbing, Elizabeth, page 112
Fitch, Shirley, page 109
Greve, Marie Louise, page 108
Grossman, Mary Ellen, page 104
Hancock, Donnette, page 107
Hanlon, Anna, page 103
Hermann, Lillian, page 99
Kerschner, T-Ann, page 107
Magers, Faye A., page 105
Mann, Yvonne, page 98
McConnell, Jenni, page 106
Miller, Deborah A., page 105
Milner, Judy, page 107
Peters, Wendi, page 100
Rankin, Valerie, page 105
Schnackenberg, Norma,
    page 102
Senic, Ida, page 100
Urbain, Arlene, page 103
White, Roberta T., page 113

PASTAS
First Place
Niepoetter, Susan, page 123
Second Place
Stever, Doreen, page 117
Third Place
Durham, Grace, page 116
Honorable Mention
Allen, Candace, page 117
Alsmeyer, Jeanne, page 119
Bernet, Mayanne, page 116
Brietzke, Stefanie, page 123
Bryan, Robbie, page 125
Givens, Sherry, page 119
Miller, Kristine, page 120
Moody, Sandra E., page 118
Pello, Lorraine, page 125
Russell, Donna S., page 121
Sherman, Diane M., page 122

VEGETARIAN DISHES
First Place
Martinez, Ruth, page 129
Second Place
Lunn, Juanita, page 131
Third Place
Rutkowski, Nan, page 130
Honorable Mention
Dionne, Yvonne, page 131
Kirkpatrick, Lorraine L.,
        page 128
Leonard-Bowen, Clara,
        page 128
Maffucci, Dianna, page 129
Mason, Cheryl, page 127
McClintock, Fran, page 126
Plache, Gail M., page 128
Roberts, Tracey, page 129
Shafer, Kathleen J., page 129
Sneddon, Barbara, page 131
Ulibarri, Gwen, page 126
Wilkens, Bette, page 130
Wilson, Frances, page 132
Wong, Diana, page 130

SWIFT SIDE DISHES
First Place
Cheseldine, Helen, page 139
Second Place
Osborn, Pamela, page 137
Third Place
Bird, Shirley J., page 140
Honorable Mention
Allison, Shelly, page 137

Cable, Candy, page 139
Cline, Carolyn M., page 142
Dell-Imaginé, Toni, page 139
Gilkey, Norma, page 140
Grim, Sonia K., page 134
Hill, Mary L., page 134
Hoepker, Joyce, page 140
Long, Wanda, page 136
Moore, Herberta G., page 137
Perusek, Marian K., page 138
Smith, Norma, page 135
Stein, Barb, page 141

BREADS
First Place
McClure, Alice R., page 146
Second Place
Buzby, Mildred, page 152
Third Place
Davies, Myrtle, page 147
Honorable Mention
Ashley, Jane Ann, page 154
Borger, Dee, page 145
Bromell, Rosy W., page 154
Esson, Vera, page 150
Goldberg, Mary Helen,
        page 144
Judy, Shonda, page 151
Leduc, Nancy, page 151
MacLeod, Shirley, page 143
O'Bryan, Ellen A., page 146
Pullins, Janeen, page 147
Soard, Patricia R., page 152
Walker, Tami, page 150

DELIGHTFUL DESSERTS
First Place
Grod, Conni, page 173
Second Place
Crumley, Brenda, page 173
Third Place
Bearb, Maureen, page 162
Honorable Mention
Anderson, Barbara, page 173
Anderson, Linda, page 179
Booker, Susan, page 161
Brannon, Naomi, page 165
Campana, Michaelene,
        page 166
Cray, Polly, page 163
Cryderman, Lesley, page 183
Dobbins, Mary, page 158
Foster, Jimmie Lee, page 189
Greenough, Joyce, page 179

Gump, Sharon R., page 174
Iannaci, Lauren, page 190
Klasel, Lynda, page 177
Leetsch, Connie, page 186
Pion, Myrtle, page 182
Rompf, Sandra, page 184
Simay, Flora L., page 162
Spalding, Gwen, page 158
Trantham, Pat, page 159
Weitz, Patricia, page 181
Welden, Carol, page 181
Windhausen, Karen,
        page 175

MEN'S SPECIALTIES
First Place
Bush, Shane Bee (grandson of
        Sara Bee-Gay), page 210
Second Place
Davito, Tony (Linda), page 209
Third Place
Nic (son-in-law of Rosemary
        Mumford), page 202
Honorable Mention
Badger, Tom (Elaine), page 196
Copeland, Michael (Kathleen),
        page 203
Eness, Vergil (Joan), page 195
Ereth, Robert (Sherran), page 205
Fair, Larry (brother of Dianne),
        page 207
Geiss, Nolan (son of Adrienne),
        page 205
Goforth, Greg (Mary), page 194
Kramer, Thomas (Cheryl),
        page 208
Kyle, Jerry (Jean), page 206
Martinez, Rick (Pamela Smith),
        page 209
McVitty, James (Peg), page 200
Morwick, Bob (Marlene),
        page 201
Palmer, Bill (Pamela), page 198
Roy, Arthur (father of Sheila
        Woodard), page 208
Stewart, Ray (Judy), page 204
Toth, Joseph (Eleanor),
        page 200
Williamson, Alan (Marianne),
        page 201
Wilson, Jerry (Anita), page 210
Worth, Scott D. (son of
        Marilyn E.), page 200
Zinn, Jim (Ruth), page 197

Index

Beta Sigma Phi Cookbooks

available from *Favorite Recipes® Press* are chock-full of home-tested recipes from Beta Sigma Phi members that earn you the best compliment of all… "More Please!"

Every cookbook includes:

☆ delicious, family-pleasing recipes

☆ lay-flat binding

☆ wipe-clean color covers

☆ easy-to-read format

☆ comprehensive index

☆ more than 1,000 recipes

To place your order, call our toll-free number
1-800-251-1520
or clip and mail the convenient form below.

BETA SIGMA PHI COOKBOOKS	Item #	Qty.	U.S. Retail Price	Canadian Retail Price	Total
Women of Good Taste	67277		$9.95	$12.95	
Simple Celebrations	68255		$9.95	$12.95	
Shipping and Handling		1	$1.95	$ 2.95	
TOTAL AMOUNT					

☐ Payment Enclosed
☐ Please Charge My ☐ MasterCard ☐ Visa
☐ Discover

Canadian orders: checks or money orders only

Signature _____

Account Number _____

Name _____

Address _____

City _____ State ____ Zip _____

No COD orders please.

Call our toll-free number for faster ordering.

Please allow 30 days for delivery.

Mail completed order form to:

Favorite Recipes® Press
P.O. Box 305147
Nashville, TN 37230